Publi   are

Dexter Whitfield

Public Services or Corporate Welfare

Rethinking the Nation State in the Global Economy

Pluto Press

First published 2001 by Pluto Press
345 Archway Road, London N6 5AA
and 22883 Quicksilver Drive,
Sterling, VA 20166–2012, USA

www.plutobooks.com

British Library Cataloguing in Publication Data
A catalogue record for this book is available from
the British Library

Library of Congress Cataloging in Publication Data
Whitfield, Dexter.
    Public services or corporate welfare : rethinking the nation state
in the global economy / Dexter Whitfield.
        p. cm.
    Includes bibliographical references and index.
    ISBN 0–7453–0855–4 (hc) — ISBN 0–7453–0856–2 (pb)
    1. Welfare state. 2. State, The. 3. Privatization. 4.
Globalization.
  I. Title.
    JC479.W483 2000
    320.1—dc21

                                                    00–008744

ISBN 978 0 7453 0856 2 paperback

10   09   08   07   06   05   04   03   02   01
10   9   8   7   6   5   4   3   2   1

Designed and produced for Pluto Press by
Chase Publishing Services, Sidmouth, EX10 9QG
Typeset from disk by Stanford DTP Services, Northampton
Printed and bound by CPI Group (UK) Ltd, Croydon, CR0 4YY

To Dorothy Calvert

Contents

List of Tables and Figures

TABLES

x

FIGURES

Abbreviations

APEC	Asia-Pacific Economic Cooperation
ASEAN	Association of South East Asian Nations
BID	Business Improvement District
CCT	Compulsory Competitive Tendering
CDC	Community Development Corporation
DETR	Department of the Environment, Transport and the Regions
DfEE	Department for Education and Employment
DSO	Direct Services Organisation
DSS	Department of Social Security
EAZ	Education Action Zone
EU	European Union
ERM	European exchange rate mechanism
ESOP	Employee Share-Ownership Plan
FDI	Foreign direct investment
FT	*Financial Times*
FTE	Full-time equivalents
GATS	General Agreement on Trade and Services
GATT	General Agreement on Tariffs and Trade
GDP	Gross domestic product
GGFD	General Government Financial Deficit
G8	Group of 8 leading industrialised countries
HAZ	Health Action Zone
ICC	International Chamber of Commerce
ICT	Information and communications technology
IFC	International Finance Corporation
ILO	International Labour Organisation
IMF	International Monetary Fund
MAI	Multilateral Agreement on Investment
MERSCOUR	Southern Cone Common Market (Latin America)
MIGA	Multilateral Investment Guarantee Agency
NAFTA	North American Free Trade Agreement
NAO	National Audit Office (UK)
NATO	North Atlantic Treaty Organisation
NGO	Non-governmental organisation

NHS	National Health Service (UK)
NPR	National Performance Review
OECD	Organisation for Economic Cooperation and Development
PFI	Private Finance Initiative
PLC	Public Limited Company (UK)
PPP	Public–Private Partnership
PSDR	Public Sector Debt Repayment (UK)
PSNB	Public Sector Net Borrowing (UK)
Quango	Quasi-autonomous non-governmental organisation (UK)
REC	Regional Electricity Company
SAL	Structural Adjustment Loan
SERPS	State Earnings-Related Pension Scheme (UK)
SOE	State-Owned Enterprise
SJPA	Social Justice Planning and Auditing
TANF	Temporary Assistance for Needy Families
TNC	Transnational corporation
TQM	Total Quality Management
UK	United Kingdom
UN	United Nations
UNCTAD	United Nations Conference on Trade and Development
UNDP	United Nations Development Programme
US	United States
VAT	Value Added Tax
VFM	Value for money
WTO	World Trade Organisation

Acknowledgements

Many people and organisations with whom I have worked over the last decade have contributed to the analysis and ideas in this book through their commitment to the provision of good quality public services, democratic accountability, equalities and social justice.

I am particularly indebted to Lee Adams, Dorothy Calvert, Karen Escott, Keith Hayman, Andy Mott, Ursula Murray, Mick Paddon and Paul Skelton who read various chapters. I hope to have done justice to their comments. I also owe special thanks to those with whom I have discussed many of the key issues, in particular Kenny Bell, John Shutt and Hilary Wainwright. Researching and writing this book alongside the demands and deadlines for critical analysis and innovation at the Centre for Public Services has been both difficult and stimulating. I thank my co-worker Karen Escott for all her support.

I would also like to thank the Public Sector Research Centre, University of New South Wales, Sydney, organisers of the Global State Conference in 1994; Al Bilik, previously President of the public sector division of the AFL-CIO, the US trade union confederation, and to Andy and Gail Mott for their hospitality during my research in Washington DC.

I appreciate the support and patience of Roger van Zwanenberg and Robert Webb at Pluto Press and copy-editor Monica O'Connor.

This book would not have been possible without the love, courage, commitment and support of Dorothy Calvert. I dedicate this book to her.

Preface

We live in an age of global and national commitments to end poverty, achieve world class regional economies, to end welfare as we know it and to provide high performance public services. At face value, few could argue with these policies because we do want an end to poverty, particularly child poverty; we want to work and live in thriving, safe and environmentally attractive regions; the welfare state must be improved to meet the needs of a multi-cultural society; and we all need good quality public services.

But in reality they are half-truths or wish-lists because global capital has no intention of making the resources available to eradicate poverty or to create full employment. To do so would create a major dysfunction of the capitalist system. And blaming and complaining to the state or focusing only on the activities of the powerful transnational companies enables private capital to evade economic and social responsibility.

Evidence of increasing financial investment, trade, takeovers and mergers, communication and cultural exchange between nations abounds, but there is a wide spectrum of views about the historical precedents, composition, causes and consequences of globalisation for nation states and international institutions. The hyperglobalisers believe that the emergence of a global marketplace with transnational investment and production creates a borderless world in which the nation state is weakened and marginalised (Ohmae, 1995). Others argue that globalisation is exaggerated, that the global economy is less integrated than it was at the end of the 19th century and that regionalisation – neighbouring nations forming trading blocs such as Europe, North America and Asia-Pacific – is more significant than globalisation (Hirst and Thompson, 1996; Boyer and Drache, 1996; Weiss, 1998). A third group claim that globalisation '... is not only, or even primarily, about economic interdependence, but about the transformation of time and space in our lives' (Giddens, 1998a, pp. 30–1). Globalisation evidently causes the reengineering of the nation state, forcing it to work in partnership with other states and transnationals and gives rise to 'new individualism'. The different models of globalisation are usefully summarised in Held et al., 1999.

The changes achieved by neo-liberal transformation and Third Way modernisation of government to date are marginal compared to the potential impact of the World Trade Organisation (WTO) marketisation agenda which, together with the World Bank, International Monetary Fund (IMF) and Organisation for Economic Cooperation and Development (OECD) investment agenda, could create vast new global markets in health, education and other services. Initially, public goods will remain 'publicly' financed by taxation but will be increasingly privately delivered. Some support services are already outsourced and the private sector is financing, building and operating an increasing proportion of new hospitals, schools, transport and other infrastructure around the world. The Third Way argument, that the core medical and teaching services will remain publicly provided, is untenable. Ultimately, 'public' services could be replaced by private provision, financed mainly by individual insurance and charges. And the idea that all the activities and services provided by the state can be marketised without privatising government itself, beggars belief.

At the root of this debate about globalisation and the nation state, is the emergence of a new post-industrial service economy, organised and operated according to neo-liberal principles and values. Public and private decisions which affect our daily lives are dominated by financial, efficiency and commercial criteria in the pursuit of market forces. Instead, we need a new political social-economy which reassesses how we value people's needs, democratises economic and city planning and regeneration, subjects projects and services to rigorous evaluation, mainstreams equity, equalities and environmental sustainability and is rooted in public investment, ownership and control. We need to rid the public sector of the commercialised reinvention and competitive performance management systems, replacing them with a new Public Service Management.

The concept of the low tax/high quality service state is an illusion. Promises of lower taxation are another half truth. Lower personal taxes on earnings are replaced by much higher taxes on spending which means that most people are being duped. Meanwhile, evasion, fraud and corruption are endemic in many countries. The 'more for less' ideology feeds the minimalist model of government and performance management in which public services are audited, inspected, monitored and surveilled to maximise productivity.

Politicians and academics examine the causes of alienation, disillusionment and disconnectedness from the political process but they fail to understand that many people feel a deep sense of policy betrayal. They are not taken in by tokenistic focus groups or service charters to patch over the continued growth of unelected, unaccountable quasi-public bodies and the centralisation of decision-making. People also object to the enforced use of private capital and cosying up to big business in order to improve local facilities. Thatcherism succeeded in creating a more selfish, individualistic 'me' society, and instead of promoting a new social and collective ideology, the Third Way's 'new individualism' appears to blame 'failing' schools, underperforming services, single mothers and the unemployed.

Public sector workers are on the receiving end both as service users and often feel undervalued at work. Years of enforced pay restraint continue, to which is added the threat of outsourcing in which staff are treated as commodities and transferred to the lowest bidder, usually resulting in job losses and wage cuts. Many frontline staff and managers have performed heroics in maintaining services, a public service ethos and minimising the impact of Tory legislation. But years of cuts, lack of investment and criticism take their toll. Instead of leading with a commitment to the public sector, we have piecemeal initiatives initiated from the back where the government stands with a big stick waiting to 'fail' those who cannot keep up or don't have the resources to do so.

Collective responsibility is also being eroded. Risk is being commodified and individualised, just as the Tories under John Major claimed they weren't privatising pensions, just personalising them! By deliberately creating fractures and fissures, the language and ideology of 'welfare' is narrowed to benefits for the needy or socially excluded in place of collective universal systems to provide comprehensive health, education and social services available to all.

Public investment must be the raison d'etre of government because private capital is incapable of fulfilling the infrastructure deficit created by two decades of declining investment. Only the state can ensure that this is continuous, equitable and meets social need.

We must understand the limits of the state, we know that the state serves the interests of the capitalist economy and cannot fulfil many social needs. It is contradictory, oppressive, secretive with fewer democratic institutions. The social economy faces similar limitations imposed by the capitalist economy, and while it offers opportunities for collective enterprise, it is not a viable alternative to comprehensive public provision. To leave capital to marketise and dismantle the welfare state at will, is not a strategy but absolute surrender.

Defensive posturing always was, and continues to be, wholly inadequate. It is intellectually, politically and economically inept. This book is not a defence of the state but a primer for improving the capacity of the state to provide, deliver and regulate capital and to provide welfare and public services in a global economy. Above all, the state and international and global institutions must be democratised.

WHAT IS UNIQUE ABOUT THIS BOOK

At the core of *Public Services or Corporate Welfare* are several fundamental issues which have, to date, been frequently ignored or dealt with superficially. This book:

- demonstrates that the state facilitates globalisation by promoting private finance of the infrastructure, the marketisation of government services and that governments can still determine both national and global policies;

- exposes how the Third Way is masking the continuity of neo-liberalism which will further reduce the capacity of the state in the global economy and restrict its ability to provide good quality public services in a modernised welfare state;
- shows how international bodies such as the United Nations, World Bank, IMF and WTO are committed to marketisation and privatisation of public services and welfare states;
- provides a comprehensive critique of modernisation of the state with a framework to understand the myriad of policy initiatives and programmes and their impact on the capacity of the state;
- presents a radical analysis of partnerships, private finance and Best Value;
- forecasts trends in the global economy and assesses the implications of the minimalist and enabling models of governance by 2020;
- explores the implications of the Third Way for welfare states and the emergence of a Corporate-Welfare Complex;
- articulates the need for an effective state in the 21st-century global economy, setting out its functions and role in a new system of global governance and stresses the importance of sustaining and improving the welfare state;
- develops a new model of public service management, placing priority on innovation, equality and investment as an alternative to the reinvention and performance management models;
- highlights the strategic approach for labour, civil society and the state to organise and mobilise to fundamentally challenge neo-liberal and Third Way hegemony.

The audience for *Public Services or Corporate Welfare* is global because all states are confronted by similar issues although they often materialise differently. Chapters 1, 2, 5 and 7 to 10 have an explicitly international perspective. Chapters 3, 4 and 6 examine the transformation agenda, its rationale, policies, the methods used to modernise government and their impact on services, jobs and the state. They focus on Britain for two important reasons. First, between 1979 and 1997, the British state was subject to radical restructuring and privatisation on a scale unparalleled among major industrialised economies. Second, since 1997 the Labour government has led the way in promoting the Third Way as an alternative to neo-liberalism which has profound lessons for other countries which have or are contemplating adopting this model.

The Labour government has pioneered private finance and partnerships for renewal of the welfare state social infrastructure in addition to the transport and communications infrastructure. Britain is exporting these largely untested policies and practices to developing countries and to the transitional economies of Central and Eastern Europe. It has also applied the US model of employment, labour market and welfare reform which has lessons and implications for other European countries. The transformation of the welfare state (Chapter 5) draws on changes to welfare regimes in Europe, the USA and Latin America.

I argued in the early 1980s that 'privatisation is more than asset stripping the public sector. It is a comprehensive strategy for permanently restructuring the welfare state and public services in the interests of capital' (Whitfield, 1983, pp. 1–2). Unfortunately, this analysis and the required counter strategies were sparsely heeded. The privatisation programme (as distinct from ad hoc sales in the 1970s) started in Britain in 1980 with competitive tendering for selected local government services, and spread to support services in the National Health Service and government departments. Privatisation of state-owned corporations started in 1981 and quickly moved to the utilities, communications and transport. In the meantime, all public bodies sold land, property and playing fields to developers or transferred residential homes, leisure centres and other assets to the social economy. Then came partnerships and private finance for everything from hospitals, schools, police stations, prisons, computer systems and even facilities and equipment for the armed forces.

This book is rooted in the public sector. I have spent 30 years working, researching and planning for public bodies and with trade union and community organisations to effect change, to improve services, jobs and equalities and to enhance democratic accountability nationally and locally. This three-dimensional perspective, combined with national and international research and analysis, provides a unique depth of experience upon which this book is based.

Introduction

The Global Corporate Agenda

A seven-item global corporate agenda provides the political, economic and social context for this book. These items are:

- The global privatisation of power and maintenance of the Washington Consensus.
- The reconfiguration and global liberalisation of public services.
- The Third Way and neo-liberalism.
- Reconfiguring the role of the state.
- Privatisation of the welfare state and the emergence of a global corporate-welfare complex.
- Increasing poverty and widening social, economic and environmental inequality.
- Corporate governance or democratic control.

They are the central political and economic policies and the power struggles which will shape nation states, regional and international institutions in the early part of the 21st century. None of these agenda items are inevitable, for they are planned, designed and implemented by governments, international organisations and multinational companies. Despite much rhetoric about the inevitability of globalisation, there *are* political choices over policies, strategies and how we want to live our lives.

Transformation and modernisation of the nation state is high on the political agenda worldwide. States must adapt to new risks, rapidly changing information and communications technology, new demands of the post-industrial service economy, urbanisation and regeneration of cities, environmental crises and increased competition between nation states. Welfare states also face the impact of demographic change, ageing populations, widening inequalities and increasing poverty. The Introduction also discusses the concept of the nation state and its role in the global economy.

The performance and stability of the global economy, the clash of political, economic and religious ideologies, increasing concern for global welfare and the environment are central issues of our time. But what of our ability, nationally and internationally, to create the conditions to sustain economic growth, to minimise war and conflict, to radically reduce poverty, to achieve social justice, to sustain the environment instead of witnessing its degradation and to increase our collective ability to attain them? After two decades of rapid internationalisation and globalisation, economic crises and neo-liberalism, we are at a conjuncture of substantive political and economic change which could dramatically enhance or reduce this capacity.

Public Services or Corporate Welfare takes stock of the achievements and failures after two decades of neo-liberalism, at what cost and for whose benefit. The stark reality is that globalisation will generate ever larger financial and environmental crises which will impose more intractable social, health, environmental and welfare demands on the state. This book is a comprehensive critique of the Third Way and Anglo-American public policy and spells out the consequences for all industrialised and developing countries. It demonstrates that the 'Third Way' is a continuum of neo-liberal transformation of the state. By 2020 the partnership or enabling models of government could replace social welfare with corporate welfare. This book makes the case for a democratic and effective state in the global economy, without which goals for ending poverty, social exclusion and renewing democracy are mere platitudes. It focuses on the ability of government and public institutions to support and sustain improved economic performance, to help create employment and to maximise social justice through welfare states. It is about our ability to turn visions into priorities, objectives and action programmes with targets. It is about choices, ownership and democratic control which have a fundamental impact on how local public services are designed and delivered.

The first six chapters of the book are analytical, the seventh forecasts trends and developments to the year 2020, the last three are prescriptive. Chapter 2 examines the facts and fiction about the scale and extent of globalisation and how this is facilitated by the state through privatisation, privately financed infrastructure and the marketisation of public services. The degree to which the state has been transformed is discussed in Chapters 3 and 4 using a template of twelve elements grouped under the function, finance, organisation and operation of the state. Chapter 5 shows how the 'reform' of the welfare state could mean a fundamental shift away from the key principles of universality and social justice, towards corporate welfare. This book uses a definition of the welfare state which encompasses pensions, family, unemployment, disability, sickness and housing benefits and services including health and social care, housing, education and training together with active labour market policies.

The effects and costs of two decades of neo-liberalism and transformation of the state are examined in Chapter 6. Chapter 7 forecasts the salient features of corporate, partnership and social economy states in 2020 showing that they will fail to meet the social and economic needs in the twenty-first century. The final three chapters set out a plan to increase the capacity of the state to fulfil its functions, responsibilities and adhere to democratic principles. A new public service management is described in Chapter 9. The final chapter outlines a strategy and the crucial role trade unions and other civil society organisations must play in facilitating the state of the future and a new era of democratic and effective government locally, nationally and internationally.

THE SEVEN-ISSUE CORPORATE AGENDA

The next section examines the seven-item corporate global agenda in more detail.

The Global Privatisation of Power and the Washington Consensus

Top of the agenda is the global privatisation of power which has three components. First, a commitment to private capital and partnerships with business. The World Bank, the IMF and the General Agreement on Tariffs and Trade (GATT – precursor to the World Trade Organisation) are collectively known as the Bretton Woods institutions, named after the ski resort where the post-war financial structure of fixed exchange rates and capital controls was established. These international organisations have constantly expanded the role of private capital through regulatory regimes, aid programmes and partnerships. They have established divisions and projects which are specifically mandated to promote an increasing role for private capital in the economies of developing and industrialised countries. For example, the World Bank's private sector divisions, the International Finance Corporation (IFC) and the Multilateral Investment Guarantee Agency (MIGA), together with the International Bank for Reconstruction and Development's guarantee programme, increasingly finance private investment in power, water, transport and economic infrastructure projects.

The primary reason for Public–Private Partnerships (PPPs) – the private sector designs, builds, finances and operates public buildings and transport systems – is not short-term financial assistance to help states out of temporary fiscal crises or to demonstrate 'business in the community' but to create new forms of capital accumulation through private ownership and control of the national and global infrastructure. PPPs ensure privatisation of the development process, not just individual infrastructure projects, and require the state to develop a new rentier relationship with capital. Even the privatisers may be privatised, for example, the British government's Private Finance Taskforce is to be transferred to the private sector and proposals have also been made to privatise the World Bank's MIGA and IFC divisions (Klein, 1998). Partnership with business is endemic in the UN system of organisations, for example, the UNDP launched Public–Private Partnerships for the Urban Environment in 1995 to promote private sector involvement through investment in environmentally sound and eco-efficient projects. It identifies 'environmental problems which can be turned into viable business opportunities.'

Second, a commitment to developing a new investment regime. International trade agreements covering goods and services are negotiated and policed by the World Trade Organisation. The Multilateral Agreement on Investment (MAI), promoted by the OECD, would have created a new blueprint for global investment and led to a paradigm shift in power to the Bretton Woods institutions and the private sector. Following opposition from several states and non-governmental organisations, the proposals were referred to the WTO in 1998, so are likely to reemerge in another guise. The MAI would have committed countries to treat foreign investors the same as domestic investors and to end favoured nation treatment. The MAI was all-embracing covering the 'establishment, acquisition, expansion, operation, management, maintenance, use, enjoyment and sale and disposition of investments'. Capital, profits and dividends would have been freely permitted to flow back to the host country, investors and key personnel allowed to enter and stay temporarily to work in support of their investments, expropriation would have been limited and compensatable, and policies to prevent capital flight prohibited. Foreign investors would have a right of entry to all economic sectors which 'essentially eliminates the borders of the nation state for the purpose of investment' (Global Trade Watch, 1998, p. 4). These conditions would apply to privatisation, ensuring asset sales are open to all and prohibiting governments retaining a degree of control through 'golden shares', voucher schemes or any form of community control. Investors (corporations and individuals) could sue for damages at international tribunals if they believed their rights were violated. But there was no provision for governments or non-governmental organisations (NGOs) to take investors to a disputes settlement.

The MAI would make it impossible for governments to restrict foreign ownership of national assets, prohibit the return of services to public ownership, lead to further deregulation and liberalisation of domestic rules and regulations under threat of legal action by TNCs, restrict economic development and regeneration subsidies and local employment clauses and threaten the local implementation of social, environmental, health and social services policies and standards. It could severely restrict national and local government economic development policies to stimulate job creation, support local initiatives and prevent capital flight. In sum, it would reduce the power of the nation state and increase the power of transnationals by providing a charter for foreign investment.

Third, a commitment to neo-liberal economic development. The private sector and international finance are rapidly becoming the prime agents of economic development. The World Bank's new Comprehensive Development Framework and social capital perspective is widening the 'development agenda' in the interests of private capital. Most international organisations and major industrialised countries are committed to the marketisation of the world economy. This is paralleled by labour market deregulation which removes or radically weakens bargaining, trade union recognition and workers' rights.

The Washington Consensus, built on US economic and political hegemony and domination of the World Bank, the International Monetary Fund and the World Trade Organisation, is extending economic and political control over the economies of the north and south, fuelled by international and global coalitions of financial and business organisations committed to neo-liberalism, and reinforced militarily through US domination of the North Atlantic Treaty Organisation (NATO) together with quantitative and technological supremacy. This is a paradigm shift in the role of these institutions. The USA has 4 per cent of the world's population but produces 22 per cent of world output (adjusted for purchasing power).

The Global Liberalisation of Public and Private Services

The second agenda item is the planned global liberalisation of public and private services by the World Trade Organisation's General Agreement for Trade in Services (GATS) which could have a substantive impact on geopolitics, welfare states and the global economy. Following the initiative of the USA, the liberalisation of trade in goods through GATT was extended to services with the first multilateral agreement on services signed in 1994. The WTO was formed the following year to further the internationalisation of trade, services, investment and intellectual property rights. The WTO is singularly concerned with ensuring the free flow of trade – social equity, health and education outcomes, working conditions and human need are not part of its remit.

GATS sets out a framework of legally binding rules governing the conduct of world trade in services to ensure transparency and the progressive removal of measures which discriminate against foreign suppliers. Nation states sign up to a commitment to open services to market access on an ongoing basis through periodic negotiations. It covers over 160 services including health, education, social services, financial services, environmental services, libraries and leisure which are widely defined; for example, education includes primary, secondary, higher and adult education. Each of these services is a multi-billion pound market hence transnationals and business interests are lobbying hard to gain access to these vast new markets (see Chapter 2). 'A contestable, competitive market in every sector in every WTO member country is the ultimate goal', stated the US Coalition of Service Industries (CSI, 1999, p. 1). The CSI, the European Services Network, the International Chamber of Commerce, the European Roundtable of Industrialists and the Transatlantic Business Dialogue ensure high levels of corporate representation in national delegations and WTO working groups (Balanya et al., 2000).

The liberalisation of goods and services is based on two key principles, *most favoured nation* which requires countries to afford the same treatment to all

GATS member states, and *national treatment* which requires foreign companies to be treated the same as national firms. Trade in services is classified in four modes, cross-border supply, consumption abroad, commercial presence (provision of services by foreign-owned companies) and the movement of personnel. GATS defines government services as those which are provided on a non-commercial basis and do not compete with other suppliers. Since virtually all public and welfare services contain at least some element of private funding and provision, the degree to which nation states can protect core services against marketisation and privatisation under the current rules is limited. The WTO has wide powers to deal with barriers to trade with a dispute settlement procedure and cross-retaliation provisions under which non-complying countries can be forced to change legislation, face retaliatory trade sanctions and/or financial penalties.

A new 'Millennium Round' of negotiations on further liberalisation was delayed by disputes and labour/NGO opposition in Seattle in 1999, although previously commenced negotiations on government procurement and subsidies continued.

Many countries, such as Britain, are committed to liberalisation behind a domestic 'modernisation' and reform agenda, building the foundations for liberalisation by introducing competitive regimes into public services, revising government procurement policies, creating purchaser–provider splits, restructuring the finance of services through per capita funding, commercial resource accounting and private finance via public–private partnerships.

Global trade in services was estimated to be $2,170 billion in 1997, over 30 per cent of world trade (Karsenty, quoted in Hufbauer and Warren, 1999) but the WTO proposals open up a new frontier for the global economy. Public and welfare services provide large long-term contracts, guaranteed markets, access to streams of investment from pensions, skilled and professional workforces, opportunities for technological change and efficiency gains from reorganisation.

A WTO agreement on financial services came into effect in March 1999 which is predicted to liberalise over 90 per cent of the world market in insurance, banking and share dealing services. It does not require countries to immediately open markets but establishes liberalisation and market access and bans new protectionist measures. Global bank assets exceeding US$41 trillion, annual insurance premiums of $2.1 trillion and share dealing of $15 trillion, indicate the scale of the market. The liberalisation of financial services and investment could 'legitimate' further US intervention in the affairs of other countries and concentrate power and foreign direct investment by US finance capital.

The service sector, particularly the public sector, is distinctive from manufacturing industry because many services must be locally delivered although the organisation supplying the service may change. Other services, both public and private, can be via telecommunications across borders requiring neither producer nor user to have physical proximity. An increasing range of functions such as corporate services, distance learning, telemedics and diagnostics, can be outsourced to locations and providers further afield. Some services, such as tourism, involve movement by consumers, usually across borders. The globalisation of services is, in part, dependent on the rate at which multinationals extend their operations across borders by winning contracts or acquiring firms which already have market share. National barriers in professional services, for example, licensing of doctors and lawyers, can usually only be overcome by takeovers and mergers. Hence the globalisation of locally delivered services, such as human services and infrastructure maintenance, requires geographic expansion by multinationals thus providing a terrain for local power struggles over the organisation and remuneration of work and the quality of services.

The effects of services liberalisation will impact in both industrialised and developing countries and ultimately result in the mass marketisation and privatisation of health, education, social care and other public/welfare services. Issues of trade and the interests of multinational companies will increasingly override public policy, distort planning, divert resources into commercial services rather than invest in sustainability, marginalise social and human needs, impose new charges and create two-tier systems.

The Third Way and Neo-liberalism

The third item on the corporate agenda is the 'Third Way' which is forging a new partnership between state and capital, a pragmatic alternative to 'old left' state intervention, public ownership and big government and to the free-market neo-liberalism of the New Right. It is '...a new modernising movement of the centre. While accepting the central socialist value of social justice, it rejects class politics, seeking a cross-class base of support' (Giddens, 1998b, pp. 18–19). Another view suggests that the Third Way's 'big idea' is that there is no big idea (Kay, 1998). Social democratic labour parties worldwide are reexamining the implications of globalisation, the dominance of neo-liberalism, the collapse of communism and the 'death of socialism'.

The Third Way/Neue Mitte manifesto agreed by Britain's Prime Minister Tony Blair and German Chancellor Gerhard Schroeder in 1999 set out a strategy for markets, taxation, public expenditure and employment. It accepts globalisation as a benign force which must be accommodated, concluding that 'the essential function of markets must be complemented and improved by political action, not hampered by it' (Blair and Schroeder, 1999). 'The enthusiastic language for the accumulation of private capital is a striking feature of the document' (Taylor, 1999, p. 412). It is more representative of New Labour PLC than a social democratic Labour Party.

The Third Way programme is built around a series of concepts such as the radical centre, a new democratic state, active civil society, the democratic family, the new mixed economy, equality as inclusion, positive welfare, the social investment state, the cosmopolitan nation and cosmopolitan democracy (Giddens, 1998a). In Britain, these concepts have been translated into degrees of devolution for Scotland and Wales, reform of the House of Lords and mayors for major cities. Restructuring government centres on 'what works', the application of performance management, the enabling model of government – a mixed economy of service providers with the emphasis on competition and regulation, not ownership. Partnerships are proliferating at the same rate as quasi-public bodies were in the early 1990s and with equal lack of democratic accountability. Business is enthusiastic for partnerships because they help to reformulate the role of the state, to ensure commercial values are reflected in contracts and projects and to enable business to influence the commodification of services such as health and education. The Third Way and 'modernisation' are intended to create competitive, flexible conditions for capital accumulation.

Third Way reform of the welfare state is intended to create a 'social investment state', shifting the emphasis from expenditure on benefits towards 'investment in human capital' through education and training. The 'failure' and 'collapse' of the welfare state to adapt and innovate is used to justify 'making services more efficient through measures such as contracting out and privatisation' (Leadbetter, 1998, p. 25). It is suggested that a vibrant civil society is essential to counter the negative impact of the market on social relations, the social costs, the commercial values and the interests of those who are not served or marginalised by market mechanisms. Reconstituting civil society and the relationship between state and capital and between citizens and services, might include reformulating central/local relationships, bypassing the local authority.

The Third Way/Neue Mitte manifesto claims that the limits of company and personal taxation have been reached and that 'taxation of hard work and enterprise should be reduced'. It argues that 'the labour market needs a low-wage sector in order to make low-skill jobs available. The tax and benefits system can replenish low incomes from employment and at the same time save on support payments for the unemployed.' In other words, the low wage strategy of employers will be legitimated and subsidised by the state, the acceptable face of corporate welfare replacing social welfare. The manifesto claims

the ability of national governments to fine-tune the economy in order to secure growth and jobs has been exaggerated. The importance of individual and business enterprise to the creation of wealth has been undervalued. The weaknesses of markets have been overstated and their strengths underestimated.

Consequently, 'the state should not row but steer; not so much control as challenge' (Blair and Schroeder, 1999, p. 4). As an example of what this means in practice, the Best Value guidance requires local authorities to consider competition for all services and activities. In 'developing markets', authorities must 'package work appropriate to the market' and must secure improved performance from mature markets, 'create the conditions in which new suppliers might take root when the current market is demonstrably weak, poorly developed and offers no credible alternative to the current supplier' with the objective of encouraging the 'competitiveness of the supply base' (DETR, 1999, p. 14). The WTO could not have said it more clearly.

Stakeholding and personal responsibility are widely promoted. 'How we shift the emphasis in corporate ethos from the company being a mere vehicle for the capital market – to be traded, bought and sold as a commodity, towards the vision of the company as a community or partnership where each employee has a stake, and where a company's responsibilities are more clearly defined' (Blair, 1996). The Third Way is in danger of creating a race to the bottom, domestically driven, and not directly caused by globalisation. Stakeholding (share ownership, employee ownership and individual funded pensions) is Labour's version of the Tories' 'Sid (Sharon) the shareholder' who was used to privatise Britain's key utilities in the 1980s.

As Hutton and others have pointed out, the Third Way 'accepts capitalism largely as it is and casts the state as the social-democratic helper of individuals to cope better – educating and training them and offering employers subsidies to employ them' (Hutton, 1998). It is also supporting the growth of corporate welfare, and is, de facto, treating the needs of business and private capital as a class of interest but it does not acknowledge a class structure of people.

Intellectually and ideologically, the Third Way continues to give primacy to economic over social and cultural values. Globalisation is often used as a vehicle by governments and capital to reiterate demands for reductions in labour costs to encourage investment and enhance profits. Hence, the Third Way is essentially a modification of, and not an alternative to, neo-liberalism and is thus fundamentally flawed.

Labour's approach is essentially managerialist, reducing vacancy levels, maximising labour market flexibility, improving the effectiveness of training, minimising unemployment; but they have developed few policies which will directly create new and additional employment.

Although there is much common agreement over the growth of electronic government (e-government), the same cannot be said for the Enabling model of government which is being constructed simultaneously, not through microprocessing, but by political and managerial ideology and faith in competition and contracts. 'E' model governance, a key part of the Third Way, is built around the enabling/entrepreneurial concept and characterised by a number of Es (see Figure 1).

The enabling model of government is built on competition to determine service provision, market forces to allocate resources and business rather than social criteria to assess performance. This leads to a purchaser–provider split, an internal market where services which cannot be contracted out are subject to an internal trading framework including charging for services,

Figure 1: **The 'E' model of government**

Function of state
- enabling
- entrepreneurial
- empowerment
- e-government
- environment

Social policy
- equalities
- equity
- employment

- efficiency
- economy
- effectiveness
Management ethos

---

market rules and trading accounts. It also means that services are increasingly based on the 'needs' of business rather than human needs in packaging contracts and partnerships.

The degree to which the Es are prioritised varies widely. Empowerment is widely promoted but is minimal because involvement is limited to consumerism and consultation. Social policy is structured around 'inclusion' and economic participation which tackles only some of the fundamental causes of inequality.

Privatisation of the Welfare State and the Emergence of a Global Corporate-Welfare Complex

A new era of privatisation is emerging, driven by globalisation, neo-liberalism, transnationals and business interests now that it is embedded in the fiscal and political ideology of many governments. While public ownership and the welfare state remain strong in most European states, the flotation and trade sale of nationalised industries and state corporations in Britain is virtually exhausted, hence the core services of the welfare state – health, education, social services, social security (pensions) and housing – form the next phase in the marketisation of the state. Welfare state expenditure is already under pressure in many countries from neo-liberal ideology promoting individualism, tax cuts and the minimalist state and through pressure from demographic change. The cost and benefit of comprehensive European welfare states will be pitted against increasing national and global financial pressures and business interests promoting the minimalist safety net model. It will make restructuring for gender and equality objectives more difficult.

Globalisation is weakening the relationship between the geography of accumulation and the provision of welfare services. In other words, profits or surplus value from the production of goods and services, property investment and financial transactions are transferred to the home base of transnational companies and investors. Similarly, the profits of pension and insurance funds invested overseas are returned to benefit pensions in the 'home' country. Taxation is therefore fragmented between the country where the investment is made, where the financial services agent is based, and the country of the investor and/or shareholder where they have a liability to pay tax on dividends. Financialisation severs the link between investment and its consequences, between production, accumulation and reproduction and is changing the spatial composition of risk and responsibility. Increased financialisation as a result of the privatisation of pensions and social insurance will accelerate this process.

Yet the provision of an educated, trained, healthy and well-housed labour force remains the responsibility of the nation state. Capital is also reliant on the state providing an economic infrastructure. Globalisation weakens employers' willingness to fund social insurance which is coupled with capital's continual desire to reduce the cost of labour. The need for social insurance and new global social policies increases as global economic integration continues. Labour market differentials, particularly between industrialised and developing countries, have meant increased pressure for the 'reform' of welfare states and the reduction of non-wage labour costs.

Capital can 'trade' responsibility for reproduction by claiming it is active economically, i.e. its economic and employment contribution replaces or substitutes for its contribution to reproduction. The marketisation of repro-duction, including transfers to individuals, means that capital sees less direct responsibility for the use of its taxes. Furthermore, corporate taxation contributes towards the cost of private provision of 'public' services. The focus is the employment relationship and benefits are linked to that on a personal basis.

The linkage between taxation and reproduction is being weakened because firms will seek to pay taxes where they can be minimised or avoided, for example, in the country of production, a subsidiary company operating elsewhere, the country where the head office is based or where the company is registered (i.e. off-shore). Companies use the global economy to maximise transfer pricing and other strategies to minimise taxation – some $2,000 billion is managed in off-shore tax havens. Globalisation has made it easier for multinationals and the wealthy to use, or threaten to use, the 'exit' option of capital flight. Multinationals often use international capital to finance their operations through the international securities market and allocate debt and investment according to national tax policies in much the same way as transfer pricing.

The mobility of capital has resulted in tax competition between nation states. Over 100 countries offer tax concessions to foreign multinationals in order to attract direct and portfolio investment.

The response of developed countries has been first, to shift the tax burden from (mobile) capital to (less mobile) labour, and second, when further increased taxation of labour becomes politically and economically difficult, to cut the social safety net. Thus, globalisation and tax competition lead to a fiscal crisis for countries that wish to continue to provide social insurance to their citizens at the same time that demographic factors and the increased income inequality, job insecurity, and income volatility that result from globalisation render such social insurance more necessary. (Avi-Yonah, 2000, p. 1)

Government revenue as a proportion of GDP increased in OECD countries from an average of 30 per cent in 1975–80 to nearly 40 per cent by the mid-1990s. Personal and corporate income taxation have remained relatively static (although the average figures mask substantial cuts in corporate tax revenue in some countries, for example, from 14.7 per cent in 1975–80 to 9.8 per cent in 1986–92 in the USA). Hence the increase in total tax revenue was financed by increased social security and consumption taxes, both borne primarily by labour. The changes are highlighted in Table 1. This shift in the burden of taxation from capital to labour is regressive because it taxes the poor more heavily than the rich, thus increasing inequality.

Table 1: **Changes in average taxation in OECD countries** (percentage of total revenue)

Type of tax	1965	1995	% change
Personal income	26	27	+4
Corporate income	9	8	−11
Social security	18	25	+39
Property	8	5	−37
General consumption	12	18	+50
Other goods and services	26	15	−42

Source: Globalisation, Tax Competition and the Fiscal Crisis of the Welfare State, R.S. Avi-Yonah, Harvard Law Review, May 2000.

A combination of globalisation, privatisation and marketisation of services has reduced the ability of the state to undertake risk. This ultimately leads to new class divisions and social disintegration as a result of those who prosper and those that lose, those who can diversify risks and those who cannot, and those that share values and those that choose not to and privatise their risk.

Privatisation of social security will rapidly accelerate globalisation as trillions of pension and social insurance funds seek the highest return on investment. This is likely to increase the turbulence of financial markets although financial institutions will scoop billions in fees. The expansion of public and private occupational pension funds has created powerful institutions which have been integrated into financial markets, rather than the welfare state. By (re)commodifying and personalising services and benefits, the risk and cost is transferred from the state and employers to individuals.

Contagion in the global economy caused by financial crises will be even greater and people's savings and pensions will be at greater risk. The increasing conflict between the mobility of capital (and ability to avoid taxation) and the immobility of labour (demanding efficient and equitable social insurance and protection against capital) will generate new conflicts and struggles. The affordability of the welfare state and public services is primarily a crisis of capital and political ideology, not in the funding or the provision of services and benefits. The emergence of new finance/service welfare transnational corporations will inevitably lead to fundamental shifts in global power. These corporations will have the power to challenge nation states on the bedrock of basic services.

The system of corporate welfare is being reconfigured so that the primacy of state policy, market intervention, regulation, taxation and public expenditure is being reorganised to extend the 'welfare' of business. The Washington Consensus and the global privatisation of power are creating a new global corporate welfare in which international bodies and nation states compete to provide the most beneficial financial, regulatory and labour market conditions for business. A new corporate-welfare complex is emerging consisting of three main elements: a contract services system and accompanying infrastructure including shared client/contractor ideology, value system and vested interests in which the state outsources an increasing range of services and functions; an owner-operator infrastructure industry; and corporate welfare consisting of a widening web of tax relief, subsidies, credits, guarantees, incentives and concessions to business. The state has always subsidised and facilitated business interests but this is being given a new priority, reinforced by partnerships and private finance, with the public sector absorbing other costs of development. Globalisation is making the taxation of corporate profits and activities more difficult, hence states are transferring costs to individuals and trying to maximise the use of resources by outsourcing (Rodrik, 1997; Garrett, 1998).

Increasing Poverty and Widening Social, Economic and Environmental Inequality

The eradication of world poverty or its reduction by half by 2015 was agreed at the World Summit for Social Development in Copenhagen, 1995, and is now supported by international bodies. However, the poor continue to bear the brunt of structural adjustment policies, economic crises and market failures. The World Bank referred to the global picture at the end of the 1990s as 'stalled progress' despite evidence that the living standards of millions in East Asia had plummeted, the number of people living in poverty in India had risen by 40 million in a decade to 340 million, inequality was rising in Latin America, while Russia, Ukraine and Sub-Saharan Africa had declining or zero growth and increasing poverty (UNDP, 1999). In the first half of the 1990s the number of undernourished people in developing countries decreased by an average of 8 million a year. This will have to increase by 150 per cent to 20 million per annum if the 1996 World Food Summit commitment to halve the number of undernourished to 400 million by 2015 is to be reached (Food and Agriculture Organisation, 1999).

By 2050, two-thirds of the world's 9 billion population is expected to live in cities, with the greatest concentrations in developing countries. 'This dramatic acceleration in urbanisation of the earth's peoples – a tripling of the world's urban population over just two generations – poses daunting challenges of social and economic destitution and severe environmental degradation' (National Science Foundation/Rutgers University, 2000, p. 1).

New economic crises, globalisation and the neo-liberal/Third Way transformation of the state will create new conflicts and fissures in society further increasing the divide between rich and poor, those in and out of work, with or without welfare benefit, and between those choosing private services and those selecting or depending on public provision in both industrialised and developing countries. Equal opportunities cannot be limited to 'creating level playing fields' because unequal participation produces greater inequality.

Global self-destruction – environmental degradation and economic crises coupled with the increasing force of natural disasters and more vulnerable populations living in shanty town poverty – could cause a chain reaction leading to global economic collapse. There are, however, renewed efforts by trade unions and NGOs around the world to try to ensure that gender, race and class and the struggle for social justice, human rights and democratic control are an integral part of the convergence agenda. Global rules, codes and policies are only a start, the question is whether they are enforceable and monitored with punitive penalties for non-implementation.

Corporate Governance or Democratic Control

The clash between corporate governance and democratic accountability is the seventh item of the global agenda. Crony capitalism is widely blamed for exacerbating the late 1990s financial crises in East Asia and Russia, hence the rapid rise of corporate governance on the development agenda and the formation of a joint World Bank/OECD Global Forum on Corporate Governance. This version of corporate governance, not surprisingly, concerns the systems by which business corporations are directed and controlled, exemplified by the OECD's principles of corporate governance covering the rights and treatment of shareholders, the role of stakeholders, disclosure and transparency, and the responsibilities of the Board (OECD, 1998a). Some of the large US pension funds, such as the California Public Employees Retirement System, have led the way in demanding improved management accountability and information disclosure. Good corporate governance is encouraged by the pensions industry to promote public trust in their products. However, one could be forgiven for considering this is little more than an attempt to root out the cowboys and crooks because they threaten progress towards global marketisation and privatisation. This version of corporate governance does not demand that companies are held accountable for the socioeconomic and environmental impact in the communities in which they operate.

But there is a third dimension, rarely reported, because a new urban governance is emerging as business is effectively extending corporate control across the public arena via partnerships, business representation on public bodies, inquiries and government committees, and social economy organisations locally, nationally and internationally. Unlike the nineteenth-century company towns which were under one company control, the twenty-first-century version is business class control because business elites hold key positions on a wide range of public bodies. Running parallel with representation is the ideological and political commitment to ensuring the primacy of business needs, objectives, interests and values prioritising agendas. The business agenda requires that the power of labour and civil society organisations be marginalised and this is accomplished by further centralisation of decision-making, reduced accountability, less transparency under the guise of 'modernisation'. Democratic renewal is focused on individualism and the atomisation of civil society through market research, postal ballots, armchair voting and personal consultation through focus groups and panels rather than representative democracy involving user, community, trade union and civil society organisations. It is about 'taking the politics out of politics' in order to legitimise 'rational' business decision-making. The privatisation of government runs parallel with the privatisation of services.

We need to ensure that this agenda is widely understood because it fundamentally affects people's lives, jobs and services.

THE NATION STATE

The form, function and future of the nation state are the central concern of this book. It is therefore essential to set out more precisely an understanding of the role of the state in the global economy. This provides the context for the discussion of globalisation in Chapter 2 and the detailed assessment of policies which have sought to transform the function, finance, organisation and management of the state in Chapters 3 and 4.

The state is a national sovereignty over a territory but it is also a form of social relations between people, institutions, markets, business and civil society which extends beyond the territory to the world economy and international bodies. The state plays a crucial role in maintaining the conditions for the means of production, distribution, communication and exchange. It:

- creates and maintains the conditions for capital accumulation – infrastructure provision, macroeconomic policies, labour market regulation, taxation, law and order and the maintenance of a healthy, educated workforce;
- ameliorates the effects and social costs of accumulation and globalisation through the provision of welfare services and benefits;
- promotes international competitiveness of indigenous capital and economic development to attract inward investment;
- controls and contains civil and labour opposition to business, state and international policies.

Nation states compete to attract and retain capital by creating the conditions, with trade and monetary policies, for profitable production of goods and services to enable capital to trade internationally. The state is constantly promoting the internationalisation of capital located within its territory and supporting initiatives which invest in capabilities to increase competitiveness, build new alliances and promote a culture of enterprise to seek competitive advantage in the world economy. It is thus exhorting internationalisation of capital and providing the means to facilitate it. 'Markets benefit from stable, strong and efficient (i.e. lean) government', according to the International Chamber of Commerce (ICC, 1998, p. 5). Markets need regulation, states regulate markets, markets need states. Globalisation does not 'bypass states' but transforms states in the interests of capital.

There are conflicts and contradictions in the role of the state in creating the conditions for capital accumulation and the reproduction of labour. Capital seeks to minimise its share of the cost of reproduction through taxation and to commodify and create new markets and opportunities for capital accumulation by delivering public services. A World Bank discussion paper on civil service reform concluded that 'a standardised view of the proper functional span and size of the state remains elusive, despite the sweeping reemergence of liberal notions of minimalist government' (World Bank, 1995, p. 3). The report concludes that 'considerably more emphasis will have to be given to longer-term management issues if sustained improvement in government administrative capacity is to take place. More attention needs to be paid to devising a coherent, overarching strategy for civil service reform, and detailing the set of tactics by which the strategic goals will be achieved' (World Bank, 1995, p. 43). However, continued privatisation, deregulation and restructuring of the state's role in the economy brings into question the state's continuing capacity to carry out the functions prescribed for it under the World Bank state model.

There is no current substitute for the nation state. In addition to its role as regulator of markets, protector of sovereignty, legal and jurisdiction and property rights and national security, it also socialises risk of last resort, coordinates national policy, relations with other states and maintains civic society. The state, however, is not benign, its form and role is determined by economic and social relations. It is a capitalist state, sometimes authoritarian, oppressive, collusive and corrupt. The notion that globalisation signals the end of the nation state, to be replaced by city regions and global governance is global babble. In fact, continued economic globalisation and global governance is only sustainable through strong, effective and democratic states.

Social, economic and technological change is imposing new demands on the state and international bodies. Continued innovation in information and communications technology is revolutionising e-commerce and e-government. The current outsourcing of IT and related services could establish computer services companies in a very powerful position within the state, particularly with further takeovers and mergers and diversification into other services. Education and training at all levels in the 'knowledge economy' will be a major growth area, as will health and social care. The ageing of the population, an increasing proportion with second- and third-tier pensions, will spur an expansion of new forms of care services. The application of biotechnology will be a major factor in the pharmaceutical and agriculture sectors challenging the regulatory powers of both state and international organisations.

It is important, however, to be wary of the discovery of new paradigms such as the 'post-welfare state' and 'post-information society' which tend to generalise and exaggerate economic and social change to justify a particular prescription. New realism, new epochs, new times, a new world order, the new economy and postmodernisms of one kind or another abound but they always seem to translate into more of the same for the poor. Most articulate a neo-liberal welfare state or new capital–labour settlement, conclude that the Keynesian welfare state has ended and advocate a new welfarism centred on privatisation and individualism.

Much change is evolutionary and while the application of new technology impacts on the production of goods and services, many state services are, and will remain, dependent on personal service. Technology can enhance the quality of service but it cannot be a substitute for personal care and involvement. We need to understand the complexity and composition of change and to avoid accepting simplistic analysis or crude economic and technological determinism which 'justifies' powerlessness of the state on the one hand and promotes fake individualism on the other.

Despite much globalisation hype, the nation state continues to play a crucial role in creating and maintaining the conditions for capital accumulation, ensuring the health, education and safety of citizens, providing a framework for social relations, and maintaining civil society. Government policy making, planning and service delivery is a potential multi-billion pound global outsourcing market, hence the neo-liberal and business agenda to redefine 'public goods' locally, nationally and globally in order to justify a new phase of privatisation and marketisation. The entrepreneurial state commodifies public services, makes and regulates markets in the interest of capital, commercialises social relations between the state, capital, labour and civil society. It promotes the transfer of public assets and services to create a 'growth sector' in local/regional economies. As a consequence, the functions, finance, organisation, operation and management of government are being restructured in five ways:

- the establishment of performance management regimes (the audit state);
- marketisation and outsourcing (the contract state);
- transfer of assets and services to quasi-public and third sector quangos (the shadow state);
- private finance and public–private partnerships to fund the infrastructure and operate core services (the partnership state);
- new forms of consumerism under the guise of democratic renewal and user choice; thus reinforcing the primacy of financial and economic policy over social and equality issues (the consultative state).

This book demonstrates that the continuation of current policies will lead to the creation of a minimalist or corporate state by 2020 with profound social, economic and democratic consequences (see Chapter 7). The weakening of centralised state power is unlikely to be substituted by increased power for municipalities or city regions.

However, financial crises and market failures have led to new opportunities to create a new public order to control and to reregulate the purpose, benefits and distribution of economic growth, the social usefulness of technological change and innovation, and to make democratic accountability a reality.

1

Public Goods, Public Risk and Power Struggles

The first part of this chapter examines the provision of global and national public goods which helps to understand why certain functions and services are publicly provided. The second part discusses the important role of risk which is being packaged and priced in order to justify partnerships and privately financed infrastructure projects. The third part provides a brief overview of the power struggles between global organisations and nation states, between multinational companies and states, between financial and industrial capital and between capital and labour. The chapter concludes that the triangular paradigm of the state, market and civil society (World Bank, 1997) is an inadequate analytical framework for understanding and assessing the consequences of globalisation.

GLOBAL AND NATIONAL PUBLIC GOODS

Public goods have two key properties. They are *non-rival* (consumption by one user does not reduce the supply available to others) and *non-excludable* (users cannot be excluded from consuming the goods). It also means that it is not possible to charge for their consumption. Local or national public goods include defence, law and order, public health, macroeconomic management, roads, parks and open spaces. Global public goods are those with benefits which extend across borders, populations groups and generations (Kaul et al., 1999). This section examines the provision of public goods, followed by a brief examination of public choice theory which is at the root of neo-liberal public policy.

Positive and negative *externalities* arise from the activities of individuals, firms, organisations and states which result in benefits (education benefiting society) or damage (air or river pollution) but they do not bear the costs. Public goods often face a double jeopardy – market failure and government failure – requiring remedial action by civil society. The state plays a crucial role in minimising negative externalities and promoting positive externalities through taxation, regulation, monitoring and inspection, planning and the provision of activities and services. States have also acted to regulate monopolies and afford consumer protection in the provision of goods and services. There are two other key attributes to public goods: they suffer from under-provision and policy is mainly determined by the nation state.

The provision of public goods is a key economic and social rationale for the state. But this is often portrayed in the narrow terms of market failure, i.e. the state providing functions which the market cannot or will not provide. This approach begins and ends with the market, thus marginalising the importance of accountability, public interest, responsibility and capability which justify state provision of public goods, and in some cases, private goods. It is a minimalist perspective, which serves to distract from market failures and inefficiencies to provide private goods and affords capital a justification to constantly reconstruct the role of markets and highlight government failure to fully provide public goods.

Global, regional and national public goods are becoming more important in determining collective and individual welfare and reducing inequality. Increasing instability of market economies, the threat of financial crises, 'the return of depression economics' (Krugman, 1999), the threat of environmental catastrophe, all place increased reliance on public goods and their interconnectedness at local, national and international levels. There are five key issues:

1. Globalisation increases the demand for public goods as a result of increased trade in goods and services. The spread of disease, food and labour standards are just two examples. There are also growing demands for international market controls to minimise fraud and corruption, to minimise negative externalities such as environmental pollution and to maximise beneficial externalities such as public health and education, and for global equity.

2. The increasing private provision of public goods by the commodification of services and public risk, the unbundling of the physical infrastructure from service provision, the private financing of public goods, creating markets for private suppliers and marketising non-core use of facilities will ultimately change the form and provision of public goods. This is precisely the WTO agenda for the liberalisation of services discussed earlier. The World Bank considers that 'although the the state still has a central role in ensuring the provision of basic services – education, health, infrastructure – it is not obvious that the state must be the only provider, or a provider at all. The state's choices about provision, financing, and regulation of these services must build on the relative strengths of markets, civil society, and state agencies' (World Bank, 1997, p. 27). This process could change the 'publicness' of public goods – for example, private provision will lead to increased business role in determining the level, quality, availability of and access to services, the terms on which they are promoted, the division into commercial and non-commercial services, the emergence of competing privately financed

services for wealthy and middle-class users resulting in further exclusion and widening inequality. These changes are mainly in local and national public goods but are likely to extend to the private provision of global public goods.

3. The private provision of global and national public goods will further marginalise global equity – it will be an *externality* of private global systems. Global public goods could widen inequalities. Globalisation is already causing new divisions in social classes and economic interests, for example indebtedness, within and between nation states creating increased demands for global public goods and equity.

4. Making private goods more public – providing development and technical assistance to countries excluded from FDI. However, this again raises the conditions imposed by international bodies which may still reinforce the private provision of public goods.

5. The need to make the public cost of private sector externalities and private sector transaction costs publicly transparent. If democratic renewal, performance management and the knowledge economy are to have any relevance, they must ensure that the full public costs and social/environmental impact of private provision, contract and market failures are regularly assessed and publicly available.

Many public goods, services and activities could, in theory, be privately provided but not without social costs, subsidies, increased inequality, stringent controls and the likelihood of increased collusion and corruption. Nations choose, in varying degrees, to identify services as public goods for public interest, security, political, social and economic reasons, and not least because of the limitations, and in some cases, the failure of market forces and private provision to meet social and public need.

Public Choice Theory

Public choice theorists gained new followers in the 1980s with the emergence of the bureau-maximisation theory (Niskanen, 1971) and new institutional economics or transitional cost theory (Williamson, 1975, 1985). Right-wing political groups and parties, business and trade organisations such as the Confederation of British Industry (Britain) and Business Roundtable (New Zealand), together with multinational industrial, service and financial capital, vigorously promoted this ideology.

Public choice or economic rationalism is focused on the role of the bureaucracy in a market economy. In summary, public choice theory claims that the growth of government is due to the private interests or ambitions of bureaucrats whose aims are directly related to the size of their budget (Niskanen, 1971). The bigger the budget, the higher the bureaucrats' salary, status and power. According to this theory, organisations produce a much larger output than is needed because of the absence of market forces. Public choice theorists believe that all but a few essential public goods should be provided by the market. Dunleavy (1991) sought to replace Niskanen's budget-maximising model with a bureau-shaping model in which he distinguishes between four types of budgets and five types of agency. Rational bureaucrats are deemed to have a choice of maximising strategies and do not solely maximise budgets.

Public choice theory has its roots in the USA and has been defined as

the economic study of non-market decision-making, or simply the application of economic to political science: the theory of the state, voting rules, voter behaviour, party politics, the bureaucracy, and so on. The methodology of public choice is that of economics, however. The basic behavioural postulate of public choice, as for economics, is that man is an egoistic, rational, utility maximiser. (Mueller, 1989, pp. 1–2)

Public choice theorists want to see public services as an integral part of the global marketplace. They seek to develop theories which prove that 'bureaucracy is bad', public is less efficient than private. They ignore the fact that the shortcomings ascribed to bureaucrats and the public sector are probably more rampant in private sector bureaucracies where self-interest, greed, exploitation, theft and corruption are often endemic.

The neo-liberal conception of the state has permeated World Bank policy making for the past two decades. This assumed that states are inherently inefficient, that state officials always act in self-interest and that state intervention has to be limited to market-friendly action such as investment in education and training, creation of a competitive climate for business, and maintaining a stable macro economy. The fact that Japan and the East Asian nations had strong interventionist states was only belatedly acknowledged.

A comprehensive review of public choice literature concluded:

Scientifically, it is another in the long line of failed attempts at a rigorous, axiomatic, general theory of government. Ideologically, many of the theorists are accused of selecting for study only those shortcomings of government which suggest reducing it rather than improving it; or else they merely search government for instances of corruption or unproductive gain-seeking and generalise them as the nature of all democratic government. (Orchard and Stretton, 1997, p. 410)

Many other analysts have been equally critical, for example 'as a general theory, Niskanen's is empirically wrong in almost all its facts' (Self, 1993, p. 34).

GLOBAL RISK OR RISKY BUSINESS

The accommodation or transfer of risk has become a central feature both for those who wish to maintain collective risk through universal public provision, and for the marketisers, who want to transfer certain risk, at a suitable cost, from the public to the private sector.

Risk is a part of everyday life, at work, travelling, in sport and leisure activities, health, making choices about savings and pensions and in personal relationships. The management of risk is centuries old, since the early insurance markets developed for overseas trade. Some risks can be eliminated or mitigated but most cannot. Technological change, particularly in financial markets and privately financed infrastructure provision, has meant a higher profile for risk management – the analysis, control, communication and monitoring of risk. Risk analysis involves identifying, quantifying and pricing risk which can usually be statistically calculated. Fire, theft or accidents occur unexpectedly but happen regularly enough to be broadly predictable and therefore insurable. Individuals, organisations and firms can choose to absorb the consequences of risk or to pay a premium to transfer risk to an insurance organisation. In some circumstances, such as motor cover, it is illegal not to have insured risk.

Keynesianism provided a way of socialising and controlling risks inherent to capital accumulation. It socialised the risks of illness, disability and unemployment and reduced the risk of civic strife and industrial strikes, sharing the costs between workers and employers. 'The welfare state can be seen as a collective and institutional response to the nature of localised risks and dangers, based on principles of rule-governed attribution of fault and blame, legally implemented compensation, actuarial insurance principles and collectively shared responsibility' (Beck, 1998, p. 15).

Business risk is more complex and difficult to predict. The reinsurance market developed to spread large-scale risk between insurance companies and financial institutions. Different financial markets provide varying degrees of risk for investment funds, for example, stocks, bonds, foreign currency and futures markets. Risk itself has become a tradable commodity. The risk attached to purchasing shares or currency can be hedged by spreading and insuring them against changes in exchange or interest rates – the spreading of, and speculation in, risk is rife. The state also provides business with different forms of insurance such as export guarantees. In the wake of Russia's debt default in 1998, the IMF called upon private sector institutions to review their financial investment risk analysis and for central banks and regulatory agencies to reassess their supervision of markets because the crisis had been in part caused by 'excessive risk-taking, excessive leverage and ultimately an unsustainable structure of financial positions' (IMF,1998, p. 15).

Giddens (1998c, p. 33) argues that the crisis of the welfare state is not purely fiscal but a 'crisis of risk management in a society dominated by a new type of risk'. But the welfare state is substantially more than a publicly owned insurance organisation providing unemployment, sickness and disability benefits. The post-war welfare state was not just about ameliorating conditions 'here and now' but creating opportunities in the future following two world wars, the failure of private health and education, mass unemployment and the defeat of fascism. This narrow 'security' categorisation conveniently ignores all the other basic functions of the welfare state such as education, health, housing and social services. The 'security' thesis implies that it would be relatively simple to replace it with private insurance.

The advocates of risk society, such as Beck, claim that the nature of risk has changed.

> The impact of modern risks and manufactured uncertainties, these modes of determining and perceiving risk, attributing causality and allocating compensation have irreversibly broken down, throwing the function and legitimacy of modern bureaucracies, states, economies and science into question. Risks which were calculable under industrial society become incalculable and unpredictable in the risk society. (Beck, 1998, p. 16)

Many PPPs are justified not solely on the lack of public finance but the need to withdraw from property management to concentrate on the provision of core services or because of new risk created by rapid technological change.

But is the future any more difficult to estimate than it was 10, 20 or 50 years ago? The Cold War has evaporated but the threat of recession, famine, civil war, nuclear and environmental disaster are ever constant. Some risks for capital have increased, for example, implementing global strategies, entering new markets, winning contracts and operating internationally against more intense competition. It has meant increased insecurity, mass unemployment, short-term contracts and casualisation of labour. The creation of risk may have outpaced the development of trust (Strange, 1996, p. 86) but it is highly questionable that the nature or composition of risk has changed so fundamentally as to make redundant many of the social mechanisms developed to accommodate it. We need more, not less, social protection to ameliorate the negative consequences of globalisation. The process of identifying, quantifying, allocating and pricing risk may be changing but this reflects a further stage in the commodification and commercialisation of risk rather than structural change in society. It is superficial justification for the Third Way and the privatisation of the welfare state.

Commodification of Risk

It is important to understand the different ways in which risk is being commodified and how capital is exploiting risk to secure new modes of accumulation by packaging, commercialising and pricing risk.

Individual risk: Restructuring the social wage by individualising second tier pensions (deferred wage), restricting the power of collective organisation and the promotion of stakeholding. Commodifying savings for fear of future non-availability or deterioration in service: encouragement of higher levels of savings for education and long-term care. Risk will be commodified so that insurance companies will have 'life services' policies for services required over a person's life rather simply than the risk of death itself.

Individualising social and family costs by commodifying and privatising the risk of unemployment, sickness and disability, insurance for elderly care, saving for education fees. Equalities and social justice are limited to equality of opportunity for individuals. Increasing personal responsibility is often presented as necessary cost containment but privatisation and marketisation are often the prime motives.

Commodifying and transferring public risk: The public sector has always borne the risk that public investment in new schools and hospitals will be adequate for the required level of future demand. Training adequate numbers of teachers and medical staff is another risk undertaken by the state. There are different types of risk such as design and construction risk (overrunning construction costs, adequate space and facilities), operational risk (escalating repair and maintenance costs), financial risk (failure to achieve rent, user fee or toll income targets, fluctuations in foreign exchange and interest rates), technological risk (equipment becomes redundant faster than expected) and residual value risk (value of the building at the end of the contract). Risk transfer involves identifying the different types of risk, allocating legal responsibility and pricing each element so that it can be recharged to the public sector. Risk is highest in the early years of an infrastructure project but decreases over time so that the later years provide continuous cash flows with declining risk. This is in sharp contrast to most industrial investment in which product obsolescence and competition from other firms increases as a product ages.

Finance capital seeks to minimalise risk and thus seeks guarantees from governments and development banks in the same way as the World Bank's Multilateral Investment Guarantee Agency (MIGA) guarantees foreign investments in developing countries from the risk of nationalisation, war and default and effectively enhances the security of investment and privatisation programmes.

The emergence of risk society has profound implications for the future of government and the welfare state. The mobility of capital, financialisation and flexible labour markets are combining to individualise risk, changing the basis of risk and therefore the role of the welfare state and the nation state: 'if you want to survive in the global capitalist market, you have to change the basic foundations of modernity: social security, the nation-state, the power of the unions and so on' (Beck, 1998, p. 11).

'Going global' by expanding and integrating regional and world markets carries major risks for companies. They must try to maintain their local markets and services while at the same time operating transnationally. This raises new threats and opportunities even for the largest companies. Some companies rapidly diversify or enter new markets only to ruthlessly demerge, close or restructure shortly afterwards because they miscalculated profitability and market access. Transnational corporations are not invincible. For example, in the 1990s, Columbia HCA and Waste Management Inc. became the world's largest hospital and waste disposal firms respectively by aggressive takeovers and overseas expansion, but have since been radically restructured following fraud investigations and takeover. Some major takeovers failed despite apparent global synergy.

> A more sober look at the crystal ball suggests a rather bumpy road toward seamlessness; intense competition among financial firms, with major bankruptcies, crises for customers and producers alike, repeated losses from overambitious investment in new technologies, financial crises leading to the socialisation of losses (à la Savings & Loans Associations) and seemingly intractable problems in reconciling the fundamental differences between contrasting financial systems. (O'Brien, 1992, quoted in Fuerbringer, 1992, pp. 47–8)

COMPETITION, POWER STRUGGLES AND ALLIANCES

Cities, regions, nations and regional trade blocs compete for international trade in goods and services and inward investment. They also 'compete' in terms of financial and market regulations, social policies and the supply of labour. The growth of multinationals and increased competition between countries to attract foreign investment often lead to cuts in labour and social standards, restructuring of national labour markets and the erosion of trade union rights (UNCTAD, 1994). The cost of labour, employers' non-wage costs, labour market regulations, productivity levels, skill levels and the activity of trade unions relative to other labour markets become increasingly important.

Power is derived from the control of resources and technology, market share, the ability to regulate and tax, the ability to withdraw labour, organise goods boycotts and to oppose damaging development. Power struggles are economic, social and political. Globalisation intensifies the power struggle for competitive advantage between multinationals competing for market share, between capital and labour and between financial and industrial capital. It encourages new alliances between companies and between the corporate sector and the state. Globalisation also intensifies power struggles between the state, national and local organisations over social policies and public spending, and between political parties and left- and right-wing interest groups. They are reflected in conflicts between trade unions, employers and government over who benefits from globalisation, demands for protectionism, who pays the social costs of internationalisation and which social groups are targeted (or more likely scapegoated) in restructuring the welfare state. Trade unions and civil society organisations react to the dynamics of globalisation by changing their structure and strategies, for example, union partnerships with employers and the formation of new organisations and alliances. These power struggles are centred in the workplace, local and welfare state services, regeneration areas and within international organisations.

Power Struggles Between Global Organisations and Nation States

Post-war industrialised countries sustained increased output and high employment, often referred to as the 'golden age', which lasted until about 1970. The oil shocks in the early 1970s and balance of payments problems in many countries, rising world interest rates and global financial deregulation led to the debt crisis in 1982. Thatcher/Reagan neo-liberalism also penetrated the World Bank where it switched from investment trickle-down to work alongside the IMF to support countries hit by the debt crisis and devised its structural adjustment loans. The Washington Consensus 'amalgamates long-standing IMF macroeconomic stabilisation policies [usually consisting of public spending cuts, high interests rates and credit restraint], the World Bank's adoption of the market deregulation and supply side economics ideas in vogue in Washington early in the Reagan period, and London's zeal for privatising public enterprises which crossed the Atlantic a few years later' (Pieper and Taylor, 1998, p. 7).

The IMF's $57 billion rescue package for South Korea's 1997 financial crisis is a classic example. South Korea accepted a package of 'reforms' which, as Rodrik notes, were unnecessary for the economy to gain renewed access to capital markets.

In effect, the financial crisis was treated as an opportunity to remould the South Korean economy in the image of a free-market economy ... That the IMF could get away with this ... is indicative of a number of novel developments in the world economy. First, even the most successful countries in the world can be brought to their knees nowadays by sudden changes in market sentiment. Second, international institutions such as the IMF (and the US government as their principal backer) can acquire tremendous leverage over the policies of smaller countries when the world economy turns sour. Third, global policy makers have come to place excessive confidence in a particular vision of what constitutes desirable economic policy. This neo-liberal model of the economy emphasises free trade and free markets, with the government's role limited to the provision of the rule of law, prudential regulation and minimal social safety nets. (Rodrik, 1999, pp. 145–6)

This is often a turbulent process beginning with government resistance to prescriptive neo-liberal economic policies, social and trade union resistance which sometimes led to riots and the overthrow of leaders and/or governments and culminating in the poor bearing the brunt of the cost while financial investors were bailed out by the IMF.

International business organisations such as the International Chamber of Commerce (ICC), the Transatlantic Business Dialogue and the World Business Council for Sustainable Development, represent all the major multinationals and are constantly influencing the WTO, OECD and the G8. 'The opening and deregulation of markets, and the modernisation and globalisation of rules and institutions relevant to business, should no longer be seen as concessions to foreign investors. A truly global framework for investment is a win-win proposition' stated the ICC's 1998 Geneva Business Declaration. It also called for examination of 'long-term imbalances in the welfare state' in countries with extensive entitlements and ageing populations and warned, 'the emergence of activist pressure groups risks weakening the effectiveness of public rules, legitimate institutions and democratic processes' (International Chamber of Commerce, 1998, p. 6).

Power Struggles and Alliances Between Multinationals and States

There are alliances and power struggles between state, multinationals and civil society over taxation, regulations and labour laws, the role of the state in macroeconomic policy and procurement policies. Multinationals seek to minimise the threat of nationalisation of their assets but are happy to negotiate state subsidies or price increases to minimise their own risk. Regulatory frameworks for sectors such as financial services, telecommunications, transport and utilities and labour market laws witness the clash between public and private interests and where there are alliances and conflicts between business, government, user/consumer groups and trade unions.

A myriad of business, trade and professional organisations operate to maintain a corporate agenda. They are in effect a shadow cabinet of government representing corporate interests and sharing a common ideology. The privatisation of basic services and utilities has ensured that business and corporate interests extend even deeper into our daily lives.

A 'transnational capitalist class' or global ruling class has emerged whose fundamental interest is the continued accumulation of private profit. They promote business and class interest through regular formal and informal dialogue with international agency and government officials and politicians but also through sponsorship of research and universities, commissioning studies and funding business, trade, public policy 'think tanks', foundations and political parties. It has four fractions comprising transnational executives/owners, globalising bureaucrats, globalising politicians and professionals, and consumerist elites (merchants and media) (Sklair, 1997). The transnational capitalist class 'gives a unity to the diverse economic interests, political organisations and cultural and ideological formations of a very disparate group of people'.

Privately financed infrastructure and public services will greatly increase the power of multinational firms to influence regulatory regimes and economic policy, particularly foreign direct investment. New alliances between construction companies, banks and financiers, IT and facilities management companies will influence how public needs are met and financed and how governments deliver services.

New financial mechanisms and funds to finance PPP schemes, similar to the investment trusts, generated by privatisation asset sales are developing. The penultimate privatisation system is one in which taxpayers fund service provision but the private sector own and manage the infrastructure and operate services. The state packages work in ways which appeal to different sections of capital, thus creating new circuits of capital by diversifying investment opportunities which were previously the prerogative of the state. The speed of change will depend on the return, risk, security and competing investment opportunities and returns. Given that finance capital is the most globalised, it could be viewed as using this as a vehicle to privatise the least globalised or privatised services.

Construction companies currently play a lead role in PPP consortia although finance and managed services firms are likely to dominate as the services content of projects increases. This may also lead to the unification of what are currently separate markets for infrastructure projects in Eastern Europe, Asia, the USA, Europe and developing countries.

The Power Struggle Between Financial and Industrial Capital

There is a constant power struggle between different forms of capital to achieve profits and dividends, defend and increase market share, minimise regulatory frameworks and to ensure business corporate interests are constantly reinforced through trade and political lobbying. There are two aspects of this struggle.

First, firms compete within the same sector for market share, contracts, the application of new technology and product innovation to give them competitive advantage and to maximise profit. Second, different sectors and regions compete for investment. Transnational companies account for about a third of global output and trade and are increasing their influence in the world economy, particularly financial services, industrial production, services, utilities and telecommunications. They form the productive core of the globalising world economy. Although there are some 40,000 multinationals which control 200,000 foreign affiliates and have total assets of US$2.1 trillion, the largest 100 companies control 60 per cent of these assets. Two-thirds of the parent firms of multinationals are based in 14 industrialised countries. The vast majority of corporations are multinational, not fully transnational; for example, over 65 per cent of Microsoft's turnover is from its US home market.

It is important to keep the relative size of multinationals in perspective. The six largest nation states in terms of annual revenue, ranged from $1600 billion to $225 billion for the USA, Germany, Japan, UK, Italy and France, far exceeding that of the six largest transnationals, General Motors, Ford, Royal Dutch/Shell, Mitsui, Exxon and Wal-Mart, in terms of annual turnover – $168 billion–$118 billion (1998). Nevertheless, these transnationals have annual turnover greater than the revenues of over 180 nation states. Another measure is to compare assets which shows that General Electric, Ford and General Motors (all US) directly own assets valued at $272 billion, $258 billion and $222 billion in contrast to the $515 billion, $500 billion and $400 billion assets under management of the top three financial investment companies, Fidelity Investments (USA), Groupe AXA (France) and the Union Bank of Switzerland respectively (*Financial Times*, 28 January 1999a).

Mergers and alliances have been driven by the need to operate globally; the large consultancy and accountancy firms have diversified into legal, computing and other professional services to complement core activities such as auditing, tax advice, insolvency and management consultancy; computer firms such as IBM and Electronic Data Systems diversified into management consultancy. Arthur Andersen moved into investment banking. PricewaterhouseCoopers is building a global law firm with 3,000 lawyers and $1 billion annual fees by 2004, mainly by acquisition. The changing nature of management consultancy work includes reengineering with much longer assignments working directly inside companies and the provision of outsourcing services. They also assist TNCs to globalise their operations and enter new markets such as China, and undertaking major strategic work for governments in Central and Eastern Europe. Consultants and financial advisers are the new imperialists imposing their policies and values in the design, finance and operation of infrastructure and public service projects around the world.

Transnationals seek market share through rapid growth by acquisition and diversification by entering new markets and exiting others. For example, the Canadian group Laidlaw built up a large share of the North American waste disposal market and expanded its transportation businesses acquiring school bus companies. In 1996 it sold its waste management business to Allied Waste for $1.2 billion, acquired Scotts Hospitality for $662 million, adding 6,000 school buses. The following year it sold the hazardous waste division for $400 million then acquired American Medical Response for $1.1 billion to become America's largest ambulance operator only three years after entering the annual $30 billion market. Some companies combine industrial production, consumer and financial services, for example, General Electric (GE Capital) and Ford.

The turbulent corporatisation of US healthcare has included the conversion of non-profit health organisations into profit-making companies and increasing links between insurance companies and hospital companies. A profits squeeze in US Health Maintenance Organisations (HMOs) in 1996 spurned a series of takeovers and mergers. Home-care sector mergers increased rapidly and the drugs sector witnessed several large takeovers in 1995–8 including Glaxo's $14.3 billion takeover of Wellcome, Hoechst's $7.1 billion deal with Merrell Dow, Pharmacia's $6.3 billion takeover of Upjohn. Outsourcing of integrated health facilities management is increasing.

The privatisation process has created new opportunities for multinational companies and consultants to consolidate market position, opened up new markets which have facilitated diversification and the acquisition of smaller firms. Newly privatised national firms have expanded overseas to become multinational companies.

The Power Struggle Between Capital and Labour

Concern over the employment and wage consequences of footloose capital has tended to obscure the employers' thrust to reduce non-wage social costs, in effect their contribution to funding the welfare state. Labour costs account for only 5–10 per cent of production costs in developed countries thus eroding the competitive advantage of relocating production in low wage non-unionised economies. Multinationals usually seek a skilled labour force with relatively high productivity, a social and physical infrastructure together with a suitable financial and tax regime. The development of flexible production methods, the need for physical proximity and more integrated production networks to minimise the effect of currency fluctuations has mitigated against global sourcing. It highlights the disparity between the mobility of capital and the immobility of labour.

However, labour costs are a significantly larger proportion of service sector costs, but because most are place-based, only certain support services can be outsourced. Developing countries and low waged regions of industrialised countries are attracting services such as data processing, software programming and business services. The drive to reduce wage costs in support services in health, social services and education in industrialised countries is mainly due to national, not global, policies.

Employers' constant attempts to reduce labour costs need to be distinguished from competitive pressures between countries and regions exacerbated by globalisation. In the USA, a 20-year wage freeze meant that real take-home pay for production and non-supervisory workers, representing more than 80 per cent of all wage and salary employees, declined by more than 10 per cent since the early 1980s. Since the North American Free Trade Agreement (NAFTA) took effect the net export deficit with Mexico and Canada accounted for 440,172 US job losses between 1994 and 1998

(Economic Policy Institute, 1999). Outsourcing is reported to have accounted for 30 per cent to 50 per cent of the decrease in unskilled labour's share of US wage income between 1979 and 1990 (Feenstra and Hanson, 1996). Gordon concluded that 'the trade-and-wages argument provides at best a partial explanation of the wage squeeze and probably not a major one', citing deregulation, downsizing, the declining bargaining power of trade unions and technological change (Gordon, 1996, p. 196).

Differences in labour costs are typically due to lower levels of labour productivity in the exporting countries. In addition, 'a significant share of international economic activity does not occur through the market but is "internalised" (through ownership) or "quasi-internalised" (through alliances, networks and subcontracting) within firms and between them' (Campbell, 1994, p. 192). The switch from mass production is often overstated and/or confused with branding (badging similar products) and niche marketing. The enormous growth in the vast surpluses of capital, managed but not owned by financial institutions, is helping to define new organisational forms of the firm and new patterns of ownership and control.

The Labour government's response is to make welfare more flexible and therefore mobile but this is very restricted mobility within the overall terms of global, regional, national and local labour markets. The vast bulk of labour is not mobile, nor will it be. The ability and right of movement already exists within Europe. So international mobility is with capital, not labour. Making labour mobile with personalised welfare systems will have limited effect – in fact the benefits are not to labour but to privatisation and the financial interests driving it.

The state has played a key role in increasing labour market insecurity through deregulation and marketisation resulting in contractorisation, wage cuts, casualisation, and the loss of welfare benefits by driving down working hours below the National Insurance minimum threshold, thus making workers ineligible for state pension and other benefits. This practice was carried out both by the state and private firms (Escott and Whitfield, 1995). Governments have also imposed legislation to reduce the power of trade unions, and some states continue to operate repressive regimes against trade union organisations.

Labour costs have three components – wage rates, service conditions such as sickness, pensions and holidays and social contributions towards the cost of the welfare state. Globalisation has given multinationals more flexibility in deciding where to locate their operations, over jobs, terms and conditions, union recognition and investment policies. Globalisation transforms the employment relationship but only where work can be relocated – manufacturing and non-place-based services (Rodrik, 1997). It raises a number of questions, for example, what proportion of the tax base is footloose, what is the variation in demand for skilled and unskilled labour, and the extent to which labour can be substituted by other workers across national borders by outsourcing and foreign direct investment. Many public services can only be delivered locally, although skilled workers can be substituted with unskilled workers.

An OECD study found that there was no simple link between the tax burden and the level of unemployment and reported varying evidence that labour taxation influenced real wages and whether the level of employers' payroll taxes were significant or not (OECD 1999f). There are marked differences between countries in employers' social security contributions. For example, employers' contributions were zero or negible in Australia and Denmark; a group consisting of Britain, USA, Canada and Finland required moderate contributions in contrast to Belgium, Germany, Japan, the Netherlands, Norway and Sweden where costs were between 10 and 20 per cent of total labour costs but less than the even higher rates applicable in France, Italy and Spain.

Rodrik concludes that globalisation presents a dilemma because

> it results in increased demands on the state to provide social insurance while reducing the ability of the state to perform that role effectively. Consequently, as globalisation proceeds, the social consensus required to maintain domestic markets open to international trade is endangered. With domestic political support for trade eroding, a return to old-style protectionism becomes a serious possibility. (Rodrik, 1997, p. 53)

RECONFIGURING THE STATE–MARKET–CIVIL SOCIETY PARADIGM

Nation states have surrendered a degree of sovereignty by creating powerful international organisations (UN, WTO, OECD), multilateral treaties (NATO), regional trading blocs such as NAFTA and APEC, clubs (Group of 8 major industrialised countries) or in the case of Europe, a degree of economic and political union (see Chapter 6). Greater cooperation and convergence is evident as states jointly negotiate regulatory frameworks and cross-border trade. However, economic and military intervention is also more evident, for example, by industrialised countries in developing and transition economies, reinforced by the global policing role of the USA, IMF and World Bank.

The IMF, the World Bank Group and the Asian, African and European development banks have played a crucial role in economic globalisation. The expansion of their organisational structures to promote and facilitate private investment, the uniform adoption of neo-liberal policies, and the widening policy agenda stretching from financial and structural adjustment to the microeconomic and domestic policy agenda have had a highly influential role in promoting, imposing and sustaining financial and economic globalisation on nation states. Control over macroeconomic policies has been sought to ensure payment of interest on debt. Internationalisation also occurs as states privatise and deregulate their economies which in turn attracts foreign investment, encourages mergers and takeovers and helps multinationals to increase their share of public service contracts. However, the internationalisation of the economy, the state, civil society and culture is uneven and many developing countries are being marginalised and impoverished.

Political parties and government bodies increasingly look overseas for policies and best practice, for example, the OECD's international promotion of performance management and Britain's New Deal are modelled on US practice. Transnational companies force competition between states, regions and cities for inward investment which in turn requires them to develop global corporate intelligence and forges common action on taxation.

Capital is constantly searching for new markets and new modes of accumulation, consequently the speed, scale and depth of internationalisation varies between regions and nations and between manufacturing, services and finance capital. Some products or commodities have global markets, for example, oil, while the car industry has global production and sourcing but distinct national markets. Many services, for example, legal services, medicine and accountancy, have distinct national markets with qualification and professional practice entry regulations.

The internationalisation of civil society is demonstrated by the growth in the number, spread and power of NGOs operating across borders and increasing involvement in UN conferences and international summits on issues of the environment, human rights, women and debt relief evidence. Trade unions increasingly participate in regional and worldwide federations and organise internationally through transnational company works councils and combined shop stewards' committees.

Social Capital and Civil Society

Civil society consists of a vast array of organisations and activities promoting self-education, citizenship, art, culture and social interaction. However, many advocates of the rebirth of civil society look to the third sector, self-management and mutuality, as a means of replacing the national welfare state with community provision. A particular form of civil society is being promoted where the division between work and community is rigorously maintained in order to foster consumerist politics in civil society.

The social economy consists of cooperatives, social enterprises, mutuals, trusts, community and other organisations involved in economic development, manufacturing and service provision either in parallel to or as an alternative to state provision. In many developing countries, NGOs play a key role in delivering public services. In Britain, the social economy has become an alternative provider as a result of outsourcing, the transfer of functions to new organisations and the diversion of large sums of public expenditure.

The World Bank, international development agencies, governments and many NGOs have enthusiastically embraced the concept of social capital. However, there are widely differing perspectives on what social capital means (Fine, 1999a, 1999b). One view includes anything which is non-physical, financial or human capital relevant to the development process in the interface between the state and civil society. This definition includes community life, school reform, environmentalism, information networks and community organising. So social capital can cover virtually anything which is not a tangible asset and focuses on the strength of civil society or the family. A more limited view considers social capital as a multidimensional attribute of an individual, dependent on the number and strength of personal relationships, group membership influencing the development of social capital for individuals which in turn motivates human behaviour, particularly family-building behaviour (Astone et al., 1999).

The World Bank promotes social capital as a vital precondition for effective privatisation, for example, creating an acceptable legal, political and social environment which enables sales to take place without obstruction. Furthermore, 'the poor's social capital, derived primarily from family and neighbours, can serve as an important day-to-day "safety net", but the social capital possessed by the rich enables them to further their interests' (www.worldbank.org/poverty/scapital). Thus securing access to markets is vitally important for the economic advancement of the poor. 'Incorporating the poor' into the design and implementation of development projects improves targeting and loyalty. Social capital can help to merge the interests of the public, private and civil sectors and thus maximise development opportunities by providing the glue that binds partnerships. Superficially, the World Bank is looking to add a social dimension to policy and project evaluation. However, the attachment to a sociological and microeconomic theory of social capital has far-reaching ramifications for the development process and the role of the state. Social capital is being constructed and promoted as a means of reinforcing market capitalism, devoid of community power structure analysis and the political economy of class and capital.

The World Bank devised a triangular state–market–civil society model with three subsets consisting of private voluntary organisations, NGOs and cooperatives, and employers' organisations, trade unions and professional associations.

The attempt by the World Development Report 1997 to reappraise the role of the state in the global economy merely served to expose some contradictions in neo-liberal ideology and World Bank policy (World Bank, 1997). The report claimed to increase the effectiveness of the state but promoted privatisation and competition in the provision of public goods and services. Not surprisingly, it adopted the enabling model of government and applauded new public management in Britain and New Zealand. It was primarily concerned with the economic effectiveness of the state yet failed to address increasing corporate power, vested interests and the role of financial and service capital in the marketisation of the state.

The World Development Report 1997 identified three levels of functions of the state and categorised these in terms of addressing market failure and improving equity:

Minimal functions – providing public goods (defence, law and order, property rights, macroeconomic management and public health) and protecting the poor (anti-poverty programmes and disaster relief).

Intermediate functions – addressing externalities (basic education and environmental protection), regulating monopoly (utility regulation and anti-trust policy), overcoming imperfect information (insurance – health, life, pensions, financial regulation and consumer protection) and providing social insurance (redistributive pensions, family allowances and unemployment insurance).

Activist functions – coordinating private activity (fostering markets and cluster initiatives) and redistribution (asset redistribution) (World Bank, 1997)

This model is centred on market failure, the state should ensure the provision of only those activities which the market cannot or only partially can provide, and is thus a minimalist economist approach to human needs.

SUMMARY

There is growing recognition of the importance of global public goods to complement national and local public goods which are a key rationale for the state. However, capital, most international organisations and some nation states are encouraging their provision by the private sector. The emergence of a 'risk society', risk management and the commodification and transfer of public risk to the private sector, together with individualisation of social and family costs, have important implications for the state, public services and users. Both these issues are part of the competition and power struggles between global institutions, nation states, multinational companies, trade unions and community and non-governmental organisations.

2

Nation States: Facilitating and Accommodating Globalisation

Nation states play a key role in the globalisation process. Global economic integration is largely driven and underwritten by governments through legislation, policy and regulatory decisions, or by the lack of them nationally and internationally. However, a nation state's ability to act alone is increasingly constrained. National macroeconomic policies are increasingly forged in cooperation with neighbouring countries as part of regional trade groups, such as Europe, NAFTA and APEC. Nation states are also constrained by financial markets – unilateral policy and regulatory action is likely to result in destabilising currency speculation.

The first part of this chapter describes the different facets and contradictions of globalisation which is neither homogeneous nor uniform and has equally important economic, political, social and cultural dimensions. The second part demonstrates how global institutions and nation states facilitate globalisation by privatisation, privately financed infrastructure and the marketisation of government services.

GLOBALISATION, REGIONALISATION AND THE NATION STATE

Globalisation was given a new impetus by the collapse of the Bretton Woods system of capital controls in the late 1970s and by the continuing growth of investment capital from pension funds and savings. The growth in world trade in goods and services coupled with the accelerating pace of international economic integration, the dismantling of protectionist barriers and the continuing fall in transport and communication costs were also very influential. New information and communications technologies have helped to speed access to, and knowledge of, products and services through global advertising, marketing and branding. These new systems have played a key role in enabling financial markets to operate globally. Global intelligence and information, such as sector analysis, market data and corporate financial performance are an increasingly valuable commodity. The organisation of firms is changing too, as a consequence of the integration of production, consumer and financial services alongside increased outsourcing and subcontracting. But economic globalisation does not automatically lead to internationalisation of the state; it can equally produce nationalistic and protectionist responses by nation states.

Not all capital is mobile, for example, money invested in real estate and other assets cannot usually be extracted quickly. Manufacturing production is not as mobile as many people imagine because access to markets, productivity levels and quality of the infrastructure are usually as, or more, important as wage costs and relocation may be uneconomic. Entry and exit from the service sector is constrained by contracts and ownership of local firms, agencies and property.

Globalisation is not simply the growth of markets, companies, organisations or shared ideology on a world scale but encompasses the political, social, cultural and ecological spheres of human activity. These systemic connections affect the dynamics of globalisation, accelerating or reformulating the process of internationalisation, regionalisation and localisation and the economic and social relations between states, capital, labour and civic society. The individual and cumulative effect of these transformative changes could be far-reaching by 2020 (see Chapter 7).

Transformative change is threatened by continuing economic, political and environmental crises, the shock waves of contagion threaten both developing and industrialised countries. The East Asian economic crisis plunged Indonesia, South Korea, Malaysia and Thailand into financial meltdown in 1997–8 while the Japanese economic recession deepened. The Russian financial default and Brazil's economic crisis followed shortly thereafter. Many major infrastructure projects were halted or delayed with the collapse of currency and property markets. These crises were preceded by the Mexican crisis in 1995, European ERM (1992–3), US bond market (1994) and the collapse of financial institutions such as BCCI (1991), Barings' Bank (1995) and the earlier staggering losses by the US Savings & Loans Associations and the Japanese property market. These crises or massive frauds were rooted in financial deregulation and liberalisation and endemic corruption in both private and public sectors. We need no reminder that the threat is not confined to economic or financial collapse but equally to environmental catastrophe, witness the 1998 East Asian smog as a result of forest defoliation by timber companies.

Globalisation is not a relentless, unstoppable process but has conflicts and contradictions. This section examines the different aspects of globalisation and its contradictions so that we can more fully understand its impact on the nation state.

Globalisation: Fact and Fiction

Globalisation is not new. Evidence suggests that globalisation in the 19th and 20th centuries has similar impacts with inequality rising in rich countries and falling in poor countries. These trends were partly responsible for the inter-war retreat when globalisation virtually ceased between 1913 and 1950 (Williamson, 1996). Globalisation is reported to account for a third to a half of the rise in inequality in the USA and other OECD countries since 1970 (Borjas and Ramey, 1994; Wood, 1994).

Developments and trends in the 1990s have accelerated globalisation. World trade increased annually, averaging over 6 per cent, supported by continued trade liberalisation and tariff reductions (OECD, 1999a). However, the speed, boundaries, mobility, transferability, communications links and transaction costs vary considerably for different sections of capital. The flow of investment to developing countries increased markedly but there was a radical shift from government development aid to private foreign direct investment (mainly transnational companies investing in production, mergers and acquisitions and property). Institutional investment (pension funds, insurance and investment companies) achieved annual double figure growth, thus having a profound impact on financial markets. Transnationalisation of manufacturing and service companies accelerated through increasing mergers and acquisitions. Finally, privatisation and deregulation were widespread in utilities, telecoms and infrastructure.

Global convergence but regional consolidation: Internationalisation and economic integration are propelled by the growth in world trade in goods and services, foreign direct investment (which usually involves management control through substantial equity capital) by multinational corporations and booming portfolio investment (investment normally not exceeding 10 per cent of a company's equity capital) from institutional investment. The formation of regional trading blocs, such as the European Union and NAFTA, represent a degree of political integration as well as combining economic interests. Other regional organisations such as APEC promote open trade and economic cooperation but are not legally binding. However, there is also a trend towards national self-determination, for example in Central and Eastern Europe, although US foreign policy, EU, IMF and World Bank conditions ultimately determine the degree of 'independence'. Thus globalisation means inclusion for wealthy nations but exclusion for the poorest. Diversification and multi-culturalism have increased but political/religious struggles have become more intense.

Homogenisation continues but differences remain: It was differential rates of profit, investment returns and currency exchange which underpinned capital flight and the 'financial meltdown' of East Asian 'tiger economies' in 1997. Wide disparities remain between industrialised and developing countries as a result of imperialism and exploitation which create 'new' opportunities for international capital. The world is not a single global market but a series of markets at different stages of development, for example, some goods and services markets are international in contrast to 'national' markets in other services. There are wide differences within services, for example, health where pharmaceuticals markets are worldwide, yet the provision of health services is nationally focused mainly because of differences in welfare state regimes.

Market forces and political choices: Globalisation is in part driven by the capitalist economic system, i.e. market forces driving international trade, foreign investment and speculation and partly by advances in technology and communications. Neo-liberal governments have played a key role in determining the extent to which national economies are integrated in the international economy. The Thatcher/Reagan era, followed by the fall of communism and the hegemony of the capitalist economic system, and the domination of centre-right politics have been very influential in continued globalisation of the world economy.

Improved global security but capitalist crises continue: Although the end of the Cold War era led to capitalism becoming a more dominant world system, political and economic security is subject to even larger shock waves and recession – the 1990s was a decade of major financial crises – Mexico (1994/5), East Asia (1997), Russia (1998) and recession in Japan. They had an enormous impact on national economies. It has been estimated that, for example, the financial and banking crises in Argentina (1989–92), Chile (1981–7), Mexico (1994–present) and Japan (1990s) cost 55 per cent, 41 per cent, 15 per cent and 10 per cent respectively of GDP (Wyplosz, 1998). The finance and banking, stock market and property debt from Thailand's financial meltdown in 1997/8 was estimated at $200 billion, the equivalent of a year's economic output (Bretton Woods Committee, 1999). Between 1975 and 1998 there were currency crises in 87 countries and banking crises in 69 countries (*Financial Times*, 21 October 1998).

Corruption and fraud are also being internationalised and are endemic in many countries. Rapid growth in East Asia attracted large capital flows because of the prospect of higher returns but ultimately resulted in over-investment and over-capacity, an endemic feature of the capitalist economic system. The subsequent 1998 collapse and rescue of the hedge fund, Long Term Capital Management, which had a peak balance sheet exposure of US$200 billion against equity capital of a mere US$4.8 billion, confirms that crony capitalism is not confined to East Asia.

Growing world trade but poorer countries marginalised: Despite increasing world trade, the 48 least developed countries, with 600 million people, a tenth of the world population, are increasingly marginalised in the world economy. Slower growth rates, falling commodity prices as a result of the Asian crisis, large debts and limited capital investment are often compounded by natural disasters. The annual interest payments on the external debt of developing countries is twice the amount received in official aid. For example, debt-servicing accounts for more than half of Mozambique's government revenue and five times its expenditure on health and education. The outflow of profit and interest from the Third World in 1980 was $35.1 billion and $24.0 billion respectively but by 1994 interest payments had soared to $64.5 billion while the outflow of profits declined to $25.4 billion. Meanwhile, the rapid growth of stock markets in developing countries with weak regulatory regimes and the increasing use of companies registered in tax havens has facilitated the laundering of an estimated $300–$500 billion annually on international money markets.

Cross-border financial flows soar but not for public services: Foreign Direct Investment (FDI) soared from $25 billion to $644 billion between 1973 and 1998, exceeding the growth in international trade. Services account for three-fifths of foreign direct investment and a quarter of global trade. More than two-thirds of inward foreign direct investment and 90 per cent of outward FDI is between industrialised countries. Five countries, the USA, Germany, Britain, Japan and France, accounted for two-thirds of FDI outflows in the 1980–95 period. In other words, most multinational investment is not flowing to developing countries but is between the richer industrialised countries. Investment in the poorest countries continued to decline and economic globalisation results in an ever increasing share of prosperity to the wealthy in the north and south (UNCTAD, 1994). It is widening inequalities between countries and marginalising the least developed countries. Official (government) development finance declined from nearly $56 billion (56 per cent of net flows) in 1990 to $41 billion (14 per cent of net flows) in 1996 (World Bank, 1999c).

In sum, globalisation proponents have overstated the magnitude of change, and hence the degree to which production is being transnationalised. For all the talk of huge global investment flows, three stubborn facts remain. First, as a proportion of long-term capital flows, FDI has been declining, not growing, over the past decade; and, second, most long-term capital transfers are of the 'arms-length' portfolio variety. Finally, of the direct form of foreign investment, a major part goes towards non-manufacturing investment and to the acquisition of existing rather than new assets – all of which have minimal significance for the transnationalisation of production. (Weiss, 1998, p. 175)

While developing countries have benefited from increased capital investment, it has been concentrated in private development and export orientated manufacturing. Public works and social development projects have been starved of funds. Official aid declined significantly in real terms (as a percentage of donor countries' GNP) and relatively, accounting for just 15 per cent of foreign direct investment (FDI) inflows in 1997. World investment has soared but mainly between industrialised countries. Nearly two-thirds of FDI accounts for changing ownership in takeovers and privatisation and to low wage economy service sectors such as tourism. Much portfolio investment is short term.

Furthermore, IMF and World Bank structural adjustment funding has been contingent on savage cuts in public spending, privatisation and liberalisation. As a consequence of the IMF bail-out in 1997, Thailand is implementing a 'Privatisation Master Plan' which covers communications, water, transport, energy and oil together with 42 enterprises in banking, commercial and agriculture sectors engaged in 'non-core government functions'. Brazil privatised its telecoms system, Telebras, in a US$19 billion sell-off in July 1998, 63.6 per cent financed by foreign investors. Three months later in the wake of the Russian default and with capital exiting at a rate of US$1 billion a day, the Brazilian government negotiated a US$41.5 billion fiscal adjustment plan with the IMF. The plan requires increased pensions contributions for civil servants and savings from social security reforms. With no private sector involvement, the plan has been heavily criticised as another bail-out of foreign investors.

Manufacturing focus but service economy reality: Services account for almost 80 per cent of GDP and employment in OECD countries and the slow decline in manufacturing is set to continue. In Britain, the rise of the service economy has been dramatic – manufacturing's share of GDP fell from 33 per cent to 20 per cent between 1970 and 1997 while services rose from 52 per cent to 67 per cent in the same period. However, manufacturing still accounts for 60 per cent of exports. The start of detailed negotiations on GATS in 2000 is likely to launch an intense battle over access for professionals and immigration laws, recognition of national qualifications and trade in services.

Free-market capitalism but nationalisation when convenient: There are some glaring contradictions between policy and practice even in countries which are bastions of free enterprise. For example, during the 1998 financial turmoil, the Hong Kong Monetary Authority bought £10 billion shares on the Hong Kong stock market to deter speculation against its currency. This resulted in partial nationalisation of the economy with the government owning substantial shares in major transnationals such as HSBC Holdings (9 per cent) and Hong Kong Telephone (7 per cent) (*Financial Times*, 4 July 1998). By June 1999 the value of the portfolio of shares had risen 84 per cent. Chilean banks were privatised, renationalised and reprivatised within two decades and despite the neo-liberal stance, the government retained control of the strategic copper industry, nationalised by Allende, which accounted for nearly half of Chile's export revenues.

Footloose but strong geographic and national base: Although corporations operate internationally, they remain home orientated for the bulk of their business activities. Many are technically multinational rather than transnational (Hirst and Thompson, 1996). Not all manufacturing is footloose – the integration of manufacturing and services in many products, market access and delivery of specialised products and the place-based nature of many services means that mobility must be kept in perspective. The production of manufacturing and services is being internationalised, yet service delivery is being decentralised.

Money makes the world go around but ...: The abandonment of fixed exchange rates in the early 1970s and removal of capital controls led the average daily trade in the global foreign exchange market to soar from US$15 billion in 1973 to US$1,900 billion in 1998. Financial liberalisation encouraged the growth of speculation for short-term profit rather than productive investment. Monetary and financial flows linked to trade of goods and services account for only 2–3 per cent of financial transactions; the rest is speculation. For example, the vast bulk of foreign capital inflows in Thailand did not go into the more productive sectors of the economy such as manufacturing and agriculture but went principally to fuel asset inflation in the stock market and property speculation. By the end of 1996 Bangkok had over $20 billion of unsold residential and commercial property (Bello, 1998a). Liberalisation and globalisation have speeded up both investment in and capital flight from economies in trouble. In addition to the US$105 billion foreign capital flight from East Asia between 1996 and 1997, a further $31 billion was transferred out of South Korea, Indonesia, Malaysia, Thailand and the Philippines by domestic firms and wealthy families, of which two-thirds were off-the-books transactions.

The globalisation of capital has been predominantly in bonds and loans; equities accounted for only 7 per cent of the US$1,769 billion raised on international capital markets in 1997. Financial globalisation should not be exaggerated, as there are still national markets for mortgages and many other financial products and substantive differences in national financial regulatory regimes persist.

Capital is mobile but labour is relatively immobile: Finance capital is highly mobile but labour markets are regulated nationally and the migration of labour is strictly controlled. For example, US business has flooded over the Mexican border to exploit cheap labour but the US government, under the NAFTA agreement, spends $4.2 billion annually patrolling the border with 7,000 agents to prevent Mexicans illegally entering the USA. Only some 30 million workers or 1.5 per cent of the global workforce work in another country. Transnationals employ 73 million workers representing about 10 per cent of paid non-farm jobs worldwide and nearly 20 per cent of jobs in industrialised countries. However, the cost of labour, its skills and level of organisation is transmitted around the world. Employers use this information to try to suppress wage demands, reduce non-wage social costs and to transform the labour process by introducing new technology and/or changing working practices by threatening to relocate their operations to low wage countries. Meanwhile, governments have sought to weaken trade union organisation and bargaining powers in order to attract inward investment.

Devolution but centralisation: Democracy is preached but rarely practised. Most global organisations and national governments stress the importance of civil society but the centralisation of public policy-making, decentralisation to unelected bodies and consultation rather than involvement are the norm. The World Bank calls for decisions to be made at the lowest practicable level but does little about the democratisation and governance of global institutions.

Welfare benefits of globalisation but increased social costs: The OECD and World Bank claim that increasing economic integration and convergence in the global economy will have economic welfare benefits for all countries. Increased trade, foreign investment and open markets stimulate efficiency, growth and rising incomes (OECD, 1999a). But human poverty remains endemic. About 840 million people are malnourished, 1.3 billion people live on incomes of less than $1 (1987 PPP$) a day, a similar number do not have access to clean water and one in seven children of primary school age is out of school (UNDP, 1999). Globalisation is uneven and unstable with flows of investment and disinvestment causing economic crises and dysfunctioning markets. These in turn cause rising human insecurity in terms of access to employment, food and health care and threaten environmental, community and political security. Inequality is increasing both between and within regions and countries. The 1998 UNCTAD Trade and Development report repeated the previous year's warning

> of a potential backlash against the contradictions of a globalising world. When a colossal global market failure and measures taken to bail out creditors are paid for at the expense of the living standards of ordinary people, and of stability and development in the debtor developing countries concerned, who is to say that justice has been served? In East Asia the trend of decades of rising incomes has been reversed, and unemployment, underemployment and poverty are reaching alarming levels. Many of the lost jobs have been in sectors that had helped to reduce poverty by absorbing low-skilled workers from the countryside. (UNCTAD, 1998, p. 3)

An additional 52 million people fell into poverty in Indonesia, South Korea and Thailand as unemployment and food prices soared while health and social spending was cut.

Publicly denounce the state but privately demand and accept corporate welfare: Right-wing organisations and big business have mounted a constant stream of criticism of 'big government', the need to 'roll back the frontiers of the state' and have heaped abuse on welfare recipients. Big business has bankrolled organisations and politicians to peddle one-sided analysis, half-truths and right-wing propaganda. At the same time they have also been ensuring that governments reduce corporate taxes, deregulate and have extracted massive subsidies and tax reliefs for investment they would undertake anyway (see Chapter 5 for an analysis of corporate welfare).

New public management but private management in reality: Although performance management is dressed up to be 'new public management', it is in effect 'old private' management underpinned by commercial values, business organisational structures and competitive tendering (see Chapters 3 and 4).

Finally, it is speculation, not science: The 1997–8 East Asian financial crisis is a case in point. A UN study of market participants – equity, bond and foreign exchange traders, investment strategists, merchant bankers, economists, credit analysts and credit rating agencies – revealed that most were aware of certain problems but 'chose to ignore, or at least downplay, these consider-ations to focus on the positive aspects of the region'. Massive capital flows to the region were accelerating in the autumn of 1997 but turned into a net outflow as the crisis deepened.

The study also revealed that:

> Market participants do not know if the failure of the 'Asian economic miracle' was a failure of a 'crony-capitalism' or a variety of free-market entrepreneurial capitalism that had somehow gone very wrong. They do not know why they had taken on such excessive and risk taking positions in East Asia, whether it was an example of market failure, or whether the markets had failed. Market participants do not know whether these speculative excesses were an exception or the product of normal competitive pressures.
>
> Market participants do not know if flexible exchange rates would have prevented the crisis from engulfing the region, or this was due to free capital mobility.

The crisis had forced many market participants 'to question not just the wisdom of further financial market liberalisation and globalisation, but even more significantly, the very viability and stability of today's globalised and largely unregulated financial markets themselves' (Rude, 1998, pp. 23–4).

We can conclude that globalisation is contradictory, volatile and the cause and effect of changes in public policy. We now need to examine the specific role of the state in supporting and accelerating the globalisation process.

HOW THE STATE FACILITATES GLOBALISATION

This section focuses on ways in which the state plays an important role creating and regulating the conditions for globalisation. The first part shows how the internationalisation of privatisation has provided opportunities for financial institutions, consultants and advisers and transnational companies to widen and deepen their global presence and extend market share in key sectors of the global economy. The second part highlights the state role in opening up the public infrastructure for private investment and partnership. The final section details the plans to marketise government services globally.

The extent to which inward investment rather than indigenous growth is promoted, the extent of deregulation and other macroeconomic policies have a significant influence. Some states, such as Japan, Singapore, Korea and Taiwan, are increasingly acting as 'catalytic states' providing a wide array of incentives 'to finance overseas investment, to promote technology alliances between national and foreign firms, and to encourage regional relocation of production networks' (Weiss, 1998, p. 20–1). But the focus is always on state intervention in the economy and state policy for the corporate sector. However, privatisation has become a central means of undermining the post-war capital–labour settlement, of state withdrawal from the provision of the infrastructure and the sharing of social costs, shifting the cost burden on to individuals while providing capital with new markets and new forms of accumulation. Thus government policies of commodifying public services, creating new markets and selling state assets such as utilities, telecommunications and transport on international money markets, private infrastructure investment and partnerships, directly impact on the form and speed of globalisation. It is happening in other spheres of the economy, for example, the corporate expropriation of important plant, animal and microbial species 'to privatise life forms through the extension of patent protection represents a qualitatively new form of the private appropriation of social resources' and another challenge for state and international regulation and intervention (King and Stabinsky, 1998, p. 75).

Since 1979, some 140 governments have eliminated exchange controls affecting imports of goods and services and some 1,330 investment treaties have been negotiated involving 162 countries. States are bound up in a web of multinational trade and financial treaties, agreements and membership of regional and worldwide bodies.

Both industrialised and developing countries deregulated financial markets in the 1970s and 1980s which removed barriers to cross-border movement of financial assets and led to a vast increase in the volume of money circulating in the international money market. Deregulation increased speculation in foreign exchange markets thus restricting the ability of governments to control fiscal policies. It also enabled transnational companies to establish integrated production networks to reduce their exposure to currency fluctuations and fuelled takeovers and mergers. Deregulation helps to create a common, more uniform, framework which makes it harder for individual states to impose specific stringent regulations. This also enables capital to argue for policy and regulatory initiatives which favour its interests.

The Internationalisation of Privatisation

Privatisation has widened from Chile and Britain in the 1970s to most industrialised and developing countries. Gross global privatisation receipts totalled nearly $850 billion between 1990 and 1999 with OECD countries accounting for 70 per cent (see Table 2.1) although they fell 27 per cent in 1998. Annual global privatisation proceeds increased fivefold from US$33,340 million in 1990 to US$157,455 million in 1997 with Australia, Britain, France, Italy, Japan and Mexico having large asset sales. Proceeds from non-OECD countries increased nearly tenfold compared to the threefold OECD increase. The poorest region in the world, Sub-Sarahan Africa, did not escape World Bank/IMF strictures. More than 2,300 mainly small privatisations between 1988 and 1996 were concentrated in Mozambique, Angola and Zambia (Campbell-White and Bhatia, 1998). Although profitability increased, 'the removal of subsidies to parastatals has added to inflationary pressures, often forcing the poor to pay more for utility services, transport and food' (*Financial Times*, 2 October 1998).

Deregulation, demonopolisation, privatisation and the reform of trade and foreign investment regimes have been central to the high levels of international direct investment in the 1990s. The recent wave of international mergers among telecommunications and airline companies is testament to the tremendous impetus to FDI given by deregulation. An even greater impetus worldwide has come about through privatisation, with significant shares in, and sometimes control of, privatised firms going to foreign investors. ... In many countries, particularly in smaller OECD countries and in the developing world, the sale of public companies to foreign investors has been the primary source of inward investment in recent years. (OECD, 1997a, p. 15)

The bulk of privatisation has been in telecoms, financial services, utilities and transport. However, OECD financial data exclude the mass privatisation schemes in Central and Eastern Europe and the Treuhandanstalt asset sales in Germany between 1990 and 1994. This narrow definition of privatisation covers only the sale of industrial state-owned enterprises and excludes contracting out, public/private partnerships, franchising and the privatisation of the welfare state. The global total for the 1990–2000 period, taking into account all privatisation methods, is estimated at $2,000 billion.

Privatisation facilitates globalisation in several ways:

Table 2.1: **Gross global privatisation proceeds 1990–99** (US$bn)

	1990	1991	1992	1993	1994	1995	1996	1997	1998	1999*	Total
OECD	24,824	37,599	16,757	55,134	47,838	53,048	70,081	100,300	85,886	100,765	592,232
Other countries	8,516	11,605	17,458	17,983	18,436	14,551	22,026	57,155	45,153	44,000	256,883
Global total	33,340	48,020	34,215	73,117	66,274	67,599	92,107	157,455	131,039	144,765	849,115

Source: *Financial Market Trends*, No. 76, June 2000.
* Estimate

Foreign investment: Marketisation and outsourcing of public services enables foreign firms to tender for contracts or to acquire firms with contracts to gain market share. Similarly, assets sold via trade sales to foreign companies, for example, Wisconsin Rail's acquisition of freight operations in Britain and New Zealand, have enabled companies to widen their international operations. Flotations and share offers are sold internationally, helping to consolidate emerging capital markets and increase opportunities for foreign investment. Flow of surplus value and profits exported back to industrialised countries.

Economic integration: Privatisation and marketisation were used to integrate Central and Eastern Europe into the global economy. Deregulation and liberalisation create market conditions for global capital.

Growth of multinationals: Privatisation projects have enabled banks, financial institutions, lawyers, management consultants and advisers to sell their expertise overseas thus widening their network of offices. Companies created by privatisation have invested overseas in core activities and diversification.

New alliances: Infrastructure projects have generated partnerships and alliances between finance capital, construction and facilities management companies which have in turn sought to enter new markets overseas. Infrastructure-related land and property development has attracted international investment.

The combined effect of these developments has been to broaden, deepen and to accelerate the globalisation process.

Increased globalisation of financial markets, particularly emerging markets in developing countries, has also reinforced the power of the corporate sector and wealthy families in developing countries. Major state assets such as telecommunications, electricity, gas and water services and other publicly owned corporations in both OECD and developing countries are usually sold via international share offerings. Between 40 per cent and 50 per cent of Britain's telecom, energy and water shares were sold internationally. In 1995, 50 per cent of privatisations in OECD countries were sold to foreign investors compared to 34 and 33 per cent respectively for 1994 and 1993. TNCs have acquired many assets through trade sales, mergers and takeovers or by involvement in privately financed infrastructure projects. Trade sales account for nearly a fifth of global privatisation receipts. A core group of multinational firms, financial institutions and consultancies have dominated sale preparation, restructuring, financial and legal advice.

The IMF and the World Bank played a major role in requiring developing countries to adopt privatisation, marketisation and deregulation of their economies as a precondition for structural adjustment loans, debt restructuring and 'reform' programmes (Whitfield, 1985,1992). The aim was to integrate these economies into the global world economy. The OECD notes that

> privatisation was pursued far more rigorously by developing countries than by OECD countries, usually as part of broader programmes of stabilisation, deregulation and structural reform. These programmes, often implemented with the support of the IMF and World Bank, sought to substitute market discipline for the previous static-protectionist development regimes, which were seen as having led to unsatisfactory economic results. (OECD, 1996a, p. 13)

The OECD presents privatisation as a win-win-win policy but it relies heavily on evidence from member governments which is often exaggerated and lacking verification although this does not seem to deter the endless repetition of claims (see Chapter 6). Employment, socioeconomic and environmental impact analysis is virtually non-existent or flawed.

Privatisation and Foreign Investment

Between 1988 and 1994, foreign investors accounted for about 42 per cent of the total proceeds from privatisation, of which FDI accounted for two-thirds of foreign investment with the remainder coming from portfolio equity investment. Some 39 per cent of total FDI in Europe and Central Asia came from privatisation in the same period, compared with 15.1 per cent in Latin America and 2.0 per cent in South Asia. Privatisation policies also attracted additional foreign and domestic investment, in a ratio of three to one, because it signalled government commitment to the private sector (Bouton and Sumlinski, 1996). Privatisation has been a dominant part of FDI in Central and Eastern Europe, accounting for the bulk of inflows to the Czech Republic, Croatia, Bulgaria, Moldova between 1995 and 1997 and Hungary where it declined from 68 per cent to 13 per cent in the same period.

The same financial institutions which are at the source of the debt problem, are now facilitating the sale of assets, in the name of 'reform'.

Many financial institutions have set up new investment trusts to 'facilitate' the sale of government assets on a worldwide basis and provide a channel through which investors, primarily in industrialised countries, can invest in flotations on a global basis. For example, the Guinness Flight Global Privatisation Fund invested £100 million in telecoms, electricity, banking and other privatised companies mainly in Britain and continental Europe. The promotional material to investors describes the 'privatisation effect' – that after privatisation management's interests align with those of shareholders, increasing efficiency and profitability, privatised companies tend to have dominant market positions, many being monopolies; they have robust balance sheets, strong asset backing and high dividend yields; governments

Table 2.2: **FDI from privatisation (asset sales) in developing countries 1989–94**

Region	FDI from privatisation [a]($m)	Share of region's FDI inflows (%)
North Africa and Middle East	447.3	2.9
Sub-Sarahan Africa	948.4	7.6
East Asia and the Pacific	2,739.0	1.5
South Asia	87.0	2.1
Latin America and the Caribbean	13,391.6	14.2
Central and Eastern Europe[b]	8,578.0	48.5

Source: *World Investment Report 1996*, UNCTAD, 1996. [a]1991–4 period
[b]Covers asset sales but not privately financed infrastructure projects.

price shares cheaply to ensure success and tend to sell them off in favourable market conditions (see Whitfield, 1992 for details of British privatisation), so much for 'failing' nationalised industries and public ownership.

Cross-border mergers and acquisitions accounted for 64 per cent of FDI in 1998 compared to 42 per cent in 1992. They accounted for the bulk of the increase in FDI and pushed the total of cross-border mergers and acquisitions worldwide to a record $411 billion in 1998. United Kingdom FDI inflows between 1992 and 1997 totalled $126,275 billion over six years but foreign acquisition of privatised companies accounted for a significant proportion. Globally, cross-border mergers and acquisitions in three service sectors subject to extensive privatisation, namely the distribution of electricity and water, the production of electricity and gas and telecommunications, had increased by 2,035 per cent in the 1991–7 period (see Table 2.3). The increased size of cross-border deals and soaring share prices accounted for only part of this enormous increase. Combining FDI takeover, merger and privatisation investment, it is clear that a large part of FDI is devoted to merely changing ownership.

Savings, pensions and insurance payments play an increasingly influential role in financing foreign direct investment and privatisation. The spectacular growth of institutional investment by pension funds, insurance companies and investment companies (portfolio investment) increased total institutional assets in the main regions in the OECD from $3,200 billion in 1981 (38 per cent of GDP) to $24,400 billion in 1995 (106.5 per cent of GDP). Insurance companies had 36 per cent of total holdings in 1995 followed by pension funds (25 per cent), investment companies (23 per cent) and other forms of institutional saving accounting for 16 per cent. The composition of funds varies widely between bonds, loans, shares and other investments.

Table 2.3: **Growth of cross-border mergers and acquisitions in privatised service sectors 1991–7** (US$m)

Sector	1991	1992	1993	1994	1995	1996	1997
Electricity and water distribution	350	8,848	10,320	10,541	17,490	25,419	32,337
Production and distribution of gas, electricity and other forms of energy	212	8,823	9,482	10,506	16,039	24,203	32,103
Postal serv. and telecommunications	3,400	2,572	17,062	8,958	17,921	15,529	20,154
Total	3,962	20,243	36,864	30,005	51,450	65,151	84,594

Source: *World Investment Report 1998*, Annex table B.9, UNCTAD, 1998.

Portfolio investment in developing countries has increased since the early 1990s but is subject to significant yearly fluctuations as a result of the Mexican 1994 and East Asian 1997 financial crises. Portfolio investment has far exceeded FDI in Latin America since 1992 and in some Asian countries.

The USA has a 57 per cent share of the world investment fund market (1996). The OECD points to a fundamental change in that 'savings are being shifted away from regulated and insured banking institutions to entities that are sometimes not insured and that operate in different regulatory regimes and have different investment objectives. This rising internationalisation of savings has a profound impact on the structure and functioning of the world's capital markets' (OECD, 1999b). Control over these capital flows is crucial – pension funds have limited trustee control, insurance is usually individualised with companies having the freedom to invest, mutual and investments trusts provide investors with a choice of funds and sectors although investment decisions are entirely the prerogative of the fund. The increasing power of pension funds influences capital markets and ultimately corporate governance. Some countries, notably Britain and the Netherlands, have a high proportion of international and equity assets while others focus on domestic investment (see Chapter 5). Savings and pension investment is expected to continue to increase, driven by rising standards of living, people living longer, the decline in the value of state pensions and subsequent growth in second tier pensions, aided by financial service companies exploiting the use of information and communications technology.

The state plays a central role in the provision of social insurance and the welfare state and the terms upon which employers contribute to these costs. The financialisation of capital – the preoccupation or dominance of finance capital over economic growth and investment in production – has been fuelled by the rapid rise in employees' savings and deferred wages (pensions). Financial and property investment has often been more profitable than investment in production. Financial outlets sought to maximise returns and try to avoid catastrophe of any massive devaluation. This is encouraging globalisation of state policies of privatisation, deregulation (Amin, 1997, p. 253).

PRIVATELY FINANCED INFRASTRUCTURE AND SUSTAINABLE DEVELOPMENT: MORTGAGING THE FUTURE

We now turn our focus to the rapid growth of privately funded infrastructure projects and partnerships. Following a short period of nationalisation and expropriation in the 1965–75 decade, infrastructure investment was regarded with uncertainty. The 1980s debt crisis led to capital budgets absorbing a disproportionate share of spending cuts, particularly in Latin America. Spending cuts led to poorly maintained infrastructure which was unable to keep pace with growth and urbanisation as a result of migration into cities. This led to fiscal conflict between social and infrastructure provision. Developing countries now seek foreign investment to improve their infrastructure and international competitiveness because of continued budgetary constraints and the substantial resources needed to finance projects.

Privately financed infrastructure has grown rapidly in developing countries while Britain is setting a precedent in Western Europe with the private finance initiative applied throughout the public sector. Full privatisation is claimed to provide the answer in some countries but continuing reservations about its long-term effects have led to the development of variants of the design, build, finance and operate transfer models. This is part of a wider agenda to shift the role of government from owner and producer to facilitator and regulator, to promote private sector participation in physical and social infrastructure including basic services to the poor and creating an enabling environment and incentives to make markets work better (Asian Development Bank, 1999).

Private sector involvement in infrastructure projects takes various forms:

- outright privatisation;
- build-operate-transfer projects – the private sector designs, builds, finances and operates a facility for a defined period after which ownership and operation pass to the government;
- build-own-operate – similar to above but ownership and operation remain with the private sector;
- build-transfer-operate – the private sector operates and shares revenues with government, ownership passes to government after completion.

Infrastructure schemes are funded by debt (loans from financial institutions, parent companies and the issue of bonds), by equity (equity or profits from parent firm or affiliates or direct investment funds) or by non-equity contributions such as technical know-how, sharing the cost of research and development, trade credits or in-kind such as equipment. Rates of return for privatisation projects are two to three times higher in emerging economies than in OECD countries, for example, roads (10–30 per cent), power (15–30 per cent), telecommunications (20–30 per cent) and ports (7–20 per cent) (Durchslag et al., 1994). Utilities and transport are already privatised in Britain hence PPPs include a wide range of government services including defence and security support activities, transport, government offices, hospitals, schools and other welfare state infrastructure facilities. Projects are generally smaller than those in developing countries and have reduced risk because the private sector is less reliant on user charges for transport tolls or increasing state subsidised utility prices.

The World Bank believes the public sector is less efficient in managing new infrastructure activities so 'the time has come for private actors to provide what were once assumed to be purely public services' (Ferreira and Khatami,

1995 p. vi). Infrastructure investment is considered essential to underpin the productivity of labour and capital, facilitating growth, safeguarding existing infrastructure investment, attracting production and foreign investment in the context of continuing regionalisation and globalisation. Developing countries rely on foreign investment because of the shortage of domestic savings and have to minimise actual and perceived risks, give appropriate guarantees and show commitment to 'approved' macroeconomic and public sector reform.

Privately financed infrastructure and partnership projects have traditionally been promoted and implemented on a sectoral basis such as transport, utilities and communications by the World Bank, development banks and governments. PPPs are usually justified by the lack of public finance, gaining access to private sector technical know-how and project management skills. However, this is a very narrow perspective for three reasons. First, it focuses on the pros and cons of a particular section of infrastructure and tends to understate the related development opportunities created for PPP consortia. Second, it does not take account of the extension of PPPs to the welfare state infrastructure (schools, hospitals and housing) and defence and security (IT and military support). Third, partnership is now promoted as the way forward for regeneration and urban development. What is at stake is not simply the supply and distribution of power and water or the provision of toll roads but ownership and control of development opportunities and new markets created by the provision and operation of the infrastructure by private capital.

The 1998 APEC Public-Business/Private Sector Dialogue on Infrastructure and Sustainable Development highlighted the limitations of a utility/transport perspective in creating partnerships for sustainable cities and the rural economy (APEC, 1998). In other words, the real agenda is about maximising capital accumulation in cities in the industrialised north and the mega cities created by rapid urbanisation in developing countries. Individual infrastructure projects are being replaced by private sector finance and management of the economic and urban development process in zones or territories, forging a new alliance between state and capital. It is a new developmental paradigm and raises key questions of who will own and control cities/regions in the future. It is rooted in capital accumulation, marketisation of the state, private land and property ownership and corporate governance in the developmental, regeneration and urbanisation processes. Palliatives of eradicating poverty, social inclusion and social capital only serve to obscure the shift in global forces.

A similar marketisation of environmental sustainability is being promoted by the UN and other agencies. United Nations Development Programme (UNDP) papers refer to the need to 'convert the non-market benefits of environmental conservation into cash flows' to establish global markets to enable the private sector to 'appropriate the economic value of non-market benefits' (Pearce, 1997, p. 1). Policy appears to be based on a combination of sweeping criticism of publicly operated infrastructure but uncritical acceptance of private sector involvement and the promotion of privatisation and marketisation as the central means of achieving environmental sustainability.

Infrastructure concessions or franchises were common in railways, canals, ports and utilities in the nineteenth century. Since then, the state has funded infrastructure and had a central role in identifying needs, strategic planning and procuring construction. The decline in infrastructure investment started in Britain and the USA in the late 1970s with major cuts in capital programmes, speeding up the spiral of decline and enlarging the infrastructure deficit in roads, schools, hospitals, aggravated by the neglect of maintenance. For example, in the USA, real non-defence public capital stock rose between 1977 and 1997 at only half the rate it had between 1955 and 1977 (Levy and Cadette, 1998).

The political and business interests which demanded drastic spending cuts over the last two decades are the same interests which are demanding infrastructure privatisation today. They are intent on making infrastructure investment commercially viable by incorporating user charges, demanding World Bank and government guarantees and increasing channels for pension fund and savings investment. In developing countries this process goes hand in hand with the development of domestic capital markets to increase the volume and improve the terms of domestic savings for financing infrastructure (World Bank, 1994a, p. 4). Private control of key parts of the infrastructure enables capital to influence regional planning, industrial and commercial development and promote a business agenda. However, there is a key contradiction because the same interests demanding public disinvestment and privatisation also rely on a comprehensive infrastructure for business and for the state to be responsible for crises and externalities. They also rely on the state to manage the transition between public, public/private and private infrastructure ownership.

Private investment in infrastructure in developing countries accelerated from a very low level a decade ago rising to $27 billion in 1996, about 10 per cent of total infrastructure investment, although it has since levelled off. The World Bank reported an upsurge in private involvement in infrastructure projects in the 1980s:

> The principal new infrastructure entrepreneurs are international firms seeking business in developing countries and operating often in association with local companies. These firms bring to bear not only their management expertise and technical skills, but also their credit standing and ability to finance investments in developing countries. Major electric, telecommunications, and water utilities in industrial countries face slowly growing demand and increased competition (following deregulation) in their home markets. As a result, they are vigorously seeking high-yielding investments in developing countries. (World Bank, 1994, p. 42)

Between 1984 and 1995, 86 industrial and developing countries privatised 547 infrastructure companies valued at $357 billion. The private sector participated in a further 570 greenfield projects valued at $300 billion in a similar number of countries. The World Bank definition of economic infrastructure covers public utilities: power (30 per cent of projects), telecommunications (28 per cent), water and sanitation (18 per cent), gas supply (6 per cent), public works: road transport (8 per cent), and other transport: railways (2 per cent), buses, ports and waterways (5 per cent) and airports (3 per cent). Foreign investment accounted for 51 per cent of the total infrastructure privatisation revenue between 1988 and 1995 with the highest level of foreign investment in telecoms (67 per cent), utilities (39 per cent) and transport averaging 29 per cent (UNCTAD, 1996). The World Bank database is tracking over 2,250 potential projects, 85 per cent of which are greenfield. A country analysis of signed deals shows the USA leading both in terms of the number and value of projects with the bulk of projects occurring in emerging economies (see Table 2.4).

Table 2.4: **Signed project deals by country, 1996**

Country	No. of signed projects	Value of signed projects ($bn)
USA	103	49
Hong Kong	36	19
Indonesia	72	14
UK	41	13
Australia	44	13
Thailand	31	9
China	64	8
India	28	7
Germany	9	6
Brazil	23	6

Source: Dailami and Klein, 1998

Between 1990 and 1997 over 630 privately financed water/sewage and electricity projects, valued at US$131 billion, were launched in developing countries (Table 2.5). Three transnational companies account for the bulk of the water projects. In addition, there were 191 privately financed mass transit and express highway projects in Asia alone at the end of 1998.

Since the early 1990s many countries have taken measures to deregulate and liberalise foreign investment in infrastructure projects, particularly relaxing regulations to encourage BOT (Build-Operate-Transfer) schemes. Nevertheless, such investments are still considered complex and perceived as high risk, consequently investors demand high rates of return which normally means higher user charges. Multilateral institutions such as MIGA

Table 2.5: **Investment in infrastructure projects with private participation in developing countries 1990–8** (US$ million)

	1990	1991	1992	1993	1994	1995	1996	1997	1998	Total
Sector										
Telecommunications	6.6	13.1	7.9	10.9	19.5	20.1	33.4	49.6	53.1	214.0
Energy	1.6	1.2	11.1	14.3	17.1	23.9	34.9	46.2	26.8	177.1
Transport	7.5	3.1	5.7	7.4	7.6	7.5	13.1	16.3	14.0	82.2
Water and sanitation	0.0	0.1	1.8	7.3	0.8	1.4	2.0	8.4	1.5	23.3
Region										
East Asia and Pacific	2.3	4.0	8.7	15.9	17.3	20.4	31.5	37.6	9.5	147.2
Europe and Central Asia	0.1	0.3	0.5	1.6	3.9	8.4	10.7	15.3	11.3	52.0
Latin America and Caribbean	12.9	12.3	17.1	18.0	18.4	19.0	27.4	45.1	66.3	236.5
Middle East and North Africa	0.0	0.0	0.0	3.3	0.3	0.1	0.3	5.2	3.6	12.8
South Asia	0.3	0.8	0.1	1.2	4.3	4.0	11.4	13.7	2.3	38.1
Sub-Saharan Africa	0.0	0.0	0.1	0.0	0.7	1.0	2.0	3.5	2.3	9.6
Total	15.6	17.4	26.6	39.9	44.9	52.9	83.3	120.4	95.3	496.2

Source: Recent Trends in Private Participation in Infrastructure, Public Policy for the Private Sector, Note No. 196, September 1998.
Note: Some totals do not add up due to rounding.

provide 'contracts of guarantee' for foreign investors which rose from 4 to 12 per cent of MIGA's portfolio by 1996, a third of new applications being infrastructure projects. Similarly, the British government introduced legislation in 1997 which provides financial guarantees for PFI projects irrespective of other public spending commitments or needs. The World Bank supports private infrastructure through loans to governments to define and implement projects – 215 loans were approved between 1988 and 1998 with a PPP component – and the International Finance Corporation, a bank subsidiary, participates directly in private projects through loans or equity, supporting 30 projects in 1998 alone.

Table 2.6: **Growth in private cross-border flows to infrastructure** (US$ billion)

	1988	1989	1990	1991	1992	1993	1994	1995	1996
Loans	0.1	0.8	1.4	0.1	1.5	6.3	6.0	11.1	7.7
Bonds	0	0.2	0.5	0.7	1.1	3.9	5.8	3.3	7.2
Equity	0	0	0.1	2.6	3.1	2.1	3.9	1.3	5.4
Total	0.1	0.9	2.0	3.5	5.8	12.3	15.7	15.6	20.3

Source: Dealing with Public Risk in Private Infrastructure, World Bank, 1997.
Note: Some totals do not add up due to rounding.

The 'past decade has witnessed radical shifts in previously accepted paradigms about the nature of public goods and public services, "natural monopolies" and the respective roles of the public and private sectors'. Private investment, under the 'right conditions', allowed 'fiscally constrained governments to concentrate on their own efforts far more selectively and effectively than before' (World Bank, 1994a, p. 89).

The World Bank supports the development of local capital markets to fund infrastructure projects either by bond finance or contractual savings in pension funds and insurance companies. For example, Chile's privatised pension funds have funded the privatisation of utilities including the Santiago subway system, holding between 10 and 35 per cent of project equity. Similarly, the Philippines' social security system has created a 4 billion peso fund, administered by local banks, to invest in power projects. Despite these trends, the World Bank expects 'moving from today's still heavy dependence on public financing to tomorrow's system of more private sponsorship is likely to be a long and sometimes painful process' (World Bank, 1994a, p. 108).

STATES MAKE MARKETS

The final part of this chapter outlines the way in which nation states are facilitating the marketisation of government services and thus increasing globalisation.

Public services are part of the service sector which includes business and financial services, construction, transportation, communications, leisure and tourism. Changes in the production, organisation and financing of private services impact on government services and vice versa. The composition of services has changed with the expansion of professional and technical services, education, health care, banking and insurance but others have declined, such as the repair and maintenance of new products. Information and communications technologies enable the 'codification of knowledge' thus allowing services to be inventoried and traded internationally.

Outsourcing or contracting out extends marketisation of the state, providing further opportunities for transnational companies; it facilitates transfer of work to other locations; provides opportunities for capital to finance investment in new equipment, property and partnership; and has an ideological spin-off in promoting private provision.

Competitive tendering or market testing started with individual service contracts, then related services, followed by the emergence of facilities management contracts covering a package of support services. Multi-service contracts are increasingly common. Foreign-based transnational companies increased their market share in Britain from 16 to 45 per cent by 1997 (Local Government Management Board, 1998).

The US government spends an estimated $175 billion annually on contracted supplies. In Britain, central and local government, including the NHS, expenditure on goods and services in 1997–8 was £158 billion (excluding grants and debt interest) and £15 billion capital expenditure (excluding PPP projects). An increasing part of the economy is subject to market forces. The scale of new 'markets' is enormous which accounts for the intensive lobbying by private sector trade and business organisations for global markets and minimal regulation:

- The annual global education market is estimated at $2,000 billion with the US and British markets valued at $700 billion (2000) and £60 billion (1998) respectively (EduVentures, 1999). Public expenditure in OECD countries accounts for an average of 80 per cent of total education spending. It accounted for 89 per cent of total education expenditure in developed countries and 75 per cent in developing countries according to a World Bank survey of 41 countries (Patrinos, 1999). Children are big business – US retailers estimate that girls between seven and 14 spend $24 billion annually and influence a further $66 billion parental purchases (*Financial Times*, 26 September 1999).

- Total world health expenditure was estimated at $2,225 billion in the mid-1990s, of which 90 per cent was accounted for by OECD countries. Hospital services represent between 40 and 50 per cent of expenditure, pharmaceuticals between 30 and 40 per cent with outpatients accounting for the remainder (World Trade Organisation, 1998a). The proportion of private provision varies widely between countries. UNCTAD estimates much higher levels of expenditure – $3,000 billion for the OECD or about $3,330 billion worldwide.
- The global telecoms industry, services and equipment, is expected to grow to $1,000 billion in 2000. The WTO liberalisation agreement in 1997 has accelerated privatisation and a wave of mergers and takeovers in both industrialised and developing countries. Six transnationals, with a market capitalisation of over $150 billion, already dominate the market
- US municipal water services have annual sales of about $50 billion, the private sector operates only 10 per cent of a highly fragmented market in which there is substantial scope to achieve economies of scale.
- The waste management market in five European countries (UK, Germany, Italy, France and Spain) was worth £18 billion in 1995 with the public sector share varying between 40 and 50 per cent. The European Union market is forecast to reach £41 billion by 2005 (Public Services International Research Unit, 1998).

The variation in the mobility of public services has already been noted. The relocation of administrative functions in welfare state agencies to the regions, facilitated by improved information and communications technology, is an example of this mobility. Much design and specialist work in construction, transportation and engineering projects is often 'flown in' or performed elsewhere. Competition in professional services is only partly based on the cost of labour because technical ability, innovation and a comprehensive service are usually more important together with higher levels of productivity. The service is static but contractors, increasingly multinationals, are highly mobile.

Despite claims that privatisation and contracting out markets remain dominated by private corporations on a single-country basis, transnational companies had a substantial market share before tendering began in 1989 and it has helped them increase their market share. The claim that 'national political idiosyncrasies constitute irremovable barriers to the development of broader transnational corporations dominating public service production' is simply untrue (Dunleavy, 1994, p. 37). Transnational companies such as Serco, ISS, EDS and Stagecoach have entered new markets and countries with relative ease.

GLOBALISATION OF PUBLIC MANAGEMENT

Public management reform has been internationalised by the promotion of reforms in Britain, the USA and New Zealand, by the World Bank and IMF as part of structural adjustment policies and by the promotion of performance management by the OECD's Public Management Service. The latter is focused on results, a greater client focus and accountability, the creation of competitive markets to provide more cost effective alternatives to direct provision, building internal markets and the use of market-based instruments, separation of purchaser and provider functions and decentralised management (OECD, 1998a). The internationalisation of public management provides a common operating system for transnationals thus eroding local, cultural and ethnic traditions, facilitates international benchmarking comparisons and opens up a massive national/local state market tendering goods and services for capital. It provides a degree of common organisational structures, business values, marketisation, user charges and performance assessment. Service and finance capital want to improve and consolidate government management systems in order to safeguard their infrastructure investments. Convergence of public management has occurred despite wide differences in national politics, institutions, legal systems and traditions. The OECD maintains that 'a nation's public management policy is a matter of concern to its partners because it affects efficiency and policy effectiveness' ... and 'policies must increasingly be made more consistent or competitive with trends in main trading partners' (OECD, 1996d, p. 4).

Multinationals also pressurise nation states to standardise public service organisation and procurement and the packaging of services in order to achieve economies of scale. The state is also forced to try to achieve comparable private sector productivity, ignoring fundamental differences in the values, function and organisation of the public sector. Restructuring the labour process is the real agenda behind the mask of service quality.

The continued internationalisation of management consultancy also helped to promote particular reform methods and the transfer of private corporate management into the public sector. Downsizing, a focus on core competence, outsourcing and customer care have been essential ingredients in the internationalisation of business management.

SUMMARY

In short, government policies have a major impact on the scale and speed of globalisation, particularly through privatisation of nationalised industries/state-owned corporations, privately financed infrastructure projects and marketisation of the public sector. It is not simply a matter of globalisation impacting on the state, but state policies shape the scope and form of globalisation.

3

Modernising the State: A Third Way for Competition

No organisation, public or private, can remain organisationally or operationally static. Continuous change is essential to ensure economic and social progress, to improve the effectiveness of services, to harness information and communications technology and to increase organisational capacity.

This chapter and Chapter 4 examine the transformation agenda, its rationale, policies and the methods used to modernise government. They focus on Britain for two important reasons. First, between 1979 and 1997, the British state was subject to radical restructuring and privatisation on a scale unparalleled among major industrialised economies. Restructuring in New Zealand went further and deeper but, as a relatively small economy, was not as influential as Thatcherism. Second, since 1997 the Labour government has led the way in promoting the Third Way as an alternative to neo-liberalism. It has led the world in private finance and partnerships for renewal of the welfare state social infrastructure as well as the transport and communications infrastructure. It is also continuing the restructuring of the welfare state, largely copying US reforms. This has serious implications for other European countries.

The analysis extends over two chapters. This chapter begins by examining the roots and objectives of transformation, summarises the critique of nationalisation and develops a theory of transformative change and a political economy typology of transformation. The remainder of the chapter is divided into two parts. The first examines changes in the function of the state (economic management, the commodification of services, and privatisation, outsourcing and transfers). The second describes changes in how the state finances these activities (the restructuring of public finance and partnership/private finance). Chapter 4 takes a similar approach to assess organisational and operational change.

THE ROOTS OF TRANSFORMATION AND MODERNISATION

Reform was not an invention of Thatcherism. Cycles of reform, initiated by periodic government commissions throughout the twentieth century, have sought to reorganise central and local government and encourage the adoption of new management techniques. The planning programming and budgeting system, corporate planning and public participation in planning were examples in the 1970s. Traditionally, restructuring has been carried out by the state, within the state with an emphasis on reorganisation, operational systems and integrating new responsibilities rather than changing functions or transferring ownership. But the 1979 Conservative government sought to radically transform the state by privatising and outsourcing functions, hence restructuring was different in scope, intensity and enforcement than previous reform initiatives.

Restructuring has gained momentum in five overlapping phases:

1. efficiency, competition and privatisation (early 1980s);
2. organisational change – agencies, quangos, transfer of services (late 1980s);
3. competitive tendering and consumerism (early 1990s);
4. partnership and private finance (mid-1990s);
5. performance management and devolution (late 1990s/early 2000).

Britain set a precedent in the 1980s for the sheer scale of its privatisation programme. Most OECD countries, under the umbrella of performance management, practised similar policies although with different objectives because of political, legal and cultural differences (Pollitt and Summa, 1997). Britain does not have a constitution nor is there administrative law which governs the management of routine work of the civil service. This allowed Thatcher to use the power of the executive to require the formation of Next Steps Agencies and market testing throughout the civil service and the NHS. Legislation was required, however, for competitive tendering in local government and the privatisation of major assets. In contrast, administrative law in most European countries made such wide and rapid change almost impossible (Ridley, 1996).

Civil service reform is an important feature of World Bank structural adjustment and economic management programmes in developing countries. 'Governments in many developing countries are unable to manage and finance their civil services ... which are frequently too large, too expensive, and insufficiently productive; and civil servants, especially those in managerial positions, get few incentives and are poorly motivated' (World Bank, 1995a, p. 1). The reforms concentrated on short-term cost containment measures such as reducing ghost workers and posts, implementing early retirement and voluntary departure programmes and equalising and simplifying salary structures. Equally important, civil service reform is needed to ensure that the Bank's privatisation, deregulation and commercialisation policies are vigorously pursued.

Criticism of Nationalisation

By the early 1970s public services in Britain, particularly the nationalised industries, required reform which, following a period of rapid post-war growth and investment, was inevitable. Democratic accountability was weak, often characterised by poor management in bureaucratic, hierarchical and often unresponsive organisations. There were few attempts to involve users or employees and information disclosure was restricted. Some programmes, such as the local government slum clearance 'machine' (and the building interests which supported it), had ignored local needs as it rolled from clearance areas into potential improvement areas. Many new, often high rise, estates lacked basic facilities. The policy was only stopped after several years of continuous action by tenants and residents' campaigns demanding the retention and improvement of their homes. Public sector trade union density was high but industrial democracy was weak and fragmented. Spending cuts in the late 1970s, imposed as a result of IMF intervention, drastically slowed down the building of new schools, hospitals, transport and community facilities.

Internal reform was a feasible alternative but the Tories characteristically exploited service dissatisfaction to enforce privatisation. It is now common practice to portray nationalisation as a 'failure from any standpoint' (Foster and Plowden, 1996, p. xi) and to describe services as 'inefficient'. But this exaggerated criticism fails to recognise that if they were so bad, how were they privatised so quickly and why were investors so eager to acquire shares? The government spent millions preparing public assets for sale but not on improving services.

There have been two virtually separate debates in progress about the future of the state. The first is about the size and role of government, its functions and how they should be financed. The second is how the state should be managed and government made more effective. The problem is that the 'solutions' offered rarely connect the two together. New approaches to public management cannot be developed independently of the role and function of the state, yet this is precisely what has happened. There are quite different skills, resources and management strategies required by a state directly providing a comprehensive range of services compared to an enabling state monitoring contracts and regulating markets.

The pressure for reform was both internal and external. There has been an abject lack of understanding of global and local capital (financial, service and industrial) interests in the restructuring of public services and the welfare state. The fact that multinational service companies, trade associations and the large management consultancies had a vested interest in the marketisation and privatisation of the state appears to have been ignored. A common interest has been all too apparent between officers and Elected Members using 'independent' consultants to justify outsourcing and restructuring while the consultants have peddled their so-called 'independence' to maintain the flow of contracts and their ideological commitment to marketisation of the public sector. The restructuring of labour has equally been understated. Some analysts have been intent on trying to find a public administration rationale for overtly political motives, while others have focused more superficially on 'fat cats', company donations to political parties or vested interests in the award of contracts.

The 'management of government' has become a diversion from tackling the important issues of governance, extending democratic control and accountability and implementing social justice strategies. The promise of efficiency 'savings' from contracting and downsizing put the spotlight on departmental budgets thus avoiding debate about public finance as a whole. Many of these changes are not exclusive to the public sector since private firms have been downsizing, outsourcing, selling subsidiaries and refocusing on their core competencies. But the scale and depth of public sector transformation and modernisation is unparalleled.

THE OBJECTIVES OF TRANSFORMATION AND MODERNISATION

A wide ranging analysis of government and the Conservative Party revealed the following objectives:

1. To transform ownership: increasing private ownership of key economic assets in order to increase productivity, efficiency and to create the conditions for economic growth; to make the achievement of socialism more difficult, and to simultaneously discredit public ownership and collective provision, placing greater responsibility on the family and individuals for the reproduction of labour and the costs of caring.
2. To marketise public services: creating new markets for private capital in the finance and operation of public services, the welfare state and the urban infrastructure.
3. To transform the labour process and reduce the power of trade unions.
4. To reduce public expenditure in order to cut personal and corporate taxation. Strict central control of public sector pay was a key government objective, starting with a cash limits policy between 1980 and 1985, followed by a more relaxed policy based in 'merit, skill and geography' between 1985 and 1990, major organisational change in the 1990–2 period encouraged decentralised pay bargaining, and centralised public sector-wide pay limits with further decentralisation of pay bargaining from 1992.
5. To maximise accumulation by deregulation and new systems to control local government activities and spending.
6. To create a smaller, more efficient and better managed state. To increase management accountability for performance, improved labour productivity, the wider use of new technology and strengthen management's 'right to manage' through devolved organisational structures with their

own budgets, performance measures and giving managers the power to hire and fire as part of more 'flexible' labour policies.

7. To maintain political control: centralising power, under the guise of rolling back the frontiers of the state, and maintaining neo-liberal hegemony.

The Conservatives claimed that since services were run in the interests of producers, i.e. the staff, rather than users, curbing the influence of trade unions was justified. A reduction and eventual elimination of better employment terms and conditions in the public sector was another objective. Their strategy was to separate quality of service from the quality of employment and to claim that who delivered the service was irrelevant.

Labour's Modernisation Agenda

Europe, devolution and industrial relations are three main policy differences between Labour and Conservative governments. The Labour government's objectives for public services and the welfare state have been cloaked in the rhetoric of the 'Third Way' and modernisation. Some of the objectives are hidden behind public statements proclaiming 'what matters is what works', and indisputably agreeable but vague statements about modernisation and renewal.

Blair's new vision for local government identified three reasons for change: locality's lack of a sense of direction, a lack of coherence in delivering local services, and wide variation in the quality of local services. But 'there is no future in the old model of councils trying to plan and and run most services' (DETR, 1998a, p. 5, John Prescott in Foreword and Introduction). Instead local government is expected to create a Third Way in which local authorities will develop a vision for their locality, provide a focus for partnership and 'guarantee services for all' yet directly deliver only 'some services'.

A key difference is Labour's commitment to democratic renewal and innovation in council structures. However, democratic renewal is primarily about improving voter turnout and reinventing individual participation, since there is scant evidence of commitment and resources for community development, improving democratic accountability of user and community organisations or to strengthen civil society other than to encourage the takeover of service delivery. The government is assuming that users will support them against the interests of the providers and the 'underperforming' or 'failing' local authorities. There is slightly less emphasis on the dogmatic drive towards private ownership and more emphasis on partnership with business and welfare state pluralism.

Labour's modernisation project is based on minimum reversal of Tory legislation. In practice, this has meant the continuation of Conservative style transformation although some policies are repackaged and justified by different objectives. The Labour government continued the commitment to:

- the transition to a performance-competition state in which, albeit voluntary, competitive tendering is legitimised across the public sector, not limited to defined services;
- a national programme of privatisation, although on a smaller scale;
- externalisation and transfer of local government (which is continuing at the same, if not faster, rate primarily because of Labour's belief in the enabling model) has been institutionalised in the Best Value regime;
- escalating corporatisation and commercialisation of the state, with increasing use of company structures;
- substantially increased role for private capital funding of the infrastructure and public services;
- a flexible labour market;
- a greater commitment to promote fairness and flexibility but making redistribution and equality matters of local choice.

The Conservative era had its three Es – efficiency, economy and effectiveness (but not equality, employment, equity, or environment). Labour promotes the four Cs – challenge, compare, consult and demonstrating competitiveness – as a management process, but the same three Es form the statutory definition of Best Value! (Local Government Act 1999).

Promoting and Resisting Transformation

The Thatcher strategy was to establish new quasi-public organisations, such as Training and Enterprise Councils and NHS Trusts, which were then packed with government approved appointees. At the same time these organisations had terms of reference and budgets which gave them little scope other than to implement Tory policies.

Some policies, particularly Compulsory Competitive Tendering (CCT) and market testing, were resisted by many managers, trade unions and users. This alliance of interests materialised in a few authorities with trade unions and users taking action with the tacit support of some managers, for example, Newcastle school meals campaign in 1988–9 which won improvements in the range and quality of meals through joint trade union and community pressure. Generally, resistance took the form of developing best practice, ensuring specifications reflected user needs, minimising competition and maximising demands on contractors within the scope of the legislation. This was the heroic period when some committed managers had to fight hard to maintain and implement corporate policies and faced internal opposition from other officers and Members who acquiesced to the Tory agenda. Also ranged against them were senior civil servants (the civil service was also subject to widespread market testing), business and trade organisations, right-wing bodies such as the Adam Smith Institute, Institute for Economic Affairs and their coterie of academics. They have been 'replaced' by similarly constituted right-of-centre Labour organisations such as the New Local Government Network.

Successive Conservative governments attempted to diminish the power of the professional classes whom they saw as a major block to their reform programme. The aim was to increase the power of managers, hence the emphasis on performance management and the establishment of a strong business role in decision-making. Not surprisingly, power struggles ensued between policy makers and managers and between managers and professional staff over the implementation of government policy.

The state is responsible for a wide range of interrelated services. It is extremely difficult to coordinate service delivery, develop integrated policies for a diverse range of interrelated issues, manage networks of organisations and meet changing demands with limited resources. It has to be innovative and creative yet carry out statutory duties with regular clockwork. There is no perfect organisational or operational model, hence this will always be a point of conflict between political and economic interests.

It is all too easy to focus exclusively on particular aspects of transformation such as privatisation and competitive tendering or to consider their impact in particular services. This approach ignores the wider significance of such policies and how they interact across services. A political economy typology of transformation and modernisation identifies twelve processes grouped under the function, finance, organisation and operation of the state (see Figure 3.1). There is some degree of interaction between these policies and they have set in motion new developments, opportunities, conflicts and opposition, in a sense their own dynamics. This will become clear in the sections which assess the scope and implementation of these policies in the remainder of this chapter and Chapter 4.

A Theory of the Transformation Process

Although the transformation process may sometimes appear to be disjointed or uncoordinated, seven interrelated processes can be clearly identified:

Destabilisation: Unrelenting criticism of public services, often by generalising individual failures, while simultaneously ignoring achievements, the cause of genuine problems and scale of social needs, is intended to undermine confidence in public provision. It portrays the public sector as inflexible and inefficient, problematic and having an inability to reform. Uncertainty, insecurity and doubts about the future role of public bodies sets in. It often involves the replacement of senior management and widespread use of management consultants. Severing the relationship between users and producers, between service quality and employment, increased use of agency and casualised labour, all help to weaken staff, trade union and organisational resistance.

Disinvestment: Public spending cuts and new centralised financial controls result in continued under-investment in the infrastructure. Repairs, refurbishment and replacement needs are deliberately ignored or given low priority, simultaneously creating 'need' and demonstrating public sector 'inadequacy' in the minds of users, staff and the public. The process of retrenchment begins with spending cuts and targeting, extends to changing universal to selective systems, focusing on core services at the expense of support and other activities, and switching public resources to alternative providers. Third Way modernisation requires that Best Value performance and transaction costs are accommodated within existing budgets.

Restructuring and commodification: Activities and functions are redefined, services repackaged, subsidiaries sold and activities curtailed, service delivery is decentralised but strategic policy is centralised, and opting out and transfers lead to fracturing of services and organisations.

Marketisation and privatisation: Legislation is usually required to establish new funding arrangements, the imposition of highly regulated competition within the state sector (in contrast to arm's-length regulation of privatised services), regulatory frameworks for new markets and a more restricted role for public sector bodies in direct service provision. Services are packaged into contracts to meet the requirements of the market, not social and user needs.

New organisations and organisational restructuring: New organisations and structures are designed to accommodate the new policy agenda in which unified services are divided into purchaser and provider functions and to bridge the public–private divide. Organisational change reinforces management control to challenge traditional professional interests, particularly in health and education. Zones, projects and initiatives apply specific rules which are the gateway to public and private sector resources. These rules often include client/contractor or purchaser/provider structures and competitive tendering.

New managerial and operational systems: New operational rules, changed value systems and business involvement are moulded into 'modernisation' of the public sector to make it 'fit' to implement the new agenda.

New funding competitions: Regeneration resources have increasingly been allocated to local authorities via competitive bidding. Similarly, they must compete for private funding and approval of infrastructure projects.

The imposition of many of these policies was experimental and crude. Despite the political rhetoric, there was scant research evidence to show that they would be effective and there were few attempts to quantify their full public cost. There was also a blatant disregard for social and economic equity. The process of commodifying services is discussed later in this chapter and the private sector response to transformation is examined in Chapter 5.

Changes in organisational structures, management systems, a shift in power at the workplace, the establishment of new values and practices, lead to convergence between public–private when business values become all pervasive. This conjuncture is at different stages in the USA, Canada and other European countries. The rest of this chapter examines the function and organisation of the state while Chapter 4 examines the operation and management of the state and its finance.

Figure 3.1: **A political economy typology of transformation and modernisation**

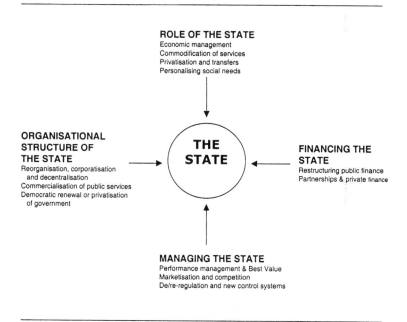

ROLE OF THE STATE
Economic management
Commodification of services
Privatisation and transfers
Personalising social needs

ORGANISATIONAL
STRUCTURE OF
THE STATE
Reorganisation, corporatisation
  and decentralisation
Commercialisation of public services
Democratic renewal or privatisation
  of government

THE
STATE

FINANCING THE
STATE
Restructuring public finance
Partnerships & private finance

MANAGING THE STATE
Performance management & Best Value
Marketisation and competition
De/re-regulation and new control systems

ROLE OF THE STATE

The functions of the state are examined under four headings: economic management; the commodification of services and assets; and privatisation, outsourcing, transfers and personalising social needs.

Economic Management

The management of the economy provided the framework for transformation. A new economic orthodoxy emerged in the 1980s based on controlling inflation primarily by interest rates accompanied by a tight reign on public sector pay and total public spending; encouraging the restructuring of the economy, in particular manufacturing industry, to cut income tax and reduce public sector borrowing, to improve productivity through closures and downsizing; reducing direct state intervention and creating the financial, regulatory and labour market conditions for business; wide ranging deregulation including the removal of capital controls to allow the free flow of capital, and reform of trade unions and labour markets.

Social policy was dominated by the trickle-down theory and the emergence of a so-called property and share owning 'classless society'. The financial strategy has encompassed reducing state expenditure relative to GDP, selling public assets, transferring taxation from income to consumption, centralising control of public spending and an internal drive to increase efficiency and better targeting of resources. The consequences of this strategy are well documented, for example, see Hutton (1995) and Hay (1999).

A right-wing analysis of the Conservative years conceded that 'while most of the government's macro-economic gambles failed miserably, micro-economic radicalism paid off handsomely through privatisation, improved industrial relations and decoupling the UK from the European tendency to excessive government budgets' (Crafts, 1998, p. 35).

Labour's Macroeconomic Strategy

The Third Way strategy was described in the Introduction. The 1997 Labour government continued the commitment to macroeconomic stability and the control of inflation. Labour adopted the Conservatives' public expenditure plans for the first two years of the administration and went further than the Tories in handing over responsibility for setting interest rates to the Bank of England. Hay charts the bipartisan convergence of economic, industrial, welfare and family policy in Britain between 1992 and 1997 and demonstrates that 'the Labour Government conceives neither of the need for, *nor indeed the possibility of*, such an alternative to the ascendant neo-liberalism of the times' (Hay, 1999, p. 135).

Commodifying Services

Commodification describes the process of shaping and packaging services into saleable and marketable items, separating them from other activities, specifying their content and establishing a pricing structure. Their form and content is determined by market forces rather than public policy so that they can be traded, tendered and made the subject of a contract.

Services, property assets, products and public sector organisations and agencies have been subjected to commodification. The commodification of risk in infrastructure projects was discussed in Chapter 2. The aim is to make public requirements and collective needs private and to seek to satisfy them individually. Community care is one example. The NHS and Community Care Act 1990 made local authorities primarily responsible for assessing need and coordinating care in the community in a context of increasing demand for home care services, budget cuts and legislation which encouraged the growth of private care. The home help service has been divided into 'personal care' and 'domestic assistance' activities. Families, neighbours and volunteers are encouraged to take over the household activities. Other examples included the increase in prescription charges from £0.20p in 1979 to £6.00 in 2000 (making it cheaper to buy some products over-the-counter), and the abolition of free dental and eye tests (the latter restored for the elderly by Labour).

The public flotation of the utilities was another example. Unwanted subsidiary companies were sold, debts written off, assets valued cheaply, and free and discounted shares helped to ensure a price advantage, a marketable product and a 'successful' sale. Commodification changes expectations and values, particularly municipal or civic values. The climate of cuts has meant fewer resources, changing priorities to 'protect front-line services' such as education, and less public presence, such as staff in parks and public places.

Commodification creates new markets for capital and facilitates diversification. Single service contracts are declining as the servicing of entire buildings, the environment or groups of services are drawn together under the umbrella of facilities management contracts. In principle, this has many advantages and eliminates the false division of services required by compulsory tendering. However, it has major implications for the labour process and trade unions – see Chapter 6.

Commodification provides new modes of accumulation for capital and new markets permit capital to profit from the provision of services previously provided by the state. Services subject to competition are often packaged to prioritise the interests of contractors rather than service or user needs. Even service user complaints have been commodified, with financial compensation (train companies) or free use (swimming pools) offered in response to service failures which are inevitably costed and built into financial planning, fare structures and charges. Compensation usually bears no relation to the value of the service to the individual or the community. Most people prefer resources to be devoted to good quality services rather than tokenistic compensation. The economics of complaints are similar to those for contracts where it is often more profitable to bear a degree of financial penalties for service failures rather than striving to provide a better quality service.

Services which were previously privately delivered are now being recommodified or repackaged to facilitate private delivery once again. The commodification process is limitless. Some services may appear to be rooted in the public sector today, both technically and politically; however, changes in demands and market forces could facilitate commodification later. Privately financed services enable capital to have a more direct role in the commodification of services. Private capital already effectively controls the supply of land, design and construction processes but now also influences the packaging and supply of finance, the operation of services and the use of surplus assets. Commodification becomes a permanent function of government with the state taking on the role of a 'privatisation or estate agency', a model adopted in many developing countries.

Education is being commodified by the separation of training, courses, supplementary activities from core teaching, i.e. the segmentation of teaching into particular products which can be specified and thus delivered by other contractors, organisations or individuals; the separation of school buildings and their maintenance from the core service provided within them and thus between core and non-core staff; and schools are being established as individual entities, separate from the Local Education Authority (LEA) and collective educational planning. Individual school performance has become a key factor determining the school's 'attractiveness' and 'market position'.

The core/peripheral workforce model, increased use of temporary/casual staff and the use of self-employed/contract workers indicates that labour is also being commodified. Work, production and service schedules and staffing requirements are disaggregated with tasks allocated solely on the employer's minimal requirements.

Ideology and Language

The transformation process generates new concepts and language. The *enabling* model of government which is *provider neutral* implies that there is no difference between public, private or voluntary provision. It also panders to the right's claim that in-house services are, by definition, provider led. It also marginalises employment and equalities policies. Local authorities and public bodies have *corporate* policies but the corporate sector usually means big business. There are terms which are increasingly ideologically confusing such as Clinton's '*market democracy*' (Molnar, 1996) and the British government's attempt to develop '*a culture of business-friendly enforcement*' through Local Business Partnerships under Labour's Better Regulation Initiative. The '*stakeholder economy*' *and* '*don't say no to business*' have significant implications. Internationally, phrases such as '*sustainable development*', '*alleviating or eradicating poverty*', '*ecological and environmental sustainability*' and '*development finance*' are widely used with the assumption that policies and investment automatically produce 'development', reduce poverty and improve the environment.

We have to be very clear about terms and definitions to prevent evasion and deception. A 'non-tiered National Health Service free at the point of use' could mean a privately operated NHS but still providing free care. Similarly, 'a solid state pension as the first building block in the pension system' could mean that the state pension is publicly funded but operated by private firms and/or has a declining role as part of a privately dominated three-pillar pension structure. The advocates of stakeholding usually avoid any reference to publicly funded and provided services. So language does matter.

Language is an important tool to facilitate changes in the principles or erode the value of universality, solidarity and redistribution and to move from collective provision to individual responsibility. A new language has emerged – risk transfer, bankability, business case – to justify partnership and private finance projects in the public sector. Labour's emphasis on 'what matters is what works' places priority on achieving success first, with the means being of secondary importance. Procurement, commissioning and brokerage are now part of the Third Way language.

Deficits or Dividends

Critiques of public policy commonly refer to 'deficits' such as a democratic deficit (Stewart, 1993), economic deficit (Elliott and Atkinson, 1998), cultural (Kelsey, 1995) or development and design deficits (Jervis and Richards, 1997). There is a 'parenting deficit' (Etzioni, 1993), 'social exclusion' and resource, needs and infrastructure deficits. Just about anything can be branded a deficit but this approach is somewhat negative. Instead, we should be identifying the democratic dividend or advantage which can be gleaned from critiques and turned into demands and benefits to be gained from particular policies.

Privatisation and Transfer

The Conservatives often justified privatisation in terms of 'rolling back the frontiers of the state' but this is a false description masking increased central control and the redirection of resources to business. While the sale of state-owned corporations, land and property has been the financial driving force, different forms of privatisation support other aspects of transformation of the state, for example competitive tendering and state subsidies for private services increase marketisation. The state has always bought and sold property, purchased services and encouraged enterprise but the scale of privatisation in the past two decades has been unparalleled.

If one thing has been consistent over the past two decades, it is the relentless rolling process of privatisation. What is unthinkable to privatise today becomes feasible tomorrow and a reality shortly thereafter. A political economy typology identifies eight forms of privatisation and deregulation – private ownership, the private production of public services, private finance, the transfer of services, increased domestic/family responsibility, deregulation, liberalisation and re-regulation, the expansion of private services, and the commercialisation of public services (see Table 3.1).

The rapid rationalisation and restructuring of nationalised industries and manufacturing industries in the early 1980s included closures of pits, shipyards, steel plants, hospitals and factories, contributing to mass unemployment and the decline of communities and regions. Direct state

Table 3.1 **Privatisation typology**

Type of privatisation	Method	Political/social/ economic objectives	Effect on the state
Private ownership	Sale of state-owned companies and utilities Sale of housing, property and land	Extend property and company ownership including shareholding. Increase government income to enable tax cuts or maintain services which would otherwise be cut	Increased income from asset sales and thus scope for tax cuts. Management of increasingly residualised services
Private production of public services	Contracting out/outsourcing, externalisation and franchising	Reduce costs. Create new markets for private firms, weaken trade union organisation	Increased monitoring, less achievement of corporate policies
Private finance	Private Finance Initiative – design, build, finance and operate infrastructure projects/joint ventures. Increased user charges and replacing grants with loans	Access to private capital and expertise	State becomes lessee of facilities, long-term financial commitment, provider of only core services

Transfer of services	Services repackaged and transferred to trusts and non-profit organisations	Increase business role in policy and delivery of services. Reduce costs by transfer of employment responsibility	Reduced range of directly provided services. More quangos
Increase domestic/family responsibility	Reducing scope of services and assuming family (women) take over responsibility for care of elderly and children	Financial savings, promote family and social capital	Service reductions and targeting
Deregulation, liberalisation and re-regulation	Withdrawal and watering down of regulations	Allow business greater freedom to carry out development, hire and fire staff and provide services	Reduced powers to intervene, reliance on market forces
Expansion of private services	Withdrawal/reduction of public service to spur private sector	Increase competition with public sector	Public services marginalised. Benefits, subsidies, vouchers paid to private sector
Commercialisation of public sector	Modelling public sector on private firm. Increased use of business criteria and values. Operating internal market	Market forces applied more widely across the public sector. Create the conditions for further privatisation and deregulation	Increasingly fragmented provision. Difficulty dealing with social values and public interest

intervention in industrial sectors and/or firms was curtailed as resources were targeted internally to financially and politically sustain the privatisation and marketisation programme. The Thatcher government instead focused on share giveaways, debt write-offs, tax concessions and fees to financiers rather than investment in the areas ravaged by decline and closures. Economic management centred on reducing inflation with no commitment to maintain high and stable levels of employment. Wage restraint, labour market reform and reduced corporate taxation were considered essential to create more productive and profitable economic conditions and inward investment.

Alleged efficiency improvement has been one of the main claims made to justify privatisation. Privatisation originated as a political and financial strategy and the economic rationale was appended later after the Tories had won a second general election in 1983 (Whitfield, 1992). It has become institutionalised under the centre-right political consensus of the three main political parties, although differences remain over which services could be privatised. The rationale for privatisation changed from its initial focus on the state withdrawing from ownership of the utilities and nationalised industries to one which is not dependent on the state directly operating services or owning the facilities in which they are provided. The state provision of services has always been a compromise between public and private sectors, for example, public housing relied on acquiring privately owned land and construction by private builders or the role of consultants and 'pay beds' in the NHS. Private sector management and business processes were imposed on the public sector to facilitate further asset stripping.

Gas, water, electricity, telecommunications and state owned companies such as British Airways, British Aerospace and Associated British Ports were sold through stock market flotations with emphasis placed on 'people's capitalism' to widen share ownership. The privatisation programme also encouraged land and property sales, particularly council houses of which 2.2 million were sold between 1979 and 1999. These sales were accompanied by 100 local authority full or partial stock transfers (over 400,000 dwellings) to housing associations. Almost 5,000 school playing fields were sold for development in the last ten years of the Conservative government. Gross privatisation receipts in the period 1979–99 were nearly £125 billion with the utilities and energy sector accounting for £25 billion, telecommunications £16 billion, with land and property sales accounting for half the total (see Table 3.2)

The 1990s privatisation programme completed the sale of most of the remaining nationalised industries and shifted the emphasis to the sale and transfer of local authority services, franchising the rail network and imposing competition in all public bodies. Other forms of privatisation included the payment of residential care allowances to the elderly in private residential care homes, which increased from £11 million in 1977–8 to £2.6 billion by 1993 and led to the rapid growth of a state-financed private care sector. The private pensions industry grew rapidly after the government allowed opting out of the State Earnings-Related Pension Scheme with concessions on national insurance. Student tuition fees and training and nursery vouchers were examples of other forms of privatisation. By 1997, 14 central government agencies, employing over 8,000 staff, had been sold mainly to firms such as EDS, Capita Group and Serco.

Table 3.2: **Summary of privatisation in Britain between 1979 and 1997**

Sector	Scope of privatisation	Gross proceeds £m
Utilities and energy	Gas, Water, Electricity, Nuclear Power, British Coal	24,260
Telecommunications	British Telecom, Cable & Wireless	16,110
Industrial companies	British Steel, British Aerospace, Rolls Royce, Rover Group	4,660
Transport	BA, BAA, Associated British Ports, British Rail, National Bus	2,442
Oil	BP, Enterprise Oil, Britoil, Wytch Farm	8,980
Sale of land and property	Council housing, MOD married quarters, New Towns	62,000
Total		123,140

Sources: Whitfield, 1992, Tables 6.4, 6.5, 6.7; National Audit Office reports on privatisations 1992–98; Public Expenditure: Statistical Analyses 2000–01, HM Treasury, Cm 4601, April 2000.

Privatisation was pre-dated by extensive restructuring which usually involved establishing new company structures and accounting policies (restating higher profits, reducing tax liabilities, writing-off debts and losses) and selling unwanted subsidiaries on an unprecedented scale (Whitfield, 1992).

Privatisation receipts became an integral part of the government's budget process, both financially and ideologically. Asset sales acquired a coterie of city advisers and consultants keen to maintain the profitable advice, a highly exportable commodity. Privatisation has been a political diversion because the sale of assets gives the appearance of investment when in fact all that is happening is a change of ownership. This helped to mask deep cuts in public spending, particularly on Britain's infrastructure.

Labour has replaced the Conservative overt objectives with pragmatism and partnership, a less strident ideological commitment but equally widespread creation of opportunities for private accumulation. Following the publication of the National Asset Register in 1997, Labour has continued with a national privatisation programme with £4 billion annual receipts planned between 1998 and 2001. Planned sales include the National Air Traffic Services, a further tranche of student loans, Belfast Port, the Commonwealth Development Corporation and the Royal Mint.

By 2000, over 100 local authorities had externalised DSOs, technical services, financial and ICT services, transferred leisure, arts and residential care to trusts and/or transferred all or part of their housing stock to housing associations. The privatisation of 15 Next Steps Agencies brought the total number of externalised services to 327 which involved the transfer of 68,150 staff to private firms or to non-profit organisations (see Table 3.3). Externalisation is primarily motivated by financial savings and access to private capital for repairs and improvements. Although European law affords transferred staff a degree of protection, it does not apply to new staff and most private contractors have inferior terms and conditions. It enables the employer to restructure with more flexible working patterns. Some local authorities have colluded with private firms by accepting tenders based on substantial staffing cuts and changes to terms and conditions within weeks or months of commencing a contract.

Table 3.3: **Privatisation and transfer of services and agencies (1990–2000)**

	No. of services	No. of staff
Local government		
DSOs, technical services, financial and ICT	160	35,000
Leisure, arts and residential care trusts	50	15,000
Large scale housing stock transfers	102	6,750
Civil service		
Next Steps Agencies	15	11,400
Total	327	68,150

Source: Centre for Public Services, 1998b, updated by author.

Privatisation started with individual assets, such as companies and houses, and grew to include housing estates and ultimately a local authority's entire stock. The scale of externalisation is illustrated by one city, Sheffield, which had previously campaigned against Conservative policies. By 1999, Sheffield City Council had established a network of five trusts for sports facilities, parks, theatres, museums and galleries with a series of subsidiary trusts and trading companies for other services such as residential care. It has also outsourced financial, IT and housing benefit services, closed its employment department and launched a city centre and schools PFI projects.

A new wave of transfers and externalisation of functions to private, non-profit and voluntary organisations is under way as the answer to 'failing' services, cost cutting, narrowly defined Best Value and the apparent termination of council housing as a tenure and subsequent transfer to social landlords. Outsourcing contracts has increased under Labour with many multi-service contracts transferring 500 or more staff. The annual council housing transfer programme has been increased from 30,000 to 140,00 per annum and the floodgates could open as several major cities, Glasgow, Birmingham, Coventry and Sunderland, plan total stock transfers. Transfer receipts, net of debt repayment and other costs, increased from £44 million in 1996–7 (the last year of Conservative government) to £116 million in 1998–9 after two years of the Labour administration (*Housing Today*, 2 September 1999). If transfers rise to 300,000 homes per annum, council housing will cease to exist within a decade. Councils are being forced to consider transfer because of lack of government funding and an ideological shift in favour of a unified social housing sector. Labour adopted Tory plans to massively expand housing associations when they came to power in 1974. Both governments systematically switched public resources from council housing to housing associations. Labour is poised to complete the demise of council housing.

The privatisation, transfer, outsourcing and partnership methods are summarised in Figure 3.2.

Education is another service where marketisation and privatisation is creating a 'new education economy'. The role of LEAs has come in for savage criticism from the government and the Office for Standards in Education (OFSTED). Education authorities are responsible for strategic management of the education service including planning and allocating resources, access (school places and transport), support for school improvement, special education services and offering services to schools. Whilst many LEAs have been slow to innovate and improve services (paying 'lip service' to school autonomy with a 'nostalgia for control' according to OFSTED) the response to this problem is familiar: don't fix it but privatise, centralise, threaten abolition and use management consultants to justify these decisions.

Of 44 LEA inspections by OFSTED in 1999, some 40 per cent of authorities were claimed to have 'significant weaknesses'. Inspections in other authorities in 2000 increased the list of 'failing LEAs'. The government responded by:

- *Using powers to intervene in authorities by directing them to outsource and privatise education services.* Leeds City Council is being stripped of its education responsibilities which are being transferred to a public/private company. In 1999 the London Boroughs of Hackney and Islington outsourced LEA services worth over £100 million over seven years to Nord Anglia and Cambridge Educational Services respectively.

Figure 3.2: **Methods used to privatise services**

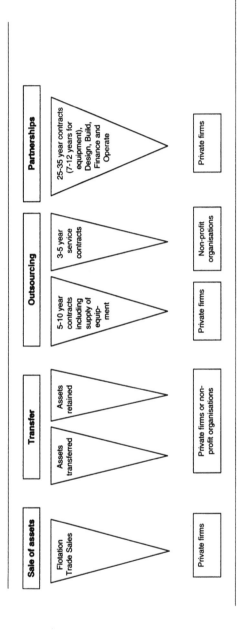

Sale of assets	Transfer		Outsourcing		Partnerships
Flotation Trade Sales	Assets transferred	Assets retained	5-10 year contracts including supply of equipment	3-5 year service contracts	25-35 year contracts (7-12 years for equipment), Design, Build, Finance and Operate
Private firms	Private firms or non-profit organisations		Private firms	Non-profit organisations	Private firms

- *Inviting management consultants and education service contractors to carry out these interventions.* The select list of consultants includes Pricewaterhouse Coopers, Deloitte Touche, KPMG and Ernst & Young and the contractors list includes four other LEAs and firms such as Group 4 (security and private prison operator), Serco and WS Atkins. Three firms, Capita, Nord Anglia and Cambridge Education Associates are on both lists.
- *Supporting a pilot procurement 'brokerage' scheme* in Rotherham, devised by management consultants Office of Public Management, which will enable schools to purchase services such as payroll, IT, management and curriculum support, school meals and cleaning directly from private firms. The brokerage will be run by representatives from private sector consultants, business, head teachers and the DfEE. The DfEE believes it 'could have significant implications for stimulating the market for schools services both regionally and nationally'. (DfEE, 2000).
- *Channelling additional investment to schools directly* from central government and threatening to bypass local authorities by separating school funding and LEA funding as part of its 'frontline first' initiative. Transfer of LEA functions to the new 47 sub-regional Learning and Skills Councils which replace TECs, has also been mooted.

These government initiatives, together with business involvement in EAZ, PPP/PFI schemes for school buildings and private management of 'failing schools', signal the rapid expansion of the education market (see p. 119). The business of education is booming with 30 takeovers worth £1 billion in a 16 month period between 1999–2000. Britain is providing a model for the World Bank's EdInvest service which facilitates private investment in education in developing countries and the global education market.

'Strategic partnership' is the new mantra under which local authorities outsource a large array of services, defined by ICT and related activities, education services, central services and/or customer services, to a 'partner' company. Several local authorities such as Liverpool, Middlesbrough, Bedfordshire, Blackburn and Cumbria are transferring or seconding between 500–1500 staff to private firms or joint venture companies.

Access to private capital and/or information technology are a minor part of the rationale for 'strategic partnership'. The driving force is primarily 'the modernisation agenda' and the belief that partnerships with private companies are *per se* the only way forward. The feast of large multi-million pound long term contracts under Labour makes the Tories CCT regime look like a roadside picnic.

The implications of 'strategic partnerships' are more far reaching than PPPs, because under the guise of partnership, markets, competition and procurement are embedded into core public services in the heart of local government placing companies in a powerful position and able to manoeuvre for additional services.

Personalising Social Need

Diluting people's expectations of government so as to encourage greater reliance on market, family or individual provision was a key Conservative objective. The state has been an ideological battleground in terms of public versus private ownership and in-house provision versus private contractors. The concept of the 'enabling state' has been at the heart of this ideological confrontation, a model of government in which the state facilitates and supports but services are primarily provided through the private and social economy. Three key trends have emerged: individualising, localising and neutralising service delivery.

'Consumer sovereignty' is promoted as an individual right, not a collective one. The Citizens Charter and the promotion of customer care with service standards and complaints procedures has resulted in service users being treated as individual purchasers of services, confining the relationship to the point of service delivery or consumption. The end, not the means is what counts, governments have claimed. The interface between service delivery and the user is thus depoliticised. Need and class are deliberately ignored as consumers are treated as a homogeneous group of individuals with little or no collective identity. The user is encouraged to think only of how the service relates to them personally. The creation of 'one-stop-shops' and call centres are a service improvement but equally a further manifestation of individual consumption. Government is seeking to privatise operational failures to prevent them becoming public issues around which people might organise and campaign.

The commercialisation of services leads to individual grievances being channelled into corporate structures where they are dealt with as separate complaints within the organisation. This has obvious advantages for management responding to and containing issues. The focus is almost exclusively on narrowly defined quality of service delivery. Standards will be increasingly set by market forces and business criteria. Marketisation and tendering also mean that users have to deal with both contractor and client.

'Opting out' of publicly provided services such as education and health fragments and destabilises public services and encourages a narrower, more localised and more self-interested concern. It is a consumerist version of democracy and democratic rights. The individualisation of identity, concern and action becomes more and more focused on the home, reinforced by 'family values'. Local problems and issues smother the wider policy issues and people's organisational abilities are more frequently channelled into event-based organising and fund raising for school and hospital equipment rather than organising people to take political action. It also ignores the state–citizen relationship and democratic accountability (see Chapter 5).

Furthermore, the users' relationship with the state is commercialised with users perceiving little or no difference between business-orientated public and private services, thus paving the way for further privatisation (Centre for Public Services, 1998).

The erosion of commitment to in-house services and adoption of 'what matters, what works' is in effect neutralising the provision of service delivery. 'Third Way' advocates claim that the quality of service at the point of delivery is most important, not who delivers the service. But this approach assumes that competition between contractors is per se a 'good thing' and the well-chronicled negative consequences and high transaction costs are outweighed by advantages – see Chapter 6. It also implies that there is no distinctive public sector ethos and marginalises employment conditions, creating a clear divide between production and consumption.

FINANCING THE STATE

This section examines the restructuring of public finance, which has focused on imposing new centralised controls on public spending in addition to cuts, and the rapid move to partnerships and private finance into the public sector.

Restructuring Public Finance

Globalisation and neo-liberalism have created pressures to radically reform taxation which has led to the redistribution of taxation and demands to reduce public spending. Reagan cut US business rates from 46 to 34 per cent in 1986, corporation tax in Britain was systematically reduced from 52 to 30 per cent between 1982 and 1999 and Germany reduced corporate taxation from 37 to 25 per cent between 1980 and 1994. The redirection of taxation is demonstrated by Canada where individuals contributed 29 per cent of taxation income compared with the corporate sector's 18 per cent in 1966 but by 1996 the individual/corporate ratio was 43/10 (Canadian Union of Public Employees, 1998). Companies and the self-employed contributed 13.1 per cent of Germany's tax burden in 1983 but it had more than halved to 5.7 per cent by 1995 (Martin and Schumann, 1997).

State Expenditure
A combination of financial controls, cuts in public spending and the proceeds of privatisation helped the Conservative government to partly achieve its objective of reducing government spending as a proportion of national income. It was 42 per cent in 1979–80, rose during the recession in the early 1980s, hovered at 38–39 per cent until the early 1990s when it rose to 43 per cent, only to decline to 39 per cent in 1998–9. Privatisation proceeds reached a high of £8.2 billion in 1992–3, totalling some £71 billion (1995–6 prices) in the 1979–98 period (excluding housing – see Table 3.2). These proceeds helped to keep the Public Sector Borrowing Requirement lower

than it would otherwise have been and, combined with a transfer of taxation from incomes to consumer expenditure, provided the means for cuts in personal income and corporate taxation.

State expenditure in Britain as a proportion of GDP declined 4.5 per cent between 1991 and 1997, second only to New Zealand's large decrease and in contrast to very marginal reductions or increases in other countries (see Table 3.4).

Table 3.4: **State expenditure as a proportion of GDP**

Country	1981	1990	1997	% change 1981–97
Sweden	62.6	59.1	62.3	−0.3
Denmark	–	54.5	54.4	−0.1
France	48.6	49.8	54.1	+5.5
Italy	46.3	53.6	50.6	+4.3
Germany	48.7	45.1	47.7	−1.0
New Zealand	–	57.5	45.9	−11.6
Norway	43.6	49.7	44.7	+1.1
Canada	40.5	46.7	42.6	+2.1
UK	44.2	39.9	39.7	−4.5
Australia	31.3	34.8	35.5	+4.2
Japan	32.8	31.3	35.2	+2.4
USA	31.7	32.8	32.0	+0.3

Source: OECD Economic Outlook, No. 63, June 1998.

New Control Mechanisms

Increased centralisation of spending controls has been a key feature of government in the past two decades. The switch to the disastrous poll tax, later replaced by the council tax, together with the nationalisation of business rates (property tax) has reduced the scope for local financial decision-making. Central government determines each local authority's expenditure through a Standing Spending Assessment coupled with a financial clawback if the authority 'overspends' and regulations limit the income local authorities can generate. Strict control of allowances for additional statutory responsibilities, inflation and pay awards enforce budget cuts and hence 'efficiency savings'. The proportion of locally funded local expenditure rose rapidly from 22 per cent in 1981–2 to 34 per cent a decade later (Challis, 2000). It fell to 21 per cent as a result of the £140 reduction in poll tax bills (which cost £4.25 billion and was funded by a 2.5 per cent increase in VAT) and the introduction of council tax. Locally funded expenditure is rising again, reaching 24 per cent in 1999–2000. Pearce and Martin estimate that the proportion of GDP devoted to local government in the 1980s and early 1990s fell by about a fifth, equivalent to £6 billion annually by 1990–1, thus making a mockery of the 'additionality' claimed for regeneration and poverty initiatives (Pearce and Martin, 1996, p. 86).

The Audit Commission, the Accounts Commission in Scotland (responsible for local government and later the NHS) and the National Audit Office (central government) were established in the early 1980s and expanded public sector auditing. Financial audit was extended to Value For Money (VFM) audits based on the 3 Es – efficiency, economy and effectiveness. In practice, VFM became another form of regulation and control, dominated by accountants. The National Audit Office similarly audited asset sales within a narrow financial and regulatory framework. Financial audit is limited to accountancy matters concerning how money is spent, not who benefits or the value and effectiveness of the outcomes of the services and activities carried out. It is money focused with the state merely controlling flows of payments to contractors and user payments, taxes and fees.

Another key issue is the alleged neutrality of audit and the auditors. Even this has been outsourced – 40 out of 104 Metropolitan Councils, London Boroughs and County Councils were audited by private firms in 1996–7 – three firms, Coopers & Lybrand, Price Waterhouse and KPMG had three-quarters of these contracts. There were many examples of firms engaging in what are normally defined as management consultancy activities in the same authority which they were responsible for auditing. The same firms advise transnational corporations on tax avoidance and off balance sheet financing – of course, all are strictly separate operations.

Quangos have generally been centrally financed and a number of Funding Councils were set up to allocate public money to the education sector. Quango budgets were, in effect, ringfenced and the new organisations were able to retain surpluses and build up reserves of public money outside of democratic control. For example, the 74 Training and Enterprise Councils in England held over £285 million in accumulated reserves at 31 March 1997, a 10 per cent increase on the previous year. Many LMS schools have accumulated reserves although they often bear little relation to educational needs.

Transfers and opting out were promoted because they usually produced a capital receipt and access to private capital. For example, the transfer of local authority housing stock to housing associations was part of a dual strategy – achieving an immediate cash injection and access to private capital for investment coupled with rent rises to much higher levels than would have been politically possible within the local authority sector. There has been little evidence of financial savings in the NHS (Pollitt et al., 1997).

The use of the National Lottery for funding arts and culture, sports and leisure facilities, community and 'non-core' health and educational activities has in effect nationalised and privatised the finance of these activities. The award of lottery grants lacks democratic accountability and is another example of transferring taxation from income to consumption.

Changing Boundaries Between Public/Private Welfare

There have been significant changes in the financing of public/private services since 1979. The proportion of publicly provided services has declined from 60.8 per cent in 1979–80 to 51.4 per cent in 1995–6, a decline of over 15 per cent. The proportion of different forms of privately financed services increased from 27.8 per cent to 31.4 per cent in the same period (see Table 3.5).

Table 3.5: **Changes in provision, finance and decision of public/private welfare**

Category	% in 1979/80	% in 1995/96
Public provision, finance and decision	53.6	48.7
Public provision and finance, private decision	4.7	1.4
Public provision, private finance, public decision	2.4	1.2
Public provision, private finance and decision	0.1	0.1
Total	60.8	51.4
Private provision, public finance and decision	4.0	8.7
Private provision, public finance, private decision	9.9	9.8
Private provision and finance, public decision	0.4	0.9
Private provision, finance and decision	24.9	29.2
Total	39.2	48.6

Source: *Boundaries Between Public and Private Welfare: A Typology and Map of Services*, Tania Burchardt, Centre for Analysis of Social Exclusion, LSE, 1997.

Different Forms of Private Finance

User charges: NHS prescription charges soared from 20p in 1979 to £6.00 by 2000 although 80 per cent of prescriptions are dispensed to exempt groups such as children, the elderly and claimants. Dental charges have also increased steeply with non-exempt patients paying 80 per cent of the cost of NHS dental check-ups and treatment. Funding for sight tests was withdrawn in 1989 and these are now carried out privately at an average cost of £13.20. Most local authorities have introduced charges for home care services. Student loans were introduced in 1990 and the means tested maintenance grant for living expenses was abolished in 1999. More students are forced to work part-time. Not surprisingly, the number of over-21s applying for degree courses declined by 11 per cent in 1998, as did the proportion of applicants from unskilled and skilled manual households.

Private use of public facilities: The NHS has over 3,000 pay beds and is the single largest supplier of private health care in Britain. Revenue from private patients increased in the 1970s and soared by 230 per cent between 1979/80 and 1995/6.

Withdrawal of services: NHS eye frames were restricted to children, low income and special needs in 1985 and shortly thereafter replaced by vouchers. NHS dentists are increasingly difficult to locate as an increasing proportion of dentists attend only private patients.

Subsidies and rebates: Opting out of SERPS was encouraged from 1986 with over 5 million people receiving rebates on National Insurance contributions for personal pensions.

Tax relief: Tax relief on private medical insurance contracts for individuals aged 60 or over increased from £40 million in 1990–1 to £110 million in 1996–7, yet the number of contracts only increased 20 per cent to 600,000 in the same period.

Discounts: Council tenants had up to 50 per cent discounts for the purchase of their homes under the Right to Buy legislation which totalled £24.2 billion in the 1979/80–1996/7 period.

Internal Drive to Increase Efficiency and Better Targeting of Resources

The control and allocation of public expenditure, particularly to local government, has been a very important means of enforcing the transformation of the state. Public spending cuts have been used to impose a political discipline on public bodies as much as for their economic function. Management by objectives and accountable management were basic themes following the Fulton Report in 1968. The Financial Management Initiative was launched in central government in 1982 and included setting objectives and management by results, the delegation of budgets, the creation of cost centres to establish management accountability together with better management accounting systems and training. The Audit Commission, formed in 1983, strove to apply the 3Es (efficiency, economy and effectiveness) in local government, and later in the NHS, although efficiency and cost dominated the agenda.

The Labour government's Comprehensive Spending Review provided the basis for the 1999–2002 spending programme. The terms of reference included examining the scope for further efficiency improvements and the scope for disposal of 'surplus assets'.

The focus on the distribution of the cake has prevented debate on the appropriate size of the cake and the required level of taxation. Increased expenditure has been limited to additional income as a result of higher than expected growth in the economy, further internal efficiency savings or raids on the contingency reserve.

Despite public spending controls and cuts, central government has spared no expense to implement transformation. It is ironic that central government is only too happy to ignore its own increased costs as a consequence of local public bodies implementing policies enforced by government (see Chapter 6).

Competitive bidding within a centralised system has increasingly been used in the 1990s to allocate resources for regeneration (City Challenge and the Single Regeneration Budget), housing and local capital investment. Bidding represents a retreat from matching scarce resources to social need (Stanton, 1996) and is a means of enforcing central government policy objectives on local government, provides limited new investment because it masks cuts in mainline programmes and incurs a high financial, institutional and opportunity cost in bidding. The system has led to increased community involvement but they are faced with a *fait accompli* of accepting government policy with limited flexibility in local implementation or no resources at all.

Accountancy Changes

The 1990 NHS reforms also introduced resource or accrual accounting, following its adoption in Australia and New Zealand. It is being introduced through central and local government in 2001. In theory, accrual output-based budgeting is a process through which public bodies are funded and monitored on the basis of performance outputs and full costs and liabilities. The claimed advantages are that it is customer focused, based on the supply of services/products, separates purchaser and provider, reflects full accrual costs, gives clear choices to the buyer, provides a sound basis for internal resource allocation and focuses on outputs and outcomes (Guthrie and Carlin, 1999). However, there has been extensive criticism that a commercial accountancy system is not applicable to the public sector (Jones, 1996). The NHS capital charging regime 'imposed new financial duties on NHS trusts, modelled on the relation between a private sector corporation and its bankers and shareholders. The duties require trusts to pay for the use of capital. In effect, hospitals are being taxed to provide capital' (Gaffney et al., 1999, p. 49).

Partnerships and Private Finance

The Introduction described how the growth of privately financed infrastructure and partnerships is one of the major transformative issues confronting the nation state in the global economy. Global trends in infrastructure privatisation were examined in Chapter 2. This section examines the far-reaching political development of partnerships and private finance in Britain. The impact on services, jobs and the public sector is revealed in Chapter 6.

Infrastructure investment in Britain declined dramatically after the 1973 oil crisis and International Monetary Fund intervention three years later. Both Labour and Conservative governments imposed substantive cuts in public sector capital spending programmes. Net public sector investment under the Labour government, £29.9 billion (5.8 per cent of GDP) in 1974–5, more than halved by the end of the decade and plummeted to a mere 0.4 per cent of GDP in 1988–9, increasing in the early 1990s, to decline again to only 0.6 per cent of GDP for the first three years of the Labour government (HM Treasury, 2000). The decline in public sector investment in the last two decades occurred at the same time as the government had unprecedented privatisation receipts and North Sea Oil revenues and public money which has been squandered on tax cuts for business and the wealthy.

By the mid-1980s a spate of studies by the Confederation of British Industry, the Federation of Civil Engineering Contractors and the now defunct National Economic Development Council had exposed the deteriorating state of the infrastructure and assessed the potential impact of further cuts in capital spending. The major contractors and construction industry bodies demanded increased government capital expenditure and relaxation of the External Financing Limits on nationalised industries and PSBR controls. There was little reference to the use of private finance. The Conservative government doubled the road building programme to £12 billion and proposed that additional road schemes could be built and operated by the private sector in 'corridors of opportunity'. The Treasury's Ryrie rules, which required a matching reduction in public funding in response to private funding of infrastructure projects, were relaxed in 1989. Some British companies were involved in some commercially unsuccessful private infrastructure projects overseas, but the Thatcher government insisted that privately financed schemes should not be subsidised. A number of private sector transport schemes including the rail link to the Channel Tunnel, a second Severn Bridge, a rail link to Heathrow and the Docklands Light Railway extension were developed at this time.

By 1990, with much of the basic transport and utility infrastructure in private ownership or planned for privatisation, contractors were lukewarm over the prospect of private roads and turned to other sectors such as hospitals, prisons and urban development where they believed they obtained higher returns and accessed 'surplus' land and property for development.

The Private Finance Initiative was launched in November 1992, a financial mechanism to obtain private finance which could satisfy political need to increase investment in the infrastructure without affecting public borrowing, guarantee large contracts for construction companies and new investment opportunities for finance capital. Most politicians had a short-term perspective but capital was looking longer term. The 'crisis' in the flow of PFI projects between 1995 and 1997 was partly caused by demands for state financial guarantees and partly because PFI consortia were flexing their muscle to ensure contracts reflected their interests. In one sense, there is an inevitability about PFI given the Conservatives' privatisation and economic policies in the 1980s. The privatisation 'machine' was never going to stop, at least not of its own accord. PFI is privatisation by stealth, privatising those parts which could not, at least politically, be sold off as complete services. It is the route to the ultimate marketisation and privatisation of health, education and social services.

'Taxpayers no longer need to own hospital buildings' claimed the Treasury (Private Finance Panel, 1996, p. 7). The Labour government embraced PPPs with fervour: 'Privatisation was their solution. Modernisation is ours. PPPs are central to that modernisation process ...' stated Alan Milburn, Secretary of State for Health (Milburn, 1999, p. 27). Labour's commitment is rooted in four claims:

- The government is using private capital as an addition to public investment 'to close the all-too-clear gap that exists between the quality of our public sector buildings and facilities and those of the private sector' (ibid.).
- The public sector needs the commercial expertise to help manage the complex investment processes in IT, transport and other services. 'By introducing private sector investors who put up their own capital, skills and experience, the public sector gets the benefit of commercial disciplines, innovations and efficiencies' (ibid.).
- PPPs result in better services and better value for money, i.e. efficiency savings.
- The switch to focus on outcomes, not inputs, means that the risks of delivering outputs are transferred to the private sector, for example, 'the government no longer needs to build roads because it can purchase miles of maintained highway' (ibid.). Outcomes, not ownership is the new mantra, thus freeing public services from 'the straightjacket of monopoly control' (ibid.).

The case for PPP/PFI has shifted from a financial justification to one where the value for money argument is paramount, coupled with the belief that the private sector is superior to the public sector in terms of management, expertise, efficiency and quality. Both the National Audit Office report (NAO, 1999) and the Andersen report for the Treasury Taskforce (Arthur Andersen, 2000) made unsubstantiated claims of 10–20 per cent efficiency savings. Although the Treasury continues its fiscal stringency to ensure that PFI is the prime way to finance capital schemes, PPP/PFI projects are considered an essential part of the modernising public services agenda.

While Labour initially increased public sector capital expenditure from £3.3 billion in 1998–9 to £8.7 billion in 2001–2 (at 1997–8 prices), this was only 1 per cent of GDP and totally inadequate to meet the huge infrastructure backlog (for example, NHS £2.6 billion and council housing £10 billion repairs). The extent of privatisation of Britain's infrastructure is

Table 3.6: **Infrastructure privatisation in Britain**

Privatisation completed			Privatisation agenda 2000+		
Transport	Energy and Utilities	Communications	Social infrastructure of welfare state	Defence and security	Criminal justice system
Railways	Electricity	British Telecom	Hospitals	Equipment	Prisons
Airports	Oil and Gas	Cable & Wireless	Schools	IT systems	Police stations and HQ
Ports	Water and sewage	TV transmitters	Council housing	Barracks	Magistrates and Crown courts
Bus services	Waste management		Residential homes	Training	IT and communications systems
Rapid transit	Coal mining		Libraries		Fleet management
Roads			Govt offices		Detention centres
			Sports and recreation		
			IT systems		
			Regeneration		
			Econ development		

highlighted in Table 3.6 showing that a large part of the transport, energy and utilities and communications infrastructure is owned and operated by the private sector. It left the social and welfare state, defence and criminal justice system infrastructure in the public sector which subsequently became prime targets for privatisation.

There are various types of PPP (see Chapter 2) but the most common in Britain requires the private sector to design, build, finance and operate (DBFO) facilities, usually for 25–35 years (7–15 years for equipment). It finances construction and is repaid by the state, in regular payments for the use of the buildings and for the services provided under a facilities management contract. Payments are classified as revenue, not capital and thus do not count against public borrowing and do not commence until the building is completed. It thus has enormous short-term political appeal.

Partnerships are not new. High rise flats mushroomed across Britain in the 1950s and 1960s as construction companies made deals with local authorities committed to getting rid of the slums, and were encouraged by Conservative government special housing subsidies for high rise prefabricated housing. In the 'modern' version, contractors and financiers are guaranteed repayment of their costs but also get to own and manage facilities, generate income from private use, plus a 25–35 year repairs and maintenance contract and a bonus of negotiating which other support services they would like to provide (see also p. 108).

What Labour did for PPPs

The new Labour government acted quickly in 1997, setting up and implementing the Bates Review which recommended streamlining the PFI process. The government also rushed through legislation to clarify the powers of NHS Trusts and local authorities to enter into PFI agreements and guarantee financial payments over the life of the contract irrespective of public expenditure. In other words, PFI contract payments are ringfenced. They also established new processing and prioritising procedures for PPP projects in all government departments together with project teams and removed the requirement that all public sector capital projects be tested for private finance potential. This ensured that only 'bankable' projects were prioritised. PFI was heavily promoted in local government which had lagged well behind other sectors. The Labour government appears to have a better understanding of the needs of business than the right-wing ideologues of the previous administration!

Net public infrastructure investment is planned to increase to £19 billion per annum by 2003/4, representing 1.8 per cent of GDP. However, a further £21 billion of PFI deals are expected to be signed in the same period. By late 2000, nearly 350 PFI projects had been signed with a capital value of £25 billion. A further 227 projects were at an advanced stage. The welfare state infrastructure accounted for 19 per cent of the value of projects – see Table 3.7. However, this is a misleading indicator of the scale of PFI projects because

Table 3.7: **Sector analysis of PFI projects in Britain**

Sector	Value of signed projects (£m)	Value of projects with preferred partner (£m)	Value of projects with shortlist (£m)	Total
Welfare state	4,654	1,466	925	7,045
Transport and environment	11,628	757	647	13,032
Criminal justice	1,410	481	101	1,992
Defence	4,747	509	5,813	11,069
Other	2,653	741	40	3,434
Total	25,092	3,954	7,526	36,572

Source: *The PFI Report*, October 2000.

it excludes projects which have been centrally approved but not signed and those which have been advertised following a local decision to proceed. The combined value of these last two categories far exceeds the value of signed projects.

Private finance is presented as an alternative form of procurement by converting the payment of debt incurred in obtaining assets into revenue payments as a payment for services. This is reflected in the presentation of the capital value of PFI projects, for example, a London Borough of Haringey secondary schools project has an £87 million capital project but the total PFI payment is £233 million over 25 years. Similarly, the South Buckinghamshire NHS Trust's £45 million new hospital will in fact require a total payment of £244.7 million to United Healthcare over 30 years.

Transformation of the funding of capital expenditure: Local authority PFI schemes receive the same subsidy as public sector capital schemes via Revenue Support Grant, controlled by central government PFI credits for approved projects. PFI credits have soared from £250 million in 1997–8 to £1,600 million in 2003/4. Since the 1990 Health Service reforms, capital spending has been financed internally by NHS trusts having to make an annual surplus of income over expenditure equal to 6 per cent of the value of their assets (buildings and equipment) and to make a charge for depreciation through capital charges.

Table 3.8 illustrates how in 1997–8 and 1998–9 net capital expenditure of –£139 million and –£348 million represent a return to government from revenue, disguising the extent to which capital investment has been withdrawn (Gaffney et al., 1999). Capital spending is thus heavily dependent on NHS trusts including capital charges in prices charged to purchasers, receipts from property and land sales, and NHS trust efficiency savings.

Table 3.8: **Financial impact of health PFI projects**

Financial year	HCHS capital £m	Charges and receipts from land sales £m	Internally generated resources (capital charges) £m	Net HCHS capital expenditure £m
1995–6	1996	282	930	984
1996–7	1711	393	1000	318
1997–8	1514	446	1207	−139
1998–9	1449	561	1236	−348

Source: Gaffney et al., 1999.

Before PPPs, public bodies planned and designed infrastructure projects, raised finance, supervised construction and then operated the facilities. The private sector was usually involved in the design and construction phases. However, financial and construction markets require PPPs to compete with

Figure 3.3: **The spiral of public sector decline and opportunity for capital**

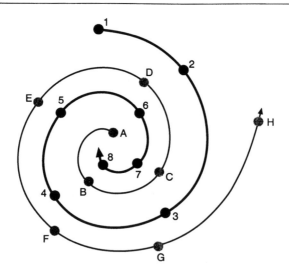

1. Business demands public spending cuts
2. Capital and revenue budgets cut
3. Repairs decline/improvement delayed
4. Physical deterioration of infrastructure
5. Pressure to use private builders/volunteers
6. User dissatisfaction grows
7. Backlog increases
8. Search for alternative private finance

A. Construction sector workload decreases/DSOs sold off
B. Contractors demand action
C. Private finance as 'additional' investment
D. Labour redesigns PFI process and gives guarantees
E. Private finance extended to welfare state and criminal justice system replacing public investment
F. Support services privatised/private use of public facilities
G. PFI dominant/public ownership marginalised
H. Core services privatised

other investment opportunities, and as the state becomes increasingly reliant (captive) on PPP projects, markets are likely to force up the cost of borrowing, construction and related costs. Furthermore, market forces will extend throughout the entire infrastructure procurement process. At the next economic crisis, public sector capital spending will again be cut and reliance on PPPs will be further embedded.

PFI consortia are refinancing deals to substantially increase profits. For example, Group 4 and construction group Carillion almost doubled their returns from the Fazakerley (now Altcourse) prison contract. Profits increased by £14.1 million (75 per cent since 1995) of which £10.7 million came from refinancing (extending the bank loan period at a reduced interest rate and early repayment of other debt), £3.4 million from completing the prison ahead of schedule and lower construction costs. The Prison Service received £1 million for additional termination liabilities.

In early 2000, Morrison Construction packaged five PFI projects in a joint venture with Edison Capital, a financial services subsidiary of the US electricity company Edison International. It is the first example of bundling PFI projects and a step towards the creation of a secondary market.

Refinancing and a secondary market of PPP/PFI projects are likely to have an increasing impact on the scope and content of PPPs generally. The PPP lobby consistently under-estimates or deliberately ignores the power that international financial capital and market forces will ultimately have in determining the provision of public services. Yet marketisation means precisely that, with market forces having a powerful influence in the division of labour, risk allocation and the provision of core services.

Spiral of Decline and Opportunity

Cuts in public sector capital spending create a downward spiral of decline starting with reduced maintenance, postponed improvements, physical deterioration of the infrastructure, rising user complaints and pressure to use alternative sources of funding (numbers 1–8 in Figure 3.3). But this process also creates a spiral of opportunity for business. As the construction sector workload decreases, contractors demand government action, privately financed schemes are permitted as 'additional' investment – then become the prime source for all capital projects, support services are privatised and an owner-operator industry mushrooms, public ownership is marginalised and eventually core services are included as PPPs become the common method of procurement and Britain's infrastructure is privatised (A–H in Figure 3.3).

Changing relationship between capital and the state: PPPs represent capital and the state forging a new relationship based on negotiated deals, long-term service contracts, shared risk and guaranteed payments irrespective of the state of public finances. CCT and market testing were almost entirely labour only contracts but PPPs require the private sector to provide both a capital asset, maintenance and a wide range of support services. Capital is further embedded in the planning and delivery of public services and extends the enabling model of government.

Transforming the procurement process: PPP imposes a new and more complex procurement process in the public sector. The PPP process is part tendering (to select a preferred bidder) and part contract negotiation in which public bodies and PPP consortia and their advisers haggle behind closed doors. It requires public bodies to develop comprehensive project appraisal and evaluation methodologies and the ability to monitor large performance contracts to ensure contract payments are performance related and that risk is fairly attributed in practice. The criteria used by the Treasury's Project Review Group, the National Audit Office and the Public Sector Comparator (merely an investment appraisal) ignore equality, employment and environmental sustainability and socioeconomic factors. Hence they do not take into account the deeper and wider implications of PFI projects.

PPPs extend marketisation of services far deeper and wider than competitive tendering ever could. It virtually eliminates in-house competition (on grounds that there is no transfer of risk if services remain in-house) and smaller companies (because of large long-term contracts and equity capital in the consortia). Transaction costs are high, up to four times those of competitive tendering, but from the multinationals' perspective, they form a useful barrier to market entry, and are ultimately funded by the public sector.

New form of contractor organisation: Competitive tendering and market testing produced two forms of contract organisation, the private firm and the in-house contracting organisation with its own trading account. PPPs require the formation of a 'special purpose vehicle' or operating company, a separate company in which the construction contractor, financial institutions and facilities management contractor have an equity stake. This company manages and operates the facility including selling spare capacity and vacant space to third parties. The combining of finance, construction and support service companies into a new owner-operator industry has been warmly welcomed by the Confederation of British Industry (see Chapters 5 and 6).

Reconfiguring services: The government emphasises that PPPs are contracts for services, not buildings, which makes the distinction between support services such as building maintenance, cleaning, catering, transport and other related services and core services such as teaching and medical treatment divisive and unsustainable in the longer term. State withdrawal from ownership and management of the infrastructure has profound implications for core services. PPP consortia will eventually include private companies bidding to manage schools and local education authorities or private health care companies.

The commodification of service provision results in social needs being subordinate to financial flows stemming from usage or activity levels, user charges and income generation. The distinctiveness of the public sector is eroded to ease transferability between public and private sectors and the former is reshaped into a residual role. It is changing the state's role in the provision of services, redefining 'public' service and 'public' employee and reducing its role from provision to underwriting, renting, procuring and regulating at an alarming rate.

Changes in construction industry: PPPs have accelerated construction industry expansion into facilities management, extending the scope of the industry from design, construction, building maintenance to a wide range of support services.

Further centralisation: The government claims that PPPs are 'services' contracts, normally for local decision-making, but the Treasury ultimately controls approvals through the Projects Review Group. This is another example of the centralisation of decision-making which will be more extensive in 2020 if PPPs continue at their current rate.

Changing nature of risk: The public sector has always borne the risk of facilities requiring adaption as service needs change, of reletting or changing the use of buildings. But, as stated earlier in this chapter, 'risk' has been commodified so that it can be identified, priced and responsibility legally attributed (see also Chapter 2). Long-terms deals are currently being signed on a static concept of risk transfer. But the nature of risk will change as the private sector gains increasing control of the infrastructure, delivery of support services and will be able to strongly influence, if not control, the supply chains of users, the growth of private services in 'public' facilities and third party use of spare capacity. Risk is identified, quantified, attributed and priced; in other words it is monetised.

Privatising the development process: Gaining control of surplus land and buildings such as school playing fields, vacant land, empty hospital buildings and so on for property development is a key part of PPP projects for the private sector. They often provide a key source of finance and profit and ensure that surplus public assets are sold for private development.

Transformation of the labour process: The government and PFI consortia claim that the higher cost of privately financed projects will be more than offset by the private sector's 'better utilisation of assets' and increased operational savings. Facilities management contracts are intended to integrate services which have often been separately tendered. Increased productivity and financial savings from support services are a core requirement for the viability of most PPPs.

PPPs and social capital: PPPs and social capital policies are central to the World Bank's strategy. However, PPPs marginalise and constrain social capital because they embed business control in the infrastructure by their virtual ownership of facilities, supply of services and development of surplus and/or adjacent land. This more frequently reduces the scope of social capital.

Reversing policy: If PFI spending was replaced by conventional forms of public funding, the selling of an extra £3–4 billion of gilts annually in current circumstances would seem to pose no problems (Robinson et al., 2000). Abolition of PPP/PFI would not affect the Treasury's current fiscal rules – the golden rule that on average over the economic cycle the government will borrow only to invest and not to fund revenue expenditure and the sustainable investment rule that public sector net debt as a proportion of GDP will be held at a stable and prudent level. Nor would abolition affect the Maastricht convergence criteria, established for countries wishing to join the European Monetary Union, which limit government borrowing (to 3 per cent of GDP) and government debt (to 60 per cent of GDP).

If the Government adopted the General Government Financial Deficit for public sector current and capital expenditure accounting, replacing the Public Sector Net Borrowing (PSNB which replaced the PSBR), public bodies could borrow to invest from the European Investment Bank (EIB) and the European Investment Fund (EIF) at low rates of interest. Following the Amsterdam Treaty in 1997, both the EIB and EIF directly fund schemes under the Special Action Programme for investment in health, education, housing, regeneration and environmental projects. Since their funds are not guaranteed by governments, they do not count against public borrowing except in Britain and the Netherlands. The PSNB is in surplus and rather than paying off national debt, the government should be investing in the infrastructure.

So there is a clear financial alternative. Given the mounting evidence of the negative effects of PPP/PFI on public service planning and provision and the flimsy evidence for value for money, this leaves the case for PPP/PFI firmly on the political and ideological terrain. We are back to the Third Way.

SUMMARY

This chapter has examined transformation in terms of the functions and financing of the state. The next chapter completes the analysis of transformation by examining the changes in the organisation, operation and management of the state.

4

Modernising the State: New Organisation and New Management?

The public sector has been subjected to extensive organisational and operational change in the past two decades. This chapter examines organisational change under three headings: reorganisation, corporatisation and decentralisation; commercialisation; and democratic renewal or the privatisation of government. Performance management and Best Value; marketisation and competition; and de/re-regulation and new control systems provide the framework for examining operational and managerial change (see Figure 3.1).

ORGANISATIONAL STRUCTURE OF THE STATE

Reorganisation, Corporatisation and Decentralisation

Much of the organisational and management change was brought about by legislative policy change. The reorganisation of local government in 1972, the abolition of the Greater London Council and the six Metropolitan Counties in 1986 and the formation of unitary councils in 1996–8, focused almost exclusively on political boundaries and the functions performed by different tiers of government. Public sector organisational change has four dimensions: *corporatisation* – public organisations are reorganised with company status which are either operated at arm's length or transferred to the private or third sector; *agentification and decentralisation* – the formation of new organisations to deliver services within the public sector; the formation of *quasi-public non-elected bodies* to deliver services; and *zonalisation* – the designation of zones, area initiatives and partnerships.

Corporatisation
Company status has been used extensively in the last 20 years to separate activities and functions from public bodies and direct democratic control. Companies have separate legal status and are controlled by directors with strict financial and operational obligations under the Companies Acts. Company status therefore separates, divides and ringfences activities and

services into a stand-alone economic entity with a separate decision-making structure, budget, accounts and responsibilities. They survive according to their balance sheet, increased productivity and diversification and, not surprisingly, are forced to adopt commercial values and practices. Most public sector companies do not have to pay dividends to shareholders but must make a surplus to finance investment.

Many public bodies formed companies for commercial income-generating activities or for specific activities such as economic development and regeneration. Local authorities were required to turn waste disposal operations into arm's-length commercial organisations following the Environmental Protection Act 1990. Municipal bus companies were operated on this basis before the Conservative government enforced their sale following the 1985 Transport Act. Polytechnics, now universities, and Further Education Colleges were transferred from local authority control to independent companies in the 1980s.

An increasing proportion of local services are now delivered and controlled by companies. The voluntary sector has also established corporate structures and companies because local authority grants have been converted to contracts to carry out specific activities and they are legally required to separate commercial activities from non-profit or charitable activities.

A hybrid organisational model has emerged, part public and part commercial, as public bodies operate one or more companies to maximise income-generating activities to supplement their core activity. For example, most universities have established subsidiary companies to maximise income from conferences and the commercial application of research or innovative products. However, increasing reliance on commercial activities could dominate the culture of the entire organisation. In this context, the hybrid organisation is transitional because the commercial organisation would merge with, or even take over, a declining number of non-commercial activities.

The holding company model is emerging in local government since many local authorities operate arm's-length companies, hold ownership of assets for use by trusts and hold shares or equity in a range of partnership companies.

Agentification and Decentralisation

The separation of client–contractor or purchaser–provider functions has had a significant organisational and managerial effect in the public sector although some authorities are eliminating the split under Best Value. The client is responsible for the budget, policies, specifying the service, evaluating tenders and monitoring contracts, while an internal or external contractor delivers the service. There has been a continuing debate about hard and soft splits and conflicts between departments. Following the Local Government Act 1988, local authorities established Direct Service Organisations (DSOs) as their contracting arm, in effect a separate department with a trading account. Some authorities have a single DSO for all contract services, for example, Newcastle City Council's Cityworks employs 5,000 staff with an annual turnover of £155 million, others have separate DSOs for environmental services, building repairs and white collar services.

Central government established some 140 Next Steps Agencies between 1988 and 1998. Fifteen agencies were privatised and some smaller ones merged. Agencies are headed by chief executives responsible for day-to-day management and staffed by civil servants. They are accountable to Ministers who set overall policy, key objectives, approve the agency's business plan, allocate resources and monitor their performance. Agencies took over responsibility for pay and conditions in April 1997. About 80 per cent of central government staff now work in agencies (Centre for Public Services, 1997). Other countries such as Sweden, Holland, Denmark and New Zealand have adopted a similar executive agency model for central government services.

Growth of Non-elected Bodies
Non-elected public bodies or non-governmental organisations have grown rapidly in the last decade. There were 6,424 quangos in 1996 (excluding government agencies) spending £60.4 billion annually which represented nearly 20 per cent of total government expenditure in 1994–5 (Hall and Weir, 1996). However, the government uses a much narrower definition of Non-Departmental Public Bodies which numbered 304 in 1998, 40 per cent fewer than in 1979 although their expenditure had risen fourfold from £6 billion to £24 billion.

There are three types of quangos. The majority are executive, implementing government policy and providing services in health, education, housing and training. Of the 5,750 executive quangos, 266 operate nationally, 318 at regional level and the remainder at local level. Regulatory quangos are mainly national bodies such as those established to supervise the privatised utilities. The third type, advisory quangos, are responsible for scientific, arts and specialist issues, for example, the Royal Fine Art Commission.

The classification of Local Public Spending Bodies (LPSBs) further confuses matters. They are unelected not-for-profit bodies whose members are not government appointed, which provide publicly funded public services. There are over 4,650 LPSBs and they include housing associations and registered social landlords, Grant Maintained Schools and higher education institutions.

Opting out of the public sector in Britain led to the growth in new organisations locally and nationally. In education, for example, a series of what has been appropriately described as new magistracies and new commissariats have been created (Morris,1994). The former included school governing bodies and the latter the Funding Agency for Schools, the Higher Education Funding Council, the Further Education Funding Council, the Office for

Standards in Education (OFSTED), and the Schools Curriculum and Assessment Authority. They are state funded with their own offices, staff and chief officers appointed by the Secretary of State. Most exercise power in place of the local education authority. Local Management of Schools (similar to Charter schools in North America) allows individual schools to operate on the basis of being a self-contained 'business' with the local authority retaining ownership of land and buildings.

Non-profit Trusts have been the vehicle for the externalisation of residential homes, leisure and arts activities, and are motivated by tax advantages being able to claim business rate reduction and reduced VAT (UNISON, 1998). They evade local government financial controls and establish a new employer to restructure terms and conditions, initially for new staff and eventually for all. A local authority often retains ownership of facilities but transfers operational control to a new employer.

The NHS internal market was structured on a purchaser/provider split with individual or groups of NHS hospitals encouraged to become independent health care Trusts, able to sell services to any feasible purchaser. Trusts can move out of national pay bargaining but few have done so. Some 57 Trusts were established in the first wave by April 1991 and this grew rapidly so that eventually all hospitals became Trusts. General practitioners (doctors) became fundholders with devolved budgets to purchase health services on behalf of patients from NHS Trusts or private hospitals. By 2000, over 100 Trusts in England alone were involved in mergers leading to further rationalisation. Yet cost savings from management overheads are estimated to be less than 1 per cent of the total budgets of the combined organisations (*Health Service Journal*, 18 November 1999).

The current pattern of Trusts, partnerships and companies in the public sector will not remain static. Economies of scale and vested interests will ensure takeovers and mergers. The interface between organisations and between services is determined by contracts through company structures, thus creating new but less distinctive boundaries within and between public, quasi-public, private and voluntary sectors. This will inevitably change the expectations, attitudes and responsibilities of elected members, managers, staff and users and cultural and social relationships within and between organisations. It also facilitates privatisation. What happens when Trusts and non-profit companies can no longer access capital on economic terms because financiers can obtain higher returns with lower risk elsewhere?

In addition to devolution in Scotland and Wales, the Labour government established nine new Regional Development Agencies (RDAs) in England, responsible for regional economic strategies bringing together inward investment, small firms, skills and training and regional development work. Their broad remit also includes administration of the Single Regeneration Budget Challenge Fund, the regeneration roles of English Partnerships and the Rural Development Commission, integrating transport planning, promoting public–private partnerships and technology transfer. Government appointed RDA boards are business-led with representation from local authorities, higher education and trade unions. Integrating functions with committed budgets, staff from disparate departments with different management cultures and interests, has been no small task.

NGOs have expanded rapidly in other countries, a sixfold increase worldwide between 1960 and 1996. They have doubled in number in Africa and Asia since the late 1980s and have grown rapidly in Central and Eastern Europe since 1989. NGOs cover a very wide range of activities including service delivery, aid relief and political campaigning. Eight federations of international NGOs control about $500 million of the annual $8 billion relief (Simmons, 1998). A wide range of quangos operate between the public and private sectors – the 'grey zone' – across Europe (Greve et al., 1999). The extent of NGO growth attributed to the takeover of services and activities previously carried out by the state is unknown.

The Rush to Create New Organisations

The government transferred the training of adults and young people and enterprise support for small and medium sized enterprises from local authorities in 1988, establishing 82 Training and Enterprise Councils in England and Wales and 22 Local Enterprise Companies in Scotland with £3 billion of public money, modelled on Private Industry Councils in the USA.

The growth of new organisations reached two peaks in the 1990s. The formation of NHS Trusts, Next Steps Agencies and Grant Maintained Schools reached a peak of 600 new organisations created in 1993. The second peak was generated by the Labour government's formation of Primary Care Groups and the spate of education, health and employment zones. Mergers are now in progress in health (49 Trusts in England merging into 21 in 1999 alone) and education (higher education institutions acquiring further education colleges).

Public sector companies, trusts and boards have several common elements. The directors normally comprise local elites and business people. Elected Members and service users have minority representation or none at all. Democratic accountability is limited yet they are all dependent on public money for the bulk of their income. Staff and trade unions have limited or no representation. Subsidiary companies carry out commercial activities (usually dominated by business and managerial appointments) or specific functions (as a vehicle to give tenants greater participation).

Modern Zones

The zonal approach has been used by government to experiment with new quasi-public organisations and the promotion of private sector involvement. The Conservative government launched Enterprise Zones, Urban Development Corporations (UDCs), the Estate Renewal Action Fund, City Challenge and the Single Regeneration Budget. For example, twelve UDCs were the centre of the government's urban regeneration policy in the 1980s.

They were designated, financed by and directly accountable to central government with extensive powers over land acquisition, finance and town planning at a time when mainstream programmes were subject to continuous cuts. 'They were regarded as government-imposed, property-orientated and dominated by the private sector – the most visible precursor of the now much reviled quangocracy' (Parkinson, 1996, p. 9). Three closed in 1995–6, the rest in March 1998.

The Labour government reinvigorated the zonal approach with health, employment, education and community safety zones and the New Deal for Communities. The first phase of 25 Education Action Zones (EAZs) are intended to raise standards in 'socially disadvantaged areas' with 'under-performing' schools. EAZs comprise two or three secondary schools one of which must become a 'specialist' school selecting up to 10 per cent of its students on the basis of 'aptitude', plus associated primary schools (maximum 20 schools). Schools can opt out of the national curriculum and national pay and conditions for teachers. EAZs are run by Action Forums comprising representatives from schools, parents, business and the local education authority with one or two Secretary of State appointees (see Democratic Renewal below).

Each zone receives an annual government grant of £750,000 with private business expected to fund and/or sponsor to the value of £250,000. Zones usually lack the presence of successful private businesses so large national firms such as BT, British Aerospace and Andersen Consulting are supporting zones, usually in kind rather than hard cash. Modelled on the limited success of the 1960s Educational Priority Areas which showed that directing resources at schools and geographic areas to 'alleviate the educational dis-advantages experienced by individual pupils was fatally flawed' (Plewis, 1998, p. 107), the government has also ignored the limited success of similar zones in France and the Netherlands.

The 26 Health Action Zones (HAZs) established by 1999 include a range of innovative approaches such as establishing healthy living centres, integrated approaches to child health or mental health. Each HAZ is a partnership between health service organisations, local authorities, community groups, charities and business and has access to New Opportunities lottery funds and freedom and flexibility to improve services. A HAZ is relatively large, covering between 180,000 and 1.1 million people. The activities of the second wave of HAZs are divided between modernising the health and social delivery system (27 per cent), community 'empowerment' (21 per cent), tackling root causes of ill health (18 per cent) or lifestyles (17 per cent) and changing the process of partnership working (Judge, 1999).

Employment Zones are part of the government's Welfare to Work strategy and cover labour market areas with high levels of long-term unemployed. Five prototype zones were launched in 1998 followed by 13 zones in April 2000. EZs will test the concept of 'personal job accounts', a sum of money which claimants can use for training, community work or job subsidy.

Employment Zones are not intended to create new jobs but to give additional support to lever the long-term unemployed into work. It is supply-side intervention and an integral part of the Welfare to Work programme.

The £800 million three-year New Deal for Communities programme is targeted for the intensive regeneration of small neighbourhoods in 17 pathfinder areas. The criteria for selection include poor job prospects, high levels of crime, rundown environment and 'no one in charge of managing the neighbourhood and coordinating the public services that affect it' (Cabinet Office, 1998a, p. 54). It introduces yet another 'local' concept of neighbourhood management which includes a neighbourhood board (involving residents, public, private and voluntary bodies), a neighbourhood manager to coordinate services, a multidisciplinary team and annual action plans.

There has been a regular exchange in zonal policies, and more recently in education policies, between Britain and the USA. The US government promoted Business Improvement Districts (BIDs), Community Development Corporations (CDCs), Empowerment and Enterprise Zones in the last two decades. BIDs are an attempt to provide better quality services in central areas, run by representatives of major employers in the area such as banks, corporations and major stores, and funded by a tax surcharge imposed on all businesses. They provide services such as refuse collection, street cleansing, security, parks maintenance and employ their own staff. For example, three Manhattan BIDs employed non-union staff on wages and conditions at just over half the equivalent City Council wage rates in 1996 (*City Limits*, 1996). CDCs provide a widening range of basic services and economic development activities at the neighbourhood level.

Local authorities in Britain and other European countries have long had city centre plans to attract and retain businesses and visitors and to coordinate redevelopment. Some have Town Centre management teams to coordinate public/private investment. Several British cities have established City Centre Management Companies alongside a campaign for Town Centre Zones (Shutt et al., 1999). Coventry is the first city centre to be completely managed by a partnership company. The City Council has transferred all its city centre functions including managing car parks (the assets will be transferred later), day-to-day city centre management, cleaning and maintenance, marketing and operating the CCTV security system. The Council has two representatives on the City Centre Management Company, the other eleven Board members are representatives of property companies, the Chamber of Commerce and retailers. The city's director of development described it as 'an exciting way of taking companies that provide public services out of the political arena, giving all sections of the community a real stake in their success' (*Financial Times*, 30 May 1997).

Pilot Home Zones, pedestrian/children-friendly areas in residential areas, were launched in 1999.

In addition to focusing on geographic areas, the zonal approach has a number of common elements:

Coordination and integration focus on management rather than a resource problem and are exacerbated by the ideology of so-called 'wicked issues' – long-term unemployment, drug abuse, poverty. The zonal approach demonstrates a lack of a multidisciplinary approach with little or no coordination in the selection of zones. Plymouth has overlapping employment, health and education zones. Coordination is only apparently an agenda item once zones are established, providing little evidence of joined-up thinking.

Financial support is only available through centrally imposed competitions or as a means of attracting or levering European funding. False claims of additional resources often mask deeper cuts in mainline spending programmes or are reliant on the injection of private capital directly by business or via partnership projects. The government is not prepared to fund a real attack on poverty so 'programme development' offers pilots, experiments and innovation in targeted areas which give the appearance of addressing root causes and divert professional and trade union criticism as everyone gets to grips with 'new' policies.

Social inclusion: Zones rarely tackle the root causes of economic and social deprivation, they have limited focus on equity and redistribution and focus only on the symptoms. The cause of social exclusion is rarely to be found within zones, and while zones are likely to improve health and educational performance, there is no guarantee that these gains will be permanent, or that the lessons, best practice and similar resources will be applied to other neighbourhoods, or that zones simply don't move the problem to another area.

New opportunities for capital: Zones are a means of legitimising private sector involvement in the provision and management of core public services. The government wants business involvement to draw on its expertise, provide new facilities and dispose of surplus assets, private funding and increased efficiency through competition. Companies gain access to new markets and customers – 'commercialising childhood', corporate publicity, an opportunity to influence the education agenda to meet the needs of employers and to profit from the technological reform of teaching (Hatcher, 1999).

Restructuring can be explored in zones to establish precedents which can later be established as national policy. For example, EAZs can opt out of the teachers' national pay scheme. Molnar notes that conflict over the reform of school 'is couched in educational terms, it is not fundamentally about education at all'. It is primarily about imposing job restructuring which 'is the key to unlock the educational market' (Molnar, 1996, p. 11). Zones enable the government to tackle professional interests which could not be achieved by traditional competitive tendering or by other educational policy initiatives. It is a form of opting out under the guise of experimentation. Education Action Zones apply performance management not just to staff but also to service users, where students have to 'work harder for longer' with no job guarantee at the end.

New tiers of governance: Education zones create a new tier of governance between school governing bodies and local education authorities and New Deal for Communities creates a new tier of urban management at neighbourhood level.

Innovation and best practice is often limited with the focus often on a physical/property led approach.

A profusion of micro-initiatives are dependent on self-help, limited community involvement, business commitment (a vested interest for private firms) and resources which do not replace cuts in mainline programmes. Public bodies are forced to share power with a plethora of other organisations in partnerships. Zones are, in effect, a microcosm of transformation.

Take Your Partners

Local government has a history of collaboration with other organisations and joint ventures with the private sector. Standard outsourcing contracts are now rebranded as partnerships. However, it is absurd to describe the relationship between the taxpayer and the state or between a public organisation and private contractor as a partnership. This is debasing the definition.

There are broadly three types of partnership. First, those between public organisations and agencies who work together on a project or tackle a common problem for which they have some level of responsibility. Second, between a public body and private firm or voluntary body to provide a specific service. Third, a consortium of public, private and/or voluntary organisations to carry out regeneration and development.

Most partnerships are sealed by contracts with companies, not committees. The state is shedding its responsibility to individuals (and to public sector workers) while at the same time intensifying its commitment to financial and service capital with long-term multi-million pound PFI contracts (see Chapter 3). Most partnerships are cloaked in secrecy with limited democratic accountability. The state and private contractors collude to protect intellectual property rights using 'commercial confidentiality' to minimise disclosure, participation, assessment of deals and public accountability. In this context, partnership is little more than negotiated privatisation and corporate welfare (see Chapter 5).

The accountability of partnerships is a major issue. Companies and private non-profit organisations are generally accountable only to shareholders and directors respectively. Partnership often involves a dilution and merging of public, private and voluntary interests. While a public body will have to maintain a commitment to matters of public interest, a partnership reflects negotiation and accommodation of different and competing interests. Some partnerships focus on the private and voluntary participants supporting and helping the local authority or health authority to achieve its objectives. Partnership by desire is being replaced by partnership by necessity. The concept of partnership implies that the state and capital are jointly concerned with the public interest and that either side can ensure that the other delivers its contribution.

Commercialising Public Services

Commercialisation of the public sector is intended to blur the boundaries between public and private sectors and to create the conditions for further marketisation and privatisation by providing a common operating system for internal trading between business. It includes the importation of business values and practices, business management systems, business planning and user charges. Commercialisation also seeks to extract surplus value or profit from the provision of public services and to legitimate market pay rates in place of national agreements. 'Success' is determined by narrowly defined business criteria such as efficiency, value for money and unit costs and relates less and less to social need and quality of provision.

Commercialisation also extends to the classroom. As competition between schools intensifies, the educational market is expanding with school–business partnerships, private management and educational and promotional material from transnational companies. US and Canadian classrooms are already inundated with 'educational' materials from banks (on finance and investment), oil companies (environmental issues) and manufacturers such as Ford (science and technology) and business sponsorship for commercial and corporate objectives.

There has been a surge of new management techniques, mainly developed for the US corporate sector, to improve quality of service and increase efficiency over the last two decades. Downsizing, outsourcing and reengineering have become management fads. Many public bodies, such as the Next Steps Agencies, have used the Business Excellence Model or Business Process Reengineering to help achieve the efficiency and market testing targets. Some managers had one eye on the potential value of the organisation and its assets and the other trying to find an appropriate management practice to improve performance. In these circumstances, managerial change was often transitional or partial.

The atomisation of the public sector into devolved units means that the prescriptive managerialism applied to private sector enterprises can be shifted into the public sector counterparts: 'excellent' schools and hospitals parallel 'excellent' companies. This cross-constituency promise of managerialism is thus a means by which under-funding claims can be defused – more is to be delivered from the same or diminished resources. (Cutler and Waine, 1997, p. 10)

Reinventing or Copying Private Sector Models

The proponents of privatisation and new public management share the same beliefs and ideology. They believe that many government activities should be transferred to the private sector, or alternatively, business practice should be imported into the public sector for those activities which cannot immediately be sold or contracted out. It is therefore not surprising that NPM has failed to develop a new or specific public service management but instead merely copied private management.

The reinvention model is not based on a definitive understanding of the differences between the public and private sectors. Although Osborne and Gaebler state that 'government cannot be run like a business' (Osborne and Gaebler, 1992, p. 21), they fail to produce a distinctive public service practice which is not based on competition and commercialisation.

Public and private sectors clearly have some common ground but there are important differences in their operating modes, regulatory framework and functions:

- The public sector is required to provide a service, not to make a profit.
- Most public sector organisations are not free to change their function, nor can they readily diversify into other activities, nor can they select their market or decide to deliver services to some users but not to others.
- They provide public and collective goods in addition to services for individuals and families and they are usually mandated to identify social needs, not just customer markets.
- Public funding is still the prime source of finance.
- Many public bodies are highly professionalised organisations employing large numbers of doctors, teachers and social workers.
- They operate to much higher levels of corporate responsibility with an expectation that equal opportunities, social inclusion and environmental sustainability are reality rather than rhetoric.
- They are required to have accountable and transparent decision-making and must bear the cost of representative democracy.
- Public bodies are required to emphasise the distinctive functions and values of government and public service in a civic and cultural sense.

Eroding the Public Service Ethos

Not surprisingly, increasing commercialisation of public services has led to the erosion of a public service ethos (defined as accountability, bureaucratic behaviour, sense of community, motivation and loyalty – Pratchett and

Wingfield, 1994). A study of over 300 staff in four local authorities identified a shift in interpretations of accountability towards contract and market accountability and increasing dissatisfaction with rules which acted as obstacles to the effective and efficient management of their 'businesses'. It also found that fragmentation of local government into business units encouraged an inward-looking culture 'that requires individuals to place the interests of their own part of the organisation above those of any wider organisational, or societal, objectives'. It also found that loyalties were moving away from a council-wide focus to cost centres and business units. 'The key feature about the emerging ethos of local government service is that it emphasises a competitive, contractual, insular and adversarial culture' (Pratchett and Wingfield, 1994, p. 34).

Renewing Democracy or Privatising Government

There have been three major policy initiatives which affected the democratic accountability of public bodies and government between 1980 and 2000. The first was the rapid expansion of quangos in the 1980s, linked in part to the creation of quasi-markets. Government policies were also designed to marginalise and restrict community action and trade union activities with new laws to restrict picketing, demonstrations and the withdrawal of funding from resource centres and community development. The ideological message of the 1980s decade was championing participation in privatisation share offers.

The second was the birth of the Citizen's Charter in 1991 with renewed emphasis on consumer complaints and user rights to compensation for service failures. It spurned an industry in quality and customer care accreditation and awards, and while it opened up channels for user views and information, it did little to improve democratic accountability. The Citizen's Charter has grown into a plethora of national and local charters based on six principles: standards, openness, information, choice, non-discrimination and accessibility. The last two were later replaced by courtesy and helpfulness, putting things right and value for money. The charter was to complement competitive tendering so as to make the producers/bureaucrats more accountable to users in the public choice theory outlined in Chapter 1. It centred on consumers' pseudo contractual relationship based on the payment of taxes, user charges or fees, i.e. monetary value rather than on citizenship rights and their expression through collective action representing common or class interests. The extent to which the relationship between users and producers has been 'reengineered' is discussed in Chapter 6 but user empowerment is illusory. They have not empowered users except to open up new channels of complaint. Charters focus on access to and the use of a service, not its provision. Charters have encouraged managers and staff into doing what they should have been doing anyway as part of good public management.

The third initiative commenced with Labour's 'democratic renewal' which included devolution for Scotland and Wales, a Royal Commission on the House of Lords, the Jenkins Report on electoral reform, the Neill Commission on party funding and Mayors for London and other major cities. It also includes more extensive public involvement in the affairs of local government by 'recognising communities by increasing their involvement in direct decision-making' and 'seeking the direct involvement of the citizen to keep the services secured by the authority up to the mark' (DETR, 1998, p. 25). However, managerialism which is intended to ensure 'involvement' is limited to consultation of individuals through focus groups rather than increasing representative democracy, attempts to increase turnout at local elections will focus on taking voting booths to supermarkets, and staff and tenant ballots limited to voting for or against the transfer of services and estates to companies and partnerships.

The transfer of government functions to quasi-public bodies is, in effect, the privatisation of power. Public policy and investment decisions are made behind closed doors. Installing token democratic representation does little to change power relationships which are usually bound by 'commercial confidentiality' and restrictions on contact with the media. This represents both institutional and operational privatisation of government. These bodies increasingly operate a form of 'government by contract' in which contractual relationships determine service delivery, forms of accountability and relationships with other public bodies. Most of these organisations are run by people who are unelected, unaccountable to, and unrepresentative of, their local communities. The Labour government has required wider representation and public access to meetings, for example, NHS Trusts. Access to quango decision-making meetings spending large sums of public money should be a basic right, and not claimed to be radical democracy.

In its first year of power, the Labour government established nearly 200 policy reviews, task forces and advisory groups. While information about, and accountability of, some of the high profile reviews has been established, there is little knowledge of the terms of reference, membership, accountability, consultation procedures and reporting timetable available for the bulk of reviews. An analysis of the membership of 30 leading task forces and advisory groups revealed that 72 per cent were men, 29 per cent were from business and 6 per cent from trade unions. Only 13 out of 449 members (0.29 per cent) were black or Asian (Platt, 1998).

Labour's plans for democratic renewal extend to users and stakeholders but not to employees. Most local authorities are eagerly arranging citizens panels and focus groups, in effect continuing the Citizen's Charter approach, which engage individuals rather than representative organisations. There are few attempts to genuinely engage, never mind empower, user and community organisations.

Staff and trade union involvement, over and above established negotiating machinery covering staffing, pay, conditions of service, health and safety, was occasional and fragmented. Trade union privatisation strategies, service improvement, job satisfaction projects and worker plans initiatives are fully assessed in Whitfield (1983 and 1992). A number of the larger, generally Labour controlled, local authorities, established tripartite working arrangements in response to CCT. This involved trade union representatives working alongside managers and elected members to review, package and specify services and evaluate tenders. The importation of TQM and other human resource management practices into the British public sector often sought to adopt the technique but without the participation of the workforce, largely because management sought to bypass and marginalise trade union organisation. Staff and trade union involvement in Best Value varies widely with many authorities committed to consultation but with limited actual involvement.

MANAGING THE STATE

Marketisation and competition, de/re-regulation and new control systems have had a substantial influence on the operation and management of the state. This has not been a seamless process. Many public organisations have simultaneously adopted 'management of change' strategies which have been a glorified way of coping with budget cuts, rationalisation and service reductions while at the same time attempting to adopt quality management systems.

Performance Management and Best Value

The OECD's Public Management Service has claimed that 'a new paradigm for public management has emerged, aimed at fostering a performance-orientated culture in a less centralised public sector' (OECD, 1995, p. 8). The term 'new public management' (NPM) is commonly used to describe the policies practised by the British and New Zealand governments since 1979 and 1984 respectively. It centres on corporatisation and commercialisation, privatisation, competition and contracting, deregulation and liberalisation, performance management and restructuring the financing of public services – the globalisation of public management is discussed on p. 62.

Performance management is characterised by:

- a closer focus on results in terms of efficiency, effectiveness and quality of service;
- the replacement of highly centralised, hierarchical organisational structures by decentralised management environment where decisions on resource allocation and service delivery are made closer to the point of delivery, and which provide scope for feedback from clients and other interest groups;

- the flexibility to explore alternatives to direct public provision and regulation that might yield more cost-effective policy outcomes;
- a greater focus on efficiency in the services provided directly by the public sector, involving the establishment of productivity targets and the creation of competitive environments within and among public sector organisations; and,
- the strengthening of strategic capacities at the centre to guide the evolution of the state and allow it to respond to external changes and diverse interests automatically, flexibly, and at least cost. (OECD, 1995, p. 8)

The OECD has simply moulded together a series of similar initiatives by member countries and repeated their claimed advantages with limited further analysis. They claim that 'corporatisation and privatisation are important policy options' and 'market-orientated arrangements, including user charging, internal markets, market testing, and contracting out, have, under certain conditions, served to ration demand, economise resource use, and produce substantial and well-documented efficiency savings. They have also contributed to enhanced quality of service and value for money' (ibid.). There is an almost total lack of recognition of other alternatives or the fact that performance management and reinvention may have any costs, disadvantages or limitations.

The renewed focus on managerialism – more for less – and the 'correct' organisational and management system is intended to maximise the use of existing resources. However, at best, this will achieve marginal gains because the core problem is the lack of substantive and consistent investment. Efficient management is not a replacement for demands for increased resources (Peters, 1996). The plethora of business models and management fads which have emerged over the past two decades is indicative of the search for increased productivity.

There has been renewed emphasis in Britain on developing a performance-orientated culture. The focus on outputs, maximising the use of information and communications technology and greater value for money are undoubtedly important targets but not when they are narrowly defined or when the means of achieving them is primarily through competition, corporatisation and privatisation. Labour's Best Value is in danger of becoming little more than the OECD's performance management or the Tories' early 1980s efficiency drive wrapped in a different language. It is widely held that performance, not process, is all important. The latter is only considered when the former is not achieved.

Performance measurement has been developed more extensively in central government's Next Steps Agencies than elsewhere in the public sector. However, 'measuring' the performance of services and benchmarking is often claimed to be relatively 'easy' when in fact it is very difficult, often subjective and easily misused if crude comparisons are made between public and private services or between organisations serving quite different demographic, cultural, economic and social needs (see Chapter 6).

Best Value is Labour's alternative to compulsory competitive tendering and comparable with the Better Quality Services initiative in central government (which is described as a means of 'creating public/private partnerships through market testing and contracting out' (Cabinet Office, 1998b, cover). All government departments have Public Service Agreements which set out objectives, performance and efficiency targets. The NHS has a Performance Assessment Framework. Best Value is, in fact, a new control mechanism, albeit with the potential for local innovation. It is driven by performance measurement and auditing with the threat of government intervention if local authorities do not achieve continuous improvement. A range of initiatives including a Cabinet Office Regulatory Impact Unit (which must be consulted on any proposal to impose a significant regulatory burden on business), a Public Services Productivity Panel (a team of mainly private sector managers working with departments to improve efficiency) and a Beacon Scheme for local authorities, schools, NHS Trusts, GP practices and government departments and agencies, all under the modernising government banner.

The Key Requirements of Best Value
Two general duties, to achieve Best Value and to consult widely, came into effect from April 2000. Authorities have to review approximately 20 per cent of their services annually so that all services are reviewed on a five-year cycle. Authorities are required to justify why and how a service is provided, to compare their performance with others using national and local indicators, to consult and engage with their local communities in reviewing services and to demonstrate competitiveness through rigorous comparison and competition. Compulsory tendering has been abolished but authorities are required to 'develop markets' by researching suppliers, engaging with potential suppliers and encouraging markets by 'packaging work appropriate to the market' (DETR, 1999, p. 14). Annual Local Performance Plans report on current performance, service improvement achievements and set targets. The District Auditor verifies and audits the Performance Plan including consultation and performance information. The Audit Commission has established a 300-strong Best Value Inspectorate which will inspect local authority Best Value reviews and work alongside other inspectorates such as the Social Services Inspectorate and OFSTED. Additional inspections can be made where an authority is deemed to have a 'failing' service or where the DETR directs the Audit Commission to do so. The Commission has estimated the cost of Best Value audits and inspections to be £43 million 2000–01 rising to £56 million in 2001–02 although the Improvement and Development Agency estimate that the 2000–01 cost could be £92 million.

The government intends to repeal Part II of the Local Government Act 1988 to allow authorities to take into account terms and conditions of employment, equal opportunities policies, training and contracting out costs in the award of contracts. Local authorities will also be subjected to a new duty to promote the economic, social and environmental well-being of the area, a duty to produce a community plan 'to secure the development of a comprehensive strategy for promoting the well-being of their area', and will have new powers to enter into partnerships with public, private and voluntary organisations.

There are opportunities under the Best Value regime for local authorities to be innovative and creative, to add their own definition to the basic requirements and to improve the coordination and integration of services and activities. They can develop genuine user/employee involvement, new methods for service review and performance assessment, minimising competitive tendering and using Best Value to make the case for more resources.

It is, however, also a substantial threat to staff and users because some councils are pressing ahead with an externalisation agenda, led by chief executives eager to impress as performance managers and enablers – the managerial careerist equivalent of the privatisation fat cats. Best Value could result in far more extensive competitive tendering than that achieved by the Conservative government because Best Value applies to all services rather than defined activities. Continued budget constraints could make 'more for less' a very negative experience for staff with increasing generic working, deskilling and changes to working practices and erosion of terms and conditions. Financial issues and efficiency measures are likely to dominate performance measurement leading to further marginalisation of equalities, health and safety and social justice issues. Involving staff in quality circles to capture their ideas while attempting to marginalise union organisation, treating users as consumers while pandering to business through partnerships, would endanger democratic renewal and the more positive aspects of Best Value.

Best Value will institutionalise comparisons with the private sector in terms of performance and cost, focus on quantifiable measures or 'public services by numbers', continue consumer consultation rather than user and employee involvement and further marginalise social justice and equal opportunities. After two decades of the commercialisation of public service management, central and local government urgently need a framework which positively promotes public service management.

Reinventing Government and the National Performance Review (USA)
A similar performance management approach has been under way in the USA. The National Performance Review (NPR) began in March 1993 when President Clinton announced a review of the workings of the federal government under the supervision of Vice President Al Gore. Britain's Best Value regime gets its inspiration from this programme while the USA has

been attempting to apply Britain's agency model for performance-based organisations.

A year earlier, the book *Reinventing Government* had caused a stir by proposing a model of 'entrepreneurial government'. 'Competition is the permanent force for innovation that Government normally lacks' (Osborne and Gaebler, 1992, p. 92) with 'enterprise management' rooted in the extension of competition as a means of forcing managers to act. The authors have total faith in the internal market because it extends commercialisation. The book was ignorant of the development of new public management in other countries.

The NPR adopted the ten principles of *Reinventing Government*:

1. competition between service providers;
2. empower citizens by pushing control out of bureaucracy into community;
3. measure performance focusing on outputs;
4. driven by missions not rules and regulations;
5. redefine clients as customers and offer them choice;
6. prevent problems rather than simply respond to them;
7. energies in earning money, not simply spending it;
8. decentralise authority embracing participatory management;
9. prefer market mechanisms to bureaucratic mechanisms;
10. focus on catalysing all sectors – public, private and voluntary (Gore, 1993).

The NPR identified the root of the problem as being 'industrial-era bureaucracies in an information age' and called for a major transformation to redesign, reinvent and reinvigorate government so that 'it works better and costs less'. It had five aims: cutting unnecessary spending, serving its customers, empowering its employees, helping communities to solve their own problems, and fostering excellence. A second phase, launched with the 1996 Clinton budget, placed greater emphasis on the consolidation of grants, devolution and privatisation. Both *Reinventing Government* and the NPR have been widely criticised for their selectivity, shallowness of analysis, superficiality of the claims for empowerment and failure to address the function of government, to name but some of the criticisms (Carroll and Lynn, 1996; Fox, 1996; Frederickson, 1996; Kettl and Dilulio, 1995; Peters and Savoie, 1996).

Marketisation and Competition

The state has played a pivotal role in the creation of new and quasi-markets in four important ways. First, services which were traditionally directly provided such as education (school management), social care (residential and domiciliary care) and council housing management have been turned into markets through legislation, regulation and payment systems. Second, services were subjected to compulsory competitive tendering in order to expand the private market, particularly professional services such as architecture, engineering, legal and financial services. Third, quasi-markets have been created to force public bodies to compete for users. Finally, competitions for resources have been extended, partly to divert attention from the real level of cuts.

The last Conservative government specifically sought to establish a social care market. It did this through a number of mechanisms such as requiring 85 per cent of special transitory grants to local authorities to be spent on the supply of services by the independent sector, continuing financial constraints on local authorities which effectively forced them to withdraw from direct provision and making Residential Care Allowance (paid by central government) for people on Income Support only available to private and voluntary homes thus further penalising local authority provision.

The Tories used CCT, large-scale stock transfers and estate renewal resource competitions to try to create a council housing management market. This failed to materialise because there were few contractors with relevant experience and most tenants preferred 'the devil we know' rather than private firms and the fear of exploitative contractor 'landlords'.

Education, or more precisely 'school management', is a potential £24 billion new market for private firms, even larger than defence procurement (see Table 4.1), forming part of a £93 billion potential new market in health care, residential and community care, council housing management and welfare state administration. There has been a clear divide between the private schools sector and the local authority education service, unlike health and social care where marketisation is more advanced. Right-wing organisations are importing private management and school–business partnership ideas from the USA, which together with PFI schemes in schools and colleges, business involvement in Education Action Zones and increasing

Table 4.1: **New public service markets in Britain**

Service	Annual value (£billion)
Local authority schools	24
Local authority residential and community care	9
Health care	6
Welfare state departmental running costs	5
Council housing management[*]	49
Total	93

Source: *Public Expenditure: Statistical Analyses 2000–01*, Cm 4601, HM Treasury, April 2000, Tables 4.5, 5.2.
[*] Glennerster, 1998, Table 5.3, data for 1995.

competition between schools, are fuelling the growth of a quasi-market. The Labour government is forcing 'failing' Local Education Authorities to outsource management and core functions. The Kings Manor School in Guildford became the first privately managed local education authority school in Britain in 1999.

The marketisation process starts with the separation or isolation of technical and support services such as training and supply staff which are then outsourced. New regulatory agencies and quangos outsource performance assessment and financial constraints force public bodies to accept financial support, equipment and sponsorship.

Competitive Tendering

Increasing the role of market forces and competition in the delivery of public services was intended to improve efficiency and productivity. Similarly increasing consumer choice was intended to impose pressures on under-performing public bodies to force them to improve standards or face closure. The Tories' strategy was to systematically erode the public sector's distinctive attributes to mirror those in the private sector and to create a common system of procurement, planning and monitoring, a basis for 'partnership' and eventual privatisation. Labour's approach is to require public services to be run in a businesslike manner, merely a change of language rather than substance.

Government departments, local authorities, the NHS and other public bodies have never been monolithic self-sufficient structures. In the post-war expansion of the public sector, most services were delivered by in-house organisations although private contractors built most new housing and facilities. Private firms supplied goods and services, such as catering supplies for school meals, with limited forays into contracts for service delivery in cleaning and refuse collection. By the late 1970s private contractors, trade associations and right-wing groups were demanding that more services be subjected to competition.

Local authorities have been required to tender or market test entire services and specific functions since 1980 although tendering was already common for construction work. The proportion of building repair and highway maintenance work to be tendered was systematically increased from 1980. Other manual services such as refuse collection, street cleansing, catering, cleaning, grounds maintenance and vehicle maintenance commenced tendering in 1989. It was later extended to sports and leisure management, parking, home to school transport, security and fire and police vehicle maintenance. White collar services, legal, finance, personnel, housing management, construction and property services had to be tendered from 1996. The combined value of services subjected to competitive tendering in local government and the civil service rose dramatically from £1,603 million in 1991 to £5,979 million by 1995 (LGMB, 1995; Cabinet Office, 1996).

NHS hospitals have been required by the NHS Executive Management Order to tender catering, domestic and laundry services since 1983. Market testing was extended on a voluntary basis, to a wide range of non-clinical services. Competitive tendering in government departments and agencies was on a more ad hoc basis until the launch of the Citizen's Charter in 1991. This required all departments to have an annual market testing and efficiency programme – covering £5.1 billion services between 1992 and 1997 – to be vetted by the Cabinet Office. Facilities management became more prevalent in the NHS (hotel service contracts) and the Ministry of Defence (management of establishments). However, in local government the 'anti-competitive' aspect of the CCT regulations and small contracts meant the government was, in effect, ignoring technical, service and market trends in order to achieve its competition objectives.

Both the breakup of the National Bus Company and the franchising of the rail network were attempts to create competition between private sector operators. These markets developed directly as a result of privatisation strategies and franchising.

Marketisation and competition impose a set of organisational and managerial requirements including the separation of client/contractor or purchaser/provider responsibilities; skills to specify services, write contracts, evaluate tenders and monitor contract performance; package contracts and quasi-contracts within market and non-competitive environments; design regulatory frameworks for the competition process with sanctions if competitors do not adhere to the rules (deregulation in some cases), trading and accountancy systems; and price services and introduce user charges.

Competitive tendering inevitably led to further privatisation despite over 70 per cent of local government contracts (by value) retained by in-house services. This was due to internal pressures in DSOs such as the decline in workload, managers wanting greater freedom and financial rewards and fear of losing a contract which would threaten the DSO's financial viability. There are also external pressures such as private firms seeking to acquire DSOs and white collar departments to increase their market share, acquire knowledge of public sector work and skills and establish national networks of offices and depots.

Some analysts have struggled over 'how to accommodate the use of market mechanisms within the management of the public service, without undermining what is specific to it' (Walsh, 1995, p. 254). Others have focused on an even more simplistic approach: 'Does the government provide services at the cheapest cost?' (McRae, 1995, p. 186). The so-called benefits identified in academic studies tended to subject partial and selective data to mathematical modelling and computer analysis.

At least one pro-contracting academic who supported claims of 20–25 per cent budget savings has changed position now that several national empirical studies have shown such claims to be grossly exaggerated (see Chapter 6). 'Contracting is neither an ideological-driven crusade, nor an ephemeral management fad. It is a manifestation of the natural, long-term evolution of the economy. Specifically, it reflects the advanced stage of development of the services sector' (Domberger and Jensen, 1997, p. 160). No evidence was supplied to justify this statement. The authors refer to the 'economic transformation' which takes place when an activity is transferred from one organisation to another. 'This transformation essentially involves the replacement of contracts of employment within the organisation with contracts for services between purchasers and providers.' On the service delivery frontline this is known as job loss and wage cuts! It is no surprise that pro-contracting academics show little interest in identifying the real source of so-called savings nor the employment, equalities and wider socio-economic costs of contracting out.

Quasi-markets for Health, Education and Social Care
The creation of internal or quasi-markets in health care, education and social care emanated from legislation at the end of the 1980s. The objective was to create market-type mechanisms requiring schools and hospitals to compete for users with services remaining free at the point of use.

Education: Local Management of Schools (LMS) requires local education authorities to delegate responsibility for finance and staff to school governing bodies. School catchment areas were scrapped to increase parental choice and competition for pupils with income tied to pupil numbers. Competition is further encouraged between schools by league tables of exam results, widely reported school inspections and the 'shaming' of 'badly performing' schools. It is predicated on competition increasing choice and performance. Schools could also opt out of local authority control by becoming grant maintained, funded directly by central government.

Higher education: The University Funding Council attempt to establish a competitive tendering system was abandoned in 1993.

Health care: The introduction of the internal or quasi-market in health care in the early 1990s involved splitting District Health Authorities into purchaser and provider units retaining responsibility only for the former, larger GP practices became fundholders to purchase services from NHS and private sector hospitals, and hospitals became self-managed 'providers' converting to trust status with freedom to decide the range and quality of services, personnel and pay matters. The Labour government abolished GP fundholding, replacing it with Primary Care Groups (most will convert to trust status) but retained the purchaser/provider split.

Social care: The reform of community care since 1993 led to the integration of funding, the assessment and coordination of care, the inspection and registration of homes, and a mixed economy of care. Local authority social service departments have become enablers rather than direct providers of care services. Central government provided financial incentives and required 85 per cent of transferred Department of Social Security funds to be spent on private and voluntary sector provision. Change was also driven by local authority spending cuts, residential care allowance not being available in local authority homes and wide differences in pay and conditions between public and the so-called independent sector.

The creation of one care market led to the attempt to create a mixed economy care market, and a tenfold increase in private/voluntary home care provision between 1992 and 1995 from 2.4 to 29.2 per cent. Community care reform intended to reverse the incentives created by social security provisions for residential care. In 1980 local authorities provided two-thirds of places but this had shrunk to a quarter by 1995 as a result of the boom in private care and closures and transfers in the local authority sector.

Although the quasi-markets described above are distinctly different, there are some common features: non-profit organisations compete for users and public contracts; markets remain publicly funded, operate under government regulations, and in reality competition and real choice is limited but they create points of entry for private firms into services previously wholly or mainly provided by the public sector; resources are allocated through internal competition and contracting rather than through planning or formula funding.

The Conservative government launched competitions for resources in which local authorities bid for allocations, with success judged not solely on social need but on the leverage of private money and the quality of private partners. The Single Regeneration Budget integrated 20 different grant schemes into a single £1.4 billion budget. The National Lottery funding of sports, leisure, arts and its extension into education, has extended competition and privatised the allocation of public resources.

Outsourcing and Contracting Out
Public and welfare state services face increasing pressure – technological ability, improved efficiency, ability to provide differentiated services to meet changing and varied client demands, and cost cutting resulting in job losses and reduced terms and conditions.

Welfare is being commodified simultaneously with these developments. Benefits are being packaged in such a way as to enable capital to contract and operate them – not simply looking for administrative efficiency but profit from added value components of job training, search and placements. Capital also receives tax breaks and payments for taking on welfare labour, i.e. paying subsidies to capital in place of benefits to claimants. The contracting out or outsourcing of existing services means that the private sector operates services on behalf of the state. The state has a provider relationship with individuals. Simultaneously, all new services and benefit schemes will be rooted in the private sector where the relationship will be between the individual and private firms. But outsourcing is not sustainable in the longer term because, as it increases, capital will seek to develop its own private welfare state products and services.

Outsourcing IT creates opportunities for companies to diversify into other related services including welfare services. Electronic Data Systems (EDS) and Andersen Consulting have major contracts to design and operate Britain's Inland Revenue and National Insurance systems respectively. IT companies are gaining control of payroll, council tax collection, housing benefits and pension administration. US corporate involvement ranges from small firms such as America Works and Maximus Inc. providing welfare, child support, job training and placement projects to transnationals such as defence contractor Lockheed Martin IMS, Andersen Consulting and IT services giant Electronic Data Systems (which processes Medicaid claims in over 20 states) seeking state-wide contracts. Lockheed Martin's Welfare Reform Initiative division has employment and training contracts and case management of welfare claimants.

Market testing in the NHS and civil service was progressed by imposing financial pressures, coupled with an ideological offensive, a policy framework and managerial 'best practice'. But the government realised compulsion was required for it to proceed in local authorities. The 1988 and 1992 Local Government Acts and regulations established a highly structured rule-bound regime identifying specific services and tendering timetable. Whenever contractors complained about contract packaging or tender evaluation, the rules were altered. But as tendering spread to white collar services, the rigid state regime did not serve the interests of private capital. CCT became outmoded because the defined services approach hindered a facilities management approach and the packaging of ICT and related services. Furthermore, the white collar 'managed services' contractors did not oppose TUPE (Transfer of Undertakings (Protection of Employment) Regulations 1981 (implementing the European Acquired Rights Directive 1997 in Britain)) to the same extent as contractors in manual services because they had a vested interest in ensuring the transfer of experienced technical and professional staff. Official contract notices are rarely for a single service but invite proposals for a package of services effectively legitimating cherry-picking by contractors. Some authorities, committed to retaining in-house services, deliberately adopt this approach to 'prove' to the government that they have considered competition but it is a dangerous game. Other local authorities now resemble the State Privatisation Offices in Central and Eastern Europe, overrun with management consultants and packaging and selling everything of 'value'. The Third Way ('what matters is what works') or the 'pick and mix' approach to the selection of providers, consolidates the contract system and further embeds competition, marketisation and privatisation throughout the public sector.

The existing penetration of public services by the private sector, sometimes for historic reasons or through recent tendering, is often used as a springboard for further privatisation. For example, the long tradition of general practitioners' (GP) services being private businesses, fully reimbursed from general taxation, has major implications for the strategic expansion of primary health care. Pressures to integrate GP and community health services, the private finance of premises and private sector property management, and the reliance on rental income from licences and subcontracts to community trusts, pharmacies, opticians, alternative medicinal practitioners and other services – essential for the viability of primary health care developments – could lead to private control of the primary health care infrastructure with dire consequences for prioritising social needs, tackling inequalities in the provision of facilities, local autonomy, diversity and flexibility (Glendinning and Bailey, 1998).

Boundaries between public, private and voluntary/social sectors are changing and becoming more complex. The distinction between provision, finance and decision used in the Rowntree study (see Chapter 3) is somewhat limited because it focuses on financial, regulation and provider issues but not ownership and control, corporate interest, employment and user preference.

The Voucher Lobby

Vouchers enable the holder to access both public and private sector schools or other services. They are highly controversial because they channel public money into private schools. While presented as increasing choice, they are a means of marketising the schools system and leave the real choice with private schools. The theory is that successful schools prosper and unsuccessful ones go to the wall. Voucher demands could arise in Britain if the middle classes exit the state system and object to paying twice through taxes and private school fees. However, voucher schemes in the USA have proved to be expensive, decrease accountability and channel public money into private schools at the expense of investing to improve public schools. There have been repeated and largely unsuccessful attempts, funded and orchestrated by right-wing organisations, to pass state legislation for voucher schemes. There are a few small schemes in Ohio and Wisconsin but these are not state-wide, being initially confined to Cleveland and Milwaukee. A nursery school voucher scheme was abolished by the Labour government in 1997.

Deregulation and Re-regulation

The last two decades have seen a mixture of deregulation, re-regulation and new regulatory regimes depending on the government's strategic and political objectives. Deregulation started with the removal of capital controls in 1979 which allowed financial institutions to move capital overseas without restriction. 'Streamlining' of the planning development process followed together with reducing and relaxing health and safety regulations and eliminating 'red tape' for business. Deregulation was extended to public transport in 1985 coupled with the sale of national and local authority bus companies.

The motives of deregulation included reducing the cost of compliance for capital and increased competition by reducing or eliminating barriers of entry. Re-regulation was motivated by political objectives by minimising opposition to deregulation and weak new regulatory regimes. Some regulation was contradictory, for example, local authorities were required to deregulate business activity but their own internal operations were subjected to a mixture of re-regulation and new regulations such as the registration and inspection of residential care homes.

There was also a wider agenda, for example, the US deregulation and breakup of AT&T in 1984 put pressure on companies to seek profits from new markets overseas, followed by privatisation of British Telecom; the 'US has managed to transform the agenda of the international political economy of communications towards deregulation to match the domestic characteristics of its own economy' (Strange, 1996, p. 104). Britain later liberalised the telecommunications market opening local, trunk and international services to competition from cable television companies, mobile networks and other firms. European Union deregulation initiatives cover airlines, telecoms and postal services as part of implementing the Single Market.

Reducing Red Tape

Reducing red tape and bureaucracy has been a constant demand of private capital which basically wants the state to regulate only to the extent to which it is necessary to ensure the proper functioning of markets. The private sector generally wants to maximise self-regulation, particularly of financial services despite the abject failure of the regulatory framework to prevent and rectify the mis-selling of pensions.

The Deregulation and Contracting Out Act 1994 gave the government an order-making power to remove or reduce regulations without requiring primary legislation. Some 37 deregulation orders had been issued by mid-1998. The Labour government converted the Conservatives' deregulation initiative into the Better Regulation Initiative to extend deregulation with more extensive consultation with business.

New Regulatory Regimes for Privatised Services and Markets

The privatisation of utilities, telecommunications and transport brought the establishment of bodies to regulate the companies, markets and prices. State regulation was a substitute for public ownership which resulted in:

- the fragmentation with each service or function having its own regulatory office;
- the limited accountability of regulatory bodies;
- confusion over socioeconomic criteria;

- institutional capability to negotiate with transnational companies and world trade bodies and to maintain up-to-date analysis of fast changing trends and developments in each sector and broader patterns of economic change.

Deregulation of the Labour Market

Deregulation at the workplace in Britain has included a fourfold increase in the qualifying period for full-time workers to claim unfair dismissal; abolition of the Fair Wages Resolution protecting staff working for private firms on government contracts; weakening and later the abolition of the Wages Councils which set minimum pay rates for 2.5 million low-paid workers. The abolition of the National Dock Labour Scheme in 1989 enabled port operators, following privatisation of the nationalised British Transport Docks Board in 1982, to compete against non-scheme ports and to casualise the workforce to meet peaks and troughs (Nolan et al., 1997, p. 167). The Conservative agenda was to deregulate for capital and re-regulate labour. Various attempts were made to deregulate public sector pay in the civil service and NHS but with limited success. Few NHS Trusts even attempted to deviate from national pay and civil service agencies could vary pay, terms and conditions only from April 1997.

The welfare state was subjected to increased regulation, for example, increased means testing, more complex regulations for eligibility, new requirements to encourage claimants into training and Welfare to Work. Some regulations were related to combating fraud but most could be classified as imposing increased discipline on the unemployed and single parents.

Deregulation and Increased Regulation of Internal Government

Despite some flagship deregulation initiatives such as Enterprise Zones and Urban Development Corporations, public services witnessed a systematic increase in tendering and contracting out regulations, with government specifying the services to be tendered and imposing strict rules on the packaging of contracts, evaluating tenders and awards of contracts. Council tenants were given the legal right to force local authorities to sell council homes.

This contrasts with the internal relaxation of regulations under the devolution of management, giving managers greater freedom in purchasing goods and services and in personnel matters. Deregulation of the management of government has centred on eliminating rules in personnel and financial matters. The big US government deregulation drive in the 1990s included simplifying procurement, the exact opposite of what happened in Britain.

Regulations were also introduced by the Conservative government to curb political activity. These ranged from restrictions prohibiting local authority expenditure on publicity which criticised the government and limiting council staff serving as Members in neighbouring authorities.

A study of regulatory bodies concluded that there was evidence of 'a growth in compliance costs commensurate with, or even greater than, the growth in direct costs of regulation inside government' (Hood et al., 1998, p. 64) The authors estimate that there are between 134 and 200 regulatory organisations, employing between 14,000 and 20,000 staff with running costs of between £800 million and £1,000 million. The 90 per cent staff increase in regulatory bodies inside the UK government between 1976 and 1995 compares with a 30 per cent and 20 per cent decline in civil service and local government staff respectively with a 106 per cent increase in annual costs.

The Conservative government substantially increased regulation of trade union activities making it more difficult to organise industrial action, support political action and collect membership dues. Specific trade union legislation increased regulatory procedures for industrial action, banned secondary action and the use of union funds for political purposes unless specifically prescribed for such purposes.

SUMMARY

This and the preceding chapter have examined the objectives, components and process of transformation of the public sector. While external influences from the continued globalisation of the world economy have had an impact, most of the transformation process has been inspired by internal political decisions and ideology. In sharp contrast to the rhetoric about the growth of global cities, governments in Britain have proscribed the financial, regulatory and managerial capacity of cities. Economic and social planning has been transferred to unelected regional bodies and the supply of welfare state services has been narrowed to focus on service delivery with policy and financial decision-making either highly centralised or localised.

Labour's modernisation programme is increasingly focused on 'citizen-centred governance' and 'people before provision' with the emphasis on 'frontline first' whereby resources are directed to individual institutions such as schools. The need for joined-up government through better integration of services and functions with more cross-cutting and holistic approaches has also led to a search for alternatives to producer-led professional attitudes and departmentalism or 'silo' forms of bureaucratic organisation. This has provoked new interest in neighbourhood management which ranges from patch coordination with 'super caretakers' to neighbourhood teams to devolved powers and resources to neighbourhoods.

However, the modernisation programme has seven fault lines. The first extends from the ideology of 'what matters is what works', neutrality on who provides services resulting in a failure to provide leadership in promoting public management. The second fault line extends through performance management with the emphasis on benchmarking, efficiency, outcomes, audit and inspection at the expense of other values and the process of provision. The third fault line is competition which is embedded in the modernisation programme, thus extending marketisation and privatisation.

PPP/PFI projects are the fourth fault line, now encompassing the welfare infrastructure, justified solely on financial grounds and the private sector's efficiency, expertise and value for money claims. The fifth fault line runs through the opposing policies of joined-up government and the transfer of core services to quangos and the proliferation of zones, contracts and initiatives. The aims of democratic renewal are weakened by more secretive cabinet government, consumerism and lack of capacity building to replace the development resources stripped from communities over the last two decades which makes involvement, let alone empowerment, improbable. This is the sixth fault line. Finally, although local government has new powers for community planning and the social, economic and environmental well-being, the combination of the fault lines reduce the capacity of local government to use these powers effectively.

The different components of the modernisation programme have a differential impact. The creation of markets, outsourcing, transfers, new quangos and PPP/PFI projects overwhelm other policies and initiatives. Good practice and innovation tend to get marginalised. A culture of modernisation is also spawned which vainly attempts to plaster over the fault lines in appeasing central government dictats.

State restructuring, marketisation and privatisation in Britain have continued with only marginal change, as evidenced in Chapters 3 and 4. The focus remains on 'government failure' instead of market failure, redistribution is marginal, and democratic renewal does not recognise the need for an organisational rather than consumerist model of civil society in order to create a counter-balance of power between capital and the state. The capacity of the state continues to be eroded as it is moulded into a corporatist (minimalist) or enabling (partnership) model of governance. The dependency culture is being reformed for the unemployed, single mothers and the working poor who are vehemently criticised for being a burden on the state, yet public resources are being used to create a new global, regional and national corporate-welfare complex in which business dependency is legitimated through taxation, subsidies and partnerships.

5

The Emerging Corporate-Welfare Complex

The welfare state has not only been subject to transformative change and modernisation but has also had to accommodate the socioeconomic consequences of globalisation, demographic change and neo-liberal business interests constantly seeking to marketise and privatise public provision to create vast new financial and services markets.

This chapter is divided into five parts. The first examines the resilience of welfare states to fundamental change, followed by a discussion of the new challenges confronting welfare states including the 'solutions' proffered by business and right-wing organisations and postmodern demands for individualism, flexibility and pluralism. The next section assesses the implications of a Third Way welfare state, and this is followed by a review of the threatened privatisation of pensions and social security. The chapter concludes with an analysis of an emerging corporate-welfare complex.

RESILIENCE TO CHANGE

Welfare states have generally been very successful in providing comprehensive education, health care, social services and benefits systems which have largely withstood post-war economic recessions, spending and investment cuts and continuous criticism. The post-war 'settlement' between capital and labour included the provision of workers' protection through statutory regulations, social security protection for unemployment and entitlement to housing and family allowances, collective bargaining, the right to organise and full employment through national economic policy. It also often included the provision of good quality housing, comprehensive education, health and social services. The state and capital also required the welfare state to maintain social order, to promote the work ethic, family values and provide a supply of low wage labour (Piven and Cloward, 1971). As such, the welfare state has always been, and will continue to be, an arena of struggle between state, capital, labour and civil society.

The welfare state is built on key principles which include social *solidarity* from one generation to another, thus distributing risk against ill health, unemployment and the cost of the social infrastructure. It also encourages social *and collective responsibility* with *redistribution from the better-off to those worse-off* and to those with greater need for medical care, family support and assistance. It is designed to afford protection from, and relief of, poverty and maintenance of a standard of living with a benefits system which encourages access to employment, training and/or education and support for people to develop their potential.

The welfare state has proved resilient to fundamental change for several very important reasons. First, the welfare state accommodates the social costs of globalisation such as the escalating social, economic and environmental effects of rapid growth and urbanisation in some regions or deindustrialisation, financial crises and unemployment in others. Mass unemployment was not a welfare state failure but a failure of the market economy. Weakening the welfare state will reduce the ability of nation states to ameliorate these impacts, reducing still further the likelihood of meeting global poverty reduction targets. Declining birth rates and increasing longevity, changing social needs, increasing income and wealth inequality and public demand for good quality health services, social care, education and training, place additional demands on the welfare state.

Many people understand that the welfare state, particularly pensions, health and education makes economic sense. British Social Attitudes surveys in the last decade have consistently shown 60 per cent or more of the public supporting increased taxes for services, particularly health and education (Appleby, 2000). The welfare state was rooted in years of struggle, exploitation and the failure of private systems to provide decent services for working people at reasonable cost, functions which are difficult to withdraw once established. Despite these strengths, the welfare state has often failed to adapt to the needs of women, black and ethnic minority communities and to develop differentiated services within universal systems. It has also been the focus of continuing national and local action by user campaigns and trade unions over welfare policies, equalities, spending cuts, and demands for more and better services.

Second, welfare states have already accommodated enormous change, for example, the ratio of active to retired workers in the USA fell from 16:1 in 1935 to 3.3:1 today and is estimated to fall to 2:1 by 2030 (Rothstein, 1999). Industrialised countries rapidly expanded education in response to the post-war baby boom. Investment was funded by economic growth and public spending decisions reflected changing social needs and priorities. Welfare state policy requires long-term planning, hence the greed and exploitative policies promoted by the right and business interests must be strongly opposed. The ageing of the population is not permanent; fertility rates will change and hence social priorities.

Third, it is politically difficult to cut costs without hurting pensioners, the disabled, the poor and the unemployed, particularly in periods of high unemployment, increasing inequalities and poverty in means-tested welfare regimes. Pensioners and the disabled account for three-quarters of the benefits budget in Britain.

Finally, although 'the absence of attractive private alternatives is often a source of strength for social programs' (Pierson, 1994, p. 181), this misses the point because the private sector has a greater immediate economic interest in the private delivery of a public welfare state out of which may emerge new commodification and marketisation strategies. This strategy avoids the risk and cost of establishing entirely new private systems. It also aligns with the transformation process model described in Chapter 3. Private systems are on the increase. A six-nation study of the role of private social benefits (mainly pensions, sickness benefits and health) showed an increase in all countries except Germany (Adema and Einerhand, 1998). The total private share of social expenditure remained low in Denmark (3.8 percent) and Sweden (5.7 per cent), followed by Germany (9.2 per cent), the Netherlands (12.4 per cent) and the UK (14.0 per cent) concluding with the USA (35.5 per cent). But these private systems also had a public cost via tax breaks for private pensions and private social benefits which accounted for 3.55 and 2.18 per cent of GDP at factor cost (1993) for the UK and USA respectively.

Some countries have recently established new welfare state systems. For example, Germany started a pay-as-you-go compulsory social insurance scheme in 1995 based on 1.7 per cent of gross earnings funded equally by employers and employees. Taiwan's universal health insurance scheme is operated by the government, funded by the employer (60 per cent), employees (30 per cent) and government (10 per cent) although the health system remains privately controlled.

Current welfare reform is likely to accelerate the erosion of the principle of universal benefits creating a two-tier approach to the deserving poor and undeserving poor. Individuals will be made responsible for an increasing proportion of risk 'protection', for example, unemployment insurance and pensions, with the consequent growth in insurance schemes, 'cradle to grave' transnational corporations and financial institutions. Outright privatisation of the welfare state, on a similar scale to the sale of the nationalised industries and utilities, was not and is still not, a feasible option in Western Europe although this has been the strategy in many Central and Eastern European and Latin American countries. Transformation and privatisation by stealth is intended to reconfigure services rather than dismantle the system.

Types of Welfare Systems

At this point it is important to briefly highlight a three-part typology of welfare regimes (Esping-Andersen, 1990, 1999). There are substantial variations within these groupings since no two welfare systems are the same and expenditure levels are a poor indicator of quality and institutional arrangements.

The *Social Democratic welfare regime* has a strong commitment to full employment, wage and gender equality through universal benefits, good quality state services particularly for children and the aged – public employees account for up to 30 per cent of the labour force, twice the OECD average (Sweden, Norway, Denmark and Finland). Scandinavia adopted a social investment strategy in the 1980s and 1990s with emphasis on work and training.

The *Conservative welfare regime* focuses on social insurance and benefits (many having separate and more generous schemes for civil servants), church and family play a key role in providing care and welfare with limited publicly provided social services. There was a labour reduction strategy in the 1980s and 1990s through early retirement/disability and discouraging married women from the labour market (Germany, France, Italy, Belgium, Austria, Netherlands, Japan).

The *Liberal welfare regime* has a high proportion of means-tested social assistance for a low income population compared to rights programmes, a narrow definition of social risk with more residualised benefits and a relatively high level of market provision of pensions, health and social care (USA, Canada, Australia, New Zealand, Britain and Ireland). Castles (1996) argues that Australia and Britain should be categorised as a liberal-labour regime because of the key role of collective bargaining. Since the early 1980s, several countries have adopted a neo-liberal strategy of reducing the social wage, deregulation, marginalising trade unions, resulting in rising poverty and inequality.

These three models illustrate radically different approaches of welfare states to women's employment and role of the family. 'Active de-familialization of welfare burdens in the social democratic regime; an essentially passive or, at most, targeted assistance approach in the liberal; and a policy of sustained familialism in Continental Europe – much less in France and Belgium, much more in Italy and Spain' (Esping-Andersen, 1999, p. 161).

NEW CHALLENGES FOR THE WELFARE STATE

In the last 20 years, welfare states in industrialised countries have had to accommodate the rise of mass unemployment, the social costs of disinvestment, falls in the employment rates for men while those for women have increased, ageing of the population, a sharp rise in the proportion of families headed by a lone parent, and a rapid increase in disability and incapacity claimants. These developments have inevitably led to questions about the affordability of the welfare state in a global economy, the compatibility of the welfare state with the needs of business and the adaptability and flexibility of welfare regimes to meet equality and multicultural demands.

The Affordability of the Welfare State in a Global Economy

Business and right-wing interests claim that the welfare state is no longer affordable because of these changes: slower economic growth, the ineffi- ciency of state provision, the lack of incentives to work, the high level of fraud and the need for new flexible and personal systems to meet the needs of the global economy in the twenty-first century. They claim that the welfare state is 'unsustainable' serving only as a transitional system 'while waiting the reconstruction of a genuine international system of savings', socialised care has evidently lost its moral and financial legitimacy and changes in the working environment will make traditional social security arrangements obsolete (Lepage, 1997 pp. 71–2).

They attempt to justify this approach on the grounds that globalisation forces employers to seek reductions in non-wage social costs and further cuts in personal and corporate taxation which in turn limit public spending, otherwise employers will simply relocate to areas of low taxation. It is therefore necessary to lift the 'burden' of the welfare state on the economy to encourage entrepreneurialism and individual responsibility. Ageing and demographic trends are being used by the Right to make exaggerated forecasts of 'boomernomics', 'generational warfare' and 'a pensions time bomb'. Business is demanding cuts in corporate taxation and non-wage social costs, irrespective of their level, in order to maximise profits. The same arguments are used to promote marketisation of the welfare state to achieve 'efficiency savings', thus creating a win-win situation for business – contracts and lower taxes!

At issue is not just affordability, but whether a comprehensive system of social welfare is compatible with the conditions and needs of the global market economy. 'With the shift to lean production and flexible workplaces, many existing social programmes are seen as a fetter on capitalist accumu- lation. Increasingly, they are regarded as being dysfunctional economically and unsustainable politically by elites everywhere' (Mishra, 1996, p. 319). Unemployment benefit is said to hamper worker mobility, universal income support is unaffordable and wasteful and high levels of taxation are a disin- centive to enterprise and investment. It is therefore necessary, it is claimed, to replace the Keynesian welfare state with post-Fordist forms of welfare which would entail shrinking the welfare state to reduce taxes, abandoning universality and targeting benefits to the needy, introducing privatisation and competition in the delivery of welfare services and developing more per- sonalised systems.

Transnational companies in ICT, financial, health, social care and insurance sectors are busy undermining public provision and organising corporately to exploit potentially vast global welfare markets. The promotion of partnerships by both the state and private sector affords further opportu- nities for capital which wants to minimise the costs of employment, maximise flexibility to hire and fire workers and establish new international markets.

This drive by business interests to privatise the welfare state is rarely recognised by analysts.

Globalisation is also forcing a degree of competition between welfare states in other countries over the strategies adopted to increase economic competitiveness, productivity, labour market flexibility and social investment. It has also led to the internationalisation of social welfare policy as the Bretton Woods institutions, OECD, UN organisations, international NGOs and corporate interests research and develop policies for pensions and social welfare regimes. The promotion of global labour and social standards, based largely on industrialised economies, also causes friction and charges of imperialism from developing countries. However, there are very large differences in the funding, benefits and services provided by welfare regimes so it is important not to overstate competitive forces.

Demographic Change, Ageing and Economic Performance

Ageing of the population is a global trend but there are significant differences in how and when it affects nation states. For example, by 2030 the proportion of those aged over 65 (as a proportion of the 15–65 age group) will reach 48 per cent and 49 per cent respectively in Italy and Germany, with Canada and Germany having growth rates in excess of 100 per cent, followed by the US with 94 per cent (see Table 5.1). The increase in the UK is forecast to be a relatively modest 59 per cent where the number of people of pensionable age is expected to increase gradually until 2011, then more rapidly until 2041 and then to decline gradually. The proportion of those aged 75–84 and 85–94 will become an increasingly significant part of the elderly population.

Table 5.1: **Ageing of population in major industrialised countries 2000–30** (% of population)

Country	2000	2010	2020	2030	% change 2000–30
Canada	18.2	20.4	28.4	39.1	115
Germany	23.8	30.3	35.4	49.2	107
United States	19.0	20.4	27.6	36.8	94
Japan	24.3	33.0	43.0	44.5	83
Italy	26.5	31.2	37.5	48.3	82
France	23.6	24.6	32.3	39.1	66
United Kingdom	24.4	25.8	31.2	38.7	59
OECD average (excl. Czech Republic)	20.9	23.5	29.8	37.7	80

Source: Family, Market and Community, OECD, 1997d.

Private insurance, it is claimed, should replace state funded care with the welfare state serving only the long-term unemployed, the old and sick. 'The fate of citizens, particularly the poor, will therefore rest heavily not on government performance but rather on the performance of market forces' (Lawrence, 1997, p. 32). Other proposals include a mass opt out programme, equivalent to giving everyone a voucher for specific welfare state services (Snowner, 1997). Another proposal is for each person to have separate 'welfare accounts' for retirement, unemployment, health (including sickness and disability insurance) and human capital (for education and training). People would make regular mandatory minimum contributions to each account which would be drawn on as and when needed. Accounts would be managed by either by the government or private financial institutions. Welfare state services would be publicly and privately provided, each sector competing for account holders' 'custom' (Orszag and Snowner, 1998, p. 5).

The OECD Secretariat claims that

> radically reducing the role of government in all domains – offers a fairly direct path to greater flexibility in the allocation of resources by individuals and firms ... the greatest virtue of such an unbounded society is its capacity to reap the full rewards of market efficiency and individual choice ... many of the technical as opposed to state-imposed obstacles to market functioning, like the cost of accurate and timely information for making transaction choices, will be largely overcome by the emerging power of the global information infrastructure. (OECD, 1997b, pp. 15–16)

A World Bank paper claims that

> public expenditure could be reduced to, perhaps, under 30% of GDP without sacrificing much in terms of social or economic objectives. ... One could argue that there is no compelling economic reason for far-reaching state involvement in these areas beyond basic social assistance e.g. in the form of a basic allowance for the poor or the unemployed, and of insurance against catastrophic events such as major illnesses or accidents for everyone. With proper reforms, most pensions, health and social insurance needs could be satisfied by the private sector. (Tanzi,1995, p. 26)

Not surprisingly, there are political and financial vested interests in promoting and preventing change. Pensioners and claimants want better benefits and construction companies want increased spending on schools and hospitals, and their demands are at least transparent. Some analysts have made simplistic claims that welfare state services have been 'appropriated by the middle classes' and hijacked by public employees in their own interests (Tanzi, 1995). The fact that business considers the welfare state as a vast potential global marketplace for capital accumulation while simultaneously trying to minimise taxation and non-wage social costs but maximising subsidies, tax reliefs and other market support mechanisms for business is rarely part of the analysis.

The threat of 'a race to the bottom' in reducing personal and corporate taxation, spurred on by transnational tax minimisation, tax avoidance and corporate welfare, threatens the funding of welfare states and public spending on health, education and social care. The 'better quality services and tax cuts' syndrome is not only false and dishonest but could endanger the very existence of the welfare state. As income tax rates are lowered, it becomes more politically and financially transparent to the public that they are paying through other means such as consumer and other indirect taxation. The growth of a multitude of payments through taxation, pensions, insurance, savings schemes, and user charges as a result of welfare pluralism results in diseconomies of scale, high administration costs and the duplication of charges. The larger the direct payment people have to make for services the more economic control they need over how and when they can afford to use them. The quality of public services is crucial to maintain middle-class support, because if they opt out in substantial numbers, it will produce a backlash against having to pay twice, i.e. through taxation and through fees for private services. Furthermore, as private funding, partnerships and private services contribute an increasing proportion of the welfare state, it is almost inevitable that the allocation of public resources will be adjusted to take into account the level of private service usage regionally and locally. This is certain to lead to further conflicts between public/private provision, withdrawals from public systems and complexity in resource allocation.

There are significant differences in social welfare expenditure between OECD countries ranging from 16 and 21 per cent of GDP in Japan and the USA respectively to 45 per cent in Sweden (see Table 5.2). Comparative figures for public social welfare expenditure in the East Asian economies of South Korea, Taiwan, Hong Kong and Singapore are 9 per cent, 11 per cent, 7 per cent and 10 per cent respectively. Differences are also evident in unemployment, pensions, family benefits and personal social services, including child care. Welfare state spending as a proportion of GDP in Britain has remained virtually unchanged for two decades rising from 24.9 per cent in 1974–5 to 25.8 per cent in 1995–6. In other words, the welfare state is not absorbing an accelerating share of national wealth, nor is it spiralling out of control. The proportion allocated to health, personal social services and social security increased while education and housing spending declined. The relentless rise in social security costs was partly related to ageing of the population and partly a result of mass unemployment. In effect, the private sector restructured and passed the cost on to the state.

The role of NGOs in the welfare state differs markedly between states and the services they provide. They account for 6.4 per cent of GDP in the USA, 4.8 per cent in Britain with most European countries varying between 2 and

4 per cent with activity concentrated in education, health and social services. Public sector payments account for 68 and 59 per cent of NGO revenues in Germany and France respectively and below 40 per cent in UK, USA and Sweden. Private sector donations were comparatively high in the UK (12 per cent) and the USA (19 per cent) (OECD, 1997d).

Table 5.2: **Social welfare public expenditure in selected OECD countries** (% of GDP, 1993)

	Japan	USA	UK	Germany	France	Sweden
Education	3.70	5.20	5.20	4.70	5.60	6.70
Health care	5.27	5.85	5.75	6.43	7.28	6.22
Old age/pensions	5.70	6.19	7.15*	11.24	11.69	10.30
Unemployment	0.36	0.79	1.78	4.34	3.33	5.84
Family benefits	0.20	0.35	1.81	1.37	2.12	2.78
Other social security	0.57	1.60	2.34	3.03	2.05	4.44
Personal social services	0.42	0.35	1.05	1.01	1.11	6.39
Housing benefits	–	–	1.84	0.24	0.92	1.17
Others	0.12	0.55	1.70	0.59	0.22	0.91
Total	16.34	20.88	28.62	32.97	34.32	44.75

Source: Jacobs (1998).
* This figure significantly overstates national data.
Note this is public expenditure – the USA spends 14% of GDP on health when private sector expenditure is included.

Simply expressing expenditure on core welfare state services as a percentage of GDP hides substantial differences in public/private provision. For example, total US health care spending is 13.9 per cent of GDP but public spending represents only 46.4 per cent of the total (see Table 5.3). Expenditure in Britain is only half the GDP figure with public expenditure accounting for 83.4 per cent of the total.

The question of who pays is aptly illustrated by Esping-Andersen's comparison of public and private social protection spending for an average family in Sweden and the USA (see Table 5.4). Although it is about 40 per cent of total household spending in both countries, expenditure in Sweden is primarily via taxation in stark contrast to the privatised US system. Of course, this analysis does not take into account the wide difference in the quality of services, the coverage (43 million people in the USA do not have health insurance), employment, equality, nor the level of poverty in each country.

Britain's position is different from other major industrialised countries because it 'industrialised first, extended its life expectancy and reduced fertility early, and has therefore come to terms with the prospects of an ageing population to a greater extent than any other nations' (Glennerster, 1999, p. 7). While the ageing of the population and the ratio to those in work will have major implications, Glennerster also points out that the age structure of Britain changed more dramatically in the twentieth century than the change which is forecast this century. This is reinforced by a Brookings Institution international study:

> The United Kingdom will face a smaller increase than in the other G-5 countries in public spending on the elderly and will accumulate substantially greater reserves in its (increasingly private) pension system. If its budget deficit is kept low, the growing accumulation in private pension accounts can help boost national saving, which in turn can increase the rate of economic growth. These policies may, however, expose workers to greater risk of low retirement incomes. Workers who invest their retirement funds recklessly or in excessively conservative, low yield securities may be forced to accept pensions that are low in comparison to their net incomes while at work. And if workers should retire after a lengthy period in which private markets yield low or negative returns, an entire cohort of them may be faced with the prospect of low retirement incomes. It is tempting to say that a shortfall in retirement income is solely a problem for the unfortunate workers, but it also might be a problem for the public budget if voters demand that public pensions or pension guarantees assure workers of good incomes in retirement. (quoted in Glennerster, 1999, p. 10)

Table 5.3: **Health expenditure in various industrialised countries** (1998)

	Total expenditure on health as % GDP	Public expenditure on health as % GDP	Public expenditure on health as % of Total
United States	13.9	6.5	46.4
Germany	10.7	8.3	77.1
France	9.6	7.1	74.3
Canada	9.1	6.4	69.7
Italy	7.6	5.3	69.9
Japan	7.2	5.7	79.9
United Kingdom	6.9	5.8	83.4
G7 average	9.7	6.6	69.6
EU average	8.0	6.1	76.5

Source: OECD, *Health Data 99: A Comparative Analysis of 29 Countries* (Paris).

Table 5.4: **Comparison of public/private welfare state costs in Sweden and USA** (1990)

	Sweden	USA
As a percentage of GDP		
Public social expenditure	33.1	14.6
Tax expenditures	0.0	1.3
Private education	0.1	2.5
Private health	1.1	8.2
Private pensions	1.8	3.0
Total	36.1	29.6
As a percentage of household expenditure		
Private health, education and pensions	2.7	18.8
Daycare (child families)	1.7	10.4
Total	4.4	29.2
Taxes	36.8	10.4
Total + taxes	41.2	39.6

Source: Esping-Andersen, 1999.

The Welfare, Jobs and Equality Trade-off

Increasing the supply of care services is crucial to increasing women's economic independence, both as part of dual income households (helping to increase services consumption and acting as an employment multiplier) and as single mothers (reducing child poverty). The social democratic de-familialisation strategy will also increase fertility rates (offsetting the impact of ageing), increase employment particularly in labour intensive services and reduce the number of people reliant on social benefits. However, increasing the supply of jobs without increasing wage inequality will be difficult, particularly in nation states which are marketising public services and driving down mainly women's wages.

As previously noted, many services are not mobile and job losses from ICT or productivity initiatives will be limited. Furthermore, the more affluent a society becomes, the greater the demand for personal service – this will be increasingly apparent in health, long-term care and life-long learning. The lifetime pattern of employment will change with periods of retraining and a wider range of full/part-time jobs and employers. However, the 'new economy' and labour market changes are often exaggerated in order to promote privatisation of the welfare state. Treating the welfare state as a monolithic and inflexible institution serves the marketisation cause. Globalisation, at least for the middle classes, enhances the choice of where to live. Being less reliant on family networks, with dual pensions and greater spending power, the availabiltiy of good quality health services, opportunities for life-long learning, safe streets, a clean environment and a range of cultural facilities becomes even more important. The performance of the local economy and quality of the environment are also likely to have greater influence on business location, thus increasing the responsibility of local government.

THE THIRD WAY WELFARE STATE

The Introduction highlighted attempts by some governments to 'end welfare as we know it' and to modernise the welfare state. This section examines the main elements of the Third Way reform of the welfare state. First, workfare gives priority to poverty reduction through employment while also maintaining a reasonable level of benefits for those who cannot find work, the disabled and the elderly. The focus on education, training and child care, coupled with the minimum wage, is intended to avoid creating a low wage economy and high levels of wage subsidies. Second, social welfare services are intended to reduce poverty, inequality and social exclusion but are simultaneously confronted by increased health and social care spending required by an ageing population, the social and economic costs of globalisation and employers' demands for cuts in non-wage social costs. Third, corporate welfare becomes more prominent as nation states and regions compete in the global economy to attract inward investment.

The US right wing promoted welfare reform under a 'Contract with America' while in Britain the Labour government proposed that 'the heart of the modern welfare state will be a new contract between the citizen and the Government, based on responsibilities and rights'. Labour's 'New Contract for Welfare' made no reference to the responsibilities of employers, placed greater emphasis on preventing poverty by the provision of high quality services, health, education, job assistance and child care, and less on social security payments. Universalism and the insurance principle are being eroded with more generous benefits targeted to the 'deserving poor'. By 2020 mutual and private providers 'will deliver a substantial share of welfare provision, particularly pensions' (DSS, 1998, p. 82). This, of course, means increasing marketising and privatisation either by outsourcing public services or by private provision replacing state provision altogether.

The Green Paper refers to four ages of welfare: the Poor Law which stopped outright destitution; the second covered the beginnings of the welfare state to alleviate poverty starting with old age pensions in 1908 up to non-contributory benefits for the disabled in the 1970s; the third age is the current, embarked on preventing poverty; and the fourth is the target to promote opportunity and develop potential.

The welfare state now faces a choice of futures. A privatised future, with the welfare state becoming a residual safety net for the poorest and most marginalised; the status quo, but with more generous benefits; or the Government's third way – promoting opportunity instead of dependence, with a welfare state providing for the mass of the people, but in new ways to fit the modern world. This is the choice for the nation. (DSS, 1998, p. 19)

The Third Way is

> a modern form of welfare that believes in empowerment not dependency. We believe that work is the best route out of poverty for those who can work. We believe in ensuring dignity and security for those who are unable to work because of disability or because of caring responsibilities, as well as for those who have retired. This system is about combining public and private provision in a new partnership for the new age. (Ibid.)

Policies Replace Principles

Labour has replaced the key principles of the welfare state with eight policy objectives: helping and encouraging people of working age to work, public and private sectors working in partnership, provision of high quality public services as a well as cash benefits, support for the disabled to lead a full life, support for families and children, specific action to attack social exclusion and poverty, the system should encourage openness and honesty with clear gateways to benefit, and provision of a flexible, efficient and easy to use system.

However, the ages of welfare are artificially constructed and the options are false because the status quo is not a viable strategy. The rejection of a minimalist privatised welfare state is a false and dishonest polarisation because partnership with private investment is privatisation. Labour's future welfare state is a mainly privatised one – there is never any reference to direct public sector provision. They do not define the scope of partnership, business involvement nor is there a framework setting out the boundaries of private provision. One can only conclude, therefore, that the entire welfare state is an open shop for business, just awaiting 'partnership' offers.

Second, the emphasis on empowerment is basically reskilling to participate in the labour market and has little to do with collective organising, action and democratic control to increase community power. Instead, it is limited to enabling individuals to participate more fully in the market economy with stakeholder pensions, job accounts and other personal schemes. The promotion of new individualism and zonalism (areas of special need) is achieved by public policy being increasingly particularistic demographically and geographically. Individual responsibility and individual (personal or institutional) failure imply that there are no system failures, only mismatched or inadequate individuals or small geographic areas. There are no class or system dysfunctions. The solutions are therefore individualistic and targeted, short-term support is provided until the problem has been ameliorated and they can participate once again. This reinforces Labour's emphasis on a managerialistic approach to local public services.

Third, although Labour has abolished the NHS internal market and nursery vouchers, competition and marketisation are an essential feature of the modernisation of the welfare state. Modernisation is in fact a continuation of the transformation commenced by the Conservative government. Labour has wholeheartedly adopted a performance management framework (see Chapters 3 and 4) in which competition and outsourcing have a central role and has created new markets with PPPs.

Fourth, social justice is limited to equality of opportunity and to mainstreaming of equalities in a limited public/private conceptualisation of the welfare state. There is an apparent lack of analysis and the means for rethinking the relationship between the state, market and family with regard to women's role in employment, service provision, the caring role within the family and participation in civil society. For example, at government behest, local authorities are marketising services such as home and residential care and transferring mainly women employees to the private and voluntary sectors where the national minimum wage replaces substantially better public sector terms and conditions. Labour's new stakeholder pension provisions, based on defined contributions, will penalise women because they are dependent on the amount, timing and a number of factors which are open to considerable risks for women carers, wives and mothers.

Finally, the supply of jobs and the quality of employment are overlooked. Simply increasing the skills of the workforce does not itself increase the supply of jobs. Workfare subsidies could simply transfer jobs from the employed to the unemployed as employers maximise the use of subsidies by recycling jobs. US workfare schemes have operated in a very tight labour market, a low wage economy and while welfare rolls fell by about 40 per cent between 1996 and 1998, major questions arise about the transferability of workfare to the European context. Furthermore, change will be limited unless the social relations and health of the staff providing welfare state services are part of the agenda, including job satisfaction, job control, innovation and development.

The Third Way is a further step towards the private delivery of public goods. The 'government does not need to own hospitals' ideology, developed by the Conservatives for public buildings, is now accepted by Labour and is being extended to services. Health and education could remain 'public services', funded by taxation, free at the point of use, but delivered entirely by private companies.

The Third Way is a closed way because it creates no opportunity to challenge the power structure of the welfare state. It reinforces business and local elites through the partnership model. Little attention is given to the democratisation of welfare state institutions. Decentralisation will be used to continue competition and market forces. The increased role for the social economy, mutuals and stakeholding has no democratic content – the assumption made is that being 'of the people' will suffice.

The lack of a long-term strategy is the most telling criticism. It has no mobilising or organising potential because it reinforces competition and market forces and is essentially a business agenda. It is convened as a policy debate, denying the history of the origins and subsequent action both critical of, and in defence of, the welfare state.

Transition to a Workfare State

Limited workfare schemes have been tried in many European countries and the USA but they now have a central role in Britain and the USA. Both Britain and the USA have adopted earned income tax credits to 'recalibrate' the welfare state, institute a work ethic and encourage the poorest into employment and training. Benefit handouts will be replaced by tax breaks which are more acceptable to the middle classes.

Labour's New Deal, financed by a windfall tax on the privatised utility companies, offers 18–24 year olds and older long-term unemployed, options for waged employment, education and training, voluntary sector work or environmental task force. It is switching government and welfare state activity and 'benefits' to subsidising the working poor, i.e. subsidising a low wage economy and to employ people in existing jobs.

After several years of wide-ranging welfare reform proposals, the US Congress approved the rather more limited but profound Personal Responsibility and Work Opportunity Act in 1996. The Act abolished the Aid to Families with Dependant Children (AFDC) programme which was financed by matching Federal and State funds, administered by states which also defined needs, eligibility and benefits. The new programme, Temporary Assistance for Needy Families (TANF), is a federal block grant, ending individual entitlement to benefit. States must ensure that an increasing percentage of adult recipients engage in approved employment, the head of each family on welfare is required to work within two years of benefits beginning. TANF assistance is limited to 60 months. The grant is capped and by 2002 states are expected to receive considerably less than they would have done under AFDC, forcing many to choose between benefits and job training and placement. The Act gives states substantial flexibility in administering TANF and several other assistance programmes by issuing vouchers or contracting their operation to private and non-profit organisations. Both TANF and the Food Stamps programme no longer require public employees to make eligibility and benefit determination decisions.

The number of US families on welfare has decreased from about 4.75 million in 1996 to 3 million two years later. Continued US economic growth has led to a tight labour market and the private sector has, at least for the present, a vested interest in investing in welfare to work partnerships.

However, more and more families are trapped in poverty in work because of low wages and the lack of sick leave and holidays in the first year of employment. Welfare rolls are declining much slower in the inner cities compared to the suburban counties, reinforcing the importance of job location otherwise an economic downturn will further disadvantage the black and ethnic communities in the inner cities (Wilson, 1996).

The context for the introduction of workfare is highly significant. Over half the US labour force have experienced an 8–12 per cent decline in wages since 1979. The rise of a low wage economy with low level growth in productivity has enabled employers to create jobs, reduce unemployment and remain profitable. In an OECD context, 'the bottom 10–20 per cent of American workers in full-time jobs are low paid compared with equivalent workers in most other countries' (OECD, 1997c, p. 7). The same study stresses that it is important 'not to oversell skills training as *the* long-run solution to all labour market problems' and that there is unlikely to be any substantial decline in the number of low productivity jobs in OECD countries in the foreseeable future.

Job creation is left to market forces and subsidies. The quality of employment is limited to employability, for example, resourcing education, training and improving productivity, and provision of an overall framework such as the European Social Chapter and the minimum wage. However, the quality is in the detail, and outsourcing and privatisation by local public bodies generally means job losses and cuts in terms and conditions. The minimum wage has three functions. It improves the income of the very low paid and it provides a minimum acceptable standard which also provides an incentive to move from benefit into work. It also minimises the level of Income Support for people in work on low wages by imposing a ceiling on the level of subsidy paid to employers who are paying low wages. The minimum wage is beneficial both for the state and for low paid workers. Furthermore, 'there is surprisingly little positive evidence to suggest that pouring public funding into higher education or vocational training has any direct effect on economic growth' (Wolf, 1999, p. 34). She argues that successive British governments have uniquely focused on 'key skills' and have copied neither the noted German apprenticeship system nor the extended general education of France, Sweden and the USA.

Tackling Social Exclusion in Britain

The Labour government's social inclusion strategy seeks to 'tackle the causes of poverty, not just the symptoms, investing in individuals and communities to help them take control of their lives and adapting action more closely to the real needs of disadvantaged communities' (DfEE, 1999, p. 3). The strategy has several themes:

Welfare to work: 'Equipping jobless people to compete for jobs, not to create jobs for jobless people' describes the training, education and work centred New Deal for young people, the long-term unemployed and lone parents. It also includes changes to the tax and benefits system to encourage people into work.

Neighbourhood renewal: The New Deal for Communities targets the most deprived neigbourhoods with £20–£50 million funding, delivered through partnerships, covering a period of up to ten years to tackle worklessness, improving health, tackling crime and raising educational achievement.

Generating enterprise in deprived communities: The 'benefits to business' theme seeks to improve business support, increasing the availability of capital and ensuring regeneration projects have a stronger enterprise component. They link other government enterprise initiatives such as employee share ownership schemes, regional venture funds, deregulation to help business, and various other tax, financial, skills and competition measures to support 'enterprise and wealth creation with social justice and fairness'.

Community self-help: Increasing volunteering and community activity, encouraging mutual support and the viability of community groups and the services they deliver form another element of the social inclusion strategy.

Family support: Providing health, education, child care and other support for families with children under four through the Sure Start programme and various educational initiatives such as mentoring, learning and ICT centres.

Tackling health inequalities: Primary Care Groups, Health Action Zones and Healthy Living Centres are supplemented by recognition of the health benefits of action and investment outside of the NHS.

Zones: The creation of over 150 Education, Health and Employment Action Zones and New Deal for Communities projects is the delivery vehicle for most of the above themes (see Chapter 3).

Joined-up government: The modernisation agenda has a strong emphasis on joined-up policy and joined-up government.

The roots of exclusion can only fully be understood as marginalisation from economic, trade union and civil society institutions as a result of poverty and the market economy. While Labour's new targeting of social exclusion with a host of innovative policies and initiatives is commendable, three observations are needed (also see Chapter 6). First, the government's strategy for reducing social exclusion is mostly supply-side initiatives and relying on macroeconomic policies to indirectly meet demand-side objectives. Second, on the one hand the government is tackling the causes of marginalisation from the market economy while on the other hand increasing competition for resources and marketising public services and the welfare state. An increasing part of the social inclusion delivery mechanism is provided by the market economy. Third, democratic renewal is limited to consumerism and consultation to facilitate and legitimate regeneration projects rather than strengthening communities' ability to organise and take political action. Poverty and social exclusion will not be radically reduced by relying on what the state and capital will deliver without a shift in power relations.

The Third Way replacement of means-tested benefits in place of universal benefits has other major consequences. It is eroding the concept of social insurance, the principle of paying into a common fund with corresponding rights to benefits when needed, which has been undermined by cuts in the value of benefits, various rule changes and contributions credited without payment. 'The silent death of national insurance' will have drastic implications for the welfare state and political implications, not least exposing the real level of taxation of standard rate taxpayers in paid employment would be more than 30p in the pound! (Timmins, 1999). Furthermore, as pensions are privatised and transfer from collective risk to individual risk money-purchased schemes, the debate over welfare state funding is likely to shift from the level of taxation to the level of dividends and profits, posing new pressures on investment strategies and markets.

PENSIONS AND SOCIAL SECURITY – THE GLOBAL MARKET

Attempts to privatise existing state pension schemes and introduce new private pensions confront social needs, equity and redistribution, the power and vested interest of financial markets and globalisation in their starkest form. This section goes into some detail to unravel the facts. Neo-liberals and business interests are seeking two fundamental changes in pensions systems.

First, demands to transfer state pension schemes from pay-as-you-go (current taxes provide today's pensions) to funded schemes (pension funds are invested in the financial markets) which would have an enormous impact on global financial flows. Second, the conversion from defined benefits to defined contribution pensions means that employers are transferring risk to the individual. The World Bank proposed far-reaching reforms with a three-tiered structure with a defined contribution, fully funded, mandatory private pension, a modest public pension scheme and a voluntary occupational or personal savings plan. The first tier provides the saving function, the second redistribution function and all three provide insurance. The bank has extolled the virtues of the Chilean model (World Bank, 1994b). These proposals have been widely criticised as being flawed in social policy terms and on theoretical and empirical evidence in terms of enhancing economic growth.

Revisions to pay-as-you-go public pension systems in several OECD countries in the last decade have included lengthening the reference period used to determine the value of pensions, indexation of benefits to net wages or prices instead of gross wages, increasing the standard age of entitlement, increasing the length of contribution periods and increasing contribution rates. The April 1998 OECD Ministerial meeting approved a set of principles to guide further reforms of pension systems including the removal of financial incentives to early retirement, more job opportunities for older workers and the provision of retirement income by a mix of tax-and-transfer systems, advance-funded systems, private savings and earnings.

The Labour government's pension proposals include abolishing the current earnings related pension scheme and replacing it, in two stages, with a flat rate second state pension, a 'stakeholder' pension with low charges and variable contributions up to £3,600 per annum and a Pooled Pension Investment (based on the US 401-K savings plans). The pensions industry has warned that employers are likely to abandon final salary schemes and switch to defined contribution stakeholder schemes and thus avoid making employers' contributions common in occupational pensions. A minimum pension guarantee of about 20 per cent of average earnings is also planned by increasing means-tested income support. Earnings inequality has widened because benefits and pensions have been linked mainly to prices, not earnings, since the early 1980s.

Privatising Social Security

Every individual would have an account into which payments are made and benefits received according to the level of insurance and state of the account. There will no longer be a National Insurance Fund but separate insurance accounts. It will be a 'benefit as you pay' rather than a welfare state. Also possible is that the reinsurance market will expand – insuring the insurance companies against loss and risk. Once this is achieved then further erosion of state funding of health, education and social services will be inevitable. The state will fund the rump, the uninsurable, the unemployable who have little or nothing in their 'account'.

The US government-appointed Advisory Council on Social Security carries out a four-yearly review of Social Security which provides pensions, disability benefits and income support to the survivors of deceased workers, some 45 million people. Social Security is a PAYG system funded by employees and employers, each currently paying 7.65 per cent (in 1999) on all wages and salaries. Income has exceeded benefit payments for many years in order to build up funds to meet the retirement of the post-war baby boom, the excess is deposited in a Trust Fund which is invested in US Treasury bonds. The current forecast projects that the Trust will have to start drawing on its reserves from 2019, these will be depleted by 2029 and by 2070 Social Security will be able to pay 69 per cent of benefits from payroll taxes. These estimates are based on conservative economic forecasts. However, the Advisory Council was sharply divided and submitted various options including privatisation and means testing to Congress.

The substantial privatisation option required 5 percentage points of the 12.4 per cent Social Security payroll tax to be diverted into a 'personal security account' which workers would decide how to invest. The government would guarantee a relatively low annual pension ($5,000 at 1996 prices) and the value of the top-up would depend on the success of their investments. Transition costs would add 1.52 per cent to the proposed shortfall over the next 75 years and would require increased taxes.

Social Security payroll taxes would be increased by 1.6 per cent which would be placed in investment accounts administered by the government under partial privatisation. Some members of the Advisory Committee proposed retention of the current system with some modest adjustments including increasing the length of computation period from 35 to 38 years, extending coverage to currently excluded state and and local government employees and investing 40 per cent of the Trust Fund in equities rather than Treasury bonds.

However, the conflict was seized on by the right and Wall Street to argue for privatisation. With an estimated $240 billion fees over the first twelve years of private sector management, the financial institutions have poured millions of dollars into pro-privatisation coalitions and media campaigns portraying a social security 'crisis'.

Critics argue that the social security system is inefficient, that it is unfair because the 'intergenerational redistribution is enormous and capricious' (Kotlikoff and Sachs, 1997, p. 2), that it is user-unfriendly because it is so complex and arcane, and that the system faces a long-term funding crisis and hence the need to raise taxes immediately to avoid huge increases later. However, there is substantial evidence and widespread public support which shows that the scheme needs amendment, not abolition (Twentieth Century Fund, 1996; Baker, 1998).

The fund management sector, financial bodies which manage pension, insurance and investment funds, are experiencing an unprecedented period of cross-border takeovers, mergers and restructuring. With a substantial growth predicted in supplementary private pension schemes in Germany, France and other European countries, further takeovers, mergers and alliances are expected as financial institutions attempt to gain a foothold in emerging and global markets (*Financial Times*, 15 November 1996).

In Europe only the UK and the Netherlands have extensive private pension funds and account for the bulk of their total value of US$2,900 billion. Germany, Switzerland, Denmark and Sweden also have substantial funds but France and Italy have relatively small private pension markets because of the high level of state pensions. Switzerland, and shortly the UK, are the only Western European countries which have compulsory contributions to a second-tier pension. A number of Eastern and Central European countries,

Poland, Hungary, Rumania, Bulgaria and Kazakhstan, have recently established multi-pillar schemes covering reformed pay-as-you-go state schemes, mandatory funded private sector pensions and voluntary third-tier savings schemes.

Within Europe, there are two main trends. First, a large increase in second-tier funded private pensions as demographic change intensifies and fiscal pressures continue. If current policies continue, one in three pensioners in Britain will be relying on means-tested benefits in 50 years time, hence the need to expand second-tier pensions. Second, changes in private sector pension fund investment patterns. The dominance of defined benefit schemes in the UK, coupled with high inflation in the 1970s and 1980s and the removal of exchange controls in 1979, led UK pension funds to maximise higher returns from equity investment. Domestic and foreign equity investment accounted for 77 per cent of UK private pension funds at the end of 1996 compared with 29 per cent, 9 per cent and 14 per cent for funds in the Netherlands, Germany and Switzerland respectively (see Table 5.5).

There are indications of a convergence between these two patterns of investment and a revision of European Union tax and investment regulations that could result in the emergence of a Pan-European pensions sector. Overseas investment by pension funds varies widely with Britain, the Netherlands and Belgium having between 29 and 35 per cent in contrast to 8, 10 and 15 per cent respectively for Germany, the USA and Japan.

> Gross flows abroad will be spurred by progress in liberalising controls on cross-border financial flows and strengthening capital markets in developing countries. Moreover, increased reliance on private pensions to fund retirement income in G-10 countries could increase the demand for higher returns. Such demands would lead investors to take greater advantage of the favourable return/risk trade-off provided by international diversification. (Bank of International Settlements, 1998, p. 29)

> Because middle-aged workers are generally able and willing to hold riskier portfolios with a higher ratio of stocks than bonds, hence the

> higher demand for stocks relative to bonds should increase the price of stocks relative to the price of bonds, and therefore reduce the rate of return to stocks relative to bonds, that is, decrease the equity premium. After the baby boomers begin to retire, savings rates would tend to fall, stock and bond prices to decline and the equity premium to rise as baby boom retirees shift their portfolios away from stocks toward bonds. (Ibid.)

> State pensions are in permanent decline: Britain's average state pension is only 23 per cent of the average wage, substantially lower than Belgium's 63 per cent, France's 56 per cent and Sweden's 54 per cent. Britain is

comparable to Canada (33 per cent), the USA and Australia (30 per cent) and Ireland (25 per cent) where private pension provision is more widespread. Most European countries have pay-as-you-go schemes which require a substantially higher proportion of GDP and are forecast to continue to rise because of ageing populations.

Table 5.5: **Asset value and allocation of European pension funds** (end 1996)

	Value of pension assets $bn	Domestic shares %	Domestic bonds %	Foreign shares %	Foreign bonds %	Property %	Cash %
UK	1,015	54	8	23	6	2	7
Netherlands	502	11	50	18	8	2	1
Germany	310	6	71	3	4	13	3
Switzerland	288	11	46	3	6	19	15

Source: *The Future for European Pensions: A Financial Times Guide*, FT, 1998.

Just because of the size of US and British funds this does not mean it will stop there and other countries will be safeguarded. More likely the reverse. The financial system will come to depend on maintaining or increasing the flow of capital into equities. This will further propel privatisation globally. The focus will become the 'return on investment' and the state of the individual's 'account' rather than entitlement and rights to benefit. The volume of cash searching to maximise returns could outpace the creation of genuine investment opportunities which would destabilise markets and increase the risk of financial meltdown.

Since the late 1980s the British government sought to encourage people to opt out of the State Earnings Related Pension Scheme by paying a fixed percentage of their National Insurance contribution into a private pension. Over 5 million have done so resulting in a £1 billion annual state subsidy.

The promotion of private pensions led to widespread mis-selling. People already in occupational schemes were persuaded to leave and start personal private pensions which have produced lower investment returns and have been recently compounded by low interest rates reducing annuity rates and the final value of the pension. Over 1.7 million private pensions are being reviewed at a cost of £10–12 billion in compensation and administrative costs which are borne by insurance and pension companies (but ultimately by savers). The performance of the regulatory body, the Personal Investment Authority, has been lamentable. Another £1 billion mis-selling scandal broke in 1998 over advice to set up Additional Voluntary Contributions outside of company pension schemes which performed poorly but provided sales commission. The growth of defined contribution (money purchase) stakeholder or individual retirement accounts in place of defined contribution (final salary) pension funds led *The Economist* to forecast that 'the days of company pensions may be genuinely numbered' (*The Economist*, 15 May 1999). They may be promoted as a new 'worker capitalism' but a money purchase pension can be only half the value of traditional final salary pensions (ibid.). Long term pension costs as a proportion of GDP are projected to remain relatively stable in Britain and Ireland (see Table 5.5). Other European countries, Italy and Germany in particular, face substantial increases in the 2020–40 period.

Table 5.6: **European pensions costs** (projection as a % of GDP)

	2000	2020	2040
Italy	12.6	15.3	21.4
Germany	11.5	12.3	18.4
Finland	9.5	15.2	18.0
Spain	9.8	11.3	16.8
Portugal	6.9	9.6	15.2
Austria	8.6	12.1	15.0
Belgium	9.7	10.7	15.0
Sweden	11.1	13.9	14.9
France	9.8	11.6	14.3
Netherlands	5.7	8.4	12.1
Denmark	6.4	9.3	11.6
UK	4.5	5.1	5.0
Ireland	2.9	2.7	2.9

Source: OECD (1998) *Maintaining Prosperity in an Ageing Society* (Paris).

Increased Administration Costs

The administrative cost of new privatised systems far exceeds the cost of public provision. Social Security administrative costs are approximately 1 per cent of benefits compared to the administrative costs of private insurance which account for between 12 and 14 per cent of annual benefit amounts (Twentieth Century Fund, 1996). Singapore's state-managed provident fund administrative costs are 0.53 per cent (Singh, 1996). Pay-as-you-go systems place liabilities on future generations but income from funded schemes is inherently uncertain because it depends on the performance of funds over several decades. They are very vulnerable to fluctuations in share prices, market or company failure and to financial failure. They succeed if investment profits exceed the substantially higher administrative costs. Another example is the annual cost of fraud, overbilling and overpriced, useless and often harmful services provided under the US health care system which is estimated at between $100 billion and $130 billion per annum.

Private Pensions: Chilean Model

Chile privatised its state pension scheme in 1981 following a funding crisis and failure of the public scheme to meet planned benefit levels or achieve full national coverage. The private scheme requires employees to compulsorily contribute 10 per cent of their wages, up to a certain ceiling, to one of 14 private sector pension funds. Significantly, the armed forces retained their own system. Each worker has a separate account and the accumulated proceeds can be used to provide a pension or purchase an index-linked annuity from a private insurance company. Employers make no contributions. The state regulates the pension funds, has assumed responsibility for the transition between the old and new systems, provides a guaranteed minimum pension for workers with regular savings, and provides a limited number of means-tested public assistance pensions for the poor.

The pension funds also operate the invalidity and survivor's benefits scheme in which workers must contribute a further 2.5 to 3.7 per cent of wages. The pension fund reinsures the risk with an insurance company and also charges a commission of about 1.8 per cent of the insured wage. Three funds account for 65 per cent of all accounts. Four of the largest are foreign owned.

The Chilean pension scheme 'contains no elements of mutual insurance between members of the workforce; there are no links of solidarity between social groups; there are no inter-generational transfers, explicit or implicit' (Gillion and Bonilla, 1992, p. 185).

Most casual workers, rural workers, peasants and the unemployed, about 35 per cent of the labour force, do not contribute. In fact, only 56 per cent of workers affiliated to the funds make contributions, down from 74 per cent in 1982. State subsidies for the private pension funds have been at the expense of improving minimum benefits for these groups. Only 4 per cent of the self-employed contribute to the scheme. More than 1.5 million people had made no payments into their funds for more than a year. Administrative costs are substantial. They started at 9 per cent of wages or 90 per cent of contributions and have since fallen to 3 per cent of wages or 10 per cent of contributions 'which mean that the high rates of return of the portfolio will not necessarily translate into better pensions' (OECD, 1997c, p. 19).

The public cost of the scheme has been enormous. Social security accounted for 27 per cent of the social budget in 1970 but by 1989 this had soared to 52 per cent and was financed by major cuts in education and health. Transition costs were high (4–5 per cent of GDP throughout the 1980s and early 1990s) because the government had to cover increasing deficits in the old system as contributions declined, and had to transfer funds into the new scheme. 'This costly process of privatisation could be carried out without macro-economic disruptions only because the government had built up a fiscal surplus before undertaking the reforms and because it continued to keep other expenditures extremely low' (Huber, 1996, p. 167).

Fast economic growth, high interest rates and 14 years of unparalleled stock market positive returns (two privatised utilities accounted for nearly 40 per cent of the total return of the Chilean funds – OECD, 1998b) buoyed the scheme in the early stages but three years of stock market decline have resulted in fund losses, an annual return of just 1.8 per cent and reductions in the average pension.

Claims that the Chilean funds represent 'financial self-determination' and 'popular capitalism writ large' thus defy reality (*The Economist*, 12 June 1999). Although Argentina, Brazil and Uruguay reformed their pension systems with different versions of individual retirement accounts after protracted opposition, and despite IMF and World Bank support and Inter-American Development Bank's financial incentives, 'a reform like Chile's that completely eliminates a universal public benefit does not appear to be politically viable in a democratic setting' (Kay, 1999).

Fuelling Globalisation

Britain, the United States and Japan dominate world pension assets reflecting the role of funded private pension schemes in addition to government pensions. US funded pension assets are forecast to rise to $6.4 trillion by the year 2000, almost triple the 1990 figure. Pension assets in Japan and Britain will have increased to $1.8 trillion and $1.3 trillion respectively in the same period. Germany has largely unfunded pension schemes and the comparable pension assets are relatively small at $190 billion by the year 2000 (*The Economist*, 31 August 1996).

In the USA, 75 per cent of private savings are now speculated on the stock exchange, primarily a result of the high comparative returns from investment in equities, reversing the situation 20 years ago when savings accounts and fixed-interest securities were dominant.

Policies for a greater private sector role, (for example, pensions will change from 60/40 public/private to 40/60 provision) will encourage further marketisation and privatisation. Pension funds already play a key role in privatisation programmes by acquiring shares and have sizable investment in contractors tendering for public service contracts – this is what they mean by stakeholder capitalism.

The privatisation of social security/pensions globally could create a flood of investment which could in turn generate a demand for new phases of privatisation – one feeds the other. Privatisation could rapidly accelerate globalisation with billions of pension and social insurance funds seeking the highest return on investment and increasing the likelihood of financial market turmoil. Financial institutions will scoop billions in fees. Marketisation and privatisation of the welfare state is a high risk strategy which will not only demolish the social and economic infrastructure but subject pensions, savings and services to the global financial casino. In the event of a major financial collapse, the value of pensions and savings could be decimated, robbing millions and a whole generation of their living standards.

THE NEW CORPORATE-WELFARE COMPLEX

The Introduction described how a new corporate-welfare complex is emerging, with similar characteristics to the military industrial complex. The Washington Consensus is maintained in part through the Wall Street–US Treasury–IMF complex characterised by a regular exchange of personnel in top posts, shared objectives and common values (Wade and Veneroso, 1998a). The other major international financial centres of London, Frankfurt and Tokyo are also influential. The emerging corporate-welfare complex embraces the military industrial complex and similar sets of interests which support manufacturing industries. Within the state sector, a six-part corporate-welfare complex is emerging as a result of neo-liberal marketisation and privatisation (see Figure 5.1). At present they take the form of separate complexes covering health and social care, education, public service tax/benefits, environmental services, development and regeneration and the criminal justice system. Although some firms and organisations operate in more than one sector, each complex is developing differently depending on private sector penetration, the regulatory framework and public policy. Eventually, these complexes are likely to merge into one, or at most, three complexes.

The 1960s–1970s saw the emergence of a military industrial complex. The defence industry has a track record of massive cost overruns and dubious contract practices and illustrates how this 'complex' could develop a sophisticated system of contracts, vested interests and compensatory policies. A comparable 'welfare services complex' is likely to emerge consisting of transnational corporations, financial institutions, consultants, business and trade associations and politicians. Contractors develop a dependency on government contracts which leads them to search for, and gain access to, insider information and intelligence in order to pursue corporate objectives, influence the procurement process and to participate in government policy making. It also leads to contract collusion and corruption. Contractors become major employers in localities and this, in turn, is used to lever further concessions, financial contributions are made to candidates as political payoffs, and a system of common values and interests makes the triangle increasingly difficult to penetrate.

Increasing global competitiveness, regionalisation, 'Third Way' politics and the power of multinationals are forcing states to prioritise the needs of business. Corporate welfare is not new but it is being reconfigured to meet the demands of capital in a global economy and the changing relationship established by state–capital partnerships. Corporate welfare is a hidden subsidy to capital, inflating profits and enabling transnationals to minimise their own investment in new factories and offices. Corporate welfare

Figure 5.1: **The corporate-welfare complex**

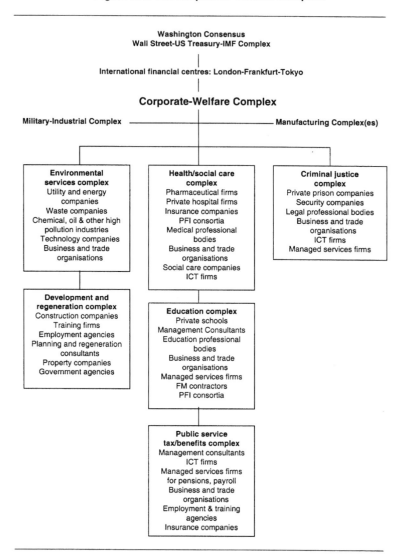

expenditure could alternatively fund substantial increases in public investment. But corporate welfare is not solely about money, it also consists of shared values and ideology, revolving doors as officials move from public to private sector jobs and vice versa and large contracts with scope for inducements and corruption.

Corporate welfare is rarely discussed or quantified, because it transcends tax policies, public expenditure, national economic policy and regional/local economic development. Corporate welfare operates through different tiers of governance ranging from local councils to global institutions such as the World Bank. It creates a shadow regime and a culture of dependency on the state by business although without the repression and insecurity of the social welfare benefits system. The corporate sector has been highly critical of the welfare state, but it has ensured its own 'welfare' regime is sustained and developed. Business and trade organisations have built a web of organisations to lobby for and to protect these subsidies, for example, US proposed cuts in corporate welfare have been fiercely resisted by the Washington lobby machine. The 'Third Way' promotes and extends corporate welfare by subsidising a low wage economy, facilitating private finance and partnerships and expanding the privatisation and marketisation of welfare state services.

The value of US corporate welfare, estimated to be $195 billion in the fiscal year 2000 in subsidies and tax breaks, exceeds the cost of the social welfare state, excluding pensions and medical care (Citizens for Tax Justice, 1999). We noted earlier the replacement of the Aid to Families with Dependant Children (AFDC) programme but the acronym lives on through 'aid for dependent corporations', the needy recipients include General Motors, Boeing, Citibank to name but a few. More than a tenth of US Congress 1999 tax cuts, totalling $792 billion over ten years, are new subsidies to corporations.

Corporate welfare should not be confused with corporate involvement in the poverty industry whereby major companies such as Ford Motor Credit Co, Credit Acceptance Corporation and Cash America Investments provide consumer finance, refinancing, credit insurance, electrical goods rental and pawn shops, earning high returns in poor neighbourhoods (Hudson, 1996).

Globalisation is expanding the corporate welfare system because firms are in a stronger position to extract subsidies to locate plants and the new emphasis on workfare provides business with yet more subsidies and tax concessions for training and employment schemes. The state usually absorbs the social or transaction costs of globalisation such as unemployment caused by relocation, subsidises inward investment and grant-aids research and development. Local government and other agencies also provide inward investment subsidies, training grants and meet the social costs of investment or closure.

The corporate-welfare complex is composed of three elements:

- a contract services system which includes shared client/contractor ideology, value system and vested interests in which the state outsources an increasing range of services and functions;
- an owner-operator infrastructure industry;
- a system of tax reliefs, subsidies and concessions to business.

Contract Services System and Transnationals

The internationalisation of production and services, coupled with sector agreements to open up competition, for example in telecoms, utilities and air transport, has resulted in more extensive cross-border acquisitions, mergers and alliances. Alliance capitalism has led to joint transnational investment in research, product development and distribution because of the high costs of competing globally and keeping pace with technological change. The past decade has seen several important changes in the structure and organisation of multinational companies. Larger service companies now promote facilities management rather than individual services, construction companies are diversifying into FM, management consultants are expanding their range of professional services, while major manufacturing companies combine production, financial and service subsidiaries.

Continued outsourcing, partnership and private finance projects, and the commercialisation or hiving off of segments of services, for example, inspections and performance assessments, 'failing schools', job placement and training schemes, staff agencies, all provide points of market entry for large and small firms. The next decade is likely to see several developments:

New alliances between transnational service companies and financial capital: The acquisition of health, education and other service suppliers by financial services companies such as insurance firms will gather pace. US and European managed care and insurance companies have expanded into Latin America as countries have privatised health care and pensions, attracted by social security systems which combine health care and retirement benefits for workers in large private and public enterprises (Stocker et al., 1999, p. 1134). 'Access to capital in public sector social security funds has become an important incentive for investment by multinational corporations' and the growing upper middle class of Latin America constitutes a potential new market for managed care (ibid.). Continued negotiation of the WTO's General Agreement on Trade in Services is likely to speed up the marketisation and privatisation of public sector provision.

Switch to funded pensions and social care: The financial institutions are promoting the switch from pay-as-you-go to funded pension schemes because it opens a vast global market controlling savings and investment with relatively high fees administering millions of accounts in place of the cost effective government administered systems. Insurance companies need to break the monopoly of public systems in order to develop 'welfare products' for health, education, training, unemployment, sickness and other insurance-based schemes.

Private delivery of public goods: The major IT and managed service companies gain a significant market share of public sector ICT contracts, diversify, and extend the managed services concept deep into the welfare state.

Corporate takeovers of non-profit organisations: The corporatisation of building societies in Britain and US Blue Cross health insurance is likely to continue. Non-profit organisations may develop chains of decentralised health facilities and schools, such as Health Maintenance Organisations and Educational Management Organisations, in order to achieve economies of scale lost in the process of decentralisation and to provide some form of protection against corporate takeovers. Voluntary and non-profit organisations will be increasingly constrained by a lack of investment finance, a shortage of managerial and technical skills, conflict between advocacy and service delivery, and subjected to severe competitive pressures from private companies.

Service management is likely to mirror the construction sector where key firms supply only project management expertise and subcontract the bulk of the work. Value added is obtained by provision of professional and technical expertise and the package of services provided, not in the delivery of basic services which are subcontracted to local firms as a means of suppressing wages and minimising trade union membership. Parallel deskilling of the local state will occur which will be stripped of many client functions to become an agent between government and transnationals.

An Owner-operator Infrastructure Industry

Eliminating the public–private divide: Global firms of management consultants and managed services multinationals employ doctors and health specialists, teachers and educationalists as they extend infrastructure provision to core service delivery. The vast new potential infrastructure market enables companies to operate public and private systems side by side, ultimately leading to the growth of individual privately funded privatised systems.

The emergence of an owner-operator industry with global infrastructure firms combining design, construction and operational services will lead to takeovers and mergers of infrastructure consortia and a secondary market in PPP finance. Infrastructure subsidiaries may eventually mirror the privatised utilities. 'It is just that schools and hospitals start off as individual assets. They are not businesses in the way water and electricity are. But in five or ten years' time these assets will emerge as major utility businesses providing schools and hospitals and roads to the public sector' (*Financial Times*, 17 July 1997).

A System of Tax Reliefs, Subsidies and Concessions to Business

The third element of the corporate-welfare complex is a range of tax reliefs, subsidies and concessions which fall into six categories (see Table 5.7).

Table 5.7: **Types and purpose of corporate welfare**

Types of corporate welfare	Purpose
Tax relief	Reduce taxation and increase business profits
Economic development subsidies/incentives	Reduce cost of development and new plants
Labour market and wage subsidies	Reduce cost of employment
Regulatory frameworks	Reduce risk by government guarantees
Bail-outs	Subsidise exports and overseas investment
Privatisation	Obtain assets cheaply, new markets for business

1. Taxation

Reducing taxes on profits: Corporate taxation has been steadily reduced in many countries, reducing the overall tax burden borne by companies (see Chapter 3). Transnational companies are adept at manipulating different levels of taxation between countries by transfer pricing. They vary the prices attributed to raw materials and production costs, research and development costs are attributed to a country irrespective of where they occurred, or they assign 'ownership' of valuable assets such as patents, and thus a large share of total profits, in countries where they are eligible for tax breaks.

Tax avoidance is legitimately backed by tax sections in all the main law and accountancy firms – a Treasury and Customs & Excise Inquiry revealed that corporate tax planning and avoidance cost the British Exchequer an estimated £2 billion in 1995–6. Money laundering, the transfer of illegally obtained money through third parties to conceal its source, has been estimated to be $500 billion worldwide or 2 per cent of global GDP.

Rupert Murdoch's News Corporation and its subsidiaries paid only $238 million in corporate taxes worldwide in the four years to June 1998, an effective tax rate of 6 per cent despite corporate tax rates of 36 per cent, 35 per cent and 30 per cent in Australia, America and Britain respectively where the firm operates (*The Economist*, 20 March 1999). Murdoch's main British holding company, Newscorp Investments, made profits of £1.4 billion over eleven years but paid no net British corporation tax, achieved by the complex use of offshore tax havens, tax loopholes and shunting profits, losses and costs between companies.

Although corporate America had a pretax profit rate of 11 per cent in 1995, a sample of ten companies which laid off 134,450 workers in the 1993–5 period received $8.3 billion federal tax subsidies thus reducing their effective tax rates well below the 35 per cent corporate rate. Corporations also gain from accelerated depreciation which allows them to deduct the cost of buildings and equipment faster than they wear out from profits, thus reducing taxation (Citizens for Tax Justice, 1995).

The cost of corporate tax breaks in 2000 include $74 billion capital gains and $6.6 billion business meals and entertainment concessions (see Table 5.8).

Tax relief to support markets: Tax concessions are often provided to individuals to support particular markets and hence aid capital accumulation. For example, tax relief on share option schemes and private health insurance are intended to support private markets.

Economic development tax concessions: These are a useful tool to encourage local economic and social investment but they are widely abused by firms to maximise concessions, commitments often remain unfulfilled with public bodies afraid to impose stringent sanctions because of intensified competition. Aid is usually accompanied by additional financial support through tax concessions, grants, debt write-offs and public investment in the surrounding infrastructure. Promises are plentiful but there is usually little or no enforcement.

Large firms win tax breaks and incentives to either remain in a city or to establish new facilities. A study of 122 audits of economic development programmes in 44 US states found primitive monitoring, infrequent evaluation, lack of data ('garbage in, garbage out') and little auditing of effectiveness (Good Jobs First, 2000). The cost of job creation by English Partnerships, a British regeneration agency, were revealed to be an average £23,000, more than twice the level claimed by the agency (House of Commons, 2000b).

BMW held the British government to ransom over the future of the Rover car plant at Longbridge, demanding a £150 million state subsidy to finance 'modernisation' and to prevent relocation to Hungary. Birmingham City Council gave the company a three-year property tax holiday worth a further £12 million. None of these prevented BMW from later threatening closure and eventually selling Rover to a consortium.

All these tax policies have the effect of reducing government revenue and restricting public expenditure.

Table 5.8: **Cost of US tax breaks for business and investment in 2000**

Type of tax concession	Total $bn
Capital gains (except homes)	73.9
Accelerated depreciation	36.9
Insurance companies and products	29.9
Multinational preferences	13.5
Tax-free bonds, private[*]	9.0
Business meals and entertainment	6.6
Other business and investment	25.1
Total	194.9

Source: Citizens for Tax Justice, 1999. [*] Excludes $16.5 billion cost of public purpose bonds

2. Wage and other Subsidies/Incentives

Labour market subsidies: In the USA, Canada and Britain earnings top-up and income support programmes for employed people have expanded rapidly and are based on the premise that being in paid employment is not sufficient to provide a minimum acceptable standard of living. Welfare benefit is transferred from the claimant to the employer for waged labour in return for employment at the same or marginally increased income compared to what they would have received if unemployed. Some employers top up wages and genuinely train but many do not. These policies appear to support the working poor but they are de facto wage and income subsidies to employers, thus supporting a low wage economy.

Market subsidies: Britain's privatised railway system is a classic example. The government created a 'market' which was dependent on companies receiving state subsidies, meanwhile millions were made out of the resale of rail leasing companies. Subsidies have also been used to opt out of the public sector, for example, National Insurance rebates for those investing in private pensions and additional financial support for grant maintained schools.

Industry and sector subsidies and support: For example, government aid to the construction industries board, property advisory group, construction sponsorship directorate and the various support mechanisms in place for the defence industry.

3. Investment Guarantees and Insurance
The World Bank's MIGA guarantees private transnational investment in developing countries against risks of currency transfer, expropriation, war

Table 5.9: **State support for private infrastructure projects**

Support	Number
Multilateral banks and Export Credit Agency debt	37
Government guarantees	28
Informal agreements	28
Multilateral banks and Export Credit Agency guarantees	26
Government equity participation	18
Government debt	14
Multilateral equity participation	13
Government grants	12
Preferential tax treatment	2

Source: *Government Support to Private Infrastructure Projects in Emerging Markets*, Mansoor Dailami and Michael Klein, World Bank, 1998.

and civil disturbance. In addition, nation states have their own Export Credit Agencies which are increasingly used to provide guarantees and insurance for infrastructure projects abroad, subsidies for arms sales and various benefits for exporters, importers and international investors. Governments use an array of mechanisms to provide financial support to private infrastructure projects. A World Bank study of 78 power, transport, water/waste and telecommunications projects identified nine methods of state support (see Table 5.9).

4. Regulatory Framework

Market regulatory frameworks, particularly the pricing structures established following the privatisation of utilities, in effect guarantee minimum profit levels. They also often protect existing markets by making it very difficult for new entrants and thus limit competition and regulate the expansion of private services in competition with state services. The social relations of regulation, the way in which companies are treated in corporate welfare, are in stark contrast from the means-tested welfare state. WTO negotiations on trade in services could impose the world's biggest deregulation initiative, restricting government laws and regulations on consumer and environmental protection, labour standards, universal provision and many other public policy matters.

5. Bail-outs or the Socialisation of Losses

Governments bail out companies and financial institutions in order to safeguard markets and prevent a domino effect across the rest of the sector. The state in effect absorbs or socialises the costs so that they are borne by all taxpayers. Corporate financial crises, irrespective of the cause, raise questions about whether the activities of financial institutions and contractors should be met by the public purse.

The US government bail-out of Savings and Loans Associations, following the collapse of property deals, cost a staggering $300 billion. A study of 54 of the largest failed associations revealed that the proportion of large deposits was almost twice the industry average, hence the bail-out was most beneficial to wealthier investors. The Japanese government has spent billions in restoring the banking system and housing loan companies which had made vast loans to property speculators. Between 1995 and 1998, Mexico took responsibility for $62 billion of bad loans from the banks. The renationalisation and reprivatisation of Chilean banks was noted above. Vast sums of public money have been used to bail out firms such as Lockheed Martin (US), ironically now operating welfare contracts.

6. Privatisation

The sale and transfer of assets and services has frequently meant restructuring costs borne by the state, including debt write-offs, discounted sale prices and deliberately low valuation of assets. The state offers up for sale assets which have often previously been competing against the private sector (another example of reducing competition and restricting it to private sector conditions) or allows the private sector to diversify with preparatory work carried out and funded by the state. Many privatised companies in Britain benefited by millions of pounds from reduced corporation tax in the post-privatisation period (Whitfield, 1992, pp. 241–4). The state has become a showcase for a constant stream of land deals, contracts, partnerships and business opportunities. But corporate welfare extends well beyond support for markets or individual firms.

The Rebirth of Company Towns

The company town was a product of the industrial revolution where a company employed a large section of the local labour market, dominated the geography, the philanthropic or dictatorial owner often provided health, library and other social facilities and the design and naming of streets and buildings clearly expressed company influence. Many textile, mining and manufacturing towns in Britain and North America are a historic heritage of this era (*The Economist*, 23 December 1995).

However, the company town is reemerging, not dominated by one industry or family, but by business elites through their involvement in regeneration, partnerships, outsourcing and sponsorship of arts and culture. The local state transfers assets and defers to the needs and interests of the business sector first and foremost. Local authorities are increasingly corporatised and influenced by business elites.

SUMMARY

The Third Way welfare state is not an alternative to the neo-liberal model but merely a different method of achieving it. Third Way neutrality on service provision is false. If the public sector is not promoted and defended within a capitalist economy then it will ultimately decline and be residualised. 'What matters is what works' will lead to the disintegration and fragmentation of the welfare state. It is an ideology which is fundamentally weak and flawed. Privatisation and marketisation will continue apace unless radical action is taken.

6

The Price of Neo-Liberal Modernisation

We now come to the important task of assessing the impact of two decades of transformative change on government, state functions, services and public sector employment. This chapter examines the effects of neo-liberal transformation and Third Way modernisation, described in detail in Chapters 3 and 4, under ten headings – macroeconomic impact, asset stripping and high transaction costs, employment, democratic accountability, fragmenting the state, social justice, service quality, performance state paradigm, ownership and control, and partnerships and private finance. The evidence is primarily from Britain although it draws on the impact of privatisation and outsourcing from other countries. It concludes with an assessment of the impact of transformation on the capacity of the state.

MACROECONOMIC IMPACT

The macroeconomic impact of transformation is summarised below:

Increasing poverty: The number of children growing up in poverty in Britain has increased dramatically since 1979, rising from 1.2 million to 4 million children living in households with less than half the average income in 1995–6 (HM Treasury, 1999). This proportion is well above other European countries. An OECD analysis of labour market policies noted that 'increases in the incidence of low-paid employment have been limited to countries with relatively low levels of labour market regulation and decentralised wage-setting institutions, for example the United Kingdom and the United States' (OECD, 1997c, p. 4).

Widening inequality: Inequality in Britain rose by a third between 1977 and 1996–7, reflecting rising inequality in incomes from work, occupational pensions and investment income. Earnings inequality increased for both men and women as wages for the highest paid rose much faster than for the lowest paid. Health inequalities widened in terms of mortality, morbidity and in the socioeconomic determinants of health (Acheson Report, 1998). The number of workless households increased from 9 per cent in 1979 to 20 per cent in

1995–6, as did the number of two-earner households. A survey of poverty and income distribution (employment, pensions, other social transfers and capital) in the European Union revealed that the poorest 10 per cent of the population in Britain receive only 3 per cent of total income while the richest 10 per cent enjoy 26 per cent, one of highest levels of inequality in Europe (EUROSTAT, 1998).

Investment: Some privatised utilities reduced investment immediately after flotation, for example, capital expenditure in British Gas declined in real terms and although British Telecom's increased this was accounted for by increased capital spending overseas (Whitfield, 1992). BT's capital investment declined from 30 per cent of turnover in 1980 to 16 per cent in 1994 (Markou and Waddams Price, 1997). Cuts in public sector capital programmes led to the continuing rundown and decline of Britain's infrastructure including schools, hospitals and road maintenance.

Research and development decline: The transformation of the state and the promotion of an enterprise economy did little to enhance research and development investment in Britain. Gross expenditure increased only 4 per cent between 1988 and 1995 with the proportion funded by government (which accounts for nearly two-fifths of the total) declining by 5 per cent, higher education increasing 10 per cent, business enterprise remaining virtually static and the proportion from abroad increasing 61 per cent (Duffus and Gooding, 1997). R & D in BT and British Gas declined after privatisation (Whitfield, 1992).

Losses from diversification: The 22 privatised regional electricity and water companies adopted a policy of post-privatisation diversification into other activities which resulted in their collectively writing off £1 billion of their £1.5 billion investment in the early 1990s (Newbury and Pollit, 1997).

Declining asset base: The net wealth of the public sector was 61.0 per cent of GDP in 1989–90 but plummeted to 5.0 per cent in 1997–8 as liabilities outstripped growth in government assets (HM Treasury, 1998a).

Lower taxation: Personal income tax rates were reduced but the overall level of personal taxation increased as taxation was shifted from income to consumption. Corporation tax was cut from 52 to 32 per cent in the 1992–7 period.

Competitive culture: The imposition of market forces has meant that different forms of competition are now endemic, ranging from the National Lottery to the allocation of regeneration funds. Resources are no longer allocated according to social need but competitions, replacing social need in allocating resources for community and sports facilities, decisions about who provides public services, access to schools and so on. But there is no evidence that competing for contracts, grants and resources improves their effectiveness or contributes to Britain's overall competitiveness.

The privatisation dividend: The combined results of three worldwide empirical privatisation studies examined 211 companies from 42 countries and 56 different industries, covering the 1961–89, 1980–92 and 1990–6 periods. The studies adopted the same methodology and sample selection criteria and covered banking and finance (36 companies), electric utilities (30), telecommunications (22), petroleum (18), steel (14) and airlines (11). They documented significant increases in profitability, output, operating efficiency, dividend payments, capital expenditure (in absolute terms but not relative to sales) but diverged with regard to the employment impact with two reporting an increase and one a decrease (D'Souza and Megginson, 1999). Of 164 firms in the employment sample, 49.3 per cent had a decrease in employment. However, none of the studies take account of takeovers and mergers and judge privatisation solely on financial and operating data obtained from annual reports and databases. They attempt to prove increased financial performance but shed no light on how this was obtained, for example, debt write-offs, continuing subsidies, tax relief, price increases and other measures have been a common feature of post-privatisation performance in Britain (Whitfield, 1992). An internal review of the World Bank's support for public sector reform and privatisation revealed that 38 per cent were 'unsatisfactory' and that 'the causes of poor performance lie as much with Bank incentives, procedures and culture as with conditions within the recipient country' (Wilks, 1997).

ASSET STRIPPING AND HIGH TRANSACTION COSTS

This section investigates the undervaluing of public assets and the high transaction costs of privatisation and outsourcing.

Many assets were sold at a fraction of their historic or current replacement cost because the sale price was based on the financial market's valuation of their future earnings, not the net asset value to the public. British Gas' net assets at the time of privatisation were estimated to be £12 billion yet it was sold for less than half this amount (£5.6 billion). Even the limited methodology of comparing 21 privatisation flotations' share price at flotation compared with the price at the end of the first week of trading reveals a £13,564 million increase in market value or undervaluation of public assets. This included some startling increases such as BT (£3,329 million), regional electricity companies (£2,619 million), water companies (£2,358 million) and Rolls Royce (£926 million). The average discount or undervaluing at the end of the first week of share trading was 28 per cent (see Table 6.1).

Table 6.1: **How public assets in Britain were undervalued**

Company	Increase in share price at end of first week of trading %	Increased value or undervaluing of the company (£m)
British Airports Authority	+19	233
British Airways	+68	612
British Gas	+29	1,576
British Telecom	+85	3,329
National Power	+40	535
Powergen	+40	328
12 Regional electricity cos	+51	2,619
Rolls Royce	+68	926
Scottish Power	+15	303
Scottish Hydro-Electric	+22	202
10 Water companies	+45	2,358
Railtrack	+10	190
9 Others (to 1996)	+11	141
Total	+28	13,351

Source: Whitfield 1992, and various press reports, 1992–96.

But this is not the full story. There were many other examples where public assets were grossly undervalued. In order to create competition, British Rail was dismembered for privatisation. Railtrack took over responsibility for track and signalling, three rail leasing companies own the rolling stock, some 11,260 trains and carriages are leased to 24 operating companies, there are 13 rail maintenance contracts, seven maintenance depots, five freight companies and so on. The National Audit Office calculated that under continuing public ownership the three rail leasing companies, Angel, Evershott and Porterbrook, were valued at £2,900 million but were sold for £1,743 million (National Audit Office, 1998a). In the year leading up to the sale, the three companies had an annual turnover of £797 million with pre-tax profits of £332 million and employed only 150 staff. Seven months after privatisation, Porterbrook was acquired by Stagecoach Holdings for £826 million, a 56 per cent increase, while Evershott shareholders made a 40 per cent profit on its sale to HSBC Holdings. Nearly a year later Angel, originally sold to GRS Holdings, was resold to the Royal Bank of Scotland for £696 million, a 58 per cent rise. The rail leasing companies' combined market valuation had risen £910 million in less than two years.

Railtrack was sold for £1,904 million in 1996, preceded by an £869 million net debt write-off. The shares were priced at 390p but within a year they had reached 620p and by early 1999 were over 1,600p valuing the company at £8 billion, four times its original sale price (National Audit Office, 1998b). Wisconsin Rail (US) acquired the bulk of British Rail's freight operations paying £249 million for four companies and receiving £242 million net subsidy, partly related to committed usage fees to Eurotunnel.

There were many others. National Transcommunications Ltd (NTL) was sold to Mercury Asset Management for a mere £70 million in 1991 when its real value was at least £270 million, 'a story of greed and ambition, where the taxpayer lost out and the National Audit Office stood by and did nothing' (*Business Age*, 1993). The National Grid was transferred to the twelve regional electricity companies (RECs) prior to their privatisation in 1990. Five years later the companies decided to sell the Grid and its Pumped Storage Business (a source of hydro electric power at times of peak demand) to exploit its increased value. The market value of the RECs had increased from £5 billion to £14 billion in five years, with the Grid increasing by £2,974 million. The government demanded that electricity consumers should also benefit and a one-off £52 discount on bills was negotiated; in fact only £31 was financed from the flotation of the Grid, the rest came from taxpayers because the discount reduced the taxable profits of the RECs (National Audit Office, 1998c). The deal included a £300 million valuation of Pumped Storage but two weeks after the flotation the RECs sold it for £680 million to Mission Energy (US). After funding the discount, tax and other payments, the RECs obtained £330 million cash from the sale.

In only four cases, the first Britoil share sale, British Energy, the second Cable & Wireless and the 1987 BP share sale, did share prices fall immediately after privatisation. The short-term losses were borne by the underwriters but all share prices subsequently rose substantially enabling them to recoup the paper losses.

Debt Write-offs

Privatisation analyses rarely take account of the £28,270 million debt write-offs between 1980 and 1996 for assets privatised in this period, primarily relating to British Steel, British Telecom, the water companies, British Coal and Railtrack. The public sector also bore the cost of restructuring prior to privatisation. British Steel, British Airways, Rover and Rolls Royce alone incurred £1,425 million rationalisation and restructuring costs in the four years prior to their sale (Whitfield, 1992). In another example, the Department of Trade and Industry incurred £121 million restructuring costs (covering relocation, redundancies and separation) on the restructuring of the commercial operations of the UK Atomic Energy Authority to form AEA Technology between 1993 and 1996 (National Audit Office, 1998d). Flotation receipts were £228 million but the restructuring costs were not considered to be sale costs. Within two years the market value of the company had more than doubled.

Post-privatisation Financial Performance

Many companies' post-privatisation financial performance was cushioned by a range of financial perks and benefits (Whitfield, 1992). They included much reduced corporation tax (National Freight paid virtually no taxes for six years after privatisation), reduced interest charges as a result of capital restructuring and debt write-offs (BT's interest payments in the five years after privatisation were £1,167 million less than the same period before its sale), many companies gained from pension fund contribution holidays (four companies, British Telecom, British Gas, British Aerospace and Cable & Wireless boosted their profits by over £1 billion in the four-year period after privatisation). These arrangements helped ensure healthy profits, financed dividend payments to shareholders and gave the appearance that privatisation was successful.

User Charges

User charges in six out of nine services have increased in real terms over the last fifteen years (see Table 6.2). Although the costs of gas, electricity and

Table 6.2: **Service price increases** (in real terms)

	% increase/decrease in real terms since privatisation
Water charges[1]	+55
Bus fares[2]	+26
Rail fares[3]	+26
NHS prescription charges[4]	+1,000
Council rents[5]	+27
Housing Association rents[6]	+38
BT line rental[7]	+8
regulated tariffs	−40
Gas regulated tariffs[8]	−20
Electricity[9]	−25

Sources:
1. between 1988/89 and 1998/99 (House of Commons Research Paper 00/7)
2. between 1985/86 and 1997/98 (House of Commons Research Paper 99/59)
3. between 1985/86 and 1997/98 (House of Commons Research Paper 99/105)
4. between 1979 and 1997 (Glennerster, 1998)
5. between 1991/92 and 1997/98 (House of Commons Research Paper 98/69)
6. between1991/92 and 1996/97 (House of Commons Research Paper 98/69)
7. between 1984 and 1996 (Markou and Wadhams Price, 1997)
8. between 1986/87 and 1996/97 (House of Commons Research Paper 00/7)
9. between 1989/90 and 1998/99 (House of Commons Research Paper 00/7)

telephones have reduced markedly, those for water, bus, rail, rents and prescription charges have increased substantially. In some cases the period before privatisation had an important bearing on post-privatisation price changes. For example, the real costs of electricity for domestic customers

> had fallen by nearly 14 per cent between 1983/84 and 1987/88 and were then raised in anticipation of flotation. Privatisation actually led to higher domestic electricity prices initially and the unit cost to domestic consumers could have fallen by around 8 per cent on the basis of falling coal costs alone. In the first quarter of 1994 domestic electricity prices were over 30 per cent higher than the average of 1988. (Markou and Wadhams Price, 1997, p. 21).

Expenditure on Changing Ownership

Over £5 billion was spent transferring ownership of public companies, land and property in the 1979–99 period (inclusive of consultants' financial and legal advisers' fees, free and discounted share offers (see Whitfield, 1992 and NAO reports 1992–9). The first 40 council housing stock transfers in the early 1990s cost £80.5 million in fees and commissions (5% per cent of the purchase price) just to change ownership. Subsequent transfers have pushed this figure to over £150 million. The Labour government is removing barriers to transfers by introducing new subsidy arrangements to facilitate the termination of council housing even in authorities where the value of the stock is less than the outstanding debt.

Accumulation of Surpluses

The formation of new unelected bodies has not only increased institutional fragmentation but has also led to the accumulation of substantial reserves as organisations protect their budgets and retain underspends. LMS schools had accumulated £546 million reserves by 1998 and Training and Enterprise Councils had £259 million reserves in 1996. Meanwhile, most local authorities have been forced to make substantial spending cuts.

Transaction and Public Cost of Tendering: The Savings Myth

The transformation of the welfare state incurs a wide range of costs. The concept of transaction costs can be used to identify the cost of contracts between economic organisations, public and private (Williamson, 1985). Organisations incur three types of transaction costs:

Transitional costs include the cost of setting up trading organisations, management consultants' fees, cost of preparing specifications, evaluating tenders and the market testing process. Advisers' fees in privatisation are another cost. Bribery is an important transaction cost in some countries.

Periodic costs include the cost of reviewing and implementing organisational change, creating new business units or adapting to new regulations.

Permanent costs include client/purchasing costs, additional costs of controlling and monitoring contracts and the loss of economies of scale with the duplication of personnel, financial and support services.

Between 1979 and 1997 the Tories claimed cost savings of 20–25 per cent from competitive tendering in local and central government (Cabinet Office, 1995a). However, this figure was never substantiated by research but was widely quoted as fact. For example, the OECD stated boldly that 'the UK, for example, has obtained typical savings of 25 per cent from its market testing' (OECD, 1995, p. 41). However, Competing for Quality programme forms, which departments and agencies have to complete annually, contained no reference to costs (Cabinet Office, 1995b).

Savings and cost reductions are normally only assessed within the scope of a contract or project. Other departmental, organisational, government and public sector costs 'external' to the contract are rarely quantified. Savings are exaggerated for two main reasons. First, most savings figures are based on claims or forecasts and are not actual savings verified by research. Once claims are made they are recycled without much due care and attention because they serve a political purpose. Savings are popular because they can be rolled up into a single quantifiable figure which can be used to legitimate change and to counter the negative consequences of job losses. Second, savings rarely take the full transaction costs into account. However, studies in Britain have exposed the real value of savings.

The central government Competing for Quality programme in Britain covered £5 billion of departmental and agency activities between 1992 and 1997. The 'efficiency savings' under this programme included the abolition of a service or activity, privatisation, strategic contracting out, market testing and internal restructuring. But efficiency was so broadly defined that it was impossible to determine the level of genuine improvements in managerial and service productivity. Competitive tendering accounted for over 90 per cent by value of this programme and was the continuing focus of the costs and savings debate (Centre for Public Services, 1997a).

'Expected savings' were notified by departments at the start of each contract but a government study revealed that 'actual savings varied from expected savings in 37% of cases' mainly due to changing requirements and 'the failure of the specification to reflect the actual work required'. This 'highlights the highly theoretical nature of savings projections made at the time of evaluation'. Process costs for market testing were 11 per cent annually of the original costs. The cost of the Competing for Quality programme was estimated to be five times greater than the cost estimates made only a year previously. The value of work subjected to market testing in the 1992–5 period was £1,841 million with annual tendering costs of £202 million. The report concluded that 'any activity where potential savings are less than 10% is not likely to be worth putting to competition on cost grounds alone' (Cabinet Office, 1996, para 3.39).

After taking tendering costs into account the average expected saving from market testing was 12 per cent. The study recommended that projects with an annual cost below £250,000 should not be put out to competition and those between £250,000 and £500,000 should be looked at critically to see if an alternative approach could provide better value for money. Some 45 per cent of the Competing for Quality programme covered services valued at less than £500,000!

The US National Performance Review (NPR) used the same crude roll up of savings, mainly by multiplying the total number of job losses by the average annual cost of a federal employee. NPR claimed estimated savings of $137 billion consisting of $44.3 billion from recommendations targeted at individual agencies, $67.5 billion claimed from government-wide initiatives such as 'reinventing Federal procurement' and $24.9 billion mainly from the auction of the Federal Communications Commission's wireless licences. However, a General Accounting Office review covering two-thirds of the agency savings concluded that 'NPR claimed savings from agency-specific recommendations that could not be fully attributed to its efforts. In general, the savings estimates we reviewed could not be replicated, and there was no way to substantiate the savings claimed' (GAO, 1999, p. 13).

The Public Cost of Competitive Tendering

Three major studies have examined local government competitive tendering savings in Britain and all demolished the 25 per cent savings claims. The first study found average cost savings in service budgets of 6.5 per cent in 40 local authorities after comparing the costs of the service before and after competition (DOE, 1993). A follow-up study covered 34 authorities and revealed retendering savings of just over 8 per cent (DOE, 1997).

The third national study, the Equal Opportunities Commission study into the gender impact of competitive tendering, was the only one based on detailed employment data and developed a model to assess the overall public costs of competitive tendering. It took account of the effect on government income and expenditure from changes in unemployment and welfare benefits, taxes, the loss of non-wage social contributions, corporate taxes and the impact on the local economy. Although local authorities' budgets produced £124 million 'savings' in 39 authorities, the full social and tendering costs totalled £250.1 million, leaving a net cost of £126 million per annum for four services in 39 local authorities (including most of the major cities) – equivalent to a 16 per cent cost. The government was, in effect, subsidising competitive tendering since it was responsible for 97 per cent of the costs. In other words, for every £1 million of 'savings' claimed, it cost the government and the public purse £2 million (Escott and Whitfield, 1995).

Transaction costs for the public sector and developers in private infrastructure projects, including feasibility studies, tendering, contract formulation, financing and project implementation 'are usually about 3 to 5 per cent in well-developed policy environments' or up to 10 per cent in pioneering schemes (World Bank, 1996, p. 2).

EMPLOYMENT IMPACT

Public service workers have taken the brunt of state transformation. Between 1981 and 1996 public sector employment fell 28 per cent with nationalised industries and other public corporations declining 78 per cent as a result of restructuring and privatisation (see Table 6.3). Central government employment fell by 23 per cent, the falling number of civil servants was used as evidence of increased efficiency and 'rolling back the frontiers of the state'. Long-term comparisons of employment data are highly complicated because of the transfer of activities to quangos, trusts and outsourcing across the public sector. The data conceal the number of staff transferred to private contractors and the number of staff actually engaged on public sector work. For example, 11,924 civil service staff were transferred to private contractors between April 1992 and March 1995. The cost of labour is simply hidden under different budget headings.

Table 6.3: **Change in public sector employment** (headcount, thousands)

	1981	1996	Change	% change
Public sector	7,185	5,150	−2,035	−28.3
Public corporations	1,867	410	−1,457	−78.0
Central government	878	676	−202	−23.0
Local authorities	2,899	2,651	−248	−8.6
National Health Service	1,207	1,192	−15	−1.2

Source: Economic Trends No. 520, March 1997, HMSO.

Civil service employment, included in the central government figures in Table 6.3, decreased 35 per cent in the 1979–98 period from 743,000 to 481,000 and included a 134 per cent increase in casual staff to nearly 18,000.

US Federal employment provides another example of the growth of the shadow state. The Federal civilian workforce declined from 2.1 million to 1.9 million employees between 1984 and 1996 ('the end of big government' claimed Clinton) but when contracted out, grant created jobs and other sectors are included there were 17 million full-time equivalent employees engaged in supplying goods and services to the US government in 1996 (Light, 1999). The overall total declined by 1 million jobs between 1984 and 1996 but if Defence Department cuts are excluded, the shadow state actually increased by 610,000 jobs, mainly through service contracts.

Substantial job losses have been incurred both before and after privatisation of nationalised industries and utilities (ILO, 1999). However, reliable workforce totals and employment change data are difficult to obtain because of the increasing practice of outsourcing by both public and private sectors. It is therefore difficult to distinguish job losses and job transfers. Job losses in Britain accounted for half of the jobs lost in the energy sector in Western Europe since 1990 (ILO, 1999). Some 156,346 jobs were lost in electricity and gas in Europe in the 1990–5 period alone. Britain's record includes a 60 per cent reduction (55,100 jobs) in gas between 1986 and 1997, a 33 per cent reduction (46,480 jobs) in electricity generating and distribution jobs between 1989 and 1995/6, and a 21.5 per cent (8,599 jobs) reduction in core employment in water services between 1990 and 1999 (Hall and Lobina, 1999).

An Equal Opportunities Commission (EOC) study identified 12,587 job losses in four services provided by 39 local authorities in the 1989–94 period, equivalent to 74,010 job losses nationally (Escott and Whitfield, 1995). Women accounted for 96 per cent of the net job loss in building cleaning, education catering, refuse collection and sports and leisure management. Cuts in hours have forced many women to take on several part-time jobs in order to try to maintain their earnings. A similar study of health and education tendering in Northern Ireland identified an overall 14 per cent job loss for women compared to 6 per cent for men, with contracting out to private firms resulting in a 37 per cent job loss compared to 11 per cent for contracts won by in-house services (Equal Opportunities Commission for Northern Ireland, 1996). Both studies also quantified cuts in working hours, increased use of temporary workers, loss of holiday pay, wage cuts, particularly in contracted out services, and a differential and adverse impact on women.

Tendering of London's bus services in the 1980s led to wage cuts averaging 14 per cent which accounted for £110 million of the £135 million cost savings (Kennedy, 1997). A decade after bus deregulation, passenger numbers had declined 36 per cent nationally and average earnings of bus and coach drivers had slumped from £5.70 per hour to £5.03 in 1994. At the start of the same period they earned 98 per cent of the average manual wage but this fell to 80 per cent (House of Commons Library, 1995).

Another example of the pressure on wages was highlighted by the House of Commons Public Accounts Committee inquiry into the use of PPP in the prison service following the National Audit Office report into the Bridgend and Fazakerley PPP prisons. Richard Tilt, Director General of the Prison

Service, reported that 'running costs in the private sector were 8%–15% lower, although the public sector was slowly closing the gap. He went on to point out that a security officer in a Securicor prison costs £14,000 a year for a 44 hour week, whilst an HMP Prison Officer costs £20,000 a year for a 38 hour week' (House of Commons, 1998). On this basis, a private prison with 500 staff would be £75 million cheaper over a 25-year period. The Prison Service submission showed the difference in staffing costs was greater than the total saving, thus proving that construction costs were actually higher than in the public sector. Wage cuts do not, of course, represent efficiency gains but transfers between managers, shareholders and taxpayers depending on the form of privatisation and the type of service.

The rapid expansion of private care in the last two decades has exploited women workers. Two 1997 surveys covering 1,270 and 187 nursing and residential homes (39,000 and 7,440 staff) respectively, revealed low hourly pay rates (half of all employees in the PSPRU survey earned under £3.50 an hour), increasing casualisation, reliance on untrained staff, between 15 and 17 days holiday and most employers did not provide a pension scheme for manual staff (PSPRU, 1997; Centre for Public Services/Fawcett Society, 1997).

Most major cities and towns have a number of private finance/partnership projects in different parts of the public sector, for example, schools, hospitals, roads, regeneration, police, central government agencies, at different stages of development. The Private Finance Initiative is estimated to result in 150,000 transfers and 30,000 job losses between 1998 and 2007 (Association of Direct Labour Organisations, 1999). The cumulative effect of these projects will be more substantial than the comparative loss of CCT or market testing contracts by the same public bodies. As DSOs and technical service departments come under increasing pressure from PPP projects and the transfer of other services, it is only a matter of time before they are acquired by PPP consortia. The loss of further contracts would threaten the DSOs' viability and help the contractor consolidate its market position. Some projects will primarily affect white collar staff, some projects will affect mainly building repair and maintenance work, while others will affect the full range of support services. The combined impact of these projects on jobs, pay and conditions could be substantive. These projects will have a wider impact on employment in each city. Local economy research studies have shown that a multiplier of between 1.15 and 1.24 is applicable to contracting situations and takes into account both jobs lost and the impact of reductions in terms and conditions (Centre for Public Services, 1995b). For every 4–5 jobs lost in local government, a further job is lost in the local economy.

Studies in other countries have revealed the same consequences of outsourcing. Privatisation resulted in a 25–49 per cent loss of wages and benefits (including health benefits, holiday entitlement and pensions) for entry level parking attendants, cashiers, security and custodial staff previously employed by the City of Chicago (Chicago Institute on Urban

Poverty,1997). Eight out of ten senior level jobs also experienced wage and benefit cuts of between 9 per cent and 46 per cent. The cuts reduced wages for nine out of ten entry level job descriptions to below the Federal poverty level thus entitling workers to Federal Earned Income Tax Credit, Food Stamps, heating assistance and free or subsidised school meals. Nine out of ten senior staff were entitled to substantial Federal Earned Income Tax Credit. This is further evidence of the way that outsourcing is subsidised by government.

Local government employment in Victoria, Australia, fell 30 per cent from 46,200 to 32,400 in the 1993–8 period as a result of council amalgamations (reduced from 211 to 78), rate capping and the introduction of CCT in 1994. A study of 249 Local Area Workplace Agreements, negotiated between local councils and in-house service providers, concluded that although basic wage rates remained largely unchanged, over half the agreements increased working hours and two-thirds altered the spread of working hours (Walsh and O'Flynn, 1999). Overall income levels were reduced because of the reduction or removal of overtime rates, premium rates for public holidays and special allowances. Another study of New South Wales government building cleaners transferred to private contractors revealed that the competitive environment had resulted in increased disharmony, tension and intolerance in the way cleaners related to each other and fear of job loss led to a dramatic increase in extra unpaid cleaning (Fraser, 1997).

A review of the impact of privatisation in Argentina, Chile, Mexico, Malaysia, Turkey, Ghana and other mixed economies revealed minimal employment impact in competitive enterprises but very high job losses both before and after privatisation in heavily subsidised and uncompetitive enterprises (Kikeri, 1998). The privatisation of telecoms, electricity, gas, water and sanitation and energy in Argentina led to 111,000 job losses (50 per cent) with similar losses revealed in a study of 218 privatised Mexican firms. In some cases, trade unions negotiated above average wage increases for remaining workers although with much revised labour contracts.

The Benefits of Transfer Regulations

The European Acquired Rights Directive provides a degree of protection for workers subjected to privatisation and contracting out. However, despite the initial frenzied opposition from contractors, the private sector has recognised the usefulness of the regulations which guarantee the transfer of experienced staff and 'intellectual capital of the service'. There are loopholes in the regulations which do not apply to new employees, hence legalising a two-tier wage structure, and changes to staffing levels, pay and conditions can be made if justifiable for 'economic, technical or organisational' reasons.

DEMOCRATIC ACCOUNTABILITY AND USER/EMPLOYEE INVOLVEMENT

Democratic renewal and empowering civil society are part of the transformation agenda but what is the reality? The promotion of decentralisation and 'community empowerment' gives the appearance of more participative government at local level but decision-making at central and local government predetermines spending and policy issues. Representation has increased at local level, for example, LMS schools and regeneration projects but under rules tightly defined by central government. Consequently, local decisions are largely about the management of increasingly scarce resources. Devolution and decentralisation have required a redistribution of responsibilities within local authorities but this does not automatically lead to democratisation and a redistribution of power to users and community organisations.

Political accountability was found to be almost negligible in self-managed units nor was there any extensive evidence of an increase in consumer power (Pollitt, 1997). 'Parents, patients and tenants were nowhere mentioned as major influences on management decision-making. At several research sites "consumer power" was said to be unimportant or even non-existent' (Pollitt et al., 1997, pp. 2–3). Furthermore, democratic accountability was rarely mentioned by any of the respondents in this research.

There have been few attempts to genuinely involve staff and users in the planning, design and management of services. Charters and complaints systems are designed for individual consumers. Public bodies have increasingly turned to market research in order to determine users' needs and opinions. Management maintains control and determines the issues on which opinions will be sought. It is ultimately about power relations and the focus on consumerism is intended to maintain the status quo. Power is limited and constrained by the consumption relationship. It is also determined by users' perception of what can be organised and the extent to which they can influence public policy. It can lead to the deskilling of people's ability to collectively discuss, debate and understand service delivery issues.

Customers, clients and citizens are quite different (Whitfield, 1992; Centre for Public Services, 1998). The state cannot claim that all government services should be 'customer driven' because this would conflict with many of the regulatory functions of government. The process of government and service delivery is an intregal part of the quality of public services. Rules and regulations are most often in existence to ensure equal opportunities, fairness and equality of treatment, to prevent fraud and graft and to ensure the authority's statutory duties are fulfilled – 'one person's red tape is another's due process' (Savoie, 1996).

Consultation alone is wholly inadequate because it is limited to expressing views, being heard but having limited impact on the outcome. It is usually a means of 'asserting public opinion and then containing it through engineered consensus' and 'manipulating the employee or user/consumer to accept and implement organisational objectives' (Chandler, 1997). Involvement enables staff to influence decision-making in the planning, management and operation of services.

The delegation of power to vary service delivery must take place within public policy and statutory parameters. Experimentation, getting things wrong and financial consequences have a different impact in the public sector particularly when this concerns people's weekly income from state benefits and their access to housing, education, health and social services. Managerial devolution in Next Steps Agencies had to take place within centralised policies of privatisation, market testing and annual efficiency targets leaving limited room to manoeuvre.

Academics and social policy-makers have sometimes referred to 'the centrality of the customer in the remaking of organisations' as part of the new managerialism. But the new breed of business managers and accountants have been at the centre of the new public sector management. These managers have used the 'cause' of customers as a means of strengthening their own position and forcing public bodies to adopt business and commercial practices. Customers have gained no additional power other than some additional channels to lodge complaints. In fact users have been redefined as 'customers' to precisely limit and curtail their involvement in public services. Consumers act individually both in expressing choice and preferences and in complaining. But citizenship defined solely by the rights and powers afforded through consumption represents a very narrow perspective and limited responsibilities of both users and service providers. The implication under this model of citizenship is that if you do not have children then you bear no responsibility for the provision and quality of education. The consumption model of citizenship is the atomised individual buying services as and when needed from the marketplace.

Workforce Involvement

Workers are often blamed for service failures which are the result of poor management and/or spending cuts. Overcoming resistance to change, developing trust and building mutual independence are difficult if the workplace has a history of conflict and mistrust. Staff may resist change because they fear the diminution of authority, loss of control and loss of jobs; lack of understanding of why change is necessary, or cultural and class differences may make acceptance difficult. Employees' doubts and resistance to performance management are usually related to their view of management's ability and attitudes.

Middle managers may fear the loss of their jobs and will therefore be reluctant participants. It may mean a changed role of middle managers from 'experts' to facilitators and they may resist performance management, or at least the employee involvement aspects, because it threatens their power relationship. Some may see it as an opportunity for a greater say in decision-making, taking on the quality mantle, becoming a spokesperson for the customer and hence maintaining, and in some cases, strengthening their power base (Munro, 1995).

Despite the rhetoric, performance management and human relation techniques intensify work and increase managerial surveillance and control. Workers are not in fact empowered but more 'self-regulation' or 'controlled empowerment' is imposed on the workforce together with self-monitoring on such matters as absenteeism and lateness.

The prescriptive rhetorical and almost evangelical encouragement for empowerment is not supported by empirical evidence. A survey of 4,500 union activists in Britain revealed a critical mismatch between policy formulation and the daily experience of work. Furthermore, 'the effects of measures intended to enhance employee commitment are undermined by those arising from measures to increase competitiveness through work intensification' and 'the introduction of measures to raise employee commitment has not been accompanied by a fundamental shift in management behaviour' (Waddington and Whitson, 1996). 'Management are opting for those elements of workplace change that have the least effect on workplace power relations', for example, team briefings.

FRAGMENTING THE STATE

Transformation has fragmented the state in several important ways. *Institutional fragmentation* occurs when an organisation is divided into a larger number of operational units which are then loosely centrally coordinated. Managing disparate, often narrowly focused, units of government raises additional management problems such as concentration on internal management, incentives and devolving power but too little focus on the wider picture. Increasing fragmentation of government is largely regarded as the price to be paid for the 'benefits' but it has major implications for the way these organisations are governed, for users, staff and trade unions.

Organisational and managerial fragmentation: Internal fragmentation with the separation of client and contractor functions and the formation of business units. Control is exercised by contracting, franchising, partnership and regulation rather than traditional hierarchical structures. It has also led to short-term, narrowly defined service or business planning, more competitive inter-organisational relations, the loss of responsiveness to implementing corporate policies, decreasing accountability as responsibility is transferred to contractors and non-elected bodies, and the loss of economies of scale with smaller organisations sourcing goods and services from the private sector. Fragmentation also leads to more contracting out and greater reliance on management consultants.

Competitive tendering led to *service fragmentation* as services were packaged for tendering. The rate at which contracts are extended to new areas of work exceeds the rate at which contracts are consolidating. User needs are narrowly defined because of the limited responsibility and purpose of each organisation. Policy coordination and integration of services are more difficult and time consuming given the larger number of organisations responsible only for prescribed parts or specific services, thus making it harder to integrate services and adopt multidisciplinary working. Fiscal policy has forced centralisation of the budgetary process with departments and sections permitted wider scope but with reduced resources, in effect decentralising the difficult choices and cuts decisions to those most affected by them and making longer term planning more difficult.

The launch of health, education and employment zones, new community and PFI projects attempts to target resources but rather than creating 'joined-up government' leads to *policy/project fragmentation*. Institutional, organisational and service fragmentation results in a multiplicity of employers or *employer fragmentation* which causes difficulties for trade union bargaining and representation, performance monitoring and data collection.

The formation of agencies and transfer of responsibility to quasi-public bodies, trusts and arm's-length companies, privatisation and public/private partnerships has led to *workplace fragmentation* with staff working in smaller geographically dispersed units. Multi-site working, split shifts and the loss of enhanced payments for unsocial hours has also become more widespread. Local bargaining fragments negotiations and causes more conflict/competition between unions at the workplace. The ability to negotiate varies. *Fragmentation of trade union organisation* means bigger unions but fragmented at the workplace with different agendas.

A *'shadow state'* is being created consisting of a network of contract and research grants employing ever larger numbers of staff in universities and research institutions working on government contracts, management consultants, private contractors together with agency and temporary staff all doing work previously done by directly employed staff.

Similar trends are evident in the USA where public bodies have to administer a plethora of service programmes. These have multiplied in the last 35 years. For example, 132 Federal grant programmes in 1960 had mushroomed to 640 by 1995. Grants for payments to individuals represented 35.5 per cent of Federal aid in 1960 but rose to 62 per cent by 1995 (Walker, 1996). The obsession with balanced budgets, elimination of deficits, the redefinition of the relationship between Federal and State power and requirements for super-majorities for Congressional tax increases reduces Federal government flexibility and responsiveness, and eliminates leverage over State and local authorities. 'Disempowering the federal government will also remove the only effective check against the large organisations that dominate modern life' (Brinkley, 1997, p. 1). The USA could become a Balkanised republic with 50 semi-autonomous State governments and new agencies as a result of the disempowering of Federal government and 'will accentuate the regional, economic, religious, ethnic and racial differences that already divide us' (Brinkley, 1997, p. 2).

EQUALITY AND SOCIAL JUSTICE

During the 1980s most public bodies adopted corporate equal opportunities policies, so the issue became one of implementation and monitoring. However, the commercialisation of public services, particularly competitive tendering, produced a widening gap between policy and practice. CCT regulations limited the examination of contractors' equal opportunities employment policies in the award and operation of contracts. Not surprisingly, CCT in local government and market testing in the National Health Service were found to be discriminatory (Escott and Whitfield, 1995; Equal Opportunities Commission for Northern Ireland, 1996). Furthermore, the debate has largely been about access to services and employment rather than a social justice perspective encompassing economic and class interests.

Labour's social inclusion policy, encompassing many important initiatives, was described in Chapter 5. Three major contradictions regarding supply and demand, marketisation and community involvement were highlighted. In addition, the proliferation of zones, organisations, partnerships and companies results in fragmentation and increases the difficulties in generalising good practice. The emphasis on equality of opportunity and on supply-side initiatives inevitably means that rather limited and narrow improvements are achievable from a social justice perspective. Many local authorities are cutting services and/or imposing higher user charges on the very services deemed essential to reduce social exclusion. Government figures show that 17 per cent of individuals have little or no savings, no occupational or personal pension, nor own their own home, yet the reform of the welfare state encourages individuals to be responsible for their own welfare and future. There is increasing pressure on families, particularly women, to provide unpaid care and/or participate in unpaid voluntary work. Women are also subject to pay cuts and loss of hours in the transfer of community care from the public to private or voluntary sectors – they take the brunt of markets and spending cuts.

The Impact on Tenants

Tenants lose security of tenure and lose direct democratic accountability with stock transfers from the public sector to quangos. Rent increases are usually limited to inflation plus 1 per cent for a three- to five-year period but tenants face average annual increases of 10 per cent or more once the guarantee period ends. Changes in the rent assessment system after the guarantee period means that some tenants face very significant increases indeed. A two-tier rent structure is immediately imposed because all new tenants' rents are set at a considerably higher level – housing association rents are an average 25 per cent higher than council rents. While most repairs programmes are implemented after transfer, there is also evidence of rescheduling of repairs programmes and day-to-day repairs due to changes in income projections. So a two-tier wage structure is complemented by a two-tier rent structure.

QUALITY OF SERVICE

Despite the rhetoric of performance measures and targets, a study by Pollitt et al. (1997) revealed a 'striking lack of convincing before-and-after data ... and the extent (or absence) of reform-induced performance improvements will never be known for sure'. This research also highlighted the different dimensions to performance, different priorities accorded by politicians, managers, staff, users and the public, and the cause/effect of changes in performance.

After a decade of measuring performance with indicators and targets the process remains fraught with difficulties. A study of agency performance concluded that the bulk of the efficiency savings originated from market testing, not from the agency model; the massaging, changing the basis of information collection and selecting soft targets made it difficult to assess performance consistently over a significant timescale; it was difficult to correlate performance measures with actual consequences; and the contradictions between performance targets, for example, efficiency and quality targets, are not always taken into account making it a mixture of art and science. The report concluded that the 'genuine difficulties of measuring performance also need to be regularly and publicly acknowledged' and that 'valuable resources need to be directed at improving the quality of services rather than the performance of indicators' (Centre for Public Services, 1997a, pp. 1–2). The overall performance of government agencies in meeting targets rose in the early 1990s from 76 per cent of targets achieved to 83 per cent in 1994/5 only to decline to 75 per cent two years later. However, 'the Government does not consider that a detailed post mortem on the causes would be likely to be profitable' (Cabinet Office, 1998).

The number of service complaints has risen rapidly since privatisation and the introduction of citizen's charters and customer care systems in the early 1990s, although it is impossible to clearly identify cause and effect (see Table 6.4). Unfortunately, the culture of complaint is dominant, making a culture of appreciation in response to good quality public services a rarity.

Monitoring and evaluation is the weak link in the contract state. In the USA, due in part to the plethora of programmes, the lack of monitoring and fully fledged evaluation is endemic.

The assault on US welfare operational contracts by major IT companies was littered with mass cost-overruns, fraud, technical incompetence, extremely high error rates and other performance failures (Service Employees International Union, 1997). For example, Lockheed Martin's contract with California's child support computer system had a 163 per cent cost-overrun; Andersen Consulting's child support tracking system for Texas cost $75.1 million, 559 per cent over budget and four years behind schedule and a

Table 6.4: **Complaints in privatised services**

	1988	1989	1990	1991	1992	1993	1994	1995	1996	1997	1998	% inc.
British Gas	302	451	397	968	1,827	1,842	2,318	3,389	9,287	27,274	61,887	127
BT	23,782	31,644	38,530	41,393	41,026	23,413	30,831	29,900	29,750	35,100	42,050	20
Water Cos*			4,613	10,635	14,795	14,290	13,326	13,192	10,070	11,123	n/a	10
Electricity				14,173	15,054	10,219	8,932	7,436	6,394	5,702	5,053	–11

* For financial years April–March
Source: *Utilities Bill*, House of Commons Library Research Paper 00/7, 2000.

welfare computerisation contract with Nebraska had a 66 per cent cost-overrun and was a year late. Virginia cancelled a $45 million Medicaid contract with EDS in 1997 because the project was 20 months behind schedule, had an error rate of over 50 per cent and state officials believed EDS could not complete the project within a reasonable time period, if ever. Unisys computer contracts in Florida, Massachusetts, Wisconsin and California led to contract terminations, large financial default payments, high levels of errors and cost-overruns in the 1990s (SEIU, 1997).

THE PERFORMANCE STATE PARADIGM

The growth of performance management was described in Chapter 4. This section first examines the potential impact of the growing obsession with inspection, audit and performance assessment, followed by a critique of the separation of client/contractor or purchaser/provider functions.

A decade of performance management implementation in the USA, Australia, New Zealand and Britain has revealed the complexity and difficulty of measuring the performance of government and public services. For example, a study of five major US regulatory agencies, including the Internal Revenue Service and Federal Aviation Administration, noted various barriers and difficulties in identifying and collecting data to demonstrate performance and the complex factors which often affect results and the long-term nature of the process (Government Accounting Office, 1997). Another study involving government agencies and private firms in the USA, Canada and Britain highlighted the need for a clear conceptual framework, effective communications and accountability and a focus on intelligence rather than data compilation (National Performance Review, 1997).

Performance measurement is part science and part art. Assessing outcomes is particularly difficult because some aspects of performance are not quantifiable but are subjective, and performance can only be assessed rather than measured; the need to assess the degree of achievement of values and principles is not normally quantifiable; performance may be based on progress and not simply on completion; different measures of performance are relevant for different levels of the organisation; and there is the difficulty of comparing performance with other organisations, particularly the private sector.

Audit has traditionally been primarily concerned with fiscal accountability (legality and budgetary matters), economy (obtaining the best possible terms in the use of resources such as accepting the lowest tender) and efficiency (maximising the outputs). Power adds a fourth dimension of accountability: effectiveness (ensuring outcomes conform to the objectives) (Power, 1997). The record of assessing effectiveness is dismal. However, Power focuses on accountancy and efficiency audit thus maintaining the hegemony of the auditor/accountant and consequently failing to recognise the importance of social, economic and equality audit.

An implosion of performance measurement and audit is a distinct possibility. The growth of an 'indicator culture' is a very real threat in which 'auditable performance is an end in itself and real long term planning is impossible' (Power, 1997, p. 121). The implication that performance is focused on quality is, in reality, a mask because the real purpose is to improve productivity and increase the efficiency of state expenditure. It could also become a means of legitimating the merging of public/private wage differentials, but only where the former is higher than the latter, by increasing comparison and competition with private and voluntary providers. A further consequence of this approach is that it fragments the power and organisation of public sector trade unionism despite short-term protection through the European Acquired Rights Directive. While ostensibly making management more accountable, the lack of democratic accountability and other initiatives such as cabinet government and Beacon councils which reinforce managerial control, means that managers refocus performance management on to frontline and support staff.

Performance measurement is used to *strengthen central control* rather than empowering users – 'failing schools', 'inefficient councils' and loss-making DSOs are part of a more strident 'government by threat' (Peters, 1996, p. 122). Although 'New Public Management' (NPM) focuses on performance assessment 'some fundamental aspects of NPM reforms themselves appear to have remained almost immune from such requirements' (Pollitt et al., 1997, p. 5).

The *myth of the independent expert* is promoted more intensely. Inspectorates, such as the Audit Commission and OFSTED, are quangos with limited democratic accountability. They regularly outsource, for example, the Audit Commission subcontracts the function of District Audit to transnational accountancy and management consultancies such as Pricewaterhouse Coopers, KPMG, Deloitte Touche and Arthur Andersen. OFSTED outsources inspection work to retired teachers, agencies and companies, some of which have aspirations to take over the management and operation of schools.

The growth of performance audit is correlated with *partnerships, contracting and decentralising activities to quasi-public and third sector organisations* where it is necessary to maintain a degree of legal and financial accountability. Performance audit is important precisely because of a lack of ideological commitment to public provision, i.e. performance assessment is more important than who delivers the service and is needed precisely because there is a plethora of providers. Increasingly, audits of partnerships/PPPs will be required to assess whether contracts and agreements have been fulfilled. Increasing reliance on deregulation and self-regulation also increases the need for audit.

Auditing becomes a *management control system* with a subsequent 'loss' of a political economy approach. Social equalities and broader economic objectives are marginalised because performance audit focuses on what is quantifiable and contractual. In theory, performance measurement should match the scope of the objectives upon which the decision to undertake the investment, activity or service is based but it becomes a key means of reinforcing managerial and financial criteria. In the merging of financial and managerial audit, 'the audit explosion represents a decision to shift evaluative cultures away from social scientific towards managerial knowledge bases' (Power, 1997, p. 67). It is highly dependent on information and monitoring and evaluation systems which will require a major overhaul in most public bodies.

The *rules of audit* and the statutory remit of organisations responsible for performance measurement will be used to *limit the scope of audit*. For example, National Audit Office reviews of privatisation are restricted to assessing whether the sale was carried out according to the government's privatisation rules and best practice established by previous audits, studiously avoiding key policy matters and using conservative cost analysis. 'In the audit society the power to define and institutionalise auditable performance reduces evaluation to auditing' (Power, 1997, p. 119).

Auditing is also being *extended to political activity* as Distict Auditors are responsible for auditing the Best Value consultation process. This will almost certainly reinforce consultation through focus groups and panels rather than involvement of community and trade union organisations. How do the auditors assess the inevitable lobbying of focus groups and juries by tenants and community campaigns?

Audit has always had a risk reduction function to ensure financial and legal duties are adhered to in the public interest. However, audit will have a new function in *assessing risk* as PPPs proliferate. The public sector is required to transfer risk as a condition of PPPs while the private sector seeks to minimise investment and operational risk.

The Best Value regime offers the means to assess social needs and the wider impact of public and private policies in addition to assessing the performance of existing activities and services. However, there is little evidence of this being adopted. Social audit, assessing the wider impact of policies and investment decisions such as the community and economic consequences of closures or privatisation (Whitfield, 1992), has never been adopted into mainstream evaluation or impact analysis. The government, the Audit Commission and the Accounts Commission in Scotland originally refused to define Best Value on the grounds that because it was a process a definition was not necessary. However, the legislation had to define the statutory duty to achieve Best Value which is limited to 'economy, efficiency and effective-ness' (Local Government Act 1999). In other words, little has changed since the birth of the Audit Commission in 1983 which had the same remit.

The Contract State

A client–contractor or purchaser–provider split is claimed to provide a clarity of purpose, preventing the subversion of user interests by staff and trade unions; reducing conflict of interests by separating the setting of objectives and specification from service delivery; strengthening opportunities for quality control, improving monitoring and compliance, transparency of funding and supporting customer care and individual redress. But the complexity of government cannot usually be reduced to a specification and a contract.

The separation of responsibilities has a number of problems. Policy formulation, implementation and evaluation are not separate or distinct processes. The first requires constant adaptation and continuous development based on the experience of service delivery and the identification of changing needs. Learning organisations are needed with continuing cooperation and interaction between policy-making and implementation. The split means two sets of competing, and in some cases, confrontational relationships and power struggles. Information about changing needs, user views of the service, contract performance and service development is often subject to 'ownership' disputes. The so-called vested interests of providers (staff and trade unions) are replaced by external vested interests of business elites and transnational companies. The fact that users sometimes have vested interests, which are in direct conflict with the public interest and corporate policies, is glossed over.

Contracting most public goods does not offer users genuine choice, only client managers. Contracting results in putting price before quality, high transaction costs, job losses and a reduction in the quality of employment and widening inequalities. It often results in a loss of trade union representation and organisation, the European Acquired Rights Directive notwithstanding. It means a loss of in-house capacity and skills, a transfer of decision-making and power from elected representatives to officers, an expansion and extension of market systems and a loss of flexibility and innovation constrained by the contract system. It also results in pressure to continuously widen the range of services outsourced to gain further economies of scale, notwithstanding the growth of a vested interest group of contractor associations and threat of increased corruption and collusion between bidders.

Contracting imposes a degree of rigidity because management by contract results in a loss of flexibility. Contracts can never be complete. They fragment rather than integrate service delivery and although variations, renegotiation and retendering are options, they impose further transaction costs. Corporate policies are implemented on a contract by contract basis resulting in fragmentation and placing a heavy reliance on client monitoring, itself highly vulnerable to spending cuts, to enforce the contract.

Entrepreneurialism and market mechanisms conflict with the core values of the public sector and safeguarding public interest. Over-prescriptive public sector rules and procedures inhibit innovation. They were not 'invented to inhibit entrepreneurial activity but were seen as a price to pay to inhibit malpractice' (Jordan, 1994, p. 274). The claim that entrepreneurial managers should have the 'right to fail' (Osborne and Gaebler, 1992) is politically crass and naive, and clearly not in the public interest. Taxpayers are not prepared to accept that managers should treat public money in the same way as private money. The private sector makes mistakes and wastes millions on failed schemes but little is heard about them so long as companies continue to be profitable, maintain dividends and avoid major environmental disasters. Yet business is the first to complain about the 'misuse' of public money.

OWNERSHIP AND CONTROL

The structure of share ownership in Britain has changed markedly in the last 40 years. In 1957 individuals owned 66 per cent of shares but only 28 per cent by 1981, and 20 per cent by 1996. Privatisation and demutualisation of building societies have increased the number of individuals owning shares but only slowed the decline in the percentage of shares owned by individuals.

Wider share ownership was used to legitimate the sale of publicly owned assets at discounted prices, to reassure financial markets that sales would be successful and to make renationalisation more difficult. Individual share ownership was widely promoted along with creating opportunities with free and discounted shares to enable employees to become stakeholders and to create a home and job owning democracy (Whitfield, 1992).

However, the reality was capital flight. In seven privatisations at the height of the 'popular capitalism' era, including the sale of British Telecom and British Gas, 5.4 million individual shareholders sold out in the first year alone, a mass exodus by any standards. The sale of National Power and Powergen attracted 3.25 million individual shareholders but within six months this had plummeted to 1.8 million.

On average, 52 per cent of individual shareholders sold in the first year following flotation. The value of dividends based on the average number of shares held by individuals as a percentage of the annual company wage varied between 0.07 and 0.65 in 1990, i.e. it was tiny. The cost of the share flotations also included £278 million worth of free and discounted shares to employees, which represented only between 2 and 3 per cent of the company's annual wage bill at the time of sale.

Employee ownership in privatised bus companies collapsed spectacularly in the mid-1990s. Over 20 bus companies were sold to managers/employees via Employee Share Ownership Plans (ESOPs) following bus deregulation in 1986, the breakup of the National Bus Company and the piecemeal sell-off of the Scottish Bus Group and municipal bus companies. For example, Yorkshire Rider, People's Bus (Gosport) and Busways (Newcastle) promoted 'employee ownership', yet were some of the first to sell out in the takeover spree as three national companies sought to acquire market share. Busways was acquired by staff in 1989 (directors and managers had 51 per cent and staff 49 per cent) but was sold five years later to Stagecoach for £27.5 million, almost twice the original purchase price. Staff voted 99.65 per cent in favour of the sale lured by payments of up to £13,000.

These sales highlighted two important points, First, employees collectively owned less than 50 per cent of the shares and management were effectively in control of companies. In most cases they were management, not employee, buy-outs. In addition, executive directors had special voting rights for an initial, usually five-year, period which gave them additional powers. Employees found a substantial cash windfall irresistible and the strategy for employee ownership to be a guarantee against hostile private sector bids proved to be fatally flawed.

A combination of share allocation at privatisation, the subsequent distribution of share options (purchasing company shares cheaply) and soaring salary increases provided directors and senior managers with new 'get rich quick' opportunities (*Labour Research*, 1997; Whitfield, 1992). Hence their justified branding as 'fat cats' by the media and trade unions whose members were meantime subject to large-scale redundancies.

Private Monopoly

In 1985, the public sector held 75 per cent of bus turnover, by 1997 it was 7 per cent. National Bus was divided into 72 separate units for privatisation and the 1986 bus deregulation encouraged new bus operators to tender for routes. Local bus passenger journeys continued to decline, down 23 per cent between 1985/6 and 1997/8. By 1999, three firms, Stagecoach, First Group and Arriva had a 53.3 per cent national market share with two other firms, National Express and Go-Ahead, owning another 12.4 per cent share. Locally, large operators acquired smaller independent firms by stealth, sometimes maintaining their original livery to create the impression of separate companies. Although passenger numbers have continued to fall, profits have risen as companies have raised fares but cut staff, wages, fleets, services and investment – in 1986 a fifth of the national bus fleet was more than twelve years old, now it is 55 per cent (*Observer*, 26 July 1998). Within a decade we have travelled from public and municipal ownership to competition and 'bus wars' to virtual private monopolisation. The big three bus companies also operate train services and two own regional airports. For example, Teesside had eight key operators in 1992 but two national operators, Stagecoach and Arriva, had by 1996, through acquisition and predatory pricing, established local monopoly corridors of operation with a few smaller bus companies operating niche markets of little interest to the larger firms (Bussell and Suthers, 1998/9).

The privatisation of water and sewerage services in several countries has exhibited economic problems and distortions characteristic of monopolies including management inefficiencies, restricted competition and corruption, excess pricing and restricted access, excess profits and low water quality and problems in delivering development objectives (Lobina and Hall, 1999).

PARTNERSHIPS

The global growth of PPPs and privately financed infrastructure was discussed in Chapter 2 and the expansion of PPPs to Britain's welfare state infrastructure in Chapter 3. This section examines the effect of PPPs on public finance, services and government. The financial consequences are fourfold. First, PPPs are often more expensive than publicly financed projects. For example, hospital PPPs increase the cost of hospital building. Total project costs (construction and financing costs in a sample of hospital projects) were between 18 and 60 per cent higher than the construction costs alone (see Table 6.5). PPP availability costs were between 11.2 and 18.5 per cent of the construction costs in contrast to 3.0–3.5 per cent annual interest on publicly financed projects (see Table 6.6).

Table 6.5: **Capital cost of PPP hospital projects**

Hospital	Construction cost to private sector (£m)	Total capital cost(£m)	Difference (£m)	Difference as % of construction cost
Dartford	94.0	115.0	21.5	22.8
Carlisle	64.7	85.0	20.3	31.3
Norfolk	143.5	214.0	70.5	49.1
North Durham	61.0	96.0	37.0	60.6
Greenwich	84.0	109.9	25.9	30.8
Bromley	118.0	155.0	37.0	35.8
Wellhouse	54.0	65.0	11.0	18.5

Source: Gaffney et al., 1999.
Note: The difference between construction and total capital costs is usually explained as arising from financing costs incurred by the private sector during the construction period.

Second, PPPs are being subsidised by government. Local government PPPs receive revenue support subsidy in the same way as if they were publicly financed projects – £800 million per annum is allocated up to 2001/2. The NHS effectively subsidises PPP schemes through three mechanisms – capital charges (paying the same for a reduced asset base), the capital support scheme and diverting block capital funding to PPP schemes. Ten of the first wave NHS projects receive an annual subsidy of

£7.3 million because of 'affordability' problems (Gaffney and Pollock, 1999). Accountants Chantrey Vellacott have estimated that the private sector's higher cost of borrowing costs the public sector an extra £50 million for every net £1 billion of PFI contracts (Chantrey Vellacott, 1999). They also note that an extra £10 billion public sector three-year capital spending in 1999–2002 would still leave the public finances well within the Maastricht convergence criteria.

Table 6.6: **Hospital construction and availability costs**

Hospital	Construction cost (£m)	PPP availability payment (£m)	PPP availability payment as % of construction cost
Calderdale	64.6	8.7	13.5
Carlisle	64.7	8.0	12.4
Dartford	94.0	10.5	11.2
Greenwich	84.0	11.0	13.1
North Durham	61.0	7.1	11.6
Wellhouse	54.0	10.0	18.5

Source: Gaffney et al., 1999.

Third, PPP projects commit future governments to a stream of PPP payments, totalling £83.8 billion up to 2026 (HM Treasury, 2000a). However, they only represent signed PPP deals and are relevant only if there is an immediate cessation of all prospective deals. Signed deals are a tiny fraction of projects under development and, assuming no policy changes and no change in the speed of approvals, a new stream of projects will develop annually between now and 2026. The financial commitment is more likely to be £415 billion, arrived at by assuming that the rate of project approvals in the 1997–9 period continues to 2026. The cumulative impact of PPP revenue payments will mean future governments may have to raise taxes, impose charges for services which are currently free, reduce borrowing to finance remaining public services or cut spending in non-PPP services.

> The future cash outflows under PPP contracts are analogous to future debt service requirements under the national debt, and, potentially, more onerous since they commit the public sector to procuring a specified service over a long period of time when it may well have changed its views on how or whether to provide certain core services of the welfare state. (*Financial Times*, 17 July 1997)

The true cost of individual PPPs will not be known for 25–35 years when the first contracts terminate and all the social welfare costs and benefits can be fully assessed. Government and business interests appear very concerned about the intergenerational burden of social policy commitments but sign up to PPP projects with little regard to the longer term public cost of PPPs.

Fourth, an increasing proportion of revenue budgets will be committed to PPP projects leaving a smaller proportion of budgets to deal with other non-PPP services, thus limiting an authority's ability to respond to changing social needs and urgent priorities. *Escalating project costs* are a common feature of PPPs, for example, Birmingham City Council's schools project rose from £20 million for eight schools to £65 million for ten schools prior to selecting a preferred bidder (Association of Direct Labour Organisations, 1999). The first 14 NHS projects had an average 69 per cent cost increase between the Outline Business Case and early 1999.

There is no indication that PPPs are a temporary fix, indeed, quite the opposite as they are now embedded in Third Way ideology and government programmes. Those who use the logic of capitalism to claim that the state should not own facilities and only provide services are being economical with their analysis. The concept of the private sector owning and managing the infrastructure but stopping short of providing core services is untenable. PPPs are merely a half-way position between public ownership and the total privatisation of health, education and social services.

The concept of *joint venture* is not applicable because there is no pooling of resources, the public body withdraws from property and facilities management merely paying usage and service fees as a lessee to repay the private sector's construction and operating costs.

Service Failures

The performance of the major computing PPPs has been less than successful. The catalogue of failures and cost overruns is summarised in Table 6.7. In addition, 14 local authority housing benefit and revenue contracts had caused havoc for service users, elected members and managers in 1999–2000. Three contracts had been terminated (Centre for Public Services/Middlesbrough Unison, 2000).

PPPs create artificial divisions between core and support services, for example, dividing health and education teams both between white collar and manual services and between core services and supplementary activities. Partnership consortia have an economic interest in the performance of the core service within their building. For example, a PPP consortium has a direct interest in a school's educational performance, in maintaining pupil numbers and ensuring its popularity is translated into maximising income generation from community and business use of the facilities. Conflict and tension will exist between partnership and non-partnership schools over the quality of teachers, which schools are allocated resources for new or special projects and the distribution of any future budget cuts between schools and services. Consortia will, therefore, want to ensure that they have the best teachers and minimum disruption to the running of 'the business'. Once the

Table 6.7: **Partnership and private finance failures**

Department/contract	Contractor	Problems/costs
National Insurance	Andersen Consulting	Delays and renegotiation of the contract. £53m extra cost to taxpayers – Andersen paid £4.1m in financial penalty. 172,000 potential cases of underpayment of pensions. Compensation paid to pension providers and pensioners for late rebates.
Passport Office	Siemens	£120 million contract for digital scanning, waiting times tripled. £12m extra costs incurred by agency, Siemens will pay £2.45m. Processing times reached 50 days in July 1999. Operating in only two out of six offices by 1999 start date. Cost of passport increased from £21 to £28.
Immigration and Nationality	Siemens	£100 million computing contract. Large backlog: 76,000 asylum cases and 100,000 nationality cases. Contractor penalised £4.5 million.
Northern Ireland Vehicle Licensing Agency	EDS	Abandoned in March 1996, £3.7 million written off, projects estimated 71% above forecast.
Benefits Agency/Post Office payment card	ICL	Long delays and project overtaken by new technology.
National Air Traffic Services New control centre.	Lockheed Martin	£623 million including £300 million overspend, six years late.
Metropolitan Police	EDS	Delivered 4 years late, cost £20 million including £3 million overspend.
Dartford and Gravesham NHS Trust hospital	Pentland	Claimed £17m savings but errors in cost estimates – now £5m. Supposed to be revenue neutral but budget increased by £4m per annum.

Sources: Select Committee on Public Accounts, 'Improving the Delivery of Government IT Projects', First Report, 2000. *Computer Weekly* (various).

private sector control the operational management of facilities they will be in a powerful position to influence service delivery policies. It makes a nonsense of the team approach, integrated services and joined-up government towards which almost everyone has been striving for years.

The current division between core and non-core services is unlikely to be sustainable. The concept of the public sector continuing to provide core staff and buying space in an increasing number of privately managed and operated schools is not credible. PPP consortia are also likely to want to expand the range of services provided. They are likely to make LEAs and governing bodies 'offers' regarding support services and additional teaching which will widen in scope (Whitfield, 1999). The employment impact was noted earlier in this chapter. Facilities management contracts are retendered every five to seven years to give consortia a degree of 'financial flexibility', an opportunity to impose substantial changes in the labour process and provide a 'PPP valve' to relieve financial pressure.

Private sector takeover of 'failing' services and/or authorities results in commercial values being embedded in the public sector, leading to a spiral of decline and privatisation. A two-tier public/private system will develop with the public sector increasingly marginalised and residualised. Despite the development of super-hospitals, twelve of the 14 first wave PPP projects had an average 32 per cent reduction in staffed acute beds in the 1996–7 period.

Controlling Development

Land and property deals are a fundamental part of PPP projects enabling consortia to develop 'surplus' land and building for commercial and residential use but it may take several years for the value of these assets to be realised. Ownership of key development sites adjacent to new highways, airports and ports, particularly in developing countries, will increase transnationals' influence in economic policy and direct foreign investment. Some PPP hospital developments have changed from a mix of refurbishment and new build on existing sites to large new complexes on out of town greenfield sites. The physical form and financial commitments can distort health care planning. Patients and staff are forced to bear the additional travel costs and government has to finance road improvement, traffic and transport changes.

PPPs are not simply the replacement of public by private finance but they ensure the privatisation of the development process, operational management, the disposal of surplus land and property and, in some cases, additional development generated by the initial investment (see Chapter 2). In fact, business has been a vehicle for the longer term privatisation of the core services of the welfare state. Supplying and managing the infrastructure on behalf of the state avoids having to create a private sector market in which individuals pay private insurance and fees. PPPs are a means of finance capital extracting higher returns from public services than they would otherwise by providing private capital in place of government borrowing and 'contract capital', i.e. transnational service companies and consultants securing long-term contracts. They redefine 'public service' because they can remain publicly financed but privately delivered in privately managed buildings.

Impact on Government

In Britain the treatment of assets has been 'clarified' and should revert to public ownership at the end of the contract where it is in the public interest and there is no alternative use for the asset (HM Treasury, 1999a). However, public sector capital spending may have almost vanished in 25–35 years and public bodies may not have the capacity or political commitment to assume operational and managerial responsibility for facilities. In these circumstances, another PPP seems inevitable.

The replacement of detailed input specifications by output specifications which set out broad requirements and levels of performance will inevitably mean that private interests and profit-making will squeeze out public need in the design and planning of public facilities. Public and community facilities will become business centres as the private sector seeks to maximise income generation and facilities compete for custom. It is galling for those who have long argued for community and multi-use of public facilities that it is suddenly 'public' policy but on business terms controlled and operated by the private sector.

Although the government has stated that in-house services may be involved in PPPs on grounds of efficiency, the greater the degree of in-house involvement, the less risk is transferred to the private sector. This means other risks will have to be transferred. Since PPPs are not limited to new building, contractors can take over services in other buildings on the same or other sites and the subsequent loss of work is likely to lead to the closure or sale of DSOs. PPP consortia will be well placed to asset strip public sector in-house support service organisations across a city in the process of building their own facilities management operation. The PFI also means that new/improved facilities are privately operated leaving the older ones under public control. Thus a process of marginalisation is set in train with ever increasing disparity between the two sectors.

Partnerships will accelerate marketisation and privatisation, creating an owner-operator industry which finances, builds, manages and operates the urban, transport and welfare state infrastructure. The construction company-led PPP consortia of the 2000s could be replaced by consortia dominated by financial institutions and private education, health and social service firms which could merge with facilities management firms to provide a 'holistic' service (again). The more profitable PPPs will attract takeovers from other partnership consortia – the previous Conservative government was keen to encourage a secondary market in consortia. Those that struggle financially will also be subject to sale as parent companies seek to minimise losses. Public bodies will eventually have several PPPs operated by different consortia and contract rationalisation will inevitably take place. Ultimately, they enable the private sector to achieve economies of scale by merging projects across sectors. For example, a city which has three hospital projects, a portfolio of PPP school projects, several local housing companies, leisure, road and government agency projects will experience rationalisation and job losses.

Secondary trading in projects will reinforce the power of capital over the rentier state and will have profound implications for services and democratic accountability. Schools and hospitals will be traded like other commodities. Further and higher education mergers could lead to the vertical integration of secondary schools and the creation of one-stop-shop education. This would not only provide a feeder system but also a satellite system of local or community 'educational centres' which could provide facilities for lifelong learning. Colleges and universities are organisational 'hybrids', part public, part commercial companies which could readily participate in consortia.

The PPP process is devoid of democratic accountability to users and staff, commercial confidentiality is used to prevent the release of contractual terms and conditions, the full evaluation of public sector alternatives and equalities matter is absent from government PPP guidance (Association of Direct Labour Organisations, 1999).

There has been an erosion, or redefinition, of the 'public interest'. In a climate of 'partnership' with a general political consensus about the role of private capital in the economy, policies and projects are approved with fewer fundamental questions being asked. Projects are 'assumed' to be in the public interest, or if private gain is transparent, it is approved because the public sector is getting something it needs. 'Planning gain' has been reduced merely to access to capital with no additional public benefit other than that which would otherwise have been provided by the public sector.

A new age of corruption and sleaze seems inevitable with a plethora of partnerships, joint ventures and non-accountable quasi-public organisations responsible for large sums of public and private money, despite the efforts of government to develop new codes of conduct. The key stages of the PPP process are negotiated between client and preferred consortia and advisers at meetings which take place behind closed doors under a blanket of 'commercial confidentiality'.

THE EFFECT ON STATE CAPACITY

The final section of this chapter assesses the overall effect of transformation on the capacity of the state. It is important to distinguish between fundamental transformational change and that which is a consequence of political choice. For example, has government merely lost the political will to regulate or has it lost the capacity to regulate? Do cuts in public spending reflect political decisions or has the state lost some of its power to tax and spend? Does the marginalisation of equalities and social justice reflect political choice or reduced technical capacity to implement policy change?

Retreat of the State?

It is claimed that recent changes in the role of the state represent a new paradigm, a new pattern of government. The Right make sweeping statements about the 'death' of the current model of government and the attraction of new models. 'The government-political complex, constructed over the last century, is destined inevitably for the ash heap of history' (Pinkerton, 1995, p. 9) and 'the state as an owner and deliverer of services and infrastructure is, by common consent, an antiquated concept. It places excessive demands on our economic wellbeing' (Arnold-Forster et al., p. 1). The Right believes that the state should be responsible for only certain minimal functions, carried out by private firms or the third sector. They reject the 'reinvention' of public management, instead advocating privati-sation, large budget cuts and the transfer of activities to the community. 'Only the third pillar of society, families, friends, associations, charities and the like, can provide the sort of guidance, dedicated caring, and support that can effectively deal with people's non-material needs' (Eggers and O'Leary, 1995, p. 71).

Others perceive that

> it is now self-evident that the role of the state as the provider of a wide range of public services rooted in the promise of dramatically evening up the life chances of individuals and populations is coming to an end. In education, housing, social services and social security support, the state is rapidly drawing back from previous levels of commitment, and even in the field of health care, the most supposedly inviolable part of the 'welfare state', the same story can be told. (Leonard, 1997, p. 1)

Direct state intervention in firms and industries to prevent job loss and to achieve social objectives during the 1970s was discredited by neo-liberalism. The state has limited power to prevent closures, particularly in sectors suffering world overproduction, when they are often rooted in over-ambitious or poor business decision-making rather than the search for low wage locations. Policies to promote inward investment often lead to increased state intervention, not in the affairs of the company, but in creating the conditions and financial climate within which the company can operate. International competition has enabled business to be more selective in its locational decisions and to make more comprehensive infrastructural demands. Sometimes referred to as 'hard' and 'soft' infrastructure, they can be more accurately categorised as the *financial* (taxation, property taxes, subsidies and grants), *operational* (market regulations, labour skills, governance structures, outsourcing contracts), forming part of the corporate-welfare complex described in Chapter 5, and *transport and communications infrastructures* (including information superhighways and networks). Their provision intensifies competition between cities, regions and states and conflicts in resource allocation between business and community needs in state and regional planning.

The nature of state intervention has changed from preventing closures and supporting sectors to providing a financial and operational infrastructure. To some extent intervention has widened and deepened through regulatory regimes, restructuring markets and marketising the state to create new opportunities for capital accumulation. The creation of a shadow state as a half-way house between direct provision and full privatisation is another component. Infrastructure and services are usually a local responsibility and local government bears the brunt of the social and economic costs of closures and market failures. In developing countries the local/regional state also has to accommodate rapid urbanisation. Clearly, the role of the state is being redefined and it is evident that regionalisation and globalisation lead to states adopting common policies and practices.

Has there been a change in the state's capacity to act at national, regional and international levels? The parameters within which economic policy is formed have narrowed – both the international financial markets and membership of regional trading blocs, particularly the legally binding framework of the EU and NAFTA, have narrowed the range of policy options and nation states have ceded some powers to act unilaterally. Nation states have less power in determining their monetary and exchange rate policies and must take recognisance of other states in setting regulatory regimes. However, the loss of power is at least partially compensated for by increased collective power gained from being within the 'union' or alliance and the powers gained by applying regulations which would otherwise not apply, for example, the application of the European Acquired Rights Directive which protects employees in transfers between employers.

Has there been any decrease or increase in the functions and responsibilities of the state? Strange assesses the role of the state using ten functions or responsibilities of the state, namely defending national territory, maintaining the value of the currency, choosing the appropriate form of capitalist development, correcting the tendency of market economies to cyclical booms and slumps, providing a safety net for the poor, responsibility for taxation, control over foreign trade, building the economic infrastructure, creating competitive national markets and maintaining a monopoly on the use of state power (see Chapter 8). She asserts that the state is undergoing a metamorphosis and that 'the domain of state authority in society and economy is shrinking and/or that what were once domains of authority exclusive to state authority are now being shared with other loci or sources of authority' (Strange, 1996, p. 82).

Devolving managerial power has been based on disaggregating and splitting government into smaller units and agencies to carry out specific tasks with increased managerial autonomy but within an increasingly centralised policy framework. As state capacity to act externally has reduced, it has centralised power internally. Business has increased penetration of the state apparatus through tendering, PPPs and copying private sector organisational structures and business practices. As the private sector increases its ownership and control of the urban infrastructure, the state is relegated into ensuring the provision of a business friendly financial and operational infrastructure (see Chapter 1). The separation of purchaser–provider functions, the establishment of agencies and transfer of services to arm's-length companies, partnerships and quangos have reduced and fractured lines of accountability.

The retreat from direct provision and the switch to regulation reduces the capability of the state in the longer term, primarily through the loss of technical, managerial and operational expertise. It becomes more reliant on external advisers and consultants. Ironically, the marketisation of government services makes the state, at least temporarily, more powerful in controlling business access to this vast outsourcing market. In the longer term, the state is increasingly under the control of business interests.

Has state capacity to regulate, intervene in economic and social affairs, to collect and redistribute taxation, to act in and against the market and to negotiate with transnationals changed? The cumulative impact of transformation has increased inequality, social polarisation and unemployment and reduced the 'ability' of the state to deal with the social and economic impact of globalisation. For the unemployed, single mothers, the disabled and those taking action against government or corporate policies, the state has increased its power of intervention and surveillance. In general, trade unions are a less powerful force and community development resources for civil society are focused on specific regeneration programmes.

Transformation has weakened the state's ability to regulate and control multinational companies, to deal effectively with the social and economic consequences of internationalisation, to create an infrastructure and climate to enhance the competitiveness of manufacturing and service sectors. It has weakened its ability to provide adequate protection and support to workers and trade unions in protecting the quality of working life and building international organisations. It is wrong to assume that the power of regulation is the same as the power of provision and that the state can retain its power through regulation rather than provision. It cannot have the same control over staffing, pay and conditions, quality of service, social criteria and equalities if it is not a direct provider of services.

The core functions of the state are being redirected in the interests of corporate welfare to maintain legal and regulatory frameworks essential for markets to operate and to maintain the conditions for capital accumulation. Deregulation is a policy which

> releases the strategies of large enterprises from the constraints which states' policies can otherwise represent. However, the facts show that these independent strategies of private firms do not form a coherent ensemble guaranteeing the stability of a new order. On the contrary, they create chaos and by their very nature reveal the vulnerability of the globalisation process, which may be thrown into doubt in consequence. (Amin, 1996, p. 231)

Whilst there are constraints on states imposed by international money markets and regional bodies such as Europe's Maastricht convergence criteria, states still have considerable powers over how they tax and spend. For example, an analysis of tax changes in Britain between 1996/7 and 2001/2 revealed an overall increase in the tax burden equivalent to 8 pence on the basic rate of income tax, currently 22p (3.5p from Tory measures and 4.2p from Labour's tax changes covering a range of income, corporate, welfare and consumers' taxes). It excludes one-off taxes such as Labour's £5 billion windfall tax on privatised utilities (Chantrey Vellacott DFK, 1999).

Have there been changes within the power structure of the state, between central and local government? Functions and power have been restructured between central and local government and between local government and quangos. However, privatisation of the welfare state could fundamentally change this position, speeding up globalisation as government services are opened to transnational capital and increasingly integrated into the global economy. There is a danger of the state being left with the 'poisoned chalice' (Peters,1996, p. 1), the intractable issues, and used as a last resort for the insolvable problems and those for which capital cannot make a sufficient rate of return. Centralisation, privatisation and the transfer of key interventionist activities such as regeneration, training and economic development to quangos and agencies has meant local authorities have less direct control. *Has there been any change in the way and extent to which the state represents the interests of particular groups or sectors (classes, organisations, interests)?* Marketisation, privatisation and partnerships have increased the power and influence of business in general, particularly multinational financial and service companies, in public policy and service delivery. However, it is important not to overstate this. It is more of a transitory, half-fledged power gain because the real power shift will only occur when companies have sufficient market share to be able to dictate prices and conditions.

Various analyses have concluded that the nation state is in retreat (Strange, 1996), withering away, is being hollowed out (Jessop, 1994), becoming catalytic (Weiss, 1998), or coming to an end because of the emergence of the borderless global economy (Ohmae, 1995). The world's most powerful nation state, the USA, is certainly not in retreat. The Washington Consensus ensures continued US hegemony. Nor are the other major industrialised nation states in retreat or withering away, although regions and cities within these states have more difficulty attracting and maintaining their industrial and commercial base. Many of these states have not 'lost' power but have chosen not to exercise it for political and ideological reasons. In contrast, the world's 46 least developed economies have been buffeted by globalisation, have been forced to privatise and deregulate on condition of World Bank/IMF structural adjustment loans, yet remain starved of investment.

> The thesis of the 'impotence of the state' is, then, not so much an observation of fact as a self-fulfilling prophesy. A state that acts strictly according to the rules dictated by neo-liberal ideology and the International Monetary Fund does in fact become impotent. (Kagarlitsky, 1999, p. 297)

SUMMARY

Globalisation of the world economy has imposed new demands on the state. A strong state is essential in sustaining global and regional economies and in maintaining civil society. However, because global governance is in its infancy, the state will remain the centre of governance. Increasing attention must, therefore, be paid to the means of improving democratic accountability at all levels. What happens in practice will be determined by power struggles between nation states, international bodies, transnationals in the finance, service and manufacturing sectors, trade unions and civil society organisations.

There is no evidence that transformation has been cost effective and saved public money over and above what could be reasonably expected from efficiency and productivity improvements. In fact, evidence shows that some core elements of transformation such as competitive tendering have been a substantial cost to taxpayers.

Furthermore, new problems are emerging including the control and coordination of a disparate range of agencies, contractors and partnership/joint ventures organisations; inefficiencies arising from contracting and moves to develop longer term relationships – limitations of outcomes finally realised that many aspects of public services cannot be measured; increasing fraud and corruption due to deregulation; problems trying to regulate markets and global contractors and monopoly control of some public services.

Constantly challenging the affordability and effectiveness of the welfare state undermines public confidence in its ability to meet future needs, lowers expectations and drives people into making individual choices through insurance and savings schemes. This duopoly reinforces demands for lower taxes. Yet it is the state, not business, which is held responsible for increasing inequality, system failures and unemployment.

7

The Nation State in 2020

If the twentieth century concludes 'the end of big government' era, what form of government will take its place? What will a minimalist or partnership state mean in practice, or are they different versions of the same model, simply relabelled according to political taste? What is the future of the performance management model of government promoted by Britain, the USA and the OECD? This chapter examines socioeconomic forecasts and predictions of the world economy and assesses the effects of three models of government which could develop as a result of the continuation of current policies. The purpose is not to 'think the unthinkable' but to examine the longer term impact of a 'minimalist', 'partnership' and 'enabling' government. They are not fantasy models or outrageously futuristic ideas but rooted in today's policies and practices.

The promotion of public/private partnerships and private finance has excluded any substantive analysis of the longer term consequences for public services and the welfare state. The 'supremacy' of marketisation is accompanied by constant criticism of, and a loss of vision for, a socialised welfare state. It has led to the virtual abandonment of forecasting the economic and social consequences of public policy, in contrast to economic initiatives. Thus there is little discussion concerning the shape, form and function of alternative state models.

Scenario modelling of world and corporate futures is practised by international bodies and transnational companies. It usually focuses on a broad sweep of economic, political, social and environmental issues highlighting the major trends, forces and potential future events, drawing up three or four alternative plausible outcomes, thus enabling organisations and companies to improve strategic and resource planning. There is also a growing industry in forecasting the future through science fiction and advertising, visioning a world dominated by technology but marginalising people's visions and ideas for cities, communities and services (see Chapter 9).

Thinking about the future is often one of two extremes. A short-term perspective of three to five years usually means that the agenda is narrowly focused on individual services with little discussion of the wider consequences or the overall picture. On the other hand, people do not identify with long-term 40- or 50-year projections of social and economic change which are beyond their lifetime. The year 2020 was chosen because those in their early twenties today will be in mid life and their children experiencing work, higher education or unemployment. Today's 40-year-olds will be contemplating 'retirement' and those in their early sixties today will be the very elderly in 2020. They are important stages in the life cycle and result in different social and economic needs.

Previous chapters revealed the lack of debate about the 'big idea' of government and the focus on what government should *not* do rather than on how the state could meet social needs in the twenty-first century. 'Enabling' and 'partnership' state forms are discussed and promoted as if they are inevitable. Politicians tend to debate individual policies as if a marketised and privately financed health infrastructure will have no bearing on housing and education or vice versa. At the other extreme are generalised statements about the 'stakeholder state' or posturing how the state could be used to control and regulate transnational capital. Unsubstantiated claims about the cost effectiveness of policies avoids making spending commitments, conceals ignorance of longer term consequences, promotes right-wing causes and avoids description of a deconstructed welfare state which would have little public support.

The imposition of a hybrid form of public/private management is likely to lead to further cycles of privatisation. Short-termism dominates – gaining access to capital today, to be repaid in the future to solve the under-investment crisis caused by yesterday's spending cuts. There are few grand visions (except the Right's privatised world) with policies limited solely by promises of reduced income tax (ignoring increasing consumer taxation) and claims that altruism and redistribution are dead.

NEW WORLD (DIS)ORDER

Predicting the course of political, social and economic change over the next 20 years and forecasting the state of the world and national economy in the year 2020 is extremely difficult! The nature and scale of economic crises, recession, stock market collapse, military, civic and religious wars, food or energy crises, potential nuclear disaster, global environmental catastrophe and/or the resurgence of the Right in one or more industrialised countries, developing countries or regions could have a profound impact on states, institutions and world trade. Increasing economic and political integration will mean that crises will reverberate more quickly and deeply.

The new era perspective is personified by the following statement from the Secretary-General of the OECD introducing the organisation's study, *The World in 2020.*

We stand on the threshold of a 'New Global Age', where all societies have the potential of participating actively in the world economy, where the benefits of liberalised world trade and investment could flow to all people, where the misery and poverty of much of the developing world could become a closed chapter of sad history, no longer a reality of the present. (OECD, 1997e, p. 7).

Is this positive optimism, pure hype or naive nonsense?

The OECD forecasts that the world economy provides a historic coincidence of interests for OECD and non-OECD countries which will improve worldwide welfare. It assesses 'business-as-usual' and 'high performance' models, the latter being achievable if governments move toward global free trade and liberalising international finance and labour markets. Real GDP per capita could be 80 per cent higher in 2020 than in 1995 (270 per cent higher in non-OECD countries) and unemployment rates in Europe could fall to around 5 per cent. Public finances will be under increasing pressure from population growth in non-OECD countries which will account for virtually all the increase in the world population from 5 billion (1990) to 8 billion in 2020. Ageing populations in OECD countries and China and Russia will shrink the labour force, reduce private savings and increase government expenditure for pensions and health care. There will also be a dramatic rise in the number of mega-cities, particularly in Asia. Countries will find it increasingly difficult to maintain their domestic tax base in a globalising economy.

The OECD states that

profoundly new and complex challenges of governance are emerging, with the need to find new balances between the roles of the state and other public and private actors. Changes in governance will be needed to help populations to form realisable expectations for both their economic security and their own responsibilities, if social cohesion and political stability are to be secured. (OECD, 1997f, p. 22)

The analysis focuses almost exclusively on what governments must do, thus understating the role and responsibility of transnational companies and finance capital.

Domestic reforms include strengthening competition, further deregulation of product and services markets, privatisation, more flexible labour markets and reprioritisation of social policies within existing funding levels. In other words, more of the same but applied in OECD and non-OECD countries alike.

In a follow-up study, the OECD predicts a 25-year sustained economic boom if the transition to a knowledge-based society is successful. They predict considerable employment growth through e-commerce and digital networks, a transition from 'jobs' to 'work', a paradigm shift in the structure of public/private institutions with more decentralised, networking enterprises and the emergence of more deeply integrated global markets with leading-edge companies clustered in certain regions and cities (OECD, 1999c).

'Faster, faster', the 'post-industrial revolution' and 'rough neighbours' are three 2015 scenarios developed by the Royal Institute of International Affairs (RIPA, 1996). The first predicts a wave of mergers and acquisitions under intense shareholder pressure in the first decade of the millennium. The pace of innovation and change would lead to high levels of unemployment and a tendency for the 'winner to take all' in industries, regions and nations. Despite chronic demands on welfare, self-help is the dominant ethos. Government labours under the idea of managing a demanding system at minimal cost while investing to maintain national competitiveness. The 'prevailing global ethos is individualistic, aggressively secular, materialist' (ibid.) and some countries experience economic failure leading to internal dissent and repression.

The *post-industrial revolution* rests on the ability to exploit the huge expansion of science, technology, judgement and management ability in local, focused networks across industries and geographical centres of excellence. Knowledge-based infrastructure is a key to success. There are similar but fewer demands on the state than the *faster, faster* scenario. 'Government expends great effort in defining and placing value upon the intangibles which permit clusters to form' (RIPA, 1996, p. 125). This includes investment in science, clean air, safe streets and local policy geared to understand and then create the conditions for the 'exploitation' of abstract knowledge. 'Bipolar politics is a thing of the past' with endlessly changing alliances around complex issues.

In the *rough neighbours* scenario the speed of change is unmanageable, resulting in a protracted period of instability and a vicious spiral of worsening commercial performance in industrialised countries. Unemployment rates of 15 per cent are common and the 'liberalise-privatise prescription is widely applied'. Developing countries are also hit by slow growth but are converging faster on the industrialised world. China dominates the Asian seaboard. Industrialised countries resort to trade barriers and sanctions and a gradual economic revival brings confrontation with developing countries.

> Embedded in huge conurbations in which nothing seems to work, watching the quality of life slip under crime, economic malfunction, corrupt institutions and decaying physical infrastructure, the average inhabitant of the slums of the poor nations would be excused for thinking that everything was getting ineluctably worse. Divided, uncertain, irritable, the world is confronted with a wave of environmental degradation and instability with which it is ill equipped to cope. (RIPA, 1996, p. 130)

In a study of the 'trajectory of the world system 1945–2025', Wallerstein argues that the world revolution of 1968, completed in 1989, involved a process of irreversible shift in collective social psychology. It marked the end of the dream of modernity – not the end of the search for its goals of human liberation and equality, but the end of the faith that the state within the capitalist world-economy could serve as the facilitator and guarantor of steady progress towards achieving these goals. (Wallerstein, 1996, p. 236)

Government cuts in social expenditure are occurring simultaneously with increased demand for social services and women's and ethnic minorities' demands for specifically targeted programmes. Significant cutbacks can only be achieved by hitting middle-class entitlements.

The combination of reduction of middle-strata jobs (by enterprises and by government ...) and the reduction in direct benefits to these middle strata in terms of entitlements would constitute an attack on precisely those elements who have been the political stalwarts of the liberal states of the North, and their major soldiers in the effort to contain the discontent of the lower strata. (Wallerstein, 1996 p. 236)

He suggests that in place of an underlying optimism is acute uncertainty and lingering fear. He cites five major institutional vectors, the militant organisation of groups, police order, military order, welfare and the stability of religious institutions which will be the focus of conflict and chaos out of which may emerge a new order.

While 'the welfare system is in universal contraction' (RIPA, 1996, p. 121) is a common observation by forecasters, little thought is given to the consequences of this policy or to marrying economic forecasts with the ability of the state to respond to social crises, civil strife and/or environmental disasters. Universal contraction of the welfare state alone could lead to strife and conflict and will be central in the terrain of struggle between capital, state and labour up to and beyond 2020.

Changes in the organisation of production and labour as a result of new information and communications technologies (leading to layoffs, social marginalisation and fragmentation of the relationship between work and wages); increased industrialisation of the services sector; enforced mobility and flexibility of labour; and emergence of a new mode of regulation all impact on the powers and functions of the state leading to different political models. One is based on 'liberal internationalism' international bodies such as the UN and WTO supported by the major powers in contrast to a 'new medievalism', a back-to-the-future model of the twenty-first century based on a power shift from hierarchies to networks, from centralised compulsion to voluntary association a sort of 'governance without government' in which the state is marginalised (Slaughter, 1997). Another alternative builds on the growing transgovernmentalism in which the state is desegregating into 'separate functionally distinct parts which form networks of cooperation' (ibid.). While terms such as 'global governance' hint at the possibility of increasing international consensus, the world up until 2020 is more likely to be dominated by increasing regional blocs such as the European Union and NAFTA. National economic and social policies will continue to focus the agenda.

By 2020, people will be living longer, income inequality will have widened between the rich and poor and between those with and without a decent pension (see Chapter 5). The proportion of elderly will be significantly higher in most countries. Changes in living patterns, employment and social trends will influence and shape demands on public services, the welfare state and the role of government in the economy.

The application of information and communications technology could transform public services by improving the integration, coordination and monitoring of services and access to information. IT will be more widely applied in service delivery but it is unlikely to replace frontline human services. Education, health, social services and housing will still rely heavily on a professional personal service. In an age of digitalised, customised and homogenised information, personal service is likely to be more highly valued. Furthermore, IT system failure could be even more damaging and dramatic in the future.

The 2020 State

If we look ahead to the year 2020, one of three models of the state could emerge, assuming the continued transformation of the state described in Chapters 3–5. All three models assume that the nation state will not be extinct. Which model becomes dominant will depend as much on nation state policies as the impact of continued internationalisation and globalisation.

Privatisation continues in the *Corporate or Regulatory State* until most central and local government services are outsourced or privately provided including the core welfare state services. The state funds some residual welfare services but regulation is the prime focus. Transnational companies dominate service delivery and government is essentially a collection of regulatory offices writ large. This is the minimalist or virtual state serving primarily the interests of international capital.

The *Enabling or Partnership State* retains responsibility for most welfare, central and local government services which are provided by a mixture of in-house units, private contractors, independent and voluntary organisations. However, the private sector is deeply embedded in state functions through a myriad of partnerships, joint ventures and contracts. The state is fluid, shapeless, functioning as provider, partner, client, contractor, financier and facilitator.

A *Third Sector State* is promoted as a middle ground between the 'extremes' of the state and the market, an alternative to and as a bulwark against the global economy or endemic corruption in some developing countries. There is a resurgence of mutuality with the state transferring responsibilities to community corporations, non-profit organisations and quasi-public organisations.

The models described below are written in the style of historical analysis in the year 2020.

THE CORPORATE OR MINIMALIST STATE

The corporate or minimalist state is the fulfilment of the Right's vision of minimalist, low tax government. Transformation to the minimalist state has not been smooth. The government continued to privatise public assets while welfare state responsibilities were transferred to individuals. The government has been left with only the unprofitable or uneconomic functions and even these are delivered by private contractors. Private individual provision is the norm for health, education, pensions, social services and for unemployment, sickness and disability through a myriad of insurance and savings schemes promoted by financial institutions. Further deregulation of financial services has led to global portable pensions and insurance products which can be credited and debited anywhere. State pensions and welfare benefits which have declined in real value, are operated from transnational service centres.

Middle- and working-class interests demanded the continuation of basic welfare state services and were opposed to paying the cost of individually financed provision in addition to paying for public provision through taxation. A transition period of dual financing or massive government subsidy was inevitable. The state now finances basic health, housing, education and social services only for the poor, issuing vouchers or credits for use in the private sector. There is little concern about the quality of these services. Queuing or similar negative images provide a visible threat of 'failure'. Conflicts and major confrontations, often resulting in riots and civil disorder, occur from time to time despite intensive surveillance of trade unions and community campaigns opposing government policies or corporate activities.

Transnational contractors dominate the corporate state providing 'cradle to grave' services such as health, education, social care and local environmental services. Takeovers and mergers of privatised utilities and service contractors are common across virtually all services. The rapid internationalisation of the British welfare state and public services opened up a vast market for financial and service companies who have used it as a bridgehead to other European welfare states.

The minimalist state relies heavily on regulatory regimes. Government regulatory offices impose market, price and competition regulations and controls within which the private sector operates. The ability to regulate is tempered by political interests little different from those pertaining in 2000. The state became reliant on the regulatory framework as it withdrew from direct service provision and it is no longer able to establish standards of best practice through in-house provision. Once private interests own, fund and provide services, 'excessive' regulation is continually contested by the corporate sector. The state employs a small staff to monitor, identify needs, enforce regulations and negotiate price reviews which are constantly challenged by the corporate sector on grounds of 'affordability'.

Quality of service is constrained and defined by the contracting system. The regulatory regime sets overall standards but regulators refrain from prescribing frontline service quality, leaving this to local negotiation to 'maintain flexibility' and choice. Demands for deregulation and re-regulation are commonplace. Government intervention in investment decisions is limited to financial and regulatory matters.

The focus has switched from declining levels of government spending to the relative value of the myriad of tax reliefs, allowances, subsidies, vouchers and grants. Inequality has widened. Two-tier provision is common for all basic services. Choice is determined by the ability to pay. Equal opportunities and social justice policies are marginalised and only feature where there is a commercial interest.

Basic rate income tax has been reduced to 15 per cent but the combined cost of insurance and savings schemes, income tax and indirect taxation is, on average, substantially higher than in the old publicly funded welfare state. Budgets are balanced and public spending has declined as a proportion of GDP. But there is increasing concern about the loss of revenue from corporate concessions and tax avoidance.

Local government has been reduced to a skeleton regulatory and monitoring agency. Core policy decisions are taken nationally and regionally and authorities are limited to trying to obtain special status for zones, bids and partnerships. The state's role in civic and cultural matters is limited to coordinating sponsorship and patronage by business interests and organising competitions and lotteries. Most quasi-public bodies have been privatised or wound up after being commercialised and managed by private firms. PPPs and performance management regimes were terminated several years ago as they were replaced by direct private provision and corporate welfare.

Local authorities employ a few policy, client, technical and financial officers but the bulk of work on means testing, issuing and redeeming vouchers is contracted out. It is a 'white collar state' because all manual and support services are delivered by private contractors. Many authorities even contract out monitoring and regulatory work. The government has ceased to influence labour market standards because it directly employs so few staff.

Accountability is determined by contracts and agreements between individuals and the corporate sector, particularly financial companies. Councillors, numerically halved, are mere civic functionaries. Cities are, in practice, run by elected mayors and committees of business people, corporate cities replacing nineteenth-century 'company towns'. Corporate controlled Business Improvement Districts, Service Zones, Leisure and Entertainment

Zones and Secure Housing Villages (private residential compounds controlled by security guards) have seceded from local authority control. They employ their own contractors. Local government budgets cover only small residual welfare services many of which are centrally financed and regulated. The urban infrastructure is privately owned and operated.

Virtually all development and economic initiatives are orchestrated by the private sector. The suburban city has blossomed while inner city areas have continued to decline into a spiral of decay, dwindling resources and weaker city government. Urban spaces and the public domain are also privatised, making industrial and community action more difficult because public protest usually involves trespassing on private property and confronting private security patrols.

Family values and individual responsibility are reinforced by personal financing of education, health and social services. Economic crises place the state's limited welfare role and resources under great strain. The practice of direct appeals to major firms to create local investment zones has provided replacement employment in some regions but at a cost of complete casualisation, flexibility and trade union free zones. Staff are assigned to groups of contracts, not to organisations or particular sectors such as health or local government. Social services and health make use of a large number of volunteers through the government's Social Volunteer Corps, established to engage the unemployed and early retirees in meaningful activity to earn their benefit.

THE ENABLING OR PARTNERSHIP STATE

This model represents two decades of public/private partnerships which have created a labyrinth of joint ventures, companies and contracts. Private firms have a lead role in the design, finance and supply of 'public services', infrastructure projects and welfare state services. The state purchases, facilities and most services are delivered by private contractors or voluntary organisations through 'Best Value' procurement. There is some direct public provision but most in-house contracting organisations have been sold or closed. The enabling role is not a new one, government has always facilitated and supported private and community initiatives. This worked reasonably well until the advent of privatisation and contracting. Initially, enabling was meant to encourage a diversity of technically competent suppliers.

Enabling has had little impact on the government's ability to shape and control market forces but has assisted capital accumulation and provided opportunities for firms to increase market share and profit maximisation from contracting. Those who claimed that an enabling state could still be a 'strong state' by concentrating on strategy and policy, have been proved to be wrong. The enabling model has a built-in contradiction. As enabling becomes more extensive, the core needs to centralise power in order to retain an intelligent client function and to monitor services. However, power is diffused through a plethora of contracts and local government's influence in economic management has withered.

A liberal version of enabling, in which the local state facilitates a wide range of activities in the local economy, promotes civic and cultural activities and 'a concern for anything which is the concern of local people' never materialised because spending cuts and privatisation continually narrowed the remit of the state. Enablers in the 1990s argued that 'if government retains responsibility for ensuring that needs are met, does it matter whether or not services are directly provided? Choice, cost and quality are the crucial considerations' (Institute for Public Policy Research, 1997). Others who argued for a 'hand-in-glove' approach with the private sector delivering public goods (Arnold-Forster et al., 1997) have come to regret their simplistic acceptance of the market mechanism and failure to recognise that choice is irrelevant in the supply of many public services. They believed in a mixed economy approach but transnational companies now dominate all service sectors. Cost savings have not materialised, nor have real quality improvements.

The performance management nirvana predictably declined into monetary management, the audit state was the engine which drove more externalisation, transfers and 'voluntary' competitive tendering. Although public–private partnerships initially extended across all levels of government, they were transitory. The transnational dominated owner-operator industry, created by the private financing of public services since the mid-1990s, is now owned by firms operating globally. The ability of the state to fulfil its obligations by negotiating, monitoring, controlling, regulating and enforcing private capital's partnership responsibilities was constantly questioned.

'Some partnerships have more to do with meeting current fashions in the requirements of Whitehall and Brussels funding regimes than commitment to power sharing and joint decision-making' (Pike, 1997). But what are the longer term implications of power sharing and joint decision-making between the state and private capital? Revenue commitments made in the last 20 years under PPP deals have proved very expensive, forcing deep cuts in other services not protected by contracts. Privately delivered 'public' welfare services have to compete against mainstream private services. The enabling welfare state continues to be financed primarily by taxation. However, government spending only marginally declined as a proportion of GDP primarily because of high transaction costs and the consequences of service and organisational fragmentation.

State intervention in the local economy is limited to enabling or facilitating the private sector and other organisations to provide training, employment and investment. It is purchasing fewer goods and services and employs few staff. Constant reorganising and restructuring of client functions has deskilled government and limited its ability to respond to strategic issues. The state is more akin to a holding company with interests in wholly owned agencies, partial stakes in arm's-length companies and joint ventures. The enabling state has also encouraged community and new quasi-private or 'independent' organisations. Community development corporations are considered an acceptable, indeed exciting, growth potential.

Centralisation has increased as government and private capital have defined the terms of partnership and make it a universal condition of revenue as well as capital spending allocation and grants. Having centralised control, bound and gagged local authorities, stripped them of resources but increased their responsibilities, they are now sufficiently weakened and willing to trade virtually any asset. Rather than maintaining or strengthening the role of the local state, partnership has enabled the private sector to dictate local political agendas. The state's regulatory powers are circumscribed because of its declining economic power linked to declining resources and limited land and property ownership. The right-wing version of the 'contract city' is nearly a reality, in contrast to the 'corporate city' under the preceding model.

In the early years of the millennium most services were delivered by in-house units but continued externalisation has weakened their technical capacity and financial viability. The internal market which permitted both internal and external trading proved to be theoretically and practically unsustainable. The loss of contracts externally resulted in a loss of internal economies of scale, higher unit costs and ultimately further loss of contracts. The tendering system now dominates the management and organisation of the enabling state because it is the prime means of engaging contractors to deliver services and to implement corporate and statutory responsibilities. The enabling state is modelled on commercial organisational models in which services are delivered by internal business units, agencies or joint venture companies. They run on business values and business planning with devolution of decision-making to unit managers who have responsibility for staffing and local pay bargaining.

The enabling or contract state vests more power in the firms and organisations supplying services. Monopoly suppliers are in a powerful position to influence, if not dictate, agendas and policy formulation.

Partnership has created a new market for management consultants and advisers. Local authorities have reduced professional capacity and the creation of separate private sector organisational structures requires all parties to have their own 'advisers' hence the new sector provides a bonanza for lawyers, auditors and accountants, tax advisers and management consultants.

A labyrinth of partnerships, companies and organisations are responsible for services but power rests primarily with corporate partners who own and control facilities. Performance measures and auditing have not prevented growing legal disputes and buck-passing institutionalised as a management prerequisite. Only well-organised user/community organisations with access to independent technical and policy advice are able to lever a degree of participation.

Local governance is exercised through layers or networks of partnerships and companies some covering areas, districts or entire cities or regions.

Democracy appears to be more diffuse but this is only a mirage. Enabling was intended to free local leaders from the pressures of 'managing vast municipal undertakings', to allow them to manage cities and to be innovative. They were to organise and orchestrate but not to deliver services, to concentrate on strategic planning responsibilities, set standards and monitor performance, leaving the 'details' to others. However, managers have exploited the enabling model to increase their control over 'non-strategic' policy matters and implementation, further marginalising elected members. In contrast to the minimalist state, private capital is more enmeshed in local and central government through joint ventures and partnerships. Transnationals have a vested interest in 'capturing' or leveraging power in government bodies and boards to safeguard their interests. Hence there is a constant power struggle with locally elected representatives often being relegated to rubber-stamping deals and channelling limited public resources through the contracting process.

The partnership state was little more than a half-way house on the road to the corporate state. Partnership is thus transitory, particularly in an increasingly centralised state and a weakened local government. It is a partnership of convenience. Partnerships eventually diminish because the private sector only supports them in order to take advantage of development opportunities, service contracts and to gain competitive advantage. As the power of the state weakens, capital balks at taking increasing responsibility for the continuing poverty and inequality and the failure of regeneration and employment policies. It seeks to redefine the terms of partnerships, increase the provision of private services and emphasise the state's responsibility for residualised services. Capital seeks to define the role of the state in terms of corporate welfare, redefining partnerships to maximise surplus value from development and services.

Cities are run as company towns, all key decisions are taken by boards and partnerships dominated by private business leaders. Most city centres are now entirely privately owned. The ability of the Partnership State to respond to economic crises is severely constrained by contracts and the vested interests of partners.

The audit explosion of 2000–10 still lingers on but public bodies now focus almost exclusively on policy coordination and arbitrate in disputes between contractors, partners and agencies. Vestiges of public sector trade unionism remain but local bargaining across a plethora of contracts, joint ventures and organisations consumes resources and energies and unions focus exclusively on disciplinary, grievance, legal and financial issues. The fragmented state is mirrored in fragmented trade union organisation where resources are channelled into negotiating staff transfers between employers.

THE THIRD SECTOR OR SOCIAL ECONOMY STATE

The third sector or social state was promoted as a feasible alternative to state and private sector provision. The trend towards demutualisation of non-profit organisations was reversed in 2005 when legislation guaranteed the rebirth of non-profits and volunteering. New social enterprises became key service providers, minimising the 'negative' aspects of state and private provision by harnessing the developmental and innovative aspects of the social sector as a viable non-profit alternative to the privatisation of the welfare state. Self-care and self-regulation were encouraged, the state transferred community care to local organisations, volunteers and unpaid carers under the guise of efficiency and post-Fordist rhetoric about locally-designed-flexibly-provided services. The third sector was perceived as a potential bulwark against the global economy by establishing local control, avoidance of global markets and a means of making social planning and environmental sustainability a practical reality.

The concept of a third sector or social state also gained ground in response to public sector spending cuts, profit maximising big business and fresh attempts to promote 'community' values. The 'social economy' was also promoted as a means of generating new jobs in Europe in the late 1990s when private firms were shedding jobs and governments cutting public spending. It was hoped that the social sector could provide the link between growing unmet needs and rising numbers of people needing work. But encouraging 'social entrepreneurs' and 'turning clients into owners', supporting cooperatives or issuing vouchers to users to purchase services from social providers did not create a thriving third sector. Initially, the fragmentation of this sector stemmed the tide of privatisation and marketisation. However, economies of scale and market forces pushed many local third sector organisations into regional and national mergers, in part replicating the 'old' welfare state.

The social economy consists primarily of non-profit organisations, cooperatives or companies which deliver services on behalf of the state. They range from newly established state boards or national non-profit bodies with regional and local structures, to local charitable bodies, community enterprises, public sector arm's-length companies and social non-profit organisations. The defining characteristic is the non-profit objective and 'community' control although much of the infrastructure is owned by local government and private firms.

The classification of a non-profit sector is misleading. Voluntary bodies have been described as 'self-governing private organisations, not dedicated to distributing profits to shareholders or directors, pursuing public purposes outside the formal apparatus of the state' (Salamon, 1987). Although they do not extract profit from development and management activities, they do not challenge or reduce the extraction of profit from landownership, design, construction, repair and maintenance and the supply of goods and other services. They also depend heavily on government funding and subsidies. They are not an alternative to public services, but a replacement.

Advocates of the third force or sector believed that it could be built up without threatening the existing public sector, and indeed, could be developed in alliance with it. They also believed that it could remain an 'independent' self-contained sector largely unaffected by either the pressures within the public sector such as privatisation, deregulation and commercialisation or the globalisation of services. A 'social economy' is not static and the pressure to achieve economies of scale, together with the forces that drive expansionary ambitions, have led to takeovers and mergers both within the social sector and by private firms.

The ability of a third non-profit sector to operate in an increasingly globalised economy and form a bulwark against transnational companies was never realisable. The third sector model requires a strong state to provide a regulatory ringfenced regime and a degree of protection and support. This proved inadequate to control mergers and takeovers and safeguard 'community' and local interests from predatory business interests. Multinational companies refused to relinquish their interest in services and encircled community organisations pressurising and searching for contracts. Some community service providers have only avoided financial collapse by accepting state funded audit management or takeover by quasi-public bodies.

Locally controlled trusts and non-profit companies established by the state to hive off services and restructure employment policies were originally part of the social economy although most have become highly commercialised or were sold to transnational companies to minimise further spending cuts in 2008.

Of the three models, this is the only one in which equal opportunities and social justice has a high priority. There are many more opportunities for women, ethnic minorities, gay and disabled people to develop their own services and have stronger representation on the boards of social providers.

There is limited competition for contracts between voluntary bodies. Many service agreements between government and voluntary bodies have ossified and the regulatory regime considerably weakened. Voluntary organisations have become economically dependent on government contracts and have often colluded with local government to reduce monitoring, negotiate contract renewals and reduce procedures for democratic accountability in order to cut costs.

By the late 1990s, Britain was a classic example of an expanding third sector or social economy. Housing associations were launched into a new role by a Labour government in 1974, public money was systematically switched from local government to housing associations and two decades later they were the main providers of new 'social' housing and rehabilitation. Hence growth of the the third sector has been axiomatic with the decline of public sector provision.

Employment in the third sector state is distributed across a range of national, regional and local social and community non-profit companies and organisations. Local authorities have become holding companies for a range of public sector arm's-length boards, trusts or companies set up primarily to restructure staffing levels, working practices and employment policies. The voluntary sector's chequered employer record continued and it failed to fundamentally challenge the prevailing pattern of social relations both as a service provider and as an employer. Employment terms and conditions have never matched those in the public sector in the 1990s.

The social economy resulted in more people being active in local organisations. However, a truly participative civil society has proved elusive. Most organisations continue to operate with a handful of key activists. While people are concerned about the availability and quality of services, their lifestyles and jobs limit the time they are willing and able to be personally involved in policy formulation, let alone managing service provision. The fragility of democratic control within community organisations has proved problematic. The problems of bureaucracy have been replaced by problems of coordination and democratic accountability, mirroring those associated with quangos. As local government became weaker, so has its ability to arbitrate conflict between social entrepreneurs, community non-profits, private firms and user and trade union organisations. There is little evidence to show that users and staff are more empowered in social organisations than in the 1990s.

Only a few community organisations delivering services have been able to maintain their core values and achieve economies of scale. Most have been taken over by larger organisations with commercial operational systems. Achieving innovation in relatively small-scale programmes is one thing but it is very difficult to achieve when an organisation is responsible for a myriad of services through a network of providers. Democratic and financial accountability have been major issues.

Decentralisation and devolution have been exploited by some religious, political and ethnic interests to impose socially and politically repressive local regimes. This has resulted in a number of major community conflicts.

The development of the social economy through a wide range of national and local non-profit organisations, boards and companies required a radical shift in government policy and a resurgence of community action which was not forthcoming. Although there were important regeneration initiatives and development trusts which could have set a template, most partnerships were designed by, and on terms acceptable to, private capital. Many promoters of the social economy had a romantic vision which failed to take account of trends in the world economy and the interests of transnational companies. They demonstrated a degree of political naivety about the sustainability of alternatives within a capitalist economy and differentiating change which required more fundamental political, social and economic change. Islands of community control exist on a greater scale than they did in the late 1990s but they remain fragmented. Community organisations, local projects, national and local voluntary organisations have an important role in local affairs. But this is markedly different from promoting the sector as a key provider of services or even as an equal partner with the state and private sector.

OTHER MODELS

References to other state models such as the Stakeholder, Evaluative or Audit State describe only one aspect of a 'model' which can readily be ascribed to any of the three models discussed above. The Stakeholder State promotes social responsibility through corporate governance with workplace cooperation and employee share ownership. It provides people with 'stakes' including transferable skills, ownership rights – 'which empower individuals within markets and the broader civil society by enabling them to be self-reliant and enterprising', together with long-term relationships of trust and political rights. For example, individuals have their own pension fund accounts, share stakes, savings and insurance schemes. They gain access to economic and social capital but there are few strategies and policies to enable the poor, homeless and unemployed to acquire 'stakes'.

Stakeholding is closely linked to the communitarian agenda of decentralisation, friendly societies and voluntary action and the replacement of state welfare by community support and responsibility, fitting neatly into the third sector state model. Equally, employee share ownership and private pension stakeholding could also be part of the corporate state model.

SUMMARY

Do any of these models provide a suitable framework for the nation state in 2020? The corporate model assumes a new capital–labour settlement entirely in the interests of capital. The enabling or partnership state is not sustainable because corporate interests become increasingly powerful and ensure that the state is further marginalised and a corporate/minimalist model is imposed. The third sector is likely to expand in the short term, particularly as a result of privatisation and externalisation of local services to non-profit organisations, but the powerful vested interests of transnationals will inevitably ensure that a thriving third sector never materialises in a capitalist economy.

The organisational and political strength of 'new social movements' has been greatly exaggerated. All three models will eventually force fundamental changes in taxation and public spending. There will be an appreciable shift in the composition of public spending with a rapid reduction in the minimalist state and its replacement with tax reliefs, allowances, vouchers and grants. Both corporate and consumer interests will focus on the relative value and purchasing power of tax reliefs and vouchers rather than the level of public spending. Transaction, regulatory, monitoring and administrative costs will rise because rigorous and effective regulation cannot be obtained cheaply.

None of these models is inevitable. They are planned to the extent that decisions are made to foster their growth and development, some vested interests are enhanced at the expense of others, the apparatus of the state nurtures and facilitates the process, and those involved have a common ideology although there may be disagreements on detail. The idea that globalisation is merely an economic process which inevitably means the end of the nation state is arrant nonsense. There are public choices and there are different interests which are being protected, promoted or suppressed. None of the three models has been 'designed' for a global economy and little thought has been given to whether one particular model or another will enhance, protect or weaken the power of state governance in a global economy.

There are choices. Just as the welfare state was a post-war 'settlement' with capital, so the new state form for the twenty-first century must be the basis of a new struggle and settlement. The rest of this book focuses on developing a model of the nation state for the twenty-first century.

8

Redesigning the State – New Public Order

We return to the global corporate agenda discussed in the Introduction. Previous chapters have demonstrated the need to counter the privatisation of power by international bodies and multinational corporations, the emergence of a corporate-welfare complex and the marketisation and privatisation of public services. Chapters 2–7 provided clear evidence that neo-liberalism and the Third-Way reduce the capacity of the nation state to manage the macro-economy, provide public goods, reduce poverty and to promote human development. Neo-liberal/Third Way policies transform rather than dismantle the state and seek to shift power within the state away from democratic control and the influence of civil society and trade union action, towards centrally controlled state and business-led quasi-public organisations.

The drive towards the corporate or enabling state model and the centralisation of power can only be countered by challenging the fundamental core values and rationale of the capitalist economy, by promoting alternative progressive public policies and by redesigning the state.

The first part of this chapter examines the scope for redesigning the state in a capitalist global economy. It discusses the core functions of the state and sets out a ten-point plan to increase state capacity and create a new public order. How the state is managed is equally important, and this is the subject of Chapter 9.

THE STATE IN CAPITALIST SOCIETY

The Introduction of this book described how the state plays a crucial role in maintaining the conditions for the means of production, distribution, communication and exchange. It creates and maintains the conditions for capital accumulation by providing the economic and transport infrastructure, macroeconomic policies, labour market regulation, taxation, law and order and the maintenance and control of a healthy, educated workforce. It ameliorates the effects and social costs of accumulation and globalisation through the provision of welfare services and benefits and promotes international competitiveness of indigenous capital and economic development to attract inward investment. The state, however, is not benign, its form and role are determined by economic and social relations and it has an ideological and control function in maintaining the hegemony of the capitalist economy. State power is frequently abused to curtail civil rights and democracy. The state, sometimes authoritarian, oppressive, collusive and/or corrupt, is often used as an instrument of nationalism and protectionism (Miliband, 1994).

Throughout this book I have discussed the state, capital, labour and civil society, not as separate sectors or categories but as social relations and power struggles. There are conflicts and contradictions in the way that the state creates the conditions for capital accumulation and the reproduction of labour. For example, capital seeks to minimise its share of the cost of reproduction by minimising taxation but also seeks new markets and opportunities for capital accumulation through contracts with the state to deliver public services.

The Scope for Progressive Policies

I have not set out to articulate a socialist or utopian concept of the state but to argue for what is possible now within the constraints of a capitalist economy. Nor am I proposing a comprehensive alternative economic strategy although the proposals in the next two chapters would clearly be part of such a strategy. The primary focus is how to develop a new public order.

A strategy to increase state capacity alone is not a feasible option. It must be accompanied by a fundamental challenge to the values, rationality and operational mode of the capitalist economic system (Panitch, 1994). It must expose the narrow commercial scope of business and the inadequacy of business social responsibility. These challenges must target those parts of the capitalist economy which the system cannot or is unwilling to fulfil, such as genuine democratic accountability, equity and sustainability and which consolidate the values of an alternative socialist system.

There is considerable scope for progressive policies:

- Nation states will remain powerful for the foreseeable future. States individually (and collectively within the European Union and regional groups) can adopt policies and take independent action although it is sometimes proscribed by international treaties and pacts. The economic, social, political and environmental conditions of countries vary widely with different constitutions, laws and traditions. Hence there is no universal model of the state, nor is there a single approach to reform.
- The speed and form of globalisation is not inevitable, nor does it have to take a neo-liberal form. Changes to state policies on private infrastructure, marketisation and privatisation coupled with controls on financial capital would slow the globalisation process (see Chapters 1 and 2).

- Equity and equalities, environmental sustainability, public service ethos and the quality of human development must take precedence over economic growth.
- A distinct public sector and public service ethos is essential to meet social need and to provide a barrier to rampant marketisation and privatisation. There is considerable scope to decommodify many of the services and functions already marketised and privatised (Chapters 3 and 4).
- Public Service Management provides a clear alternative to the managerial state which is being created by the transfer of state services to 'depoliticised' quasi-public bodies and the marketisation and privatisation of public goods.
- A progressive approach must focus on the power struggles between state, capital, labour and civil society.
- It is essential to oppose and to try to contain the corporate-welfare complex (see below).
- The partnership with business mania can and must be stopped. A 'strategic partnership' role for the state is not a viable option for a state which has been asset stripped, deskilled, resource starved and is reliant on competitive performance management to supply services. Creating a 'partnership with capital' has spread like a virus among international organisations such as the UN, UNDP and World Bank, national and local governments. It is sold on the grounds that it combines the strengths of both sectors in a win-win scenario, but the reality is somewhat different.

Challenging the Corporate-Welfare Complex

The centrality of the state in retaining, maintaining and extending the corporate-welfare complex was discussed in Chapter 5. So how can the redesign of the state challenge the corporate-welfare complex when the state itself is an integral part of the complex? This can be addressed in a number of ways.

First, by embedding the principles and values, democratic accountability and Social Justice Planning and Auditing (see Chapter 9) and other aspects of Public Service Management to provide an alternative framework for public organisations.

Second, stop all further marketisation of public services, press for radical change at the WTO and commence a review of all contracts with the private and voluntary sectors with the intent to renegotiate or return to direct provision. In addition, campaign for the expansion of a publicly financed and provided welfare state (health, education, housing, social services, pensions and income support) based on taxation and employer/employee social security contributions.

Third, introduce a requirement for full disclosure and transparency of all public support, aid, grants, loans and other financial or in-kind support to the private and voluntary sectors. All public organisations should be required to amend accounting systems and financial information to facilitate such regular public disclosure. The state already intervenes in the economy although redesign will require wider and deeper intervention.

Fourth, civil society and trade unions should constantly investigate local power structures including the role of companies, business organisations and elites in the decision-making process. They should also demand that any support to the private and voluntary sectors be subject to detailed scrutiny, transparency, democratic accountability, monitoring and enforcement of conditions.

Finally, the claim that the providers of services, staff and trade unions, have 'captured' services which are run in their interests, must be constantly challenged.

THE CORE FUNCTIONS OF THE STATE

International organisations and most nation states subscribe to human and social objectives and needs which are, in effect, the fundamental principles which underpin policy objectives. The huge gulf between rhetoric and reality has already been noted. The principles encompass dignity and self-determination for individuals, families and communities; maintenance of a standard of living with guarantees to food, clothing, housing and medical care to ensure participation in the economy and civil society; opportunities for all, irrespective of race, gender, age or religion, to education, training and employment; a fair distribution of wealth and resources; and understanding and respect for cultural diversity (based on Kelsey, 1995).

An economistic approach to meeting these needs limits the state to the allocation of resources, the redistribution of income and provision of a minimum safety net, the provision (although not necessarily the production) of public goods, the promotion of growth and employment and the stabilisation of economic activity. Rules, regulations and intervention are put in place to help expand the role of the market (Tanzi, 2000). The severe limits of reliance on market forces and minimal state intervention have been highlighted in earlier chapters.

A political economy approach is based on meeting social, equity, democratic, environmental and economic objectives. In this model the state has five core functions: democratic and civil society, national and international responsibilities, human needs and development, economic and fiscal management and the regulation of markets, firms and organisations (see Figure 8.1). A range of other functions, activities and services are grouped under each core function, none of which are in any order of priority.

Figure 8.1: **The core functions of the state**

Democratic and civil society
Enhance democracy and public accountability
Civil rights and freedom of information
Justice and penal system
Enhance capacity of civil society
Promote the arts, culture and heritage

National and international responsibilities
Global, regional and national policy-making
Macro economic, infrastructure and transport planning
Foreign relations
Defence and security
Protect and sustain the environment

Human needs and development
Education and learning
Public health, health and social care
Shelter and housing
Income support
Poverty reduction and social inclusion
Equalities and social justice
Identify and quantify social and economic needs
Promoting the social economy

Economic and fiscal management
Tax regulation and collection
Managing public expenditure
Investment in infrastructure
Redistribution
Regional, urban and rural planning and development control
Job creation and training
Regeneration of communities
Manage public assets effectively
Research, development and innovation

Regulation of markets, firms and organisations
Regulation of and intervention in markets
Property, land and intellectual property rights
Regulation of the labour market
Regulation of corporate sector
Regulation of public sector, social & voluntary sectors
Regulation planning, development and the environment

Increasing State Capacity

The capacity of the state to fulfil these functions is dependent on a number of factors. The state constitution, laws and regulations and those imposed by international agreements, such as the European Union's Maastricht Stability and Growth Pact, must enable the state to take different forms of action in pursuance of implementation. The state must have the autonomy to develop its own policies or persuade international partners to act jointly, adequate resources, the power to implement policies and to overcome the complexity of socioeconomic conditions and opposition from vested interests.

There are different types of capacity ranging from leadership, governance and accountability in which democratic objectives are mainstreamed in all public organisations both ideologically and practically by creating the time, resources and structures for genuine involvement in community and workplace decision-making. Economic management is dependent in part on having more control over the flows of capital and trade. Weiss focused on the 'transformative' capacity of the state 'to devise and implement policies that *augment* a society's investible surplus, as opposed to merely *redistributing* existing resources' (Weiss, 1998, p. 5; emphasis in original). She claims that the ability of the state to improve and transform the industrial economy is the most important type of state capacity for the nation state in a globalising economy. However, the ability to transform public services and the welfare state is equally important. The preparation of meaningful city, rural and regeneration plans, coordination of different agencies and organisations in the development process and the management of projects from design to completion are other examples of institutional capacity required by the state. The different types of state capacity are summarised in Table 8.1.

The quality of public organisations is another aspect of state capacity. This is dependent on the resources available to the state, the degree of integration and coordination between public sector organisations, the legitimacy and power of intervention and enforcement, the public management system and availability of skilled staff and the capability for innovation transfer and reorganisation. These qualitative factors are also dependent on the capacity and quality of the private and voluntary sectors (the quality of corporate governance and the level of fraud and corruption are key factors). The quality of democratic accountability and the rights and freedom of civil society and labour to organise, represent and take action also affect the quality of state capacity. All these factors determine the overall effectiveness of the state.

It is increasingly argued that the modern state must focus on 'strategic partnership' as a means of strengthening public control and influence. Yet a state whose assets are in freefall provides fewer, more restricted services which it directly delivers only at the margins, is likely to have reduced capacity, particularly when inequality is widening and poverty is increasing. Can a strategic partnership enforce the private sector to deliver democratic accountability, redistribution, poverty reduction, equity and environmen-

Table 8.1: **Different types of state capacity**

Different types of capacity
Leadership
Governance and accountability
Power to legislate
Develop strategies and policies
Investment
Economic management
Sustainability
Redistribution
Planning
Project management
Coordination
Development
Innovation and redesign
Management
Regulation and control
Security
Administration

tal sustainability? And once services are outsourced, will the private sector tolerate British-style Best Value performance management systems with layers of state inspection?

In the longer term, partnerships extend marketisation and privatisation and increase private control and influence in public sector decision-making. They enable the private sector to embed itself (values, priorities and vested interests) within public organisations. The claim that strategic partnerships empower the state to dictate terms and conditions of the private sector's engagement is indicative of political naivety and management practice devoid of public service ethos and principles.

Public bodies are forced to take equal account of the private 'partner' in the decision-making process and they provide capital with more direct access to the different forms of corporate welfare. They enable capital to carve out an increasing role in the development/regeneration process, infrastructure, services and functions which in turn further reduces state capacity as it is deskilled and stripped of its ability to produce public goods. Partnerships soon become a necessity to carry out all but the simple and basic tasks (see transformation process in Chapter 3). Partnership weakens, not strengthens the state.

Simply increasing the capacity of the state is not enough because enhanced state power will be used to protect the interests of capital, particularly multinational firms, and to contain and control political, civil society and labour opposition. Increasing capacity must be developed in parallel with democratic accountability, civil society and labour involvement, the principles and practice of Public Service Management and other measures discussed below.

A New Public Order

Despite these powerful constraints, it is possible to create a new public order which is more effective in providing and producing public goods and at the same time challenges the values and rationale of the capitalist economy. This public order can never be a separate protected sphere, nor can it be free of contradictions and conflicts. And capital will constantly seek to marketise and privatise its functions and services.

Some of the criticisms of the public sector are warranted but they are generally deliberately grossly overstated as a means of justifying neo-liberal and Third Way strategies. Reconfiguring the state must be substantive and sustainable but it is not starting from scratch. There are many good quality public services.

Short-term marginal change will achieve little. This means striving for the redistribution of power, increasing state institutional capacity and democratic accountability, extending international, national and local controls over capital and markets, and ensuring a more equitable share of global resources are devoted to meeting social needs. The redesign of policies, practices and structures should occur in parallel at five levels: international, regional, national, local and community. It will have to confront the question of taxation and resources. The following ten-part plan, together with Public Service Management, could radically transform public services and the welfare state for the twenty-first century.

1. Extending democratic accountability with new models of governance – the local state
2. Taxation of income, consumption and corporate profits
3. Reversing marketisation and privatisation
4. New financial and regulatory architecture to control capital
5. Promoting civil society, citizenship and the social economy
6. Maintaining universal welfare systems
7. Reducing poverty through empowerment, redistribution, equalities, regeneration and control of development
8. Creating jobs and quality employment
9. Imposing corporate governance and social accountability
10. Maintaining macroeconomic stability and investment

Each part of this plan is examined in more detail below together with further explanation of the core functions of the state.

EXTENDING DEMOCRATIC ACCOUNTABILITY AND NEW MODELS OF GOVERNANCE

The immediate revitalisation of local and regional government is required by sweeping democratisation of public and quasi-public bodies. A radical transformation could be the impetus for recharging the level and quality of democratic involvement. It would involve the transfer into public control and direct democratic accountability of all organisations which have either been transferred or opted out to the quasi-public sector. Local and regional government should have new duties and powers to invest to protect and enhance the social, economic and environmental well-being of their area.

Democratic control and accountability are fundamental principles which should underpin all public interest decision-making within public organisations and externally to users and to the wider public. It must recognise the existence of ethical questions, respond quickly to the needs of the community and the value of choice where this is feasible and desirable. The identification of social and public needs, how public money is spent, the way services are organised, operated and delivered, to whom they are targeted, are all matters of public interest and must be under direct democratic control and accountability.

A democratic dividend perspective is essential to engage the active participation of political organisations, user, community and trade union organisations in service planning. Accountability must be organised and structured through collective and individual involvement, not through share ownership or stakeholding (see Chapters 6 and 9). It should encompass genuine involvement to help lay the foundations for changes in power relations and thus the ability of civil society and labour organisations to influence the decision-making process. It should identify and remove all barriers to equal opportunities, allocate resources for community capacity building to develop analytical and participative skills to shape policy, not simply to participate in government policy implementation.

The local state

There are substantial differences in the powers, responsibilities of different levels of government and local–regional–central government relations in nation states, hence it is very difficult to generalise the functions and role of local government. However, some basic requirements include:

- powers to set and collect local taxes;
- to borrow to finance capital expenditure;
- to establish democratically accountable quasi-public corporations;
- to promote, coordinate and implement policies to improve the social, economic and environmental well-being of their area;

- to produce local and community plans for social, economic, physical and environmental development; to ensure equal opportunities are implemented in the decision-making process; equality of access to education, health and other services; measures to prevent and eliminate violence and discrimination against women, black and ethnic minorities and children; integrate equalities perspectives in legislation, policies, programmes and projects; promote and protect public health; set targets and performance assessment in all audits and inspections; and promote harmonisation of work and family responsibilities for women and men;
- to form consortia and joint working with other public bodies and organisations in the locality and region;
- to evaluate, audit and assess the impact of policies and proposals with regard to their social, economic, environmental and financial impact.

Local government should have a general power of competence to provide a wide range of activities, functions, service provision, regulation and intervention and include the ability to invest and raise finance. It would permit new alliances or consortia of public bodies to jointly provide services and would enable authorities to develop public service agencies operating across the public sector, for example, providing facilities management or support services to local authorities, NHS and education bodies and there could be more sharing or pooling arrangements covering support services such as payroll, IT and personnel. A general power of competence should encompass regeneration and development, economic development, employment and training, public health, primary health care, education and life-long learning, community and social care and enhancing civil society.

The state has an important role in not only making its internal functions more transparent and accountable but also ensuring that the private and social sector adhere to the same principles of disclosure. This should not be limited to giving information, complaint and compensation obligations and citizen 'voice' but to support and strengthen civil society in order to increase organisational and representative involvement in decision-making. The risk of capture by providers or local community elites is a minor concern when the state is increasingly serving the interests of corporate welfare.

The core functions of the state are implemented at different levels of government with organisational structures, operating and management systems (see Figure 8.2). They vary from country to country. Organisational structures need to be flatter and decentralised and structured for user and trade union involvement to reflect service user needs and public service values (see Chapter 9). Quasi-public bodies and quangos should be transferred to directly elected public bodies or restructured so that they become directly democratically accountable. It will be crucial to avoid grandiose gestures of 'public control' where the organisation proceeds as it has before. It is equally important to avoid bureaucratic controls, budget raiding and asset stripping by the host authority and the emergence of new inter-departmental rivalries.

Figure 8.2: **The organisational and operational framework of the nation state**

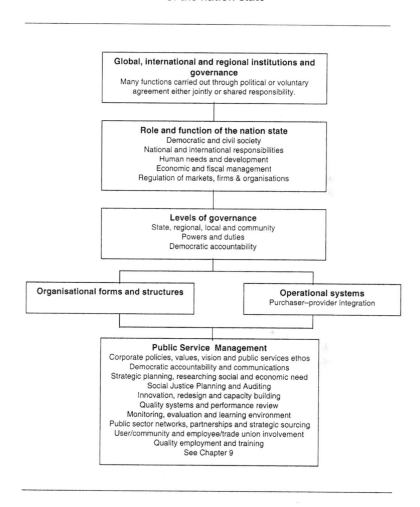

TAXATION OF INCOME, CONSUMPTION AND CORPORATE PROFITS

The impact on tax competition and recent shifts in the burden of taxation were discussed in the Introduction. It is essential that taxation, resources and the functions of the state are tackled head on in three key areas.

First, the provision of quality public goods cannot be achieved on the cheap. The concept of low taxation-small government-good quality public services is a myth as demonstrated in previous chapters. The connection between tax collection and public expenditure needs to be stronger, for example, bringing tax-raising more closely into line with the appropriate levels of service provision, reversing the trend towards national or federal tax collection for local service delivery. The state has an important role in promoting and educating for the link between taxation and quality of life, between taxation and the total cost to individuals, the efficiency and effectiveness of public provision and high individual costs of health insurance, education fees, personal pensions and other insurance costs through privatised provision. The tax base of the welfare state must be strengthened with new mechanisms for collective insurance and savings which encourage diversity and choice rather than a minimalist standard approach to contributions, savings and benefits. The state must distribute income and wealth more equitably between people and localities using taxation policies, macroeconomic planning, public expenditure, welfare state benefits, pensions and services and the corporate policies of central and local government.

Second, the corporate sector must make a full and fair contribution through taxation and at the same time minimise corporate welfare (see Chapter 5). This is an essential standard of a just and humane society and a prerequisite for the achievement of global poverty reduction and environmental sustainability objectives. Taxation systems must guarantee that taxes will be fairly based on the ability to pay with adequate resourcing of tax collection and compliance agencies to minimise evasion, fraud and corruption.

Third, tax competition between nation states must be reduced. The European Union adopted a package of measures to tackle harmful tax competition in 1997 which comprised a non-binding code of conduct on business taxation and draft directives on the taxation of savings and cross-border interest and royalty payments. A 1998 OECD study on harmful tax competition produced a series of recommendations to refrain, review and remove harmful practices and the establishment of a Forum on Harmful Tax Practices (OECD, 1998d). These codes need strengthening and monitoring. Tax fraud and evasion, money laundering and banking secrecy should be targeted through international cooperation. Proposals for a new world tax organisation should be resisted because it is likely to result in tax minimisation under the guise of harmonisation between states which would have major implications for European welfare states and developing countries.

Two other resource issues are important. More creative use can be made of pension fund investment by widening the investment criteria to encourage funding of regional and local ventures. For example, social use criteria should be part of the investment return assessments for it is pointless having high returns if a large proportion of the final pension is consumed by high cost private services on retirement. It is also contradictory when pension funds invest in the very companies leading the marketisation of public services (Whitfield, 1983).

The central–local relations are also crucial, particularly regarding the financing of local government. A local government finance system should strengthen the accountability of local councils and maximise genuine local involvement, decrease pressures for central government financial intervention, recognise the different needs of areas, provide for a fair and equitable progressive local tax, be easy to understand and transparent, facilitate 'joined-up' working and integrated approaches to service delivery within and between public organisations, encourage innovation and vision and stimulate investment (Local Government Information Unit, 2000).

REVERSING MARKETISATION AND PRIVATISATION

The state must have a substantial role in the production and maintenance of public goods in order to maintain their 'publicness' (see Chapter 1). The identification of needs, standards, the delivery process and accountability are usually integral to the supply of public goods, hence the need to minimise marketisation. Private provision will ultimately result in companies seeking to influence the contract and terms of public goods to reflect private rather than public need, they will focus on profitable parts at the expense of others, and they will develop competing private goods whenever such opportunities arise, thus marginalising public goods.

Public services should be immediately excluded from the WTO General Agreement on Trade in Services remit. WTO powers should be curtailed with emphasis placed on national and regional flexibility regarding social, employment and environmental conditions on transnationals and states (see below). The WTO should be democratised with full representation from developing countries, trade unions and NGOs. Any attempt to recall the proposals for a Multilateral Agreement on Investment should be forcefully resisted and replaced by obligatory and monitored codes of practice for socially responsible investment.

Without government strategic planning and public sector capital investment the renewal of the social and physical infrastructure will remain piecemeal and fragmented. Fundability, not social needs, will determine what gets built, where and for whom. The state has a key role to play in the provision of the physical and social infrastructure including:

1. transport – road, rail, sea and air;
2. utilities and energy – gas, electricity, water;
3. telecommunications, media and communications – support for e-government and local/regional information systems;
4. social or service infrastructure such as schools, colleges, hospitals and health centres and community care facilities;
5. cultural infrastructure – art galleries, museums, libraries, heritage;
6. economic development infrastructure such as factories and enterprise centres, sector support, innovation and product development;

7. environmental – waste disposal, sewage treatment land reclamation and environmental improvement projects.

Health, education, housing and regeneration, social services and other local facilities should be publicly financed and PPPs abolished (see p. 99). Alternative policies include increasing public sector capital spending budgets, changing public finance regulations giving public bodies greater freedom to borrow and use receipts and the GGFD framework to allow public sector corporations to invest without affecting government borrowing limits. Private finance should be restricted to major (over £500 million) infrastructure projects where joint public/private finance is required.

Why Public Ownership is so Important

The debate about public ownership and control is usually limited to who owns and controls the utilities, transport and some key industries and services. I have repeatedly argued that the privatisation and deregulation agenda has never been limited to this narrow perspective and it has been increasingly evident that it encompasses the welfare state, regeneration and the development process (Whitfield, 1983, 1985, 1992). Hence the case for ownership must cover the buildings and land required for the delivery of public services – the welfare state infrastructure; the provision of basic utilities and transport infrastructure; technical and professional expertise; research and development as well as the production of services. There are many key reasons for public ownership:

Meeting social needs: Public provision and ownership allows facilities and services to be provided according to social needs and priorities sanctioned through democratic decision-making. Cuts in capital spending have plagued planning timetables but the vagaries of private sector deals are no improvement. Despite this drawback, public provision and ownership is usually more effective in meeting needs than reliance on market forces and private finance which result in uneven and unequal provision, as evidenced by previous chapters. Public ownership also means control over the design and planning of facilities to ensure they maximise public service needs – the 'service fit' between building and internal activities. The loss of flexibility to change services and adapt buildings according to social needs and not be constrained by private ownership, complex contracts and conflicting interests of private management should not be overlooked.

Providing and producing public goods and services: There are major long-term consequences of separating the supply and ownership of the physical infrastructure from the services provided within them. Many services require integrated team working with professional, technical and support staff working collaboratively under a common unified management structure and a single employer. Once ownership is relinquished, repair and maintenance, servicing and facilities management are carried out by the private sector and a private operator will inevitably seek to widen the range of services provided resulting in the eventual privatisation of the entire service. Private ownership of buildings and part public–part private supply of services is not sustainable. Public ownership under public service management (see Chapter 9) also minimises commercial issues such as income generation from non-core activities from negatively affecting the delivery of public services.

Minimising the cost of capital: The state can borrow more cheaply and requires a much lower rate of return than the private sector because the risk of failure or non-payment is negligible. Privately funded schemes have an in-built cost of capital and profit premium which will be reflected in the quality of the overall package either through higher user charges, cuts in jobs and/or worse terms and conditions.

Coordinating regeneration and development: Public ownership of land and property is vitally important in the planning and development process, for urban renewal and regeneration, transport schemes and economic development, because it provides a level of control and negotiating power essential for implementation. Project after project has floundered precisely because of the lack of power and leverage resulting from ownership.

Some local authorities in Britain operate managed workshops for new enterprises – publicly owned and operated centres providing shared equipment which have generated a large number of businesses which would not otherwise have started or survived. The private centre alternatives are traditional industrial units managed as part of a property portfolio. This is a clear example of added value through public ownership including the availability of equipment and machinery which would not otherwise be affordable, plus provision of a secure environment with affordable rents and charges.

Providing good quality employment standards: Public ownership means higher standards of employment taking into account the pay and the wide range of conditions of service covering additional benefits, workplace conditions, training, education and employment practices in general. Doing things equitably, safely and with professional diligence takes time and resources. Public bodies also have a much better track record in implementing corporate policies, and national and international standards. Publicly owned and operated facilities also implement equal opportunities for users and staff more readily than the private sector (see Chapters 6 and 9).

Limiting market forces: Without public ownership and public investment the power of the state to fundamentally intervene in markets will be weakened. The state itself will be reliant on those same markets to purchase services and will be subservient to the needs of capital. Public ownership of the infrastructure is essential in order to ensure that it is provided according to social and economic need, not according to market forces or the motives of individual companies. The state has a key role in preventing the formation of markets in public goods.

Working towards environmental and ecological sustainability: Public ownership usually means higher standards are achieved by more rapid and fuller implementation of environmental regulations. The private sector usually relies on profitability or advantages to corporate image in adopting similar regulations.

Redistributing income and wealth: Public ownership is a key means of redistribution because it enables governments to vary provision and prices according to need and ability to pay.

Controlling the infrastructure: The market system will not provide the required level of investment, when and where it is needed at reasonable cost. All capitalist economies rely on governments to plan and develop the economic infrastructure. Public investment is crucial for productivity growth and private investment. Studies have shown that the ratio of productivity of public to private investment ranges from 1 to 3 per cent (Munnell, 1994; Holtz-Eakin et al., 1994 and Aschauer, 1990 quoted in Baker and Schafer, 1995). Every 1 million dollars of public investment stimulated between $450,000 and $500,000 of private investment (Munnell, 1994; Aschauer, 1990 and Erenburg, 1993 quoted in Baker and Schafer, 1995). Private landlords always seek market rent and profit so there is an economic case for public ownership of the infrastructure. The state will pay a higher price in the longer term via lease and rental costs than if the infrastructure had been built at cost by the state. There is also a need to regain public control of the design and planning process to ensure facilities meet social and community need (see Chapter 4).

Collectivising risk: Many elements of risk have successfully been carried by the public sector at minimum cost because they have been collectivised – the welfare state is the classic example (see Chapter 5). The public sector is much better equipped to deal with operational, demand and usage and financial risk. Residual value risk is irrelevant in publicly financed projects. Design and construction risk could be better shared by imposing more stringent procurement conditions on private contractors. The consequences of commodifying risk was discussed in Chapters 1 and 2.

Regulating through public ownership: Ownership is a means of regulation by setting standards and competing alongside private suppliers, influencing prices and market behaviour, technical development and full ownership would remove the need and cost of regulation.

Different Forms of Public Ownership

A strong public sector is a prerequisite to support and underpin different types of public organisation, ownership and control. For example, a uniform model of 100 per cent public ownership is not always desirable or effective. It is not within the scope of this book to examine the different forms and degrees of public ownership which will, by necessity, vary depending on the function and service concerned. The main options are summarised below.

Different forms of public ownership include:

- 100 per cent ownership by local (municipal), regional or central government or other public bodies including public corporations or arm's length publicly owned companies.
- Consortium or collective ownership – joint ownership with other nation states, such as within the EU or national, regional or local joint ownership by a consortium of public authorities and bodies, for example, providing services on behalf of a group of similar or neighbouring organisations.
- Strategic ownership in a joint venture with the state owning a majority (51 per cent or more) or full ownership of a key part of a service or activity.

There are also many examples of publicly owned land and facilities being leased to community and non-profit organisations, which for the last two decades has been used to outsource and transfer public services out of democratic control (see Chapters 3 and 4). However, in a changed political climate which was creating a new public order, these same mechanisms could be used to experiment with new forms of local democratic and decentralised control of state functions and services.

Different forms of collective ownership include:

- Cooperatives with user/worker members owning shares.
- Employee share ownership schemes (ESOPs) – see Chapter 6.
- Community owned and controlled non-profit organisations.

They can also be used to develop new forms of local democratic and decentralised control.

Why it Matters who Delivers the Service

This is not just about who provides services or carries out functions but the principles, values, ethos and policies determine the way in which services and activities are provided.

Integrating purchaser and provider: Planning and allocating resources, identifying, assessing and prioritising social needs, and operational management of service delivery are integral to the quality of service.

Direct democratic control and accountability of service delivery and functions: Public services are directly accountable to elected representatives and issues are more clearly in the public arena. Outsourcing often leads to client/private contractor collusion to protect the contracting decision and commercial confidentiality as a priority over service user interests. External providers are accountable first and foremost to shareholders or management boards which are usually dominated by business elites. More effective parliamentary scrutiny is needed to enhance accountability together with rigorous evaluation of policies and interests.

Better quality of service: When properly resourced, publicly delivered services can provide a higher standard of service, more responsive and flexible to changing circumstances (see Chapter 6). Private providers are much more likely to cut corners and use inferior materials because profits determine the quality of work. The quality of service is best maintained when the quality of employment is also a key objective, services and activities are integrated or joined-up through direct provision rather than via a plethora of contractors and other providers, and when equity and equalities are mainstreamed throughout the organisation, services and activities.

Maximising the scope for improvement: Evidence from detailed research in both public and private sectors indicates that a motivated and committed workforce is an essential prerequisite for achieving continuous improvement (West and Patterson, 1998). Transferring staff like commodities between employers undermines job security, a public service ethos and the conditions necessary to maximise innovation and improvement (see Chapter 9).

Coordination and integration of activities and services: Service delivery, social inclusion and anti-poverty strategies, regeneration and economic development increasingly require a multidisciplinary coordinated approach. This requires integrated teams, the pooling of skills, experience and resources between organisations in networks, partnerships, alliances and coalitions with the public sector playing a central role. It requires joined-up *government*, not joined-up contracts. The price of selectively 'cheaper' suppliers is often outweighed by the loss of connectivity and coordination of the overall service. Budget holders may claim a 'saving' but this is usually absorbed in transaction costs and service users rarely see the benefits. Achieving the vertical and horizontal integration of a democratically accountable and complex range of services and functions is often underestimated.

Working to needs, not contracts and profits: The prime purpose of publicly provided services is to meet social need. The first priority of private services is to meet the demands of the marketplace and ensure profitability for share-holders, unless of course they are being subsidised by the state.

Lower overall cost: In-house services usually have lower overall costs, on a comparative basis, after taking all client, contractor and other public costs into account (see Chapter 6). In-house provision serves to regulate prices when comparisons are made between public and other providers.

Economies of scale: The division of services into contracts reduces economies of scale and hinders sharing and distribution of resources between high/low levels of usage, urban/rural and high/low cost areas. Private and voluntary providers usually opt for areas to maximise their resources or where there is an existing market, resulting in poorer and rural areas suffering as a consequence.

Implementation of corporate policies, objectives and community needs: Although corporate policies and mission statements are common in all sectors they have a more direct and deeper impact on the quality and process in the delivery of public services. Corporate polices are most effectively implemented as part of in-house services. Full implementation requires resources, training and mainstreaming through political, managerial and operational structures with monitoring and evaluation of performance. The record of public providers is superior to the private sector.

Continuity and security: Continuity of service and knowledge of local require-ments and conditions is often an important part of service delivery. External providers can decide not to seek renewal or to abandon contracts because of financial difficulties.

Public interest: Graft and corruption appear to have few boundaries, but the greater the involvement of private firms in the delivery of public services, construction and supply of public goods, the more likelihood that there will be corruption and collusion, particularly as contracts get larger and larger.

Cost transparency: The cost of publicly provided services is generally more open to inspection (although competitive tendering regimes make this more closed). Other providers can transfer costs and prices between a range of contracts and use company law or commercial confidentiality to prevent public access to the true figures.

Quality of employment: The public sector is more likely to have a commitment to good employment terms and conditions including pay, pensions, holidays, sickness schemes, maternity/paternity leave and workplace conditions such as training and health and safety. It is more likely to give full trade union recognition for organising, representation and negotiating rights compared to weaker and partial agreements common in the private sector.

Societal and collective responsibility: It is important to retain and harness collective responsibility which encourages a sense of belonging, community and stability and improves people's health and well-being (Putman, 1993; Wilkinson, 1997). Privatisation undermines these aspirations and replaces them with individual and commercial attitudes (see commodification of services in Chapter 3).

The private sector has used outsourcing not only to reduce production costs but also to restructure work organisation and reduce the power of labour. Work is often brought back in-house once this transformation process has achieved these objectives. A similar process is happening to public services writ large, although the private sector has a much greater vested interest in extending and maintaining marketisation. The cycle will no doubt be repeated some time in the future, when a new version of modernisation will seek to reinvent public services and the welfare state with in-house services. But the risk of relying on this is uninsurable.

NEW FINANCIAL AND REGULATORY ARCHITECTURE TO CONTROL CAPITAL

The failure of neo-liberalism and the succession of financial and economic crises has led to a consensus on the need for a new financial and political architecture for the institutions, markets, regulations and practices to control economic and financial activity. It is essential that it address market failure and not just government failure. In other words, this 'architecture' must encompass new public controls, regulations and intervention in markets including the activities of multinational companies. Too many proposals focus on government policy when the ultimate cause was market failure. Within the purpose of this book it is only possible to highlight some of the changes required.

Codes of conduct and framework agreements, best practice and charters have an important role in mobilising support for policies but they have limited value unless they are accompanied by verification and enforcement by international organisations and nation states. Greater international cooperation will never be a reality unless those promoting codes and charters equally focus on increased state intervention. Globalisation and market forces will never be curtailed or controlled by voluntary codes. Greater transparency, accountability and more equitable economic growth require a new domestic and international financial architecture together with other powers to make state intervention a reality.

However, governments cannot adopt the enabling model for the internal affairs of the nation state on the one hand, but try to have a direct hands-on interventionist role internationally. Policies which reduce the capacity of the state internally also reduce its capacity in the international arena.

The starting point must be compliance and respect for the Universal Declaration of Human Rights and the six core treaties on economic, social and cultural rights; civil and political rights; racial discrimination; discrimination against women; children's rights; and torture and the conventions on genocide, refugees and labour standards. Universal ratification of the UN General Assembly Covenant is urgently needed with increased resources for enforcement and development of standards to assess compliance with the obligations.

Reform of the World Bank and IMF: Radical reform of both institutions is urgently required. The imposition of structural adjustment programmes conditional on grants and loans and stabilisation programmes in the wake of economic and financial crises should be stopped immediately, accompanied by withdrawal of the IMF's new Poverty Reduction and Growth Facility (PRGF) and poverty reduction goals (Jubilee South, 1999). The IMF has merged its structural adjustment programme into the PRFG which requires recipient countries to prepare a Poverty Reduction Strategy Paper outlining poverty reduction priorities and economic policies as the basis for all financial support. The IMF now has control of poverty reduction strategies!

The Economic Policy Institute calls for new and improved international financial institutions which should include:

- providing more grants and less loans, which would give recipient countries less incentive to raid their environment and exploit their workers to repay international loans;
- encouraging internal development over dependence on external capital flows;
- encouraging and providing assistance in the design and implementation of effective capital controls;
- requiring adherence to labor and environmental standards by international borrowers or grant recipients. International Labor Organisation certification of labor standards, for instance, could become a condition for receiving IFI grants or loans. (Economic Policy Institute, 2000)

These organisations must also be made democratically accountable, involve labour and NGO organisations and much greater transparency in decision-making and their operations.

Reform of the UN system: There is an increasing gap between the rhetoric and reality in the UN development system and a case can be made to focus on more limited priorities to increase its effectiveness and maximise the use of limited resources (Bergesen and Lunde, 1999). Different parts of the UN system are developing partnerships with business, for example, the UN's Global Compact, based on nine human rights, labour and environment principles, is aimed at gaining agreement on 'global corporate citizenship'. It is vague, non-binding and without any enforcement mechanism and another example of 'partnership' with business in which the UN leadership promised to support global free trade. Since the principles are already included in other international codes which could be more effectively verified and monitored, the Compact should be abolished.

Financial markets are intrinsically unstable which constantly threatens economic collapse and recession, hence new structures and regulatory regimes are needed urgently to control financial flows, improve disclosure and regulatory regimes. A series of measures are required:

Control of capital flows: An International Financial Transactions Tax (Tobin tax) should be imposed on foreign exchange transfers to discourage currency speculation and thus volatility in the market. A 0.1 per cent tax rate could possibly reduce speculation by up to 50 per cent and raise $200 billion tax revenues. Over 80 per cent of foreign exchange turnover involves transactions spanning a week or less and only 3 per cent directly finances trade in commodities and non-financial services. 'The other 97 per cent represent financial transactions that exploit discrepancies between inter-country interest rates and corresponding exchange rates, speculate on movements of bonds and equities in different markets, and hedge against or speculate on exchange rate changes' (Foreign Policy in Focus, 2000).

IMF requirements that countries liberalise their capital accounts as a condition for borrowing should be abolished. Capital controls, particularly on short-term capital, can help reduce capital flight, improve financial stability and reduce the need for IMF intervention as lender of last resort. Malaysia and Chile have recently used capital controls to this effect.

Debt relief for developing countries: Forty-two heavily indebted poor countries owe over $100 billion in unpayable debt to the World Bank, IMF, regional development banks and donor governments with a further $19 billion owed to commercial banks. Jubilee 2000 estimate that 28 countries need full debt cancellation plus $12 billion in aid after taking account of essential spending on health, education, infrastructure and the target of reducing by one-half the proportion of people living in extreme poverty by 2015 (Jubilee 2000,

1999). Current proposals for debt repayment by the Bretton Woods institutions and the major industrialised countries fail dismally to address these problems. Jubilee South demands that multilateral debt (owed to international financial institutions) to all South countries be cancelled, the cancellation of all bilateral (government to government) debt and stopping all loans and support to authoritarian, dictatorial, oppressive and military regimes.

New development model: This should focus on growth financed principally from domestic savings and investment, supplemented by foreign direct investment, which requires progressive taxation systems. Economic and environmental sustainability are best achieved by strengthening domestic markets rather than relying on fast track export markets.

Financial disclosure: Elimination of crony capitalism by requiring greater disclosure of bank reserves, liabilities, foreign currency trading and off-balance sheet financing.

Termination of all planned liberalisation: An immediate moratorium on all regional and international agreements which propose further liberalisation of FDI, including World Bank and IMF loan and credit approval conditions.

Financial regulatory bodies: Increased supervision, transparency and enforcement of new international and national regulatory regimes for financial institutions including banks, hedge funds, pension funds, insurance companies and investment/savings organisations and the termination of self-regulation.

New initiatives to meet Official Development Assistance targets: All donor countries to agree a timetable to meet the 0.7 per cent ODA target by 2010 and application of the 20/20 principle relating to the proportion of ODA and recipient country budgets devoted to social expenditure.

Reform of Export Credit Agencies: Project proposals should be subject to rigorous independent analysis of options and impact assessment and incorporation of human rights, social, environmental and development standards as a condition of support with transparency and accountability in financial guarantee decision-making.

Review of the role of development banks in infrastructure and development: Public investment must be increased and public control of infrastructure projects extended. A complete refocus is required to increase state capacity to plan and manage projects which harness private capital under public control.

New measures of wealth and progress: New accounting measures to incorporate natural capital, produced assets, human resources and social capital.

Adoption of European-type public sector borrowing framework: The General Government Financial Deficit excludes net borrowing by public corporations enabling local government and other public organisations to finance investment on the value of assets and revenue stream. This should encourage innovative investment models.

New savings schemes: Need to encourage personal saving and social investment through new national savings schemes and bonds targeted for infrastructure, education, health and social care facilities.

Withdrawal of public sector from scope of WTO negotiations: The exclusion of public services from the GATS negotiations has already been discussed. The Trade-Related Investment Measures (TRIMS) and the Trade-Related Intellectual Property Rights (TRIPS) agreements should be renegotiated to enable countries to impose local content requirements on foreign investors and prevent the privatisation of patenting of life forms. The WTO disputes settlement procedures must be radically redesigned to ensure they are democratic, transparent and give right of access to states and NGOs.

Implementation of the International Labour Organisation's Declaration on Fundamental Principles and Rights at Work: This includes the right for workers to form and/or join free and independent unions of their choice, to negotiate collectively wages and other employment conditions, the abolition of forced and child labour, and the prohibition of all forms of discrimination in employment. All public sector contracts and Export Credit Guarantees should be conditional on companies observing international codes of conduct, including ILO core labour standards.

Imposing codes of conduct on transnational corporations: International agreements are required which encompass corporate responsibility, social accountability, codes of conduct, labelling for labour and environmental conditions. New conditions should be imposed for economic development support and include the clawback of incentives based on the companies' performance based on a system of reverse payment (the longer they stay and maintain their commitments the smaller the repayment), the assessment of job creation targets, concern for production chains and support for local suppliers and support services, wage and benefit requirements, participation in the regional economy and local community. This will reduce the competition driving the race to the bottom and increase accountability and transparency.

Ethical trading and investment: As a major purchaser of goods and services, the public sector can play a bigger role in setting standards by boycotting goods which are produced in countries under sweat-shop conditions and promoting those produced and marketed through ethical trading agreements.

Competition policy: Merger and takeover policy should be transparent and within the political decision-making process, not hived off to business elites or academics. Competitive bidding between public organisations for grants and projects should be minimised and replaced with needs-based allocation and collaborative approaches. Competition policy should set clear limitations for private intervention in the provision and production of public goods.

Global cooperation to combat organised crime: New controls are required to counter the increased trafficking in women and children and smuggling migrants, and new laws to prevent exploitation of migrant workers.

Global anti-poverty project: Targets and funding commitments from international institutions, developed countries and transnational corporations to reduce absolute poverty, achieve universal primary education, provide universal access to basic health care services, together with access to a minimum standard of nutrition, water and sanitation.

Global social policy code:

- Universal entitlements to a share in one of the main means of livelihood of the society: land, paid employment, micro-credit. Principle of state/employer/worker financed and publicly operated pension and basic income support.
- Entitlement to income compensation when these are not available.
- Government regulated and citizenship contributed compulsory social insurance provision to pool risks and to cover for all risks (unemployment, sickness, disability, survivorship, old age).
- Equitable access to the level of health care and education affordable at the level of development.
- Mechanisms to ensure universal access to adequate water, food, sanitation, (food subsidies of basics in a market economy even if the subsidy also benefits the middle class remains an important mechanism of social solidarity).
- Tax and benefit processes that win the universal commitment of all to their funding and provision.
- Involvement of civil society institutions, local NGOs in the articulation of needs and in aspects of social provision without undermining government responsibility for the standard and regional distribution of services.
- Government mechanisms which enforce core labour standards, UN human and social rights, and regional social charters where they exist.

- Economic development strategies which are pro-poor and encourage labour growth with adequate renumeration (Deacon, 1998).

The 27 principles agreed at the United Nations Conference on Environment and Development in Rio de Janeiro, 1992, placed key tasks on the role of nation states which agreed to cooperate in a spirit of global partnership to conserve, protect and restore the health and integrity of the Earth's ecosystem. The state has a responsibility to:

- ensure that environmental audits are prepared for all major projects and policy changes;
- mainstream environmental sustainability in all public bodies with a matrix of indicators;
- regularly assess the quality of environmental assets and performance;
- promote development of brownfield and derelict sites;
- prevent pollution and causes of ill-health;
- ensure a life cycle perspective from construction to operation and maintenance to decommissioning;
- examine resource, supply, production, transport, distribution and other chains.

It is vital to integrate economic and ecological sustainability, the scope of which is summarised in Table 8.2. But this can only be achieved by state capacity to act within their jurisdiction coupled with international action to enforce agreements and codes of practice.

Table 8.2: **Goals of economic and ecological sustainability**

Economic sustainability	Ecological sustainability
Full employment	Maintaining biodiversity
Economic stability	Maintaining life-support systems
'Reasonable' economic growth	Conserving the resource base
Elimination of poverty	Reduced reliance on non-renewables
Labour force replenishment and skilling	Conserving renewables
Attainment of labour standards	Creating a secondary materials economy
Expanding social capital	Eliminating health risks
Distributive and procedural justice	Avoiding creation of new risks
Democratic participation and accountability	Protecting household and workplace safety

Source: 'Towards a Comprehensive Geographical Perspective on Urban Sustainability', Rutgers University, January 2000.

PROMOTING CIVIL SOCIETY, CITIZENSHIP AND THE SOCIAL ECONOMY

A recurring theme throughout this book has been the importance of democratic accountability and labour/civil society involvement as a means of increasing their power to affect change (see also Chapter 9). It has three elements. First, changes in the structure and management of public services to facilitate user/employee involvement. Second, public resources devoted to community development and capacity building. Third, the need for trade unions, community organisations and NGOs to be democratic and representative and adopt good practice management. The redesign of the state strategy is heavily reliant on the quality of these organisations and the extent to which they forge alliances between the different sectors.

Rebuilding the capacity of civil society will require:

- central/local state support for community research and resource centres to train and facilitate involvement, community organising, training to support involvement in public service planning, support of life-long learning, development education to increase understanding of the local–global perspective, collective research and analysis for scrutiny panels and support preparation of alternative policies (see Chapters 9 and 10);
- greater organising and action within communities;
- the formation of coalitions and alliances between community, other civil society organisations and trade union and labour organisations, with the latter recognising that they must be more proactive;
- the integration of development education into all secondary and adult education, citizenship and trade union education will encourage more substantive international alliances and joint action;
- developing local, national and global citizenship as a key state responsibility which should extend throughout education and the life-long learning system.

The social economy encompasses delivery of services, advocacy, manufacturing goods and financial services such as credit unions. It includes local initiatives responding to specific community needs which are not provided (or inadequately or at high cost) by the public or private sector. The state should facilitate the social economy via start-up finance, tax measures to encourage a role in innovation and development arising from public research and development, technical support, peppercorn rents, guaranteeing markets and purchasing agreements. Local and regional economic development strategies should concentrate on the organic growth of the social economy and community enterprise rather than expansion through the privatisation and outsourcing of public services.

MAINTAINING UNIVERSAL WELFARE SYSTEMS

The state already socialises many personal and collective risks in society both efficiently and effectively. Socialising risk is important because it is the most effective way of minimising the use of scarce resources and maximising efficiency; creating a fair and just society; minimising the administrative cost of public provision; achieving equality of opportunity, access, dignity, self-determination and security irrespective of age, gender, race, social and economic position; facilitating redistribution within a a universal system and preventing the emergence of two-tier systems (see Chapter 5). This book has highlighted the consequences of commodifying and commercialising risk in order to justify marketisation and privatisation.

The provision of education and training fulfils a human need and has an economic or reproduction function in helping to equip and prepare people for work and citizenship. Life-long learning requires a continuity of opportunities beyond further and higher education with organisations such as Europe's Workers' Educational Association playing a much more extensive role in conjunction with community colleges and other institutions. Only the government can provide the necessary leadership, resources and organisational coordination of all the different education and training interests to reskill, retrain and improve educational performance across the board.

A public health strategy must be based on the democratisation of health and social care organisations, prioritising action inequalities and poverty and recognising the importance of race, gender and class issues. Participative community planning for regeneration and services should be centred on involvement and ownership of health strategies, not mere consultation. The strategy will also require the integration of health impact assessment into policy planning and more extensive inter-agency coordination of health-related initiatives to achieve sustainable development and environment, and provide resources for public primary care infrastructure, innovation, healthy living centres, new services for children and the elderly. The quality of employment and occupational health are vital in a sector which has a record of low wage female exploitation.

The provision of good quality socialised public housing with affordable rents is important in order to meet social, health and economic objectives. It should provide a comprehensive and flexible service to meet general housing needs with security of tenure and strong and effective tenancy agreements. It must not be subject to sale. It should accommodate a variety of tenant and community management systems.

The welfare state has to provide adequate and comprehensive social security for all citizens and a minimum income. Income support through the benefits system serves as a means of achieving redistributive or social equity objectives, particularly during economic recession or financial crises.

REDUCING POVERTY THROUGH EMPOWERMENT, REDISTRIBUTION, EQUALITIES, REGENERATION AND CONTROL OF DEVELOPMENT

The Preface briefly indicated the scale of increasing world poverty and widening inequalities in industrialised and developing countries. Chapters 3–7 showed how marketisation and privatisation are increasing inequalities. Poverty reduction and social exclusion can only be tackled by increasing the capacity of the poor to struggle for power by strengthening civil society and labour organisations and by enforcing public organisations to involve them in decision making.

Policy making and budgeting must be subjected to rigorous equalities and social justice planning and auditing in order to radically improve access to, and the quality of, public services such as education, life-long learning and training. It will require additional and more stringent regulation of the capitalist economy beyond the provision of a safety net to minimise the impact of globalisation, technological change and economic/financial crises. The World Bank, UNDP and IMF initiatives consistently seek to 'empower' the poor through consultation and participation but not through organising assistance to help them take power.

It is the operation of market forces, not government, which is the prime cause of poverty. Hence, poverty reduction, irrespective of state capacity, is not solely a state responsibility. The focus on the lack of coordination or joined-up government is important in targeting and making the most effective use of resources to reduce poverty, but it does not address the root causes of poverty.

The public resources made available for policies and projects are tiny compared to social and economic need. The partnership approach creates a false impression that public and private resources are going to be combined to jointly solve the problem. To this extent, partnerships are a diversion and create an illusion that a combination of the state and market forces can end poverty. The focus of the World Bank's draft World Development Report 2000 is on assisting the poor within the market system, to ensure 'inclusive' policies are devised supported by 'safety nets' rather than welfare states.

A statutory obligation to promote equalities and social justice at all levels of government with a positive right to equal treatment and positive action is essential, and forces business to implement equal pay for work of equal value. The state should ensure growth and equity run in parallel. Each public body should have a clear statement of the organisation's commitment to implementing equal opportunities for both users and staff, have established priorities, plans and targets to eliminate inequalities and a monitoring and evaluation process.

Regeneration will only be effective if the strategic management and enforcement role of the local state maximises funding through mainline public spending to avoid regeneration being merely a system of partial replacement of spending cuts for the hardest hit. It must tackle causes as well as deal with effects, take into account social justice and geographical equity, and adopt a city-wide and regional approach to strategic issues.

CREATING JOBS AND QUALITY EMPLOYMENT

Employment strategy must cover job creation and job protection (maintaining and improving the quality of existing jobs), job and service enhancement (creating jobs by improving services and training, decentralisation and devolution) and transforming the labour process.

It is important that job creation objectives be rooted in service needs and priorities, creating jobs which are sustainable in terms of their security, training, education and career development. Growth areas include health and social care, environmental services – waste recycling, energy and a wide range of social and community services. A jobs strategy should focus on the quality of employment, be capable of implementation within a plan period, implement corporate policies such as equalities, environmental sustainability, health and safety and anti-poverty strategies.

Reversing the marketisation and privatisation will reduce job losses and wage cuts (see Chapter 6). The quality of employment should be enhanced by improving wages, benefits, security, pensions, family friendly policies, control over the work process and training and career development (see Chapter 9). Trade union recognition and organisation and the implementation of all ILO labour standards are also essential.

Transforming the labour process should be a strategic objective to both oppose and provide an alternative to the consequences of marketisation, flexible labour markets and performance management characterised by neoliberalism. Trade unions should campaign for more control over the job by devolving responsibilities, increased involvement in decisions affecting the management and operation of public organisations and promote, where relevant, task flexibility and multiskilling based on the needs of users and services. The growth of e-government will open up new opportunities for enhancing services, particularly where these extend into the production of services and beyond communications and payment systems. However, a digital divide within the workplace could open up new divisions and conflicts. Public investment should be encouraged in the application of new technology in health, education and social care (growth sectors in most economies) to develop new products and services.

IMPOSING CORPORATE GOVERNANCE AND SOCIAL ACCOUNTABILITY

This part of the ten-point plan requires the imposition of stronger and enforceable controls and conditions on capital and multinational companies. Regulation of the corporate sector must be strengthened including the regulation of companies and competition, the approval of takeovers and mergers, forms of corporate governance and implementation of international codes through legislation, regulations supported by appropriately resourced monitoring and enforcement units. There is an increasing credibility gap between corporate objectives, rhetoric and reality. The era of vacuous sound bites, idealistic objectives and meaningless mission statements which extends from the UN, multinational companies to many nation states and government departments must be constantly exposed.

The World Bank has adopted the OECD principles of corporate governance which cover the rights, equitable treatment and role of shareholders, disclosure and transparency and responsibilities of the Board. However, the review of the OECD Guidelines for Multinational Enterprises (OECD, 1999e) exposed the weaknesses of revised proposals. These were succinctly summarised by the Citizens Council on Corporate Issues (Canada). They concluded that the guidelines:

- are merely voluntary and consequently unenforceable;
- fail to go beyond the present status quo with respect to corporate responsibility by not setting strong standards for corporate behaviour and requirements for state regulation of corporations;
- place the public interest second to private interests;
- ignore the social and environmental implications of scientific and technological objectives; and
- accept the inappropriate involvement of corporations in the development of public policy with respect to corporate activity. (CCCI, 2000, p. 1)

Trade unions have also criticised the failure of the guidelines to include substantive provisions and enforcement of ILO standards, the weak implementation process and the need to apply them in non-OECD countries to prevent the creation of a two-tier system.

Maintaining conditions for private market activity covers a range of functions which create and maintain the conditions required for markets and the private sector to operate and to prevent private monopoly in the supply of services or activities. Regulatory frameworks must minimise damage caused by the unfettered private exploitation of natural resources and markets.

A similar regulatory framework is required for all utilities and services. Local authorities will need to expand their role, not merely as consumer advocates, but in regulating and enforcing more substantive and effective regulations, for example, in community care, environmental services and waste disposal. Stringent environmental health inspection is required in the provision of food and restaurants, trading standards and pricing. Regulatory systems must ensure that the process is democratic and transparent, regulatory agencies must have adequate resources to research, investigate, gather information and the ability to penalise and effect enforcement. They must also ensure that the public has full access to information.

Labour market regulations should include the implementation of codes of labour practice incorporating ILO employment statements, employment standards including minimum wage and equal pay for work of equal value and regulations to give freedom of trade unions to organise, represent, negotiate and take action. The European Acquired Rights Directive should be strengthened and copied world-wide to give employment protection for any transfers between employers. Disincentives should be eliminated to facilitate continued labour force participation by older workers.

The state also regulates the public and social/voluntary sectors. A power of general competence will broaden the scope and powers of local government, permit formation of public sector consortia within and between different tiers of government and prevent transfers from the public sector based merely on the evasion of property or valued added taxes.

MAINTAINING MACROECONOMIC STABILITY AND INVESTMENT

Sustaining human development and maintaining economic stability and investment are key nation state functions. Macroeconomic planning in the industrial, financial and service sectors provides a framework for regional economic and social planning together with local economic development policies. Management of the economy should maintain and create employment, stimulate investment and promote equity and environmental sustainability in parallel with economic growth. It must ensure that social investment is targeted at achieving these objectives rather than create the conditions for private markets. The state also has a responsibility to stabilise the economy to minimise the effect of ups and downs in financial markets and peaks and troughs in trading performance.

The state must encourage a longer term investment perspective to counter the short-termism of most financial institutions and speculators. It must impose a new financial architecture nationally to coordinate with new international regulatory frameworks and take a more strident position in setting the development framework.

Local/regional investment funds should support research and development in public, private and social sectors; development funds for innovative products and services together with organisational and managerial support structures are essential to encourage and facilitate indigenous and innovative investment.

SUMMARY

This chapter has set out the important role of the state in the twenty-first century. The next chapter presents a new framework for managing the state and operationalising the functions, activities and services described in this chapter.

9

A New Public Service Management

A new public management system is urgently needed which will increase the capacity of the state and strengthen its core competence to carry out the functions described in Chapter 8. It must also ensure that a more equitable share of global resources is devoted to meeting social needs and counter the growing corporate-welfare complex (see Chapter 5). Public management should retain and improve a distinctive public dimension rather than merely being an eclectic cocktail of commercial applications (see Chapters 3 and 4).

Public management has to operate within the conflicts and contradictions of the state in a capitalist economy as discussed in Chapters 1 and 8. Political decision-making with limited public resources will always be conflictual because the needs of capital, labour, civil society and the state can rarely be reconciled. Public management will always have to compete against business management to maintain its distinctiveness and public service ethos. Ethical frameworks and codes of conduct are essential but of limited value in the context of the increasing commercialisation of the public sector via Third Way modernisation. Only the reversal of these policies will provide a challenge to the increasing power of the corporate-welfare complex.

This chapter details a new Public Service Management which integrates the wider social, economic, political and environmental responsibilities of public bodies and the need for collaborative planning and implementation. The provision of public goods requires a management system which values the process of delivery, promotes democratic accountability and involvement and has the capacity to regulate capital. It must be capable of facilitating the implementation of the five core functions of the state: democratic and civil society, national and international responsibilities, human needs and development, economic and fiscal management and the regulation of markets, firms and organisations (see Chapter 8).

PRINCIPLES OF PUBLIC SERVICE

A number of core principles underpin Public Service Management. Several countries, for example, Australia, the USA, Portugal, Britain and New Zealand have recently drawn up various principles and standards for public service and the OECD has promoted an ethics infrastructure (OECD, 1996b) although none are fully comprehensive. Public Service Management is based on the following core principles which extend Britain's seven principles of public life (Nolan, 1995) with the addition of participation and involvement, equality and competence.

Selflessness (motivated by service rather than by profit, commitment and degree of altruism and attraction to serve the public)

Integrity (commitment to the organisation's values and objectives)

Objectivity (impartial judgment and assessment and clarity in communication)

Accountability (acceptance of legitimacy of the political institutions and processes, serving collective and community needs)

Participation and involvement (civil society and labour involvement in design, planning and policy making processes)

Openness (transparency and responsiveness)

Honesty (highest standards of probity and conduct)

Leadership (high standards and fiscal responsibility)

Equality (respecting cultural diversity and commitment to justice and fairness)

Competence (using skills and experience for the public good with a commitment to training and service improvement)

Public Service Management is new and distinctive because it is centred on:

- the effectiveness of services, investment and the process of provision, *not just on results*;
- participatory governance, *not mere consultation*;
- participatory management *inclusive of frontline staff and trade unions*;
- commitment to the improvement of in-house services by redesign and valuing staff, *not by outsourcing, competitive tendering or making markets*;
- accountability to users, civil society and labour, *not merely to business*;
- implementation of equalities, social justice and environmental sustainability as an integral part of public service provision, *not as lip-service to promote corporate image*;
- integrated management and organisational structures, *not divisive separation of purchaser and provider functions*.

Public Service Management is designed to be good quality public management practice. The aim is to define a practice which fully reflects the principles and values of public service ethos and which is free of gimmicks and fading or new fads. The priority is to establish a comprehensive management system rather than develop techniques or tools which address only particular problems. While there is often some merit in management tools such as business process re-engineering, knowledge management, total quality management and core competencies, they are designed to have limited relevance and life only to be replaced by the next and other yet-to-be-named 'wonder' practices.

The application of public service principles and values requires the organisation and management of public bodies to have a range of core competences or attributes. These are grouped under five headings, strategic role, organisational structure and culture, management practice, employees and trade unions (see Table 9.1). Local public sector trade unions are included because their capacity, strategy and quality make an important contribution to Public Service Management through a proactive and strategic approach, participative and representative organisation with education and training of members.

Limiting Bureaucracy

The complexity of state functions and activities, the need for democratic accountability and involvement, the need for due process in the allocation of welfare state benefits, grants, applications and the fulfilment of statutory obligations require public organisations to have detailed information, systematic and thorough procedures and working practices. Consultation, verification, assessment and decision-making in the context of limited resources take time and resources. Systems are also required to minimise fraud and corruption by individuals and companies. The misuse of public money is a matter of public interest whereas misuse of private money is usually hidden and responsibility limited. It is essentially a matter of priority. Public Service Management must not be diverted by the obsession of neo-liberalism and public choice theory (see Introduction) with minimising bureaucracy at any cost.

Procedures are often used by management, business, civil society organisations and trade unions to delay and frustrate the decision-making process in pursuance of their objectives or vested interests. Although checks and balances are essential, they open the public sector to criticism for being slow and burdened by red tape. Public management can and must minimise bureaucracy but it cannot be eradicated because without procedures and processes there will be limited accountability, involvement, equity or equalities.

Mainstreaming Equalities and Sustainability

Equalities mainstreaming requires that all public organisations impose equal rights and access, equal treatment and positive action into every aspect at all levels of the organisation, design, planning and implementation of policies, functions and services. Mainstreaming will only be effective if it is a statutory requirement enforced by a statutory body or commission and is

Table 9.1: **The key characteristics of Public Service Management**

Strategic role
Governmental leadership
Service improvement and redesign
Meeting human needs and demands
Valuing and measuring by users, Elected Member and front-line, managerial and
    professional staff
Good quality services and functions with regular performance review
Enhancing the environment through sustainable planning
Equity and equality mainstreaming
Support for social enterprises

Organisational structure and culture
Subsidiarity and decentralisation
Democratic accountability at all levels of public bodies
Networking with other public bodies, organisations, alliances on global, regional,
    national and local basis
Participative and responsive structures
Flatter structures

Management practice
Integration of monitoring and evaluation
Democratic and participative management
Cooperation between management and labour
Freedom from corruption, patronage and favouritism
Maintaining probity, fiduciary duty and personal confidentiality
Transparent decision-making, reporting performance and information disclosure
Application of technology for socially useful purposes
Research and investigation for needs and options
Efficient and effective use of resources
Innovative and learning environment
Social Justice Planning and Auditing
Training and staff development
Enhancing capability

Employees
Work and views valued
Commitment to public service ethos
Good quality employment – pay, conditions of service and working environment
Equality of opportunity
Family friendly policies
Job satisfaction

Trade unions
Proactive
Strategic approach
Effective organisation
Democratic accountability
Collective bargaining and negotiating
Participative and representative
Communication with members
Alliances with civil society
Education and training

inclusive of gender, race, disability, religion and political opinion, age, marital status, dependents and sexual orientation. Mainstreaming must be an integral part of all ten elements of Public Service Management as a strategy and a political process. The state has a responsibility to mainstream equalities across social and economic life, not just the transformation of public organisations (and the private and voluntary sectors). The purpose of mainstreaming is not merely to identify adverse impact and discrimination but to take account of equalities in all policies, projects and processes and to recognise diversity and difference in class, gender, age and other factors.

Environmental sustainability should be mainstreamed by inclusion in corporate objectives, the design and planning process, service reviews, performance and quality indicators and in monitoring and evaluation.

Beyond Modernisation, Performance Management and Best Value

The reinventors claim that bureaucracy is the enemy of 'good governance' but the real problem lies with the reinventors who promote contracting, privatisation and commercialisation under the guise of modernisation. The modernisers claim to be neutral on who provides services and performs the functions of government, but this is a sham in a capitalist economy because it is little more than a remit to extend outsourcing and privatisation. This approach to modernisation simply provides capital with the raison d'etre to intensify their efforts to marketise and privatise public services.

It is necessary to build public organisations which are structured on learning and innovation and to prevent retrenchment or insularity behind closed doors. Legislation and regulations provide a framework but good quality Public Service Management cannot simply be enforced through law. Similarly, adequate resources are fundamental to the level and quality of services. Increased productivity, the wider application of new technology and quality programmes cannot substitute for financial resources.

The culture of an organisation is very important. It must be free of bullying and discrimination, value and respect the contribution of staff, encourage innovation and implement corporate policies. Organisational culture is determined by shared values, norms and relationships, hence the importance of establishing the principles and values, corporate policies and priorities and the practice of Public Service Management. The improvement of administrative processes, reducing paperwork, improving forecasting, redesigning procedures for applications and approvals and changing working practices must also promote the differences and distinctiveness of public service from the private and voluntary sectors. Political and corporate leadership, employee and trade union involvement, training and development, motivation, stability and security are all essential to achieving meaningful cultural change.

Managers too readily search for new techniques and off-the-shelf answers when they should be concentrating on increasing their own capacity for imaginative and innovative action.

Too many managers are looking outside themselves for answers to their problems. They are looking for the latest theory and at what successful organisations are doing. They are trying to spot the latest trends. In reality, they would be better off engaging in some critical thinking for themselves, recognising that they and their colleagues already have a vast treasure of insight and experience, which they could and should be using. The challenge is to tap this insight and understanding in a constructive way. (Morgan, 1993, p. 23)

A BLUEPRINT FOR A NEW PUBLIC SERVICE MANAGEMENT

Public Service Management has ten elements which link together to form an integrated strategy for a radically new approach to the management of public organisations. Corporate policies, values, vision and public service ethos provide a base on which democratic accountability and use/community and employee/trade union involvement extend across the organisation. Innovation, redesign and capacity building are continuous and integral functions together with monitoring and evaluation and creating a learning rather than an inspection/competition environment. Social Justice Planning and Auditing will facilitate mainstreaming equalities and provide a means of integrating employment, social, health, environment and local economy criteria into public policy decision-making. Quality systems and performance review, quality employment and training, strategic planning and researching social and economic needs, and public sector networks, partnerships and strategic sourcing are the other key elements (see Figure 9.1). Collectively, they form a systematic and comprehensive approach to increasing the capacity of the local, regional and national state. They are the means of putting the principles and values of public service into practice. Too frequently, corporate policies and priorities are little more than grandiose mission statements, regularly ignored or violated in daily practice. We need a new system which integrates these policies into management practice and performance assessment. The remainder of this chapter describes the approach and content of each element in more detail.

Public Service Management is applicable to all public bodies including local and central government, agencies and public enterprises. Although state owned corporations usually operate in a commercial environment the adoption of public service values and practices should be an integral part of their managerial and organisational strategy.

The *organisational capacity* of public sector bodies, in addition to the technical and managerial competence of staff, is fundamental to carrying out the core functions of the state and in creating the conditions for economic growth and social progress.

Figure 9.1: **Key components of Public Service Management**

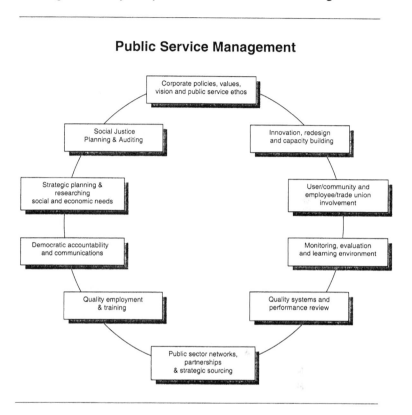

Public Service Management

Corporate policies, values, vision and public service ethos

Social Justice Planning & Auditing

Innovation, redesign and capacity building

Strategic planning & researching social and economic needs

User/community and employee/trade union involvement

Democratic accountability and communications

Monitoring, evaluation and learning environment

Quality employment & training

Quality systems and performance review

Public sector networks, partnerships & strategic sourcing

CORPORATE POLICIES, VALUES AND PUBLIC SERVICE ETHOS

A public organisation must have clarity about the functions and purpose of the organisation and its role in the local, national and international economy. It must constantly revise the vision of what it wants to achieve, ensure it is rooted in reality and harness the aims and aspirations of local people.

Strategic vision should set the framework within which strategic planning is carried out. Strategic vision usually covers a five–ten-year period and highlights the potential future development of the area, functions and services for which public bodies are responsible. For example, strategic vision for local government should identify forthcoming opportunities, how it will pursue economic development and social progress, improve the quality of life for citizens, enhance civil society, arts and culture and tackle regeneration and unemployment. These visions should be reflected in corporate policies and priorities and cascaded to service delivery and project implementation.

Developing a vision of public services in the future should be a key activity built into the organisation's public service planning, service improvement and innovation and redesign. It should include how they could be enhanced and improved, what they could offer if adequately resourced, how they could contribute to the well-being of the community and local economy. This process is difficult after two decades of cuts. It is not promoting idealism but a means of identifying the potential, increasing expectations and consolidating the values of public provision. Out of visions come goals and objectives to achieve more immediate improvements and change. Community organisations and trade unions have a responsibility to draw up their own ideas and visions, both as an important part of their strategies, and to wrest the ownership of visions from a handful of politicians, managers and business elites who are traditionally involved in this process.

All the performance management systems, for example Britain's Best Value and Better Quality Services, are primarily cost-driven or operate within a cost-centred context. New criteria and a new system of assessing performance, evaluating and accounting for public policy decision-making are urgently required. Values also affect the perception of problems and solutions, ethical behaviour and the establishment of trust. The criteria should include community and occupational health, employment, environmental sustainability, social needs, equity and equal opportunities, local economy and strengthening civil society and trade union capacity in addition to quality of service, good practice and cost effectiveness. These criteria should be used in all assessments and evaluation of policies and projects, particularly to determine adverse impact or added value.

Social Justice Planning and Auditing (SJPA) provides a means of valuing and assessing the impact of policies, budgets and projects at the planning, policy making and evaluation stages (see below). Users and employees must be actively involved in the auditing process.

Incentives form an important part of any management system, encouraging staff to adopt particular approaches or courses of action. Incentives in public services include respect and recognition of the importance of the work carried out by staff, job satisfaction, pay (but not performance related pay) and pensions, conditions of service, training and development, and involvement in policy formulation and operational management. Job Satisfaction Surveys have highlighted how staff value being treated fairly, with respect and a 'give and take' attitude (Whitfield, 1992).

Public Service Management should break the micro-management cycle of excessive rules which inhibit innovation and improved performance. This can be progressed by delegating responsibility to frontline supervisors and teams, better coordination of services and functions by more joint and collaborative working between departments and other agencies, minimising rules and regulations for sanctioning work and astute use of ICT. Equally important is the ability of the organisation to provide a sound framework for assessing all aspects of achievement and performance and recognising staff contribution by improving job satisfaction and family friendly policies.

DEMOCRATIC ACCOUNTABILITY AND COMMUNICATIONS

Reinvigorating and rebuilding democratic accountability forms the bedrock of Public Service Management. New forms of public scrutiny must be meaningful and feasible. Neo-liberal and Third Way modernisation only serve to consolidate consumerism and managerialism rather than genuine involvement (see Chapter 6).

Accountability is multi-layered and includes explaining or justifying decisions, accepting the need to rectify a problem, praise or blame, keeping and verifying correct records, providing information and redirecting responsibility when relevant. Accountability will not, like power, be willingly transferred or established. It can never be the prerogative of any management system, public or private. It depends equally on external structures and resources in addition to internal systems. Hence access to labour and community research and resource centres providing analytical, technical, organising and campaigning advice is an important part of the accountability structure.

Accountability is developed and maintained through a number of mechanisms:

Democratic structures: The structure of elected bodies should be based on the active involvement of all elected members and avoid the centralisation of policy making.

Scrutiny: Review and policy evaluation by elected members should be supported by powers to investigate and review, call evidence from within and outside the organisation and to engage independent advice.

Participation and involvement: Public organisations should have a statutory duty to involve user/community and employee/trade union representatives in all reviews, plans, audits and decision-making (see below).

Membership of boards and quasi-public organisations: The democratisation of these organisations by bringing them within the remit of democratically accountable public bodies was discussed in Chapter 8. Representatives on all public bodies and quangos, partnerships, networks and consortia should be mandated to regularly report back and account for policy decisions.

Capacity of civil society and labour to investigate and assess decisions: Accountability is partly dependent on the ability and capacity of civil society and labour organisations to be involved in decision-making processes, to carry out their own analysis of issues and develop alternative proposals.

Freedom of information and communications: Improved access to and distribution of strategic reports, reviews, audits and other basic information should be facilitated by ICT and freedom of information legislation.

Equalities and representation: Full representation of women, ethnic minorities and other groups must extend from membership of elected bodies to the methods used to engage civil society and labour organisations in the decision-making process.

Transparency of all contracts, partnerships and deals: The rules of all public organisations should require the disclosure of the main terms and conditions of all contracts, partnerships and deals. This can be achieved without undermining commercial confidentiality.

SOCIAL JUSTICE PLANNING AND AUDITING

A new methodology, Social Justice Planning and Auditing (SJPA), is required to infuse public management with the means to rigorously assess the impact of policies and projects and to develop alternative solutions. It must be mandatory, i.e. a statutory requirement for all public organisations and thus establish clear managerial accountability for mainstreaming equalities. It should be concise and expose the false and/or exaggerated claims commonly made to justify public and private policies. It is more comprehensive and powerful than cost–benefit analysis or issue-specific assessments because it integrates social, equity, health and environmental impact assessment.

SJPA is a political economy methodology to examine the macro and micro impact of public policies and both public and private investment. It is a framework to test the validity of claims and to evaluate the full consequences of policies, identifying who pays, who benefits and who may suffer any adverse consequences. It has five main components: an assessment of how policies impact on different social groups, an assessment of the direct employment and expenditure of earnings by staff employed in the organisation, indirect effect on jobs and expenditure created as a result of staff employed, identification of the social costs and benefits resulting from changes in employment and the local economy, the induced effects from further rounds of expenditure and employment generated by the purchase of locally produced goods and services; analysis of the full public sector costs resulting from changes to employment in the local economy.

SJPA is a process of examining the consequences of policy decisions, options and resource allocation on the rest of the public sector locally, regionally and nationally and on the private sector. In Britain, the Acheson Report on health inequalities recommended that all policies likely to have a direct or indirect impact on health should be subjected to a health impact assessment and formulated to reduce inequalities (Acheson Report, 1998). The impact of most decisions is not confined within organisations, public or private. The SJPA process identifies both positive and negative impacts. For example, public investment usually has benefits for all sectors including the private sector while company decisions to deindustrialise have hidden public sector costs. SJPA helps to identify these impacts, to ensure they are transparent and to amend or redesign policies to minimise adverse impact and to maximise opportunities and added value. It has become easier to claim 'savings' when the budget is focused on particular aspects of individual services and the knock-on effects of decisions and spending are not technically the responsibility of the organisation.

Social audits are a means of challenging commercial criteria and values, and developing measures which reflect the full social, political and economic impact of both public and private decisions. They should reflect the wider public and private social, economic and political 'costs' and benefits, both financial and non-financial, and not the maximisation of private or corporate wealth. SJPA complements the UNDP human development indices such as the Human Development Index, the Human Poverty Index and equality measures such as the Gender-related Development Index and Gender Empowerment Measure (UNDP, 1997).

All modelling involves calculations, estimating, and sometimes, assumptions because no one individual research project or survey can obtain all the required information in sufficient detail. However, the SJPA process requires all information to be transparent and any estimating to be recorded. The accountability built into SJPA should ensure that it reflects local values (see below).

A Public Sector Comparator is frequently used to assess the cost of public sector options in assessing outsourcing and privately financed infrastructure projects. However, the comparator is essentially an investment appraisal and does not assess the social, economic and environmental advantages/disadvantages of projects.

Local authorities, health and community care organisations have an important role in the local economy of most communities because they are among the largest employers; staff and their families represent a significant proportion of service users; decent employment conditions make an important contribution to the health of the community; they are major employers of women; they have a responsibility to provide sustainable employment and all employers have a responsibility to implement equal opportunities.

Equitable distribution or allocation is determined by the use of resources according to need, the share of benefits of economic growth and representation in civic and cultural affairs. Equality is assessed in terms of opportunity to develop skills, to learn, to be creative; of access and availability; in design, planning and relevance of a service; in the social relations of use of services; in employment, recruitment, promotion; and in participation, democratic control and representation. They apply to the public, users and to employees.

SJPA has four key functions: first, to assess the impact of policies, plans, the allocation of resources and participation/involvement with respect to race, gender, age, sexual orientation, religion, disability, political opinion, marital status, with/without dependents and class.

Second, the achievement of multi-faceted objectives is increasingly important in regeneration and service integration, hence they should be evaluated comprehensively to identify what is achievable as distinct from wish lists and rhetoric. It identifies the advantages and disadvantages of development and renewal proposals and assesses the impact on communities.

Third, investment impact analysis is increasingly important to assess the social and economic outcomes of public/private financed infrastructure projects and joint ventures.

Finally, increasing fragmentation as a result of the growth of new public, quasi-public and PPP, often single purpose, organisations means that financial, social, economic and environmental impacts should be assessed across the public sector rather than on a narrow functional remit. Claims of cost savings and benefits are meaningless in such circumstances.

SJPA is increasingly important in the public sector and public/private partnerships in a capitalist economy because the changing complexity of power within the state–capital–labour–civil society paradigm means that objectives and outcomes are in constant flux. Hence all plans, budgets, investment projects, major outsourcing and service reviews should be subjected to a SJPA audit. They must focus on process and outcomes.

The SJPA Process

The process has 13 stages which are summarised below and illustrated in Figure 9.2. The process is accountable through several mechanisms. Elected members, officers, community and trade union representatives should be established to oversee the audit and the findings fully reported and publicly available. The process will also often require research and consultation with affected organisations and groups. Finally, the process, findings and recommendations should also be open to scrutiny.

1. Identify scope of the analysis: Identify the scope of the assessment through a series of questions. Is there any evidence that new or existing policies may lead to different effects or impact on people of different religious beliefs or political opinions, men and women and other groups? The assessment should consider the indirect or knock-on effect of policies on social life, employment and the local economy, health and the environment. The SJPA can accommodate different levels of detail depending on the scope of the policies, projects or budgets under review, particularly in terms of the degree of comprehensiveness and level of detail necessary in the local economy, health and environmental impact assessments. These can vary in scope depending on the scale of the policy, project or budget being audited.

Figure 9.2: **Social Justice Planning and Auditing model**

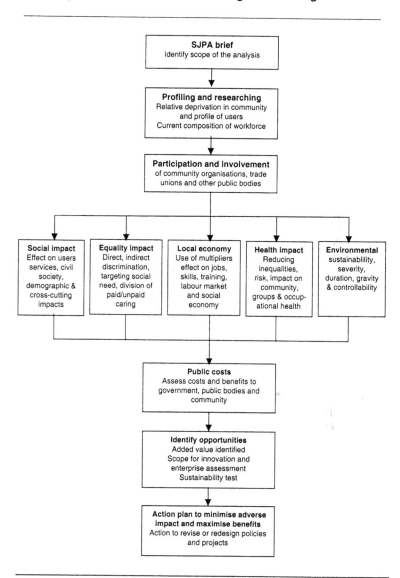

2. *Relative deprivation in community and profile of users:* Map the relative deprivation of the catchment area relating to the user and employment scope of the project. This profile should serve as a base for assessing the impact of proposals. Profile of relative deprivation and inequalities, ill-health, performance of the local economy, profile of users and potential users.

3. Current composition of workforce: The purpose is to identify the composition of the workforce in the similar manner to that for (2) above.

4. Participation and involvement of community organisations, trade unions and other public bodies: A wide range of community and local organisations, trade unions and civil society organisations should be involved in identifying and predicting how the policies, proposals or planned budget would impact on them.

5. Identify effect of proposals on services and users: Assessing the impact of proposals on services and users should be an integral part of the planning and project evaluation process. It should disaggregate the total benefit and/or loss to determine the net effect on particular services and groups of users. Differences in the quality of services can be experienced by people differentially depending on a number of factors.

6. Assess social impact: This should include assessment of opportunities for community development, improving community participation in service planning, changes in the patterns of shifts and availability of services, impact on family and child care, effect on community ownership, identity and maintaining self-organisation within the community. Assess impact on social capital, for example, education's contribution to civil society and engagement and the extent to which projects include support for the organising of civil society.

7. Equality impact: This will be in four parts. First, identifying direct discrimination, for example, any aspect of the policy, proposal of budget which impacts unequally in terms of gender, race, religion and political opinion, disability, age, marital status, dependents and sexual orientation. Second, identifying indirect discrimination, for example, whether the policy or project involves any requirements or conditions which affect one group of people differently from another, or whether it has a substantially unfavourable impact on one group compared with another. Third, identifying success/failure to target social need, for example, identify any negative impact or cause any social or economic disadvantage to any group of users, employees or their families. Finally, identifying the impact on the division of paid and unpaid caring between women and men within households and the impact on opportunities for education, training, employment and engagement in civil society.

8. Identify effect on employment and local economy: Assessment of the direct and indirect employment impact of proposals should be based on actual projected employment data. Promotional and media claims of jobs created should not be used unless they can be verified. Equally important is the classification of jobs into full/part time (based on actual projected hours) and the expected employment status, permanent, temporary or casual. Identify job losses, cuts in hours, changes to pay rates and conditions of service. Assess the impact of proposals on the local community, local authority or region with respect to public/private sectors and the social economy. Changes in staffing levels, terms and conditions, purchasing of local goods and services will have a knock-on effect on private services and the labour market. The flow of income and expenditure between central and local government, employed and unemployed, the private sector and the local economy can be assessed using the model in Figure 9.3 (Centre for Public Services, 1995b).

9. *Health impact assessment:* Identify nature of potential positive and negative health impacts of the project, the likely nature and extent of disruption caused to communities and the existence of potentially cumulative impacts. This could include changes in risk levels for health and safety at work, occupational health support, reducing health inequalities by increasing employment opportunities, quality of employment and training, reducing backlogs/delays in repairs, particularly those related to dampness, heating systems, and the contribution made by increasing environmental sustainability. A socio-environmental model of health should be used, covering biological factors, personal/family circumstances and lifestyle, social and physical environment, public services and public policy (Scott-Samuel et al., 1998). Epidemiological issues should include the probability, frequency, severity and size of health impacts.

10. *Environmental impact assessment:* Assess the impact of completion of the policy/project and budget on the quality of the environment including the implementation/construction phase. Environmental factors will cover water and air quality, noise and vibration; odours; visual quality and intrusion; landscape and agriculture; flora and fauna; river, coastal and estuary patterns; social and economic effects, and historical and archaeological interest.

11. *Assess public costs and benefits:* Projects and development often have other public sector costs and benefits. Assess increased unemployment, welfare payments and loss of national and local tax revenues, cost of special employment schemes. Use changes in employment levels and pay to determine impact on direct and indirect taxation and access to benefits. This stage should bring together all the different elements of project and public costs and the gains/adverse impact for each group/community. It should also identify the importance, scale and likelihood of predicted impacts.

12. *Innovation and enterprise assessment:* Identify scope for provision of new services and/or products by public, social and/or private sector and opportunities for venture capital or pension fund investment.

Figure 9.3: **Income and expenditure flows to and from the local economy**

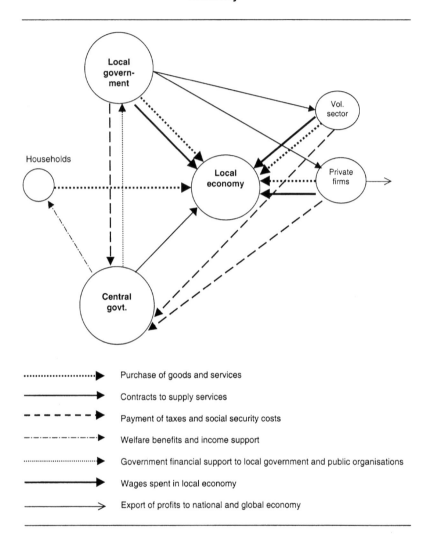

`........................▶`	Purchase of goods and services
`────────────▶`	Contracts to supply services
`─ ─ ─ ─ ─ ─ ▶`	Payment of taxes and social security costs
`─·─·─·─·─·▶`	Welfare benefits and income support
`.............................▶`	Government financial support to local government and public organisations
`────────────▶`	Wages spent in local economy
`───────────▷`	Export of profits to national and global economy

13. Action plan to minimise adverse impact and maximise benefits: The final stage of SJPA should identify any discrimination and adverse effects of policies and projects, trade-offs between positive and adverse impacts and the identification of added value – defined as a contribution over and above what would otherwise be achieved by other options or proposals. Added value should be assessed in terms of additional investment in new or extended services or facilities, health and environmental improvements or sustainability and the quality of employment. This stage should prepare proposals and any action to be taken to amend or redesign proposals to prevent or ameliorate discrimination. It should also identify how the benefits or added value of policies can be sustained.

INNOVATION, REDESIGN AND CAPACITY BUILDING

The concept of innovation and development should operate in conjunction with service improvement because they are interrelated and should be integrated into management systems and organisational structures. Innovation has three dimensions: internal innovation and transfer within the organisation, the import/export of innovation from/to other organisations and providers, and the application of ICT. Innovation should be an integral part of the organisational and managerial culture of public organisations.

The development of e-government is radically changing the collection of taxes and rents and payments such as pensions and benefits. It offers the opportunity to improve the issuing of licences, grants and regulatory approvals; the reporting of faults, problems and complaints (although not necessarily the solutions); the ability to align service provision to needs including better integration and coordination of service delivery; user access to information on services, such as availability and frequency; data and intelligence about social and economic needs; environmental controls of public facilities. However, ICT development is only one aspect of innovation and is applicable to only certain parts of state functions and services.

Research and development plays an important role in improving service delivery, developing new services and tackling special needs and problems. Learning organisations in the twenty-first century will be judged on their capacity to develop an organisational and managerial culture to foster innovation and its transfer across the organisation. Improved networking and communications systems will facilitate this process but it also requires specific management action, initially with a central team to lead, provide technical and financial support with a mainstreaming strategy. It should ensure ideas are examined, proposals developed, tested ideas are transferred throughout the organisation with full monitoring of implementation.

Innovation should encompass service provision including revised, expanded or new functions, information sources, sources of funding, new types of forms and administrative systems, use of ICT systems and software. Developing innovative new services and projects should be an integral part of policy and financial planning.

Innovation should be mainstreamed so that it is part of a continuous culture, a permanent agenda item, in which staff are encouraged and supported to develop ideas and proposals, with resources for workplace development. It is imperative that staff feel that their ideas and involvement are valued and they have the confidence to challenge management. A code of practice should detail the procedures for the development and assessment of new ideas, and attribute credit and recognition for proposals and how they can be accessed on intranets.

Innovation and transfer can be supported by having a percentage of budgets allocated to innovation and experimentation thus making it an enforceable budget heading which allows the use of savings as additional incentives for innovation allowing transfer between budgets and financial years.

USER AND EMPLOYEE/TRADE UNION INVOLVEMENT

All public bodies should be required to produce a corporate strategy on user/employee involvement which includes proposals to involve (a) service users and potential users; (b) representative civil society organisations, social economy and business organisations; (c) the public; (d) employees and trade unions. It should set out the terms of involvement, community organising and development support and a strategy to ensure women, people with disabilities, black and ethnic minorities and other equality groups are afforded equal access and representation.

It is vitally important that involvement is through both representative civil society and labour organisations, alongside participative techniques such as citizens' panels, forums and focus groups to draw on those not involved in or represented by any organisation. Political support for public policy is most effectively achieved by winning the support of representative organisations because local needs are usually more clearly represented and expressed and such organisations usually build up an understanding and experience of service delivery problems and public policy issues.

Participation and involvement should encompass monitoring and reviewing services, the design of facilities, community planning, the regeneration and development process, setting performance standards and targets, Social Justice Planning and Auditing, evaluation and scrutiny to name just the key areas.

The quality and accountability of involvement and the quality of information and views received should be a key objective. A variety of methods are available including group discussion, workshops on specific issues, public meetings or forums, small group meetings in areas or on particular issues; representation on coordinating committees and working parties; participation in workplace service improvement projects with staff; involvement in formal structures – area committees, advisory panels, neighbourhood forums and consultative user panels, citizens' juries and focus groups.

There is a direct connection between how the poor are involved in the development process in Third World nations and how the poor are involved in regeneration and social inclusion projects in industrialised countries. The World Bank's Poverty Assessment has developed into Participatory Poverty Assessment (Robb, 1999) but has simply moved from a wholly technocratic perspective to 'better defining the experience of individuals, groups and households and communities'. It falls well short of 'participatory government' which focuses on empowering the poor to achieve effective poverty reduction inclusive of a demand-driven participation, accountability and capacity building. This is powerfully summarised by Schneider who describes empowerment as:

> ... the gaining of strength in the various ways necessary to be able to move out of poverty, rather than literally 'taking over power from somebody else' at the purely political level. The use of the term in the poverty debate stems from the observation that the poor frequently lack the means which are the basis of power in a wider sense, to move out of poverty. These means include knowledge, education, organisation, rights and 'voice' (Hirschman) as well as financial and material resources. Any attempt at poverty reduction therefore has to identify for the specific case which of these means are lacking and in which ways they may be obtained. (Schneider, 1999, p. 17)

The Case for Staff Involvement

The gap between rhetoric and reality is very wide. Employee involvement or so-called 'empowerment' rarely featured in the work of the quality gurus such as Deming, Juran and Crosby and only entered Total Quality Management via the 'pop management' writers. 'This literature tends to be superficial, trivialising the conflict and tensions that exist within organisations' (Wilkinson et al., 1995, p. 9).

An organisation will be more effective and both management and staff will have greater job satisfaction if the workforce is genuinely involved in decision-making concerning organisational, managerial and operational matters. This is more effective if it is built into the industrial relations framework as opposed to being an 'add-on'. Workforce involvement is an essential means of achieving and sustaining a public service ethos within public bodies. This is supported by detailed research in the public and private sectors which concluded that 'the attitudes of the people in the organisation which seem to account for the largest part of the variation in company productivity and thereby profitability. Indeed, people and their attitudes to their jobs are the most important company assets' (Patterson et al., 1997, p. 7).

Workers should be made to feel that they can influence the delivery of services and management practice, be able to accomplish things on their own by exercising discretion and have a degree of autonomy over their work and recognition for their efforts. Workers should be given continual and meaningful training. The workforce should have the ability and freedom to organise, select its own representation and the right to be involved in service reviews and audits with access to their own advisers. The scope of involvement should encompass management and organisation of the service, implementation of corporate policies, strategic planning and development of the service, resource planning, service improvement, research and development, preparation of public service/business plans, monitoring and evaluation, and innovation and application of new technology (IDEA, forthcoming).

Old style command and control management systems stifle initiative, innovation and flexibility and ultimately limit the quality and effectiveness of services. Trade unions and management usually share some common objectives but are fundamentally opposed in others. Well-organised unions can both work cooperatively with management on redesigning the workplace *and* simultaneously campaign for improved pay and conditions.

The organisation of work and the labour process in the public sector should be radically changed to accommodate:

- frontline workers perceived as a resource rather than as a cost;
- the quality of employment valued and its relationship to the quality of service fully recognised;
- equity and equality in employment and service delivery;
- participatory management with emphasis on teamwork, consensus and cooperation and involvement in planning, management decision-making and quality improvement;
- deregulation of bureaucratic rules and delayering management structures;
- employment security which is vital for motivation, morale and commitment to implement corporate policies. Outsourcing and competitive tendering treat workers as mere commodities and undermine the conditions necessary to achieve service improvement;
- provide new incentives for workers to improve their skills;
- education, training and development (individuals and teams) to provide the tools, knowledge and confidence to facilitate involvement;
- adoption of a learning organisation approach and thus understanding and responding to the external and internal environment, valuing monitoring and evaluation, cross-functional teams and user research;
- improve the working environment.

The importance of the link between the quality of employment and the quality of services is underlined by much of the leading management thinking in Britain and the USA. It places great emphasis on the important role of the workforce in service industries and the need to develop systems which 'promote better use of the potential motivation and skills inherent in the members of an organisation' (Normann, 1991, p. 45). Normann reports that

> various studies have shown that it is almost impossible to develop and even more to maintain a particular kind of climate and relationship between front-line personnel and customers unless the same climate and

basic values prevail in the relationship between front-line personnel and their supervisors. If one behavioural code and one set of values prevails inside the organisation and another in external contacts with clients, the contact personnel will find themselves in a more or less impossible 'double bind' position. (Ibid, p. 45)

While pay and training *are* crucial issues for many front-line public service workers, involvement in the design and planning of their work is also vitally important.

Trade unions have a key role in Public Service Management because they provide a democratic representative structure, ensure that workforce concerns are voiced, bargain for jobs, pay and working conditions and promote continuous learning, training and skill development. They provide employees with a degree of organised power which is a precondition for genuine participatory management. It is crucial that trade unions maintain their independence and organisational ability to take action to protect their members' interests.

Workforce involvement in Public Service Management is either jointly with management or via independent trade union initiatives which produce recommendations and proposals that require political and managerial support for implementation. More recently, management's agenda has been driven by cuts, efficiency, outsourcing and restructuring in contrast to a union agenda driven by protecting jobs, maintaining in-house services and improving the effectiveness of services.

An agreement on employee and trade union involvement should be negotiated and include facility time and training, an information agreement, access to managers and front-line staff, a project evaluation and reporting procedure, a budget to fund initiatives (likely to be far more cost effective than most management consultants) and a commitment to create a learning culture which accepts constructive criticism and values ideas rather than competes over their ownership. It should supplement existing joint employer–trade union structures such as Works Councils or Joint Consultative Committees.

Genuine and continuing democratic accountability and involvement cannot be achieved on the cheap. Increasing the capacity of public organisations to involve user/community organisations and staff/trade unions and increasing the capacity of civil society to meaningfully engage in these processes has financial implications. Again, quality counts and costs. Involvement cannot be funded from 'efficiency savings' but must be an integral part of public management with a budget heading in all national, regional and local public bodies and a key criterion in central–local resource allocation.

There are various methods of facilitating joint management–employee/trade union involvement:

- *Workshops, team meetings or briefings* where workers meet with management to discuss current problems and ideas for service improvements ranging from improving communications, changing procedures to the application of new technology.
- *Labour–Management Committees (LMCs)* and other formally agreed participative structures with equal representation of trade unionists working jointly with management on specific projects such as reorganising work, improving job satisfaction, redesigning services and supplementing existing negotiating arrangements. LMCs are usually structured on the basis of joint control, written ground rules, direct and representative participation, frequent feedback, sharing of information and expertise, collaborative problem solving and consensus decision-making (US Department of Labor, 1996). LMCs often establish quality improvement teams of front-line staff to analyse work processes and make recommendations.
- *Service Delivery Committees, Service Development Teams and Service Review Teams* involve management and workers jointly reviewing services, working practices and procedures. There is wide variation in the scope of these initiatives but they are generally management teams with trade union representation and sometimes a user/community representative.
- *Departmental reviews:* They generally involve all departmental or section staff in identifying problems and issues using Strengths/Weaknesses/Opportunities/Threats, GAP analysis or similar techniques. They are too frequently one-off events which require follow-up initiatives such as the above.

Trade unions will normally require that all local union involvement be channelled through the local executive committee which will elect or appoint representatives. Unions should also be involved in the design, planning and distribution of communications to union members including questionnaires, surveys and proposals to engage facilitators or consultants. They will also wish to be involved in setting the agenda and will wish to ensure that proposals are negotiated through the existing bargaining arrangements.

Management must be willing to genuinely evaluate service improvement from front-line staff and trade unions.

Service improvement requires continuous learning hence all these initiatives should be supported by training. Some authorities use consultants to carry out workplace consultation, focus groups and to identify staff concerns; however, this is often intended to marginalise trade unions and usually has a negative effect on management–staff relations.

Trade unions in North America have extensive experience of 'empowerment' and new management systems (such as Total Quality Management and High Performance Workplace) and have devised a three-part strategic response to management initiatives which covers organising, researching, assessing strengths and weaknesses and education/training as a precursor to determining union strategy. The second part is centred on deciding whether to join, improve or oppose depending on whether the initiative is under way or planned. The third part includes educating and mobilising the membership, organising within teams and projects and agreeing a code of conduct, developing trade union proposals and identifying the terms and conditions of involvement (Parker and Slaughter, 1994).

Community/Trade Union Projects

Public Service Management rejects traditional staff suggestion or reward schemes because they are superficial and ineffective. Instead, it promotes properly constituted joint management–trade union–community initiatives and facilitates community and trade union organisations drawing up their own plans, proposals and strategies. The latter could include:

- *Union initiated working groups or committees* to examine job satisfaction, draw up proposals for service improvements and better training programmes.
- *Worker/community plans* by community and/or trade union organisa-tions produce proposals to counter management plans for closures, outsourcing, transfer and privatisation. In Britain, a wide variety of community and/or trade union alternative plans have provided a detailed critique of central or local government policy, business plans, Best Value service reviews, contract or project evaluation, assessed the social and economic impact on the local economy and presented alternative plans for how services should be managed and operated or for area development (Whitfield, 1992). The Centre for Public Services has worked with many public bodies, community and trade union organisations to produce alternative plans and proposals, many of which have succeeded in preventing privatisation and led to improved services.
- *Access to external trade union consultants and advisers, facilitators and training,* for example, the 'Komanco' project developed by the Swedish union SKAF, has initiated many successful restructuring and efficiency projects (Sjolander, 1996).

STRATEGIC RESEARCHING AND PLANNING SOCIAL AND ECONOMIC NEEDS

The state has a key responsibility to survey, research, collect, collate and assess information on a broad range of local and national social and economic needs, the performance of all sectors of the economy and to make this information readily accessible for educational, business and other purposes. There is often a vested interest in keeping the real level of social needs hidden from the public, fearing criticism of the organisation rather than central government or not wanting any shortfall or failure to be on the political agenda. Sometimes needs are simply obscured by technocratic language or because of a lack of hard information.

Regeneration, poverty reduction, Social Justice Planning and Auditing and designing and planning services on user needs will require public organisations to put increased priority on social research. It will also require direct engagement with civil society and labour organisations in research methodology. For example, obtaining the in-depth views and ideas of 100 service users is usually more valuable and enlightening than market research of a larger sample.

Community or area plans provide the means of translating national, regional and city policies into practice in the context of local needs, structures and aspirations. They create an opportunity to maximise the coordination of services, improvements and regeneration with the involvement of community organisations, civil society, voluntary organisations and other public agencies. Public Service Management should be underpinned by research skills including social, economic and environmental analysis, project planning and management and strategic service or business planning.

Researching trends and developments in the local, national and global economy, maintaining profiles of key local industries and services, monitoring economic activity and labour market change and assessing the local impact of policies and legislation should be integrated into management practice. High quality social and economic research are essential for SJPA and to support local government's duty to enhance the economic, social and environmental well-being of their area (see Chapter 8).

Strategic, service and financial planning should be an integral and continuing activity in every service to meet current and future needs and adapt to changes in technology and the economy. Service planning and a strategic perspective is essential to achieve more effective services, make comprehensive assessments of national and local needs, adapt to changing needs, and to plan for the future. Service planning should cover the organisation's strategic objectives, service profile and resource audit, sector or market analysis, user needs together with strategic, staffing and operational plans with arrangements for monitoring and evaluation (Centre for Public Services, 1993 details how to prepare public service plans).

Public bodies require project planning and management skills in order to ensure fast and effective implementation of projects from inception to completion. All departments, sections and units should be able to draw on internal technical, financial planning and legal advice thus minimising reliance on consultants and maximising internal organisational learning. This could be supported by a public sector consultancy operated by associations representing local and public bodies.

QUALITY SYSTEMS AND PERFORMANCE REVIEW

Quality of service and public service values and principles are inevitably interdependent in public bodies. They need to be incorporated into quality programmes, performance standards and targets. The adoption of national, professional or best practice standards for training, competence, equalities, working conditions and service-specific codes should be a minimum requirement. The quality of public services is determined by the level and range of services, access to the service, the service environment, the service relationship, quality of employment, accountability and democratic control of the service, management and organisation of the service, and monitoring and performance review (Centre for Public Services, 1993).

The widely used term 'continuous improvement' is rejected because it is only feasible if it is narrowly defined. Service improvement cannot be separated from the provision of services to meet social and economic needs and the availability of resources – 'meeting needs/improving quality' is a more useful banner. The pressure to achieve continuous improvement can lead to increased stress and bullying. It is also incompatible with the methods required to achieve more substantive innovation and improvement through Public Service Management. Furthermore, continuous improvement is associated with performance management (see Chapters 3 and 4), the widespread use of performance indicators and inspection regimes.

Performance should be assessed rather than measured because of the profound difficulties in correlating performance measures with actual consequences, the contradictions between performance targets, for example, efficiency and quality targets, variations in the basis on which information is collected and different interpretations of performance, and changes in staffing levels make some performance measures difficult to assess.

Public Service Management should have a small core set of *performance standards* (a given minimum level or good practice provision of service), selected *performance indicators* (which indicate the extent to which strategic objectives are being met, gauge the impact of projects and services or demonstrate how well a standard is being met) and *targets* (a commitment to achieve a certain level of service or use of resources within a given timescale) spanning quality, cost effectiveness, equity and sustainability. Performance assessment should be based on *inputs* – the resources used to produce a service which indicate costs and efficiency, *outputs* (count the goods and services delivered or workload),*outcomes* (indicate the impact or benefit of services) and *process* measures because the manner in which inputs are procured, outputs produced or outcomes achieved is an inherent part of the service or function performed. Assessing outcome is fraught with problems of identifying cause and effect and the influence of other policies and organisations.

Financial systems have a key role in accountability and service delivery and must reflect public service principles and values. Accrual or resource accounting and budgeting should be abolished and replaced by a system designed to reflect the funding, operational and managerial needs of public sector organisations. Departments and units should have the flexibility to move resources between budgets and financial years and to retain a fixed percentage of 'savings' from reorganising and restructuring services. They should also be able to carry over unspent budgets for research, service development, improvements or innovative projects. The financial system must sit alongside and facilitate the other nine elements of public service management, particularly SJPA, innovation transfer and performance review.

MONITORING, EVALUATION AND LEARNING ENVIRONMENT

Monitoring has a fundamental role in identifying the scope for new initiatives, learning the lessons from front-line staff and service users, designing service improvements and gathering intelligence about needs. A well-designed monitoring system will employ a range of monitoring techniques to assess performance and the achievement of corporate objectives, adequately trained staff, a recording, analysing and reporting system, compliance and default procedures and regular review of the monitoring system itself. Monitoring should not be confined to service delivery but also cover organisational and financial performance, the implementation of corporate policies, employment policies and practices, regulatory functions, project management, service plans and user/employee involvement.

Public Service Management should take account of four main types of audit and evaluation:

1. *Social Justice Planning and Auditing* assesses the potential social, economic, equity, health and environmental impact of policies, projects and options and is integrated into the policy making and resource allocation process.
2. *Policy and programme evaluation* assesses the effectiveness of policies and projects, the extent to which objectives are met, and is usually carried out during implementation and upon completion of projects.
3. *Environmental audit* assesses the impact of proposals and an organisation's performance in environmental compliance and management practices to protect the environment (can also be part of SJPA).
4. *Financial audit* assesses whether an organisation's financial duties, income and expenditure have been exercised with due process.

There are a range of techniques for reviewing services which include quality audits, benchmarking, user research, market intelligence, process mapping, gap analysis and workforce involvement in service improvement projects (Centre for Public Services, 1998).

A three-yearly needs assessment and community planning review should have five key components, namely, a needs assessment identifying unmet needs; resources which have been available in previous years and forecasts for next period to identify the resource deficit; performance assessment including achievements, problems and causes; a review of organisational and management practice; and proposals for service development.

The evaluation of policies, programmes and projects has a key role in Public Service Management because of the contribution it can make to policy formulation, strategic planning and meeting corporate objectives. A culture of evaluation should be developed supported by training, funding and dialogue and incorporated into organisational structures and management systems.

Evaluation methodology will need to recognise the importance of the context (spatial, geographical, institutional) and the social (norms, values, rules and interrelationships) in the assessment of outcomes. Determining policy effectiveness – what works for whom and in what circumstances – and learning lessons from the evaluation process are essential elements of realistic evaluation. Rigorous methods of evaluation are key to creating a learning environment as an alternative to oppressive systems of audit, inspection and surveillance or a means of justifying relentless pressure to increase performance and productivity.

The integration of monitoring, service review and evaluation is illustrated in Table 9.2.

Equalities and environmental sustainability should be an integral part of the evaluation process, for example, the assessment of the outcome of projects, reviews, policies which had specifically mainstreamed equalities, integrating equality objectives with main project objectives and with action plans compared with those which had not. It should also include research to examine the gender/equality impact of policies and projects, the availability of equality data in terms of profiles of service users, employees, equality monitoring and equality assessment of involvement and participation.

PUBLIC SECTOR NETWORKS, PARTNERSHIPS AND STRATEGIC SOURCING

Public bodies are increasingly required to collaborate and jointly provide public goods and services because of the complexity and interrelationship of issues and social needs. Networks are defined by membership, collaboration, coordination and interchange. Networks or coalitions of organisations jointly may fund and deliver services, design and implement projects, share information and coordinate functions. They have their own rules negotiated by participants.

Public bodies should design new networks to link together fragmented self-governing quasi-public organisations created by neo-liberal and Third Way modernisation by offering services, access to ICT and economies of

Table 9.2: **The evaluation context**

Performance	Monitoring scope	Review methods	Evaluation
objectives	quality of service	quality audit	causation
indicators	quality of employment	benchmarking	methodologies
standards	corporate policies	user research	participants
targets	financial performance	market intelligence	norms and values
	equalities mainstreaming	process mapping	policy effectiveness
	project management	gap analysis	outcome assessment
	service plan implementation	service planning	learning lessons
	user/employee involvement		
	sustainability		

scale. This could encourage communication, cooperation and mutuality between schools, residential homes and hospitals without centralised control. While public bodies may engage in networks which involve the private sector, social enterprises and voluntary organisations, the prime focus should be in forging public sector networks.

This concept of networks differs markedly from those promoted by academics. For example, Rhodes describes networks as a 'form of coordination and managing inter organisational links' which 'are not accountable to the state: they are self-organising' (Rhodes, 1997, pp. 52–3). Others argue that networks of public and private agencies and voluntary organisations are emerging to form a 'network society' in which network relationships are determined by cooperation, competition, coordination and coevolution (Jackson and Stainsby, 2000). Networks in these terms accept the increasing opaqueness of public–private sector boundaries and arise out of continuing the Third Way agenda, not as alternatives to it.

Public sector networks involving the social economy, civil society and trade unions will also be important in countering the power of capital and markets. Networks or federations of civil society and trade union organisations have a different function but combine many of the above attributes.

Partnerships are basically an agreement by public, private, social enterprise and/or voluntary organisations to work jointly on a specific project by pooling resources within a common agenda and action plan. However, the current hype makes a virtue out partnerships per se with the goal becoming partnership working appearing to have higher priority than the outcomes which they are intended to achieve. The current vogue in Britain to brand every project or contract 'a partnership' is in danger of devaluing and discrediting the concept. It is no coincidence that the 'new' partnerships between state and capital follow two decades in which trade unions and civil society have been weakened and marginalised.

There are certain fundamental preconditions for partnership which must include the concept of 'additionality' and must not substitute or replace the role of the state nor mask a loss of capacity. They should also include resource commitment, allocation of risk and responsibility, ownership, transparency and open book accounting, allocation of surplus, continuous performance, quality of employment and a social capital component to increase power of user/community and trade union involvement.

Collaborative arrangements, partnerships, multi-agency working groups, membership of a consortium or a network of organisations require clear and comprehensive agreements which cover strategic objectives, shared vision and priorities, resource commitments, responsibilities and the overall control and management. Responsibilities for carrying out specific tasks, policy for acquiring specialist advice and support services and the application and implementation of different organisations' corporate policies must also be included. Agreements should also cover financial matters such as investment, allocation of risk, sharing increase/decrease in the valuation of assets, the pooling of resources and budgets, and financial and resource obligations. A procedure for agreeing performance standards, targets and service reviews and implementation programmes will be required.

Partnerships should also include community, civil society and trade union representation on boards and joint committees, accountability and reporting back arrangements, access to meetings and information pooling and disclosure. The conditions for termination of a partnership or consortium and the treatment of assets will also be essential.

All public bodies need to access specialist advice and services from time to time even when they are committed to in-house provision (see Chapter 8). It is therefore essential that clear and comprehensive policies and procedures are in place, if necessary, for strategic sourcing from consultants, social enterprises, voluntary organisations and private firms.

The strategic sourcing process should include negotiating trade union and user involvement, assessing performance and reviewing the service and a commitment to submitting an in-house bid. It is essential that packaging of the contract, the specification, contract conditions and compliance requirement be based on the needs of the service and public interest criteria, not on the requirements of markets or contractors. The evaluation of proposals must be rigorous and comprehensive, covering quality performance, employment and industrial relations, training, health and safety, equalities, environmental sustainability, ethical and corporate social responsibility. The financial assessment should include all the relevant public costs including the cost of administering the tendering process, contract management and monitoring costs and other costs incurred in contracting out. It should include a full analysis of the additional costs imposed on other public sector bodies and the impact on the local economy and labour market.

QUALITY EMPLOYMENT AND TRAINING

There is an inseparable link between the quality of service and the quality of employment. Public service values and principles should be reflected in the depth and scope of the organisation's employment policy which should encompass the health and welfare of its staff in the broadest sense. Recruitment and selection procedures which take into account all the factors noted below will assist in ensuring a more committed workforce providing a consistent and good quality service. The key components of employment policy should include:

- recognition of the right to organise and collective bargaining and full implementation of all ILO standards;
- pay (not performance related), pensions and conditions of service;
- family friendly employment policies including child care provision;
- training, education and life-long learning;

- health and welfare policies including health-enhancing quality of the work environment;
- equalities mainstreaming;
- workplace involvement agreement;
- public service culture and code of ethics;
- working conditions;
- comprehensive transfer policies if work is outsourced.

The recognition of and facilities for trade unions are vitally important for industrial relations, service delivery and the fair and just treatment of staff. All public service workers should be covered by a system of industrial relations providing comprehensive employment and trade union rights and conditions of service. Staff training and career development should form an integral part of in-house service delivery with public sector management training to rebuild a distinctive public service management and to recapture public sector ethos and values. Corporate and departmental or section joint consultative committees in which consultation and involvement in decision-making is integrated into the structure and agendas at all levels are essential.

A comprehensive Code for Quality Employment should supplement existing bargaining arrangements and encompass best practice industrial relations framework with trade union recognition and facilities for repre-sentation, education, information disclosure and continuous workplace improvement. It would also provide mechanisms for the application of new technology, changes to working practices, redeployment, training and staff development, health and safety and staff health and welfare (Centre for Public Services, 1998).

Public bodies should have policies and practices which facilitate structural and organisational change and mitigate their employment impact. In addition to early retirement and voluntary severance schemes and the protection of pensions and other employee benefits, public bodies should include redeployment and retraining, access to further education, work sharing, phasing job reductions, skills assessment, counselling and employment services to help staff access new employment and advice on developing social economy alternatives.

Combined together, the ten elements of Public Service Management provide a new, distinctive and powerful means of increasing the capacity of the state to fulfil the core functions – democratic and civil society, national and international responsibilities, human needs and development, economic and fiscal management, and regulation of markets, firms and organisations in the twenty-first century.

10

New Strategies and Alliances

Public services and the welfare state sector will be a central terrain of change and conflict in the first decades of the twenty-first century. Power struggles between capital, labour, civil society and the state will intensify as marketisation and privatisation extend to the core services such as health, education and social welfare. There is evidence of a rising tide of opposition to these values and policies. Neo-liberalism and Third Way ideology appear to be well entrenched but continuing economic, political and environmental crises could destabilise or derail the modernisation agenda.

There are also fundamental flaws in the private sector's ability to provide public goods and no amount of rhetoric and propaganda about partnerships and business involvement can hide the deep fault lines.

Strategies for the twenty-first century should:

Challenge the values and rationale of the capitalist economy: This should include continually contesting the narrow economistic and competitive model of modernisation and demonstrating the relevance and viability of alternatives.

Campaign for democratic accountability, governance and involvement to increase the power of labour and civil society: Demanding the democratisation of international, national and local government, public bodies and NGOs and rethinking of state institutions to improve accountability, transparency and public management is crucial to mount maximum pressure on the capital–state relationship. Improved governance is essential to achieve sustainable human development. The internationalisation of NGOs and civil society must also be rooted in improving democratic accountability in order to improve their credibility, legitimacy and sustainability.

Strengthen the opposition to marketisation, privatisation and partnership: Two decades ago, a seven-part strategy was drawn up to oppose privatisation. It required the simultaneous application of all seven elements, namely: developing alternative plans and proposals to improve services; education and propaganda; building stronger workplace organisations and making links with workers in other places; developing coalitions and alliances; the tactical use of industrial action and negotiating machinery; direct action by workers and users and a counter-offensive against contractors already providing public services (Whitfield, 1983; 1992). This strategy has been successful in many campaigns in several countries although they are, unfortunately, the exception rather than the rule. The problem has not been the lack of a political strategy but the lack of opposition to privatisation and deregulation in principle. Two decades later, although forms of privatisation have widened and deepened, the strategy retains its relevance. Opposition to strategic partnerships and PPPs must be intensified since they have enormous impact on the accountability, quality, employment, organisation and provision of public services, the social and physical infrastructure and regeneration process. Radical alternative modernisation plans must play a central role in this strategy.

Organise and campaign against the World Trade Organisation's negotiations to restructure the role of government: This should focus on GATS, the multilateral agreements on intellectual property rights (TRIPS), trade related investment (TRIMS), government procurement (AGP) and investment regulations relating to the stalled MAI. Alternative international agreements should enhance nation state welfare systems, international collaboration to improve planning and access, share good practice, create social partnerships and improve working conditions.

Constantly press for increased public investment: More imaginative use of borrowing mechanisms such as bonds, quasi-public corporations and pension fund investment, must be conditional on meeting social use criteria and be subjected to social justice planning and auditing. The taxation=public spending=quality of public services and the welfare state=value of the social wage linkage must be at the core of these demands.

Expose the consequences and contradictions of neo-liberal modernisation, the Third Way and the private provision of public goods. Continually challenge business hegemony, vested interests and the corporate-welfare complex and demand new controls over capital with re-regulation, rigorous monitoring and evaluation.

Strengthen the organisation and formation of alliances and coalitions between labour and civil society locally, nationally and internationally. This should include organising the chain of production of public services which will increasingly extend from in-house provision to home-working to voluntary organisations and the social economy to local, national and/or international locations of private firms. More broad-based movements for economic and social justice beyond the workplace and workers' rights will be essential. The Relatives Action Group for the Elderly (RAGE) forging a community/trade union alliance in Birmingham, the continuing collaboration between

Newcastle City Council UNISON and the Newcastle Tenants Federation and the forging of a broadly based Community Alliance in the city to oppose the council's regeneration proposals and prepare an alternative plan are three excellent examples. Trade unions have a vital role in organising, representing, bargaining, educating, training, monitoring and participating in labour and civil society in an era of increasing insecurity.

Improve understanding of the global economy and research/investigative skills to analyse the key trends and developments, investigate the activities of multinationals, expose local power structures and develop analytical skills to articulate needs and alternatives. Life-long learning should reskill people for involvement in civil society and trade unions, not just for employment and education.

Combine industrial, civil and community action internationally, nationally and locally. In addition to independent action, the emphasis must be on *linking* workplace and community action, *coordinating* strategies and creating opportunities to broaden the base through national and international alliances. Trade unions must give more active support to non-workplace issues and campaigns.

Promote an alternative modernisation strategy which encompasses a new vision of government at central, regional, local and community levels. It should be centred on a radical rethinking of democratic accountability with the involvement of users, communities, staff and trade unions; new legislation and regulations which empower and resource public bodies and local government to act in the public and community interest; a new blueprint for a new public service management coupled with organisational reform of public agencies and responsibilities; a social justice strategy for poverty reduction and equalities; and a plan to rapidly enhance environmental sustainability.

Develop and promote a distinctive public management based on public service values, principles and best practice for the production and provision of public goods. It is essential to differentiate public management from the commercial and voluntary sectors, particularly by putting public service ethos, codes of conduct and quality systems into practice.

These principles and values must continue to distinguish vibrant and innovative public services from markets and profiteering, despite the constraints and limitations imposed by capitalism. They indicate the possibility of a better quality of life and a more equitable, progressive and sustainable civilisation than that dictated by markets and the capitalist economy and suggest the potential of a truly socialist alternative. They will always be worth organising and campaigning for.

Bibliography

Acheson Report (1998) 'Independent Inquiry into Inequalities in Health: Report' (Chairman: Sir Donald Acheson) (London: Stationery Office).

Adema, W. and Einerhand, M. (1998) *The Growing Role of Private Social Benefits, Labour Market and Social Policy*, Occasional Papers No. 32 (Paris: OECD).

American Federation of Government Employees (1995)*Total Quality Partnership: A Vision for the Future* (Washington, DC).

American Federation of State, County and Municipal Employees (1995)*Redesigning Government* (Washington, DC: AFSCME).

Amin, S. (1996) 'The Challenge of Globalisation' *Review of International Political Economy*, 3: 2, pp. 216–59.

Amin, S. (1997) *Capitalism in the Age of Globalisation* (London: Zed Books).

Appleby, J. (2000) 'Hypothecated Taxes', *Health Service Journal*, 2 March 2000.

Arnold-Forster, J., Lee, M. and McLeod, J. (1997) *Hand in Glove: Private Sector Delivering Public Goods*, Discussion Paper No. 30 (London: Fabian Society).

Arthur Andersen (2000) *Value for Money Drivers in the Private Finance Initiative* (London).

Ascher, C., Fruchter, N. and Berne, R. (1996)*Hard Lessons: Public Schools and Privatisation* (New York: Twentieth Century Fund).

Asian Development Bank (1999) *Private Sector Development Strategy* (Manila).

Asia-Pacific Economic Cooperation (1998)*Infrastructure and Sustainable Development: Proceedings of the 1998 APEC Public-Business/Private Sector Dialogue* (Singapore).

Association of Direct Labour Organisations (1999) *The Employment Impact of the Private Finance Initiative in Local Government* (Manchester).

Astone, N. M., Nathanson, C.A., Schoen, R. and Kim, Y. J. (1999) 'Family Demography, Social Theory and Investment in Social Capital', *Population and Development Review*, 25 (1)..

Atkinson, R. D. and Court, R. H. (1998)*The New Economy Index* (Washington, DC: Progressive Policy Institute).

Avi-Yonah, R. (2000) 'Globalization, Tax Competition and the Fiscal Crisis of the Welfare State', *Harvard Law Review*, May 2000.

Bailey, S.J. and Davidson, C. (1999) 'The Purchaser–Provider Split: Theory and UK Evidence', *Environment and Planning C: Government and Policy*, Vol. 17.

Baker, D. (1998) *Saving Social Security in Three Steps*, Briefing Paper (Washington, DC: Economic Policy Institute).

Baker, D. and Schafer, T. (1995) *The Case for Public Investment* (Washington, DC: Economic Policy Institute).

Baker, D., Epstein, G. and Pollin, R. (1998) *Globalisation and Progressive Economic Policy* (Cambridge: Cambridge University Press).

Balanya, B., Doherty, A., Hoedeman, O., Ma'anit, A. and Wesselius, E. (2000) *Europe Inc: Regional and Global Restructuring and the Rise of Corporate Power* (London: Pluto Press).

Bale, M. and Dale, T. (1998) 'Public Sector Reform in New Zealand and its Relevance to Developing Countries', *The World Bank Research Observer*, Vol. 13, No.1, February.

Bank of International Settlements (1998) *The Macroeconomic and Financial Implications of Ageing Populations* (Luxembourg). .

Barber, B. R. (1995)*Jihad vs McWorld: How Globalism and Tribalism are Reshaping the World* (New York: Ballantine).

Barratt-Brown, M. (1998)*Defending the Welfare State* (Nottingham: Spokesman Books). .

Barratt-Brown, M. (1999)*Young Person's Guide to the Global Crisis* (Nottingham: Spokesman Books).

Beck, U. (1998) 'Politics of Risk Society', in Franklin, J. ed., *The Politics of Risk Society* (Bristol: Policy Press).

Bello, W. (1998a) 'The End of a "Miracle": Speculation, Foreign Capital Dependence and the Collapse of the Southeast Asian Economies', *Multinational Monitor*, Vol.19, Nos 1 and 2.

Bello, W. (1998b) 'The Asian Economic Implosion: Causes, Dynamics and Prospects', *Race & Class*, Vol. 40 No. 2/3.

Berger, S. and Dore, R. (1996) *National Diversity and Global Capitalism* (Ithaca: Cornell University Press). .

Bergesen, H.O. and Lunde, L. (1999) *Dinosaurs or Dynamos? The United Nations and the World Bank at the Turn of the Century* (London: Earthscan).

Blackburn, R. (1999) 'Grey Capitalism and Pension Reform', *New Left Review*, No. 233, Jan./Feb.

Blair, T. (1996) 'Speech to the Singapore Business Community', Labour Party Press Release, 8 January.

Blair, T. and Schroeder, G. (1998) 'Europe: The Third Way/Die Neue Mitte' (London: Labour Party).

Blommestein, H. J. (1998) 'Pension Funds and Financial Markets', *The OECD Observer*, No. 212, June/July.

Boldrin, M., Juan J., Dolado, Juan, Jimeno, F. and Peracchi F. (1999) 'The Future of Pensions in Europe', *Economic Policy*, No. 29.

Borjas, G. and Ramey, V. (1994) 'Time-Series Evidence on the Sources of Trends in Wage Inequality', *American Economic Review*, 84, May, pp. 10–16.

Boubakri, N. and Cosset, J.C. 'The Financial and Operating Performance of Newly Privatised Firms: Evidence from Developing Countries', *Journal of Finance*, .

Bouton, L. and Sumlinski, M. (1996) 'Trends in Private Investment in Developing Countries: Statistics for 1970–95', Discussion Paper 31 (Washington, DC: International Finance Corporation).

Boyer, R. and Drache, D., eds (1996) *States Against Markets: The Limits of Globalisation* (London: Routledge).

Brahmbhatt, M. and Dadush, U. (1996) 'Disparities in Global Integration', *Finance & Development*, September (Washington, DC: IMF/World Bank).

Brenner, N. (1998) 'Global Cities, Glocal States: Global City Formation and State Territorial Restructuring in Contemporary Europe', *Review of International Political Economy*, 5:1, Spring.

Brenner, N. (1999) 'Globalisation as Reterritorialisation: The Re-scaling of Urban Governance in the European Union', *Urban Studies*, Vol. 36, No. 3.

Brenner, R. (1998) 'The Economics of Global Turbulence', *New Left Review*, No. 229.

Bretton Woods Committee (1999) *The United States and the WTO: Benefits of the Multilateral Trade System* (Washington, DC).

Brinkley, A. (1997)*The Assault on Government* (New York: Twentieth Century Fund).

Bruegel, I. (1996) 'Gendering the Polarisation Debate: A Comment on Hamnett's "Social Polarisation. Economic Restructuring and Welfare State Regimes"', *Urban Studies*, Vol. 33, No. 8. .

Burbach, R., Nunez, O. and Kagarlitsky, B. (1997) *Globalisation and its Discontents* (London: Pluto Press).

Burchardt, T., Hills, J. and Propper, C. (1999)*Private Welfare and Public Policy* (York: Joseph Rowntree Foundation).

Burnham, P. (1999) 'The Politics of Economic Management in the 1990s', *New Political Economy*, Vol. 4, No.1.

Burtless, G., Lawrence, R. Z., Litan R. E. and Shapiro, R. J. (1998)*Globaphobia: Confronting Fears About Open Trade* (Washington, DC: Brookings Institution/Progressive Policy Institute/Twentieth Century Fund).

Business Age (1993) 'Scandal: How Her Majesty's Government Threw £200 million Away', pp. 24–30, February.

Bussell, L. J. and Suthers, B. (1998/9) 'On the Buses: Bus Deregulation on Teesside, 10 Years Down the Road', *Northern Economic Review*, Winter, No. 28.

Cabinet Office (1995a) *Civil Service: Taking Forward Continuity and Change*, Cm 2748 (London: HMSO).

Cabinet Office (1995b) *Annex F, Guidance for the Development & Use of Efficiency Plans* (London: HMSO).

Cabinet Office (1996) *Competing for Quality Policy Review* (London: HMSO).

Cabinet Office (1998a) *Bringing Britain Together: A National Strategy for Neighbourhood Renewal* (London: Social Exclusion Unit).

Cabinet Office (1998b) *Better Quality Services: A Handbook on Creating Public/Private Partnerships through Market Testing and Contracting Out* (London).

Cabinet Office (2000) *Reaching Out: The Role of Central Government at Regional and Local Level* (London: Stationery Office).

Callinicos, A. (1998) 'World Capitalism at the Abyss', *International Socialism*, No. 81, Winter.

Campbell, D. (1994) 'Foreign Investment, Labour Immobility and the Quality of Employment', *International Labour Review*, Vol. 133, No. 2, pp. 185–204.

Campbell-White, O. and Bhatia, A. (1998) *Privatisation in Africa* (Washington, DC: World Bank).

Canadian Center for Policy Alternatives (1998) 'Privatising Schools: Democratic Choice or Market Demand', *Education Ltd.*, Vol. 1, No. 3.

Canadian Union of Public Employees (1998) *Public Interest vs Private Profits: The Threat of Lease-back Schools* (Ottawa).

Canadian Union of Public Employees (1999)*Hostile Takeover: Annual Report on Privatisation* (Ottawa).

Carroll, J.D. and Lynn, D.B. (1996) 'The Future of Federal Reinvention: Congressional Perspectives', *Public Administration Review*, May–June, Vol. 56, No. 3.

Carter, B. (1997) 'Restructuring State Employment: Labour and Non-Labour in the Capitalist State', *Capital & Class* No. 63, Autumn.

Castells, M. (1997) *The Power of Identity* (Oxford: Blackwell).

Castles, F. (1996) 'Needs-based Strategies of Social Protection in Australia and New Zealand', in G. Esping-Andersen (ed.) *Welfare States in Transition* (London: Sage) pp. 88–115.

Centre for Public Services (1993)*Social and Economic Audit: Royal Hospitals Trust, Belfast* (London: UNISON).

Centre for Public Services (1995a) *Calculation of the National Costs & Savings of CCT*, Research Paper No. 1 (Sheffield).

Centre for Public Services (1995b)*Secret Services: A Handbook for Investigating Local Quangos*, (London: Local Government Information Unit).

Centre for Public Services (1997a) *Strategy for Best Value* (Sheffield).

Centre for Public Services (1997b)*Reinventing Government in Britain: The Performance of the Next Steps Agencies* (Sheffield).

Centre for Public Services (1998)*User/Employee Involvement in Best Value, PFI and Partnerships* (Sheffield).

Centre for Public Services (1998a) *Best Value Implementation Handbook* (Sheffield).

Centre for Public Services (1998b) *Externalisation by Privatisation* (London: UNISON).

Centre for Public Services (1999) *Management Consultants: Best Value Handbook* (Sheffield).

Centre for Public Services/Fawcett Society (1997) *Undervalued Work, Underpaid Women: Women's Employment in Care Homes* (Sheffield).

Centre for Public Services/Middlesbrough UNISON (2000) *Contract Capital of the North* (Sheffield).

Cerny, P. G. (1997) 'Paradoxes of the Competition State: The Dynamics of Political Globalisation', *Government & Opposition*, 32, pp. 251–74.

Cerny, P. G. (1999) 'Globalising the Political and Politicising the Global: Concluding Reflections on International Political Economy as a Vocation', *New Political Economy*, Vol. 4, No.1.

Challis, P. (2000) *Local Government Finance* (London: Local Government Information Unit).

Chandler, J. (1997) 'The Citizens Charter: Empowering Users or Providers: A Rejoinder', *The Review of Policy Issues*, Summer.

Chantrey Vellacott DFK (1999) *The Private Finance Initiative: Is it Financially Flawed*, (London).

Chicago Institute on Urban Poverty (1997) *Does Privatisation Pay? A Case Study of Privatisation in Chicago* (Chicago).

Chicken, J. C. and Posner, T. (1998)*The Philosophy of Risk* (London: Thomas Telford). .

Chomsky, N. (1998) 'Power in the Global Arena', *New Left Review*, No. 230.

Chossudovsky, M. (1996)*The Globalisation of Poverty* (London: Zed Press).

Citizens Council on Corporate Issues (2000) *Submission to Review of OECD Guidelines for Multinational Enterprises* (www.oecd.org).

Citizens for Tax Justice (1995) *The Hidden Entitlements* (Washington, DC).

Citizens for Tax Justice (1999) Statement of Robert S. McIntyre, Director, House Committee on the Budget Regarding Unnecessary Business Subsidies (Washington, DC).

City Limits (1996) New York, July–Aug.

Clark, A. M., Friedman, E. J. and Hochstetler, K. (1998) 'The Sovereign Limits of Global Civil Society: A Comparison of NGO Participation in UN Conferences on the Environment, Human Rights and Women', *World Politics*, 51, October.

Clark, G. L. and Evans, J. (1998) 'The Provision of Urban Infrastructure: Financial Intermediation through Long-Term Contracts', *Urban Studies*, Vol. 35, No. 2.

Clark, G. L. and Root, A. (1999) 'Infrastructure Shortfall in the United Kingdom: The Private Finance Initiative and Government Policy', *Poltical Geography*, Vol. 18.

Clayton, R. and Pontusson, J. (1998) 'Welfare State Retrenchment Revisited: Entitlement Cuts, Public Sector Restructuring and Inegalitarian Trends in Advanced Capitalist Economies', *World Politics*, 51, October.

Coalition of Service Industries (1999) *Agenda for the Next WTO Negotiations* (Washington, DC).

Cohen, D. (1998) *The Wealth of the World and the Poverty of Nations* (London: MIT Press).

Corner House, The (1999) *Snouts in the Trough: Export Credit Agencies, Corporate Welfare and Policy Incoherence*, Briefing No. 14, Sturminster Newton.

Cox, R. with Sinclair, T.J. (1996) *Approaches to World Order* (Cambridge: Cambridge University Press).

Crafts, N. (1998) *The Conservative Government's Economic Record: An End of Term Report* (London: Institute of Economic Affairs).

Crawford, M. (1997) 'The Big Pensions Lie', *New Economy*, Vol. 5, No. 1.

Cutler, T. and Waine, W. (1997) 'The Politics of Quasi-Markets' *Critical Social Policy*, Vol. 17, No. 51.

D'Souza, J. and Megginson, W. L. (1999) 'The Financial and Operational Performance of Privatised Firms During the 1990s', *Journal of Finance*, August.

Dailami, M. and Klein, M. (1998) *Government Support to Private Infrastructure Projects in Emerging Markets* (Washington: World Bank).

Davis, M. (1999) 'Magical Urbanism: Latinos Reinvent the US Big City', *New Left Review*, No. 234.

Deacon, B. (1998) 'Towards a Socially Responsible Globalisation: International Actors and Discourses' (University of Sheffield, Globalism and Social Policy Programme).

Dean, H. and Khan, Z. (1997) 'Muslim Perspectives on Welfare', *Journal of Social Policy*, Vol. 26, No. 2, pp. 193–209.

Department for Education and Employment (1999) *Social Exclusion and the Politics of Opportunity: A Mid-Term Progress Check* (London).

Department of Social Security (1998) *A New Contract for Welfare*, Cm 3805 (London: Stationery Office).

Department of the Environment (1993) *Competition and Service: The Impact of the Local Government Act 1988* (London: HMSO).

Department of the Environment (1997) *CCT and Local Authority Blue-Collar Services* (London).

Department of the Environment, Transport & the Regions (1998) *Modernising Local Government: Local Democracy and Community Leadership* (London).

Department of the Environment, Transport & the Regions (1998a) *Modern Local Government: In Touch with the People*, Cm 4014 (London: Stationery Office).

Department of the Environment, Transport & the Regions (1999) *Local Government Act 1999: Part 1 Best Value, Circular 10/99* (London).

Department of the Environment, Transport & the Regions (2000) 'Quality and Choice: A Decent Home for All, The Housing Green Paper' (London).

Dieter, H. (1998)*Crises in Asia or Crisis of Globalisation*, Centre for the Study of Globalisation and Regionalisation, University of Warwick, Coventry.

Domberger, S. and Jenson, P. (1997) 'Gaining from Outsourcing', *New Economy*, pp. 159–63.

Drache, D. (1999)*Globalisation: Is There Anything to Fear?*, Centre for the Study of Globalisation and Regionalisation, University of Warwick, Coventry.

Duffus, G. and Gooding, P. (1997) 'Globalisation: Scope, Issues and Statistics', *Economic Trends*, No. 528, November.

Dunleavy, P. (1991) *Democracy, Bureaucracy and Public Choice: Economic Explanations in Political Science* (Brighton: Wheatsheaf).

Dunleavy, P. (1994) 'The Globalisation of Public Service Production: Can Government be "Best in World"'? *Public Policy and Administration*, Vol. 9, No. 2.

Durschlag, S., Puri, T. and Rao, A. (1994) 'The Promise of Infrastructure Privatisation', *McKinsey Quarterly*, No. 1.

Eatwell, J. and Taylor, L. (1998) *International Capital Markets and the Future of Economic Policy*, Center for Economic Policy Analysis, New York.

Economic Policy Institute (1999) *NAFTA's Pain Deepens*, Briefing Paper (Washington, DC).

Economic Policy Institute (2000) *Meltzer Report Misses the Point*, Issue Brief No. 141 (Washington, DC).

The Economist, 31 August 1996.

The Economist (1997a) 'A Survey of the World Economy; The Future of the State', 20 September.

The Economist (1997b) 'All Capitalist Now: A Survey of Fund Management', 25 October.

The Economist (1999) 15 May.

The Economist (1999) 'Latin Lessons on Pensions, 12 June.

The Economist (2000) 'A Survey of Globalisation and Tax', 29 January.

Educational International/Public Services International (1999) *The WTO and the Millennium Round: What is at Stake for Public Education* (Brussels).

EduVentures (1999) Education Industry, www.eduventures.com.

Eggers, W. and O'Leary, J. (1995) *Revolution at the Roots: Making our Government Smaller, Better and Closer to Home* (New York: The Free Press).

Eisenschitz, A. and Gough, J. (1998) 'Theorising the State in Local Economic Governance', *Regional Studies*, Vol. 32, No. 8.

Ekins, P. and Newby, L. (1998) 'Sustainable Wealth Creation at the Local Level in an Age of Globalisation', *Regional Studies*, Vol. 32, No. 9.

Elliott, L. and Atkinson, D. (1998) *The Age of Insecurity* (London: Verso).

Equal Opportunities Commission for Northern Ireland (1996) *Report on Formal Investigation into Competitive Tendering in Health and Education Services in Northern Ireland* (Belfast).

Escott, K. and Whitfield, D. (1995) *The Gender Impact of CCT in Local Government* (Manchester: Equal Opportunities Commission).

Esping-Andersen, G. (1990) *The Three Worlds of Welfare Capitalism* (Princeton: Princeton Univesity Press).

Esping-Andersen, G. (1996) *Welfare States in Transition: National Adaptions in Global Economies* (London: UNRISD/SAGE).

Esping-Andersen, G. (1999) *Social Foundations of Postindustrial Economies* (Oxford: Oxford University Press).

Estes, R. (1996) *Tyranny of the Bottom Line: Why Corporations Make Good People Do Bad Things* (San Francisco: Berrett-Koehler).

Etzioni, A. (1993) *The Spirit of Community* (London: Fontana Press).

European Bank for Reconstruction and Development (1998)*Transition Report 1998* (London).

European Commission (1998) *Job Opportunities in the Information Society*, Report to the European Council.

European Foundation for the Improvement of Living and Working Conditions (1999) *Linking Welfare and Work* (Dublin).

EUROSTAT (1998) 'A Quarter of All Income Goes to the "Richest" 10%', Press Release 69/98 (Luxembourg).

Evans, P. (1997) 'The Eclipse of the State? Reflections on Stateness in an Era of Globalisation', *World Politics*, Vol. 50, pp. 62–87, October.

Fairbrother, P. (1997) *Unions in Restructured States: Social Democracy in Australia and Economic Liberalism in the United Kingdom* (Coventry: Centre for Comparative Labour Studies, University of Warwick).

Feenstra, R. and Hanson, G. (1996) 'Globalisation, Outsourcing and Wage Inequality', *American Economic Review*, May, pp. 240–5.

Ferlie, E., Ashburner, L., Fitzgerald, L. and Pettigrew, A. (1996)*The New Public Management in Action* (Oxford: Oxford University Press).

Ferreira, D. and Khatami, K. (1995) *Financing Private Infrastructure in Developing Countries*, Discussion Paper 343 (Washington, DC: World Bank).

Field, F. (1996) *Stakeholder Welfare* (London: Institute of Economic Affairs).

Financial Times, 17 July 1997.

Financial Times, 2 October 1998.

Financial Times, 21 October 1998.

Financial Times, (1999) *FT Guide to Telecoms* (London).

Financial Times, 28 January 1999.

Financial Times 'Girl Power, Spending Power', 26 September 1999.

Financial Times, 4 September 1999.

Financial Times, 10 April 2000.

Fine, B. (1999a) 'The Development State is Dead – Long Live Social Capital', *Development and Change*, Vol. 30, No. 1, pp. 1–19.

Fine, B. (1999b) 'The World Bank and Social Capital: Bursting the Bubble', mimeo (London: SOAS, University of London).

Food and Agriculture Organisation of the United Nations (1999) *The State of Food Insecurity in the World* (Geneva).

Foreign Policy in Focus (2000) IMF: Case of a Dead Theory Walking, Vol. 5, No. 12 (Washington, DC).

Forrest, R. and Kennett, P. (1998) 'Re-reading the City: Deregulation and Neighbourhood Change', *Space & Polity*, Vol. 2, No. 1.

Foster, C. and Plowden, F. J. (1996)*The State Under Stress* (Buckingham: Open University Press).

Fox, D. (1996) 'Reinventing Government as Postmodern Symbolic Politics', *Public Administration Review*, May–June, Vol. 56, No. 3.

Frank, E. (1999) 'Rethinking Social Security Reform', *Dissent*, Fall .

Franklin, J. ed., (1998) *The Politics of Risk Society* (Cambridge: Polity Press).

Fraser, L. (1997) *Impact of Contracting Out on Female NESB Workers: Case Study of the NSW Government Cleaning Service* (Belconnen, Australia: Ethnic Communities Council of NSW).

Frederickson, H.G. (1996) 'Comparing the Reinventing Government Movement with the New Public Administration', *Public Administration Review*, May–June , Vol. 56, No. 3.

Froud, J., Haslam, C., Sukhdev J., Shaoul, J. and Williams, K. (1996) 'Stakeholder Economy? From Utility Privatisation to New Labour', *Capital & Class*, No. 60, Autumn.

Fuerbringer, J. (1992) *The Road to Globalism, International Economic Insights*, September/October (Washington, DC: Institute for International Economics).

Gaffney, D. and Pollock, A. (1997) *Can the NHS Afford the Private Finance Initiative?* (London: British Medical Association).

Gaffney, D. and Pollock, A. (1999) 'Pump-Priming the PFI: Why are Privately Financed Hospital Schemes being Subsidised?' *Public Money & Management*, Vol. 19, No. 1.

Gaffney, D., Pollock, A., Price, D. and Shaoul, J. (1999) 'NHS Capital Expenditure and the Private Finance Initiative – Expanison or Contraction?', *British Medical Journal*, July.

Gales, P. and Harding, A. (1998) 'Cities and States in Europe', *West European Politics*, Vol. 21, July.

Gamble, A. and Kelly, G. (1996) 'The New Politics of Ownership', *New Left Review*, No. 220.

Garrett, G. (1998) *Partisan Politics in the Global Economy* (Cambridge: Cambridge University Press).

Geyer, R. (1998) 'Globalisation and the (Non) Defence of the Welfare State', *West European Politics*, Vol. 21, No.3.

Giddens, A. (1998a) *The Third Way: The Renewal of Social Democracy* (Cambridge: Polity Press).

Giddens, A. (1998b) 'After the Left's Paralysis', *New Statesman*, 1 May.

Giddens, A. (1998c) 'Risk Society: The Context of British Politics', in J. Franklin (ed.) *The Politics of Risk Society* (Cambridge: Polity Press).

Gillion, C. and Bonilla, A. (1992) 'Analysis of a National Private Pension Scheme: The Case of Chile', *International Labour Review*, Vol. 131, No. 2.

Glendinning, C. and Bailey, J. (1998) 'The Private Sector and the NHS: The Case of Capital Developments in Primary Healthcare', *Policy and Politics*, Vol. 26, No. 4.

Glennerster, H. (1999) 'The Elderly: A Burden on the Economy?', *Centrepiece*, Vol. 4, No. 2.

Glennerster, H. and Hills, J. (1998) *The State of Welfare: The Economics of Social Spending* (Oxford: Oxford University Press).

Global Trade Watch (1998) 'MAI Provisions and Proposals: An Analysis of the April 1998 Text' (Washington, DC: Public Citizen).

Good Jobs First (2000) *Minding the Candy Store* (Washington DC).

Gordon, D. M. (1996) *Fat and Mean: The Corporate Squeeze of Working Americans and the Myth of Managerial Downsizing* (New York: Free Press).

Gore, A. (1993) *From Red Tape to Results: Creating a Government that Works Better and Costs Less* (New York: Plume/Penguin Books).

Gore, A. (1996) *The Best Kept Secrets in Government* (Washington, DC: National Performance Review).

Gough, I. (1996) 'Social Welfare and Competitiveness', *New Political Economy*, Vol. 1, No. 2.

Government Accounting Office (1997) 'Managing for Results: Regulatory Agencies Identified Significant Barriers to Focusing on Results', GGD-97-83 (Washington, DC).

Government Accounting Office (1999) 'NPR's Savings: Claimed Agency Savings cannot all be Attributed to NPR', GGD-99-120 (Washington, DC).

Graf, W. (1995) *The State in the Third World, Why Not Capitalism: Socialist Register 1995* (London: Merlin Press).

Grant, W. (1998) *Globalisation, Comparative Political Economy and the Economic Policies of the Blair Government* (Coventry: Centre for the Study of Globalisation and Regionalisation, University of Warwick).

Greer, A. and Hoggett, P. (1999) 'Public Policies, Private Strategies', *Public Administration*, Vol. 77, No. 2.

Greider, W. (1998) *One World, Ready or Not: The Manic Logic of Global Capitalism* (London: Penguin).

Greve, C., Flinders, M. and Van Thiel, S. (1999) 'Quangos – What's in a Name? Defining Quangos from a Comparative Perspective', *Governance*, Vol. 12, No. 2.

Guthrie, J. and Carlin, T. (1999) *A Review of Australian Experiences of Output Based Budgeting: A Critical Perspective*, Critical Management Conference, Manchester.

Hall, D. and Lobina, E. (1999) *Employment and Profit Margins in UK Water Companies: Implications for Price Regulation Proposals* (London: Public Services International Research Unit).

Hall, W. and Weir, S. (1996)*The Untouchables: Power and Accountability in the Quango State* (London: The Scarman Trust).

Hamnett, C. (1996) 'Social Polarisation, Economic Restructuring and Welfare State Regimes', *Urban Studies*, Vol. 33, No. 8.

Hatcher, R. (1998) 'Profiting from Schools: Business and Education Action Zones', *Education and Social Justice*, Vol. 1, No. 1, Autumn 1998.

Haughton, G. (1998) 'Principles and Practice of Community Economic Development', *Regional Studies*, Vol. 32, No. 9.

Hay, C. (1999) *The Political Economy of New Labour: Labouring under False Pretences* (Manchester: Manchester University Press).

Health Service Journal, 18 November 1999.

Held, D., McGrew, A., Goldblatt, D. and Perraton, T. (1999) *Global Transformation* (Cambridge: Polity Press). .

Higgott, R. and Phillips, N. (1998) *The Limits of Global Liberalisation: Lessons from Asia and Latin America* (Coventry: Centre for the Study of Globalisation and Regionalisation, University of Warwick).

Higgott, R. and Reich, S. (1998)*Globalisation and Sites of Conflict: Towards Definition and Taxonomy* (Coventry: Centre for the Study of Globalisation and Regionalisation, University of Warwick).

Hildyard, N. (1997) *The World Bank and the State: A Recipe for Change?* (London: Bretton Woods Project).

Hirst, P. (1997) *From Statism to Pluralism* (London: UCL Press).

Hirst, P. and Thompson, G. (1996) *Globalisation in Question* (Cambridge: Polity Press).

HM Treasury (1997) *Financial Statement and Budget* (London: Stationery Office).

HM Treasury (1998a) *Public Services for the Future: Modernisation, Reform, Accountability*, Cm 4181 (London: Stationery Office).

HM Treasury (1998b) *Stability and Investment for the Long Term*, Cm 3978 (London: Stationery Office).

HM Treasury (1999) *Budget 99: Building a Stronger Economic Future for Britain*, HC 298 (London: Stationery Office).

HM Treasury (1999a) News Release: Speech by the Chief Secretary to the Treasury, Alan Milburn, at the launch of the IPPR Commissin into Public/Private Partnerships, 20 September.

HM Treasury (2000) *Public Expenditure: Statistical Analyses 2000–01*, Cm 4601 (London: Stationery Office).

HM Treasury (2000a) *Public Private Partnerships: The Government's Approach* (London: Stationery Office).

HM Treasury (2000b) Financial Statement and Budget Report, HC 346 (London: Stationery Office).

Hodge, S. and Howe, J. (1999) 'Can the European Social Model Survive', *European Urban and Regional Studies*, Vol. 6, No. 2.

Hoggett, P. (1996) 'New Modes of Control in the Public Sector', *Public Administration*, Vol. 74, Spring, pp. 9–32.

Holden, C. (1999) 'Globalisation, Social Exclusion and Labour's New Work Ethic', *Critical Social Policy*, No. 61.

Holland, S. (1998) *New Dimensions to European Finance* (London: Local Government Information Unit).

Holloway, J. (1994) 'Global Capital and the National State', *Capital and Class*, No. 52.

Hood, C., James, O., Jones, G., Scott, C.and Travers, T. (1998) 'Regulation Inside Government: Where New Public Management Meets the Audit Explosion', *Public Money & Management*, April–June.

Hopkins, T. K., Wallerstein, I. et al. (1996) *The Age of Transition: Trajectory of the World-System 1945–2025* (London: Zed Books).

House of Commons (1998) Public Accounts Committee, Evidence Session, 22 January.

House of Commons (1999) *Buses*, Research Paper 99/59 (London).

House of Commons (2000) 'The Private Finance Initiative', Select Committee on Treasury, Fourth Report, March (London: Stationery Office).

House of Commons Library (1995) 'The Consequences of Bus Deregulation', Transport Committee Report (London: HMSO).

House of Commons Library (1998) *Rent Levels, Affordability and Housing Benefit*, Research Paper 98/69 (London).

House of Commons Library (1999) *The Transport Bill Part IV: Railways*, Research Paper 99/105 (London).

House of Commons Library (2000a) *Utilities Bill*, Research Paper 00/7 (London).

House of Commons Library (2000b) *English Partnerships – Assisting Local Regeneration*, Select Committee on Public Accounts, Twenty-Third Report (London).

Housing Today (1999) 'Transfer Receipts Bonanza', 2 September.

Huber, E. (1996) 'Options for Social Policy in Latin America: Neoliberal versus Social Democratic Models', in Esping-Andersen, G. (ed.) *Welfare States in Transition* (London: Sage).

Hudson, M., ed. (1996) *Merchants of Misery: How Corporate America Profits from Poverty* (Monroe, Maine: Common Courage Press).

Hudson, R. (1999) 'The Learning Economy, the Learning Firm and the Learning Region', *European Urban and Regional Studies*, Vol. 6, No. 1.

Hufbauer, G. and Warren, T. (1999) *The Globalisation of Services: What has Happened? What are the Implications?* (Washington, DC: Institute for International Economics).

Hutton, W. (1995) *The State We're In* (London: Jonathan Cape).

Hutton, W. (1997) *The State to Come* (London: Vintage).

Hutton, W. (1998) *Observer*, 20 September.

Hutton, W. and Giddens, A. (2000) *On the Edge: Living with Global Capitalism* (London: Jonathan Cape).

ICEM (1996) *Power and Counterpower: The Trade Union Response to Global Capital* (London: Pluto Press).

IDEA (forthcoming) *Employee and Trade Union Involvement in Best Value* (London).

Institute for Public Policy Research (IPPR) (1997) *In Progress Bulletin* (London).

International Bank for Reconstruction and Development/World Bank (1997) *Dealing with Public Risk in Private Infrastructure* (Washington, DC).

International Chamber of Commerce (1998) 'The Geneva Business Declaration', Statement by Helmut Maucher, President ICC, 24 September 1998, Geneva.

International Labour Organisation (1999) *Managing the Privatisation and Restructuring of Public Utilities – Water, Gas and Electricity* (Geneva).

International Monetary Fund (1998) *World Economic Outlook*, December (Washington, DC).

Iversen, T. and Wren, A. (1998) 'Equality, Employment and Budgetary Restraint: The Trilemma of the Service Economy', *World Politics*, 50, July.

Jackson, P. and Stainsby, L. (2000) 'Managing Public Sector Networked Organisations', *Public Money & Management*, Vol. 20, No. 1.

Jacobs, D. (1998) *Social Welfare Systems in East Asia: A Comparative Analysis Including Private Welfare*, Case Paper No. 10 (London: Centre for Analysis of Social Exclusion, London School of Economics).

Jervis, P. and Richards, S. (1997) 'Public Management: Raising Our Game', *Public Money and Management*, April–June.

Jessop, B. (1994) 'Post-Fordism and the State', in Amin, A. (ed.) *Post Fordism: A Reader* (Oxford: Blackwell).

Jones, G. (1996) 'Resource Accounting and Budgeting: Another False Trail?', *Public Money and Management*, June.

Jones, M. (1998) 'Restructuring the Local State: Economic Governance or Social Regulation', *Political Geography*, Vol. 17, No. 8.

Jordan, B. (1998) *The New Politics of Welfare* (London: Sage).

Jordan, G. (1994) '"Reinventing Government": But will it Work?', *Public Administration*, Vol. 72, Summer, pp. 271–9.

Jordan, L. (1999) *The Death of Development: The Converging Policy Agendas of the World Bank and the World Trade Organisation* (Washington, DC: Bank Information Center).

Jubilee 2000 (1999) *What will it Cost to Cancel Unpayable Debt?* (London).

Jubilee South (1999) *Towards a Debt-Free Millenium: South–South Summit Declaration* (Manila).

Judge, K. (1999) 'Evaluation of Health Action Zones', unpublished paper (University of Kent).

Kagarlitsky, B. (1999) 'The Challenge for the Left: Reclaiming the State', in Panitch, L. and Leys, C. (eds) *Global Capitalism Versus Democracy: Socialist Register 1999* (Woodbridge, Suffolk: Merlin Press).

Karliner, J. (1997) *The Corporate Planet: Ecology and Politics in the Age of Globalisation* (San Francisco: Sierra Club Books).

Kaul, I., Grunberg, I. and Stern, M. (1999) *Global Public Goods: International Cooperation in the 21st Century* (Oxford: Oxford University Press).

Kay, J. (1998) 'Evolutionary Politics', *Prospect*, July.

Kay, S. J. (1999) 'Unexpected Privatisations: Politics and Social Security reform in the Southern Cone', *Comparative Politics*, July, pp. 403–22.

Kelsey, J. (1995) *Economic Fundamentalism* (London: Pluto Press).

Kennedy, D. (1997) 'Who Ends Up Paying the Fare?', *New Economy*, No. 3, pp. 164–6.

Kettl, D. and Dilulio, J. J., eds (1995) *Inside the Reinvention Machine: Appraising Governmental Reform* (Washington, DC: Brookings Institution).

Kikeri, S. (1998) 'Privatisation and Labour: What happens to Workers when Governments Divest', Technical Paper No. 396 (Washington, DC: World Bank).

King, J. and Stabinsky, D. (1998) 'Biotechnology under Globalisation: The Corporate Expropriation of Plant, Animal and Microbial Species, *Race & Class*, Vol. 40, No. 2/3.

Kitson, M. and Michie, J. (1998) *Globalisation, Unemployment and Government Policy* (London: Full Employment Forum).

Klein, M. (1998) 'One Hundred Years After Bretton Woods: A Future History of the World Bank Group', in *International Financial Institutions in the 21st Century, EIB Papers*, Vol. 3, No. 2 (Luxembourg: European Investment Bank).

Korten, D. C. (1998) *Globalizing Civil Society: Reclaiming Our Right to Power* (New York: Seven Stories Press).

Kotlikoff, L.J. and Sachs, J. (1997) 'It's High Time to Privatise', *The Brookings Review*, Vol. 15, No. 3.

Kozul-Wright, R. and Rowthorn, R. (1998) 'Spoilt for Choice? Multinational Corporations and the Geography of International Production', *Oxford Review of Economic Policy*, Vol. 14, No. 2.

Krugman, P. (1999) *The Return of Depression Economics* (London: Allen Lane/The Penguin Press).

Labour Research (1997) 'An Era of Snouts in the Trough', *Labour Research*, Vol. 86, No. 5, May, pp. 11–13.

La Porta, R., Lopez-de-Silanes, F. and Shleifer, A. (1998) 'Corporate Ownership Around the World', *Journal of Finance*, October.

Lau, W.K. (1999) The '15th Congress of the Chinese Communist Party: Milestone in China's Privatisation', *Capital & Class*, No. 68, Summer.

Lawrence, R. (1997) 'Current Economic Policies: Social Implications over the Longer Term', in *Societal Cohesion and the Global Economy* (Paris: OECD).

Leadbetter, C. (1998) *The Rise of the Social Entrepreneur* (London: Demos).

Lechner, F.J. and Boli, J. (2000) *The Globalisation Reader* (Oxford: Blackwell).

Leonard, P. (1997) *Postmodern Welfare: Reconstructing an Emancipatory Project* (London: Sage).

Lepage, H. (1997) 'A Liberal Socio-Economic Scenario for the Early Twenty-First Century', in *Societal Cohesion and the Global Economy* (Paris: OECD).

Levy, S. and Cadette, W. (1998) 'Overcoming America's Infrastructure Deficit', Public Policy Brief No. 40A (Annandale-on-Hudson: Jerome Levy Economics Institute).

Light, P.C. (1999) *The True Size of Government* (Washington, DC: Brookings Institution Press).

Lobina, E. and Hall, D. (1999) *Public Sector Alternatives to Water Supply and Sewerage Privatisation: Case Studies* (London: Public Services International Research Unit).

Local Government Information Unit (1999) 'Breathing New Life into Public Housing', Special Briefing, No. 51 (London).

Local Government Information Unit (2000) *Local Democracy for the 21st Century: Finance* (London).

Local Government Management Board (1995) 'Service Delivery and Competition', Survey Report (London).

Local Government Management Board (1998) Survey Report No. 16, Service Delivery and Competition Information Service (London).

London Edinburgh Return Group (1980) *In and Against the State* (London: Pluto Press).

MacEwan, A. (1999) *Neo-liberalism or Democracy* (London: Zed Press).

McRae, H. (1995) *The World in 2020* (London: HarperCollins).

Marden, P. (1997) 'Geographies of Dissent: Globalisation, Identity and the Nation', *Political Geography*, Vol. 16, No.1.

Marfleet, P. (1998) 'Globalisation and the Third World', *International Socialism* No. 81, Winter.

Markou, E. and Waddams Price, C. (1997)*Effects of UK Utility Reform: Source and Distribution* (London: Institute for Public Policy Research).

Martin, H. P. and Schumann, H. (1997) *The Global Trap* (London: Zed Books).

Michie, J. and Grieve Smith, J., eds (1997)*Employment and Economic Performance: Jobs, Inflation and Growth* (Oxford: Oxford University Press).

Milburn, A. (1999) 'Building for the Future', *Government Opportunities*, November, pp. 24–7.

Miles, D. and Timmerman, A. (1999) 'Risk Sharing and Transition Costs in the Reform of Pension Systems in Europe', *Economic Policy*, No. 29.

Miliband, R. (1994) *Socialism for a Sceptical Age* (Cambridge: Polity Press).

Mintzberg, H. (1996) 'Managing Government: Governing Management', *Harvard Business Review*, May–June.

Mishra, J. and Akins, F. (1998) 'The Welfare State and Women: Structure, Agency and Diversity', *Social Politics*, Fall.

Mishra, R. (1996) 'The Welfare of Nations', in Boyer, R. and Drache, D. (eds) *States Against Markets* (London: Routledge).

Mjoset, L. (1999) 'Employment, Unemployment and Ageing in the Western European Welfare States', Oslo (draft).

Molnar, A. (1996) *Giving Kids the Business: The Commercialisation of America's Schools* (Boulder: Westview Press).

Morales-Gomez, D. (1999) *Transnational Social Policies: The New Development Challenges of Globalisation* (London: Earthscan).

Morgan, G. (1993) *Imaginization* (London: Sage).

Morris, P., ed. (1996) *Jobs & Justice: A Public Service Agenda for Full Employment* (London: Lawrence & Wishart/UNISON).

Morris, R. (1994) 'New Magistracies and Commissariats', *Local Government Studies*, Vol. 20, No. 2.

Mueller, D. (1989) *Public Choice II, a Revised Edition of Public Choice* (Cambridge: Cambridge University Press).

Munro, R. (1995) 'Governing the New Province of Quality: Autonomy, Accounting and the Dissemination of Accountability', in A. Wilkinson and H. Willmott (eds) *Making Quality Critical* (London: Routledge).

Murray, R. (1992) 'Towards a Flexible State', *IDS Bulletin*, Vol. 23, No. 4. .

Nathan, S. and Whitfield, D. (2000) 'PFI and Europe's Most Privatised Criminal Justice System', *The PFI Report*, February, pp. 16–17.

National Audit Office (1998a) *Privatisation of the Rolling Stock Leasing Companies*, HC 576, Session 1997/98 (London: Stationery Office).

National Audit Office (1998b) *The Flotation of Railtrack*, HC 25, Session 1998/99 (London: Stationery Office).

National Audit Office (1998c) *Obtaining a Benefit for Electricity Customers from the Flotation of the National Grid*, HC 618, Session 1997/98 (London: Stationery Office).

National Audit Office (1998d) *Sale of AEA Technology*, HC 618, Session 1997/98 (London: Stationery Office).

National Audit Office (1999) *Examining the Value for Money Deals under the Private Finance Initiative* (London: Stationery Office).

National Performance Review (1997) *Serving the American Public: Best Practices in Performance Measurment* (Washington, DC).

National Science Foundation/Rutgers University (2000) *Towards a Comprehensive Geographical Perspective on Urban Sustainability* (New Jersey).

National Union of Public and Government Employees (1999a) *How Do We Measure Economic Prosperity?* (Ottawa).

National Union of Public and Government Employees (1999b) *The Value of the Public Sector to Canada's Economy* (Ottawa).

Newbury, D. and Pollitt, M. (1997) 'The Restructuring and Privatisation of the CEGB: Was it Worth it?', *Journal of Industrial Economics*, September.

Newman, J. (1994) 'Beyond the Vision: Cultural Change in the Public Sector', *Public Money & Management*, April–June.

Niemann, M. (1998) 'Globalisation and Regionalisation from a Spatial Perspective', *Space & Polity*, Vol. 2, No.2.

Niskanen, W.A. (1971) *Bureaucracy and Representative Government* (Chicago: Aldine Atherton).

Nolan, Lord (1995) 'First Report of the Committee on Standards of Public Life', Cmnd 2850(1) (London: HMSO).

Nolan, P., Saundry, R. and Sawyer, M. (1997) 'Choppy Waves on Air and Sea: Deregulation has done Damage to Two Key Industries which is Irreversible', *New Economy*, Vol. 4, No. 3.

Normann, R. (1991)*Service Management: Strategy and Leadership in Service Business* (Chichester: Wiley).

O'Brien, Richard (1992) *The End of Geography* (London: Pinter).

Observer, 26 August 1998.

OECD (1995) *Governance in Transition: Public Management Reform in OECD Countries* (Paris).

OECD (1996a) *Financial Trends*, June (Paris).

OECD (1996b) *Ethics in the Public Service: Current Issues and Practice* (Paris).

OECD (1996c) *Performance Management in Government*, Public Management Occasional Paper No. 9 (Paris).

OECD (1996d) *Globalisation: What Challenges and Opportunities for Governments?* (Paris: PUMA).

OECD (1997a) *Financial Trends*, June (Paris).

OECD (1997b) *Societal Cohesion and the Globalising Economy: What Does the Future Hold?* (Paris).

OECD (1997c) *Labour Market Policies: New Challenges, Policies for Low-Paid Workers and Unskilled Job Seekers*, OCDE/GD (97) 160.

OECD (1997d) *Family, Market and Community: Equity and Efficiency in Social Policy* (Paris).

OECD (1997e) *The World in 2020: Towards a New Global Age* (Paris).

OECD (1997f) *Towards a New Global Age: Policy Report* (Paris).

OECD (1998a) *Corporate Governance* (Paris).

OECD (1998b) *Public Management Reform and Economic and Social Development* (Paris).

OECD (1998c) *The Chilean Pension System* (Paris: Public Management Service).

OECD (1998d) *Harmful Tax Competition: An Emerging Global Issue* (Paris).

OECD (1999a) *Open Markets Matter: The Benefits of Trade and Investment Liberalisation* (Paris).

OECD (1999b)*Financial Trends*, No. 72, February (Paris).

OECD (1999c) *Revenue Statistics 1999* (Paris).

OECD (1999d) *The Future of the Global Economy: Towards a Long Boom?* (Paris).

OECD (1999e) *Review of the OECD Guidelines for Multinational Enterprises: Framework for the Review* (Paris).

OECD (1999f) *Employment Outlook 1999* (Paris).

Ohmae, K. (1995) *The End of the Nation State: The Rise of Regional Economies* (London: HarperCollins).

Orchard, L. and Stretton, H. (1997) 'Public Choice: A Critical Survey', *Cambridge Journal of Economics*, No. 21, pp. 409–30.

Orszag, M. and Snowner, D. (1998) 'Creative Accounting' *European Economic Perspectives*, No. 16, January.

Osborne, D. and Gaebler, T. (1992) *Reinventing Government: How the Entrepreneurial Spirit is Transforming the Public Sector* (Reading, Mass: Addison-Wesley).

Osborne, D. and Plastrik, P. (1997)*Banishing Bureaucracy: The Five Strategies for Reinventing Government* (Reading, Mass: Addison-Wesley).

Panitch, L. and Leys, C., eds (1999) *Global Capitalism Versus Democracy: Socialist Register 1999* (Woodbridge, Suffolk: Merlin Press).

Panitch, L. (1994) *Globalisation and the State*, in Socialist Register, 1994 (London: Merlin Press).

Parker, M. and Slaughter, J. (1994) *Working Smart: A Union Strategy Guide for Labor–Management Participation Programs and Reengineering* (Detroit: Labor Notes).

Parkinson, M. (1996) 'Twenty-five Years of Urban Policy in Britain – Partnership, Entrepreneurialism or Competition', *Public Money & Management*, Vol. 16, No. 3.

Paterson, M. (1999) 'Globalisation, Ecology and Resistance', *New Political Economy*, Vol. 4, No. 1.

Paterson, M., West, M., Lawthom, R. and Nickell, S. (1997) *Impact of People Management Practices on Business Performance* (London: Institute of Personnel and Development).

Patrinos, H. (1999) *Market Forces in Education* (Washington DC: World Bank). .

Pearce, D. (1997) *Bridges to Sustainability: Incentives for Private Sector Financing of Sustainable Development* (London: University College).

Pearce, G. and Martin, S. (1996) 'The Measurement of Additionality: Grasping the Slippery Eel', *Local Government Studies*, Vol. 22, No. 1, pp. 78–92.

Perraton, J., Goldblatt, D., Held, D. and McGrew, A. (1997) 'The Globalisation of Economic Activity', *New Political Economy*, Vol. 2, No. 2.

Peters, B. G. (1996)*The Future of Governing: Four Emerging Models* (Kansas: University Press of Kansas).

Peters, B.G. and Savoie, D.J. (1996) 'Managing Incoherence: The Coordination and Empowerment Conundrum', *Public Administration Review*, May–June, Vol. 56, No. 3.

Phillips, N.(1998)*Globalisation and the 'Paradox of State Power': Perspectives from Latin America* (Coventry: Centre for the Study of Globalisation and Regionalisation, University of Warwick).

Piachaud, D. (1998) 'The Prospects for Poverty', *New Economy*, Vol. 5, No. 1.

Picciotto, S. (1991) 'The Internationalisation of the State', *Capital & Class*, No. 43, Spring.

Pieper, U. and Taylor, L. (1998) *The Revival of the Liberal Creed: The IMF, the World Bank and Inequality in a Globalised Economy* (New York: Center for Economic Policy Analysis).

Pierson, C. (1996) *The Modern State* (London: Routledge).

Pierson, P. (1994) *Dismantling the Welfare State?* (Cambridge: Cambridge University Press).

Pierson, P. (1996) 'The New Politics of the Welfare State', *World Politics*, Vol. 48, No. 2, pp. 143–80.

Pierson, P. (1998) 'Irrestible Forces, Immovable Objects: Post-industrial Welfare States Confront Permanent Austerity', *Journal of European Public Policy*, Vol. 5, No. 4.

Pike, A. (1997) 'Partnership Built on Understanding', *Financial Times*, 30 May.

Pinkerton, J. P. (1995)*What Comes Next: The End of Big Government and the New Paradigm Ahead* (New York: Hyperion).

Pitelis, C. (1991) 'Beyond the Nation State?: The Transnational Firm and the Nation State', *Capital & Class*, No. 43.

Piven, F. and Cloward, R. A. (1971) *Regulating the Poor* (New York: The New Press).

Piven, F. and Cloward, R. A. (1997) *The Breaking of the American Social Compact* (New York: The New Press).

Platt, S. (1998) *Government by Taskforce: A Review of the Reviews* (London: Catalyst Trust).

.

Plewis, I. (1998) 'Inequalities, Targets and Zones', *New Economy*, Vol. 5, No. 2, June.

Pollitt, C. and Summa, H. (1997) 'Trajectories of Reform: Public Management Change in Four Countries', *Public Money & Management*, January–March, pp. 7–18.

Pollitt, C., Birchall, J., and Putman, K. (1997) *Opting Out and the Experience of Self-Management in Education, Housing and Health Care* (Glasgow: Local Governance Programme of Economic & Social Research Council).

Polyani, K. (1957) *The Great Transformation: The Political and Economic Origins of Our Time* (Boston: Beacon Press).

Poole, F. (1999) 'Buses', Research Paper 99/59, House of Commons, London, June.

Powell, M. and Hewitt, M. (1998) 'The End of the Welfare State?', *Social Policy & Administration*, Vol. 32, No. 1.

Power, M. (1997) *The Audit Society: Rituals of Verification* (Oxford: Oxford University Press).

Pratchett, L. and Wingfield, M. (1994) *The Public Service Ethos in Local Government* (London: Commission for Local Democracy).

Private Finance Panel (1996) *Risk and Reward in PFI Contracts* (London).

Public Sector Privatisation Research Unit (1997) *Community Care Survey* (London).

Public Sector Research Centre (1995) *A Global State? Implications of Globalisation and Challenges for the Public Sector in Australia* (Sydney: University of New South Wales).

Public Services International (1999) *Public Services in a Globalised Economy: The PSI Alternative Strategy Revisited* (Ferney-Voltaire). .

Public Services International (1999) *The WTO and the General Agreement on Trade in Services: What's at Stake for Public Health?* (Ferney-Voltaire). .

Public Services International Research Unit (1998) *Waste Management: Europe* (London).

Putman, R. (1993) *Making Democracy Work: Civic Traditions in Modern Italy* (Princeton: Princeton University Press).

Queisser, M. (1999) *Pension Reform: Lessons from Latin America*, Policy Brief 15 (Paris: OECD).

Radice, H. (1999) 'Taking Globalisation Seriously', in Panitch, Leo and Leys, Colin (eds) *Global Capitalism Versus Democracy: Socialist Register 1999* (Woodbridge, Suffolk: Merlin Press).

Rai, S. (1998) *Engendered Development in a Global Age?* (Coventry: Centre for the Study of Globalisation and Regionalisation, University of Warwick).

Rhodes, M. (1995) '"Subversive Liberalism": Market Integration, Globalisation and the European Welfare State', *Journal of European Public Policy*, Vol. 2, No. 3 September.

Rhodes, R.A.W. (1995)*The New Governance: Governing without Government* (Swindon: Economic & Social Research Council).

Rhodes, R.A.W. (1997)*Understanding Governance: Policy Networks, Governance, Reflexivity and Accountability* (Buckingham: Open University Press).

Richards, D. G. (1997) 'The Political Economy of Neo-Liberal Reform in Latin America: A Critical Appraisal', *Capital & Class*, No. 61, Spring.

Ridley, F. (1996) 'The New Public Management in Europe: Comparative Perspectives', *Public Policy and Administration*, Vol. 11, No. 1.

Robb, C. M. (1999) *Can the Poor Influence Policy? Participatory Poverty Assessments in the Developing World* (Washington, DC: World Bank).

Robinson, P., Hawksworth, J., Broadbent, J., Laughlin, R. and Haslam, C. (2000) *The Private Finance Initiative: Saviour, Villain or Irrelevance?* (London: IPPR Commission on Public Private Partnerships).

Rodrik, D. (1997)*Has Globalisation Gone Too Far?* (Washington, DC: Institute for International Economics).

Rodrik, D. (1999) *The New Global Economy and Developing Countries: Making Openness Work* (Washington, DC: Overseas Development Council).

Rothstein, R. (1999) 'When First We Practice How to Deceive', *Dissent*, Fall.

Rowthorn, R. and Kozul-Wright, R. (1998) 'Globalisation and Economic Convergence: An Assessment', Discussion Paper 131 (Geneva: UNCTAD).

Royal Institute of International Affairs (1996)*Unsettled Times: The 1996 Chatham House Forum Report* (London).

Ruane, S. (1997) 'Public–Private Boundaries and the Transformation of the NHS', *Critical Social Policy*, No. 51, May.

Ruccio, D., Resnick, S. and Wolff, R. (1991) 'Class Beyond the Nation State', *Capital & Class*, No. 43, Spring.

Rude, C. (1998) *The 1997–98 East Asian Financial Crisis: A New York Market-Informed View* (New York: Department of Economic and Social Affairs, United Nations).

Sainsbury, D., ed. (1994) *Gendering Welfare States* (London: Sage).

Salamon, L. (1987) 'Partners in Public Service: The Scope and Theory of Government/Non-Profit Relations', in Powell, W. (ed.) *The Non-Profit Sector*, pp. 99–117 (New Haven: Yale University).

Sanderson, I. (1998) 'Beyond Performance Measurement? Assessing "Value" in Local Government', *Local Government Studies*, Vol. 24, No.4.

Sassen, S. (1998) *Globalisation and its Discontents: Essays on the New Mobility of People and Money* (New York: New Press).

Savoie, D.J. (1996) 'What is Wrong with the New Public Management', *Canadian Public Administration*, Vol. 38, No. 1.

Sawyer, M. and O'Donnell, K. (1999) *A Future for Public Ownership* (London: Lawrence and Wishart).

Schick, A. (1998) 'Why Most Developing Countries should not try New Zealand's Reforms' *The World Bank Research Observer*, Vol. 13, No. 1, February.

Schneider, H. (1999) 'Participatory Governance: The Missing Link for Poverty Reduction', Policy Brief No. 17 (Paris: OECD Development Centre).

Scholte, J. A. (1997) 'Global Capitalism and the State', *International Affairs*, Vol. 73, No. 3.

Scholte, J. A. (1999)*Global Civil Society: Changing the World?* (Coventry: Centre for the Study of Globalisation and Regionalisation, University of Warwick).

Schwartz, H. (1996) 'Small States in Big Trouble: State Reorganisation in Australia, Denmark, New Zealand and Sweden', *World Politics*, Vol. 47, No. 4, pp. 527–55.

Scott-Samuel, A., Birley, M. and Ardern, K. (1998) 'The Merseyside Guidelines for Health Impact Assessment' (Liverpool: Merseyside Health Impact Assessment Steering Group).

Select Committee on Public Accounts (2000) *Improving the Delivery of Government IT Projects, First Report* (London: Stationery Office).

Self, P. (1993) *Government by the Market?: The Politics of Public Choice* (Basingstoke: Macmillan).

Service Employees International Union (1997) *Contracting Human Services: Recurring Scandals and Bad Performance* (Washington, DC).

Shaw, M. (1997) 'The State of Globalisation: Towards a Theory of State Transformation', *International Political Economy Journal*, Vol. 4, No. 3, pp. 497–513.

Shutt, J., De Silva, P. and Muller, T. (1999) *Step Change: The Case for a Town Improvement Zone Programme* (Leeds Business School).

Simmons, P.J. (1998) 'Learning to Live with NGOs', *Foreign Affairs*, Fall.

Singh, A. (1996)*Pension Reform, the Stock Market, Capital Formation and Economic Growth: A Critical Commentary on the World Bank's Proposals* (New York: Center for Economic Policy Analysis).

Sivanandan, A. (1998) 'Globalism and the Left', *Race & Class*, Vol. 40, No. 2/3.

Sjolander, A. (1996) 'Come On! We Can Change Things', *PSI Focus*, No. 2 June (Geneva: Public Services International).

Sklair, L. (1997) 'Social Movements for Global Capitalism: The Transnational Capitalist Class in Action', *International Political Economy Journal*.

Slaughter, A. (1997) 'The Real New World Order', *Foreign Affairs*, September/October.

Snowner, D. (1997) 'Challenges to Social Cohesion and Approaches to Policy Reform', in *Social Cohesion and the Globalising Economy* (Paris: OECD).

Social Exclusion Unit (1998) *Bringing Britain Together: A National Strategy for Neighbourhoods* (London: Cabinet Office).

Soludo, C. and Rao, M.S. (1999) *Potential Social Impact of the New Global Financial Architecture* (Niskka: University of Nigeria).

Standing, G. (1997) 'Globalization, Labour Flexibility and Insecurity: The Era of Market Regulation', *European Journal of Industrial Relations*, Vol. 3, No. 1, pp. 97–137.

Stanton, R. (1996) 'The Retreat from Social Need: Competitive Bidding and Local Public Investment', *Local Economy*, November.

Steans, J. (1999) 'The Private is Global: Feminist Politics and Global Political Economy', *New Political Economy*, Vol. 4, No.1.

Steinmo, S. (1994) 'The End of Redistribution? International Pressures and Domestic Tax Policy Choices', *Challenge*, November/December, pp. 9–17.

Stewart, J. (1993) 'The Limitations of Government by Contract', *Public Money & Management*, July–September.

Stiglitz, J. (1999) 'Reforming the Global Economic Architecture: Lessons from Recent Crises', *Journal of Finance*, Vol. 54, No. 4.

Stocker, K., Waitzkin, H. and Iriart, C. (1999) 'The Exportation of Managed Care to Latin America', *New England Journal of Medicine*, 8 April, Vol. 340, No. 14.

Strange, S. (1996) *The Retreat of the State: The Diffusion of Power in the World Economy* (Cambridge: Cambridge University Press).

Swyngedouw, E. (1996) 'Reconstructing Citizenship, Re-scaling of the State and the New Authoritarianism: Closing the Belgian Mines', *Urban Studies*, Vol. 33, No. 8.

Szreter, S. (1999) 'A New Political Economy for New Labour: The Importance of Social Capital', *Renewal*, Vol. 7, No. 1.

Tanzi, V. (1995) 'The Growth of Government and the Reform of the State in Industrialised Countries', Working Paper 130 (Washington, DC: International Monetary Fund).

Tanzi, V. (1997) 'The Changing Role of the State in the Economy: A Historical Perspective', Working Paper 114 (Washington, DC: International Monetary Fund).

Tanzi, V. (1998a) 'The Demise of the Nation State', Working Paper 120 (Washington, DC: International Monetary Fund).

Tanzi, V. (1998b) 'Fundamental Determinants of Inequality and the Role of Government', Working Paper 178 (Washington, DC: International Monetary Fund).

Tanzi, V. (2000) 'The Role of the State and the Quality of the Public Sector', Working Paper 00/36 (Washington, DC: International Monetary Fund).

Taylor, R. (1999) 'Some Comments on the Blair/Schroeder "Third Way/Neue Mitte"', *Transfer: European Review of Labour and Research*, Vol. 5, No. 3.

Taylor-Gooby, P. (1996) 'The United Kingdom: Radical Departures and Political Consensus', in George, V. and Taylor-Gooby, P. (eds) *Squaring the Welfare Circle* (London: Macmillan, pp. 95–116.

Timmins, N. (1999) 'The Silent Death of National Insurance', *Financial Times*, 22 November.

Tsoukalas, K. (1999) *'Globalisation and "The Executive Committee": Reflections on the Contemporary Capitalist State'*, in *Global Capitalism Versus Democracy: Socialist Register 1999* (Woodbridge, Suffolk: Merlin Press).

Turok, I. and Edge, N. (1999)*The Jobs Gap in Britain's Cities: Employment Loss and Labour Market Consequences* (Bristol: The Policy Press).

Twentieth Century Fund (1996) *Social Security Reform, Guide to the Issues* (New York).

21st Era (1998) *21st Century Regions* (London).

UNDP (1997) *Analytical Tools for Human Development* (Geneva).

UNDP (1999) *Human Development Report, Human Development in the Age of Globalisation* (Geneva).

UNISON (1998) *Leisure and Library Trusts* (London).

United Nations Conference on Trade and Development (1994) *World Investment Report 1994* (New York: United Nations).

United Nations Conference on Trade and Development (1995) *Comparative Experiences with Privatisation: Policy Insights and Lessons Learned* (New York: United Nations).

United Nations Conference on Trade and Development (1996) *World Investment Report 1996: Investment, Trade and International Policy Arrangements* (New York: United Nations).

United Nations Conference on Trade and Development (1997) *International Trade in Health Services: A Development Perspective* (New York: United Nations).

United Nations Conference on Trade and Development (UNCTAD) (1998) *Trade and Development Report 1998* (New York: United Nations).

United Nations Population Division (1998) *World Population Prospects: The 1998 Revision* (New York: United Nations).

United Nations Research Institute for Social Development (1994) *Structural Adjustment in a Changing World* (Geneva).

United Nations Research Institute for Social Development (1995) *Adjustment, Globalisation and Social Development* (Geneva).

United Nations Research Institute for Social Development (1996) *Globalisation and Citizenship* (Geneva).

United Nations Research Institute for Social Development (1997) *Globalisation and Civil Society: NGO Influence in International Decison-Making* (Geneva).

US Department of Labor (1996) *Working Together for Public Service, Task Force on Excellence in State and Local Government through Labor–Management Cooperation* (Washington, DC).

Vandenbrouche, F. (1998) *Globalisation, Inequality and Social Democracy* (London: Institute for Public Policy Research).

Waddington, J. and Whitson, C. (1996) 'Empowerment Versus Intensification: Union Perspectives of Change at the Workplace', in P. Ackers, C. Smith and P. Smith (eds) *New Workplace and Trade Unionism* (London: Routledge.

Wade, R. and Veneroso, F. (1998) 'The Gathering World Slump and the Battle Over Capital Controls', *New Left Review*, No. 231.

Wade, R. and Veneroso, F. (1998a) *The Asian Crisis: The High Debt Model vs the Wall Street-Treasury-IMF Complex*, draft (New York: Russell Sage Foundation).

Walker, A. (1999) 'The Third Way for Pensions (by Way of Thatcherism and Avoiding Today's Pensioners)', *Critical Social Policy*, Vol. 61, pp. 511–27.

Walker, D. (1996) 'The Advent of an Ambiguous Federalism and the Emergence of New Federalism III', *Public Administraion Review*, May–June, Vol. 56, No. 3.

Wallerstein, I. (1996) 'The Global Possibilities, 1990–2025', in Hopkins, T.K. and Wallerstein, I. *The Age of Transition: Trajectory of the World-System 1945–2025*, (London: Zed Press).

Walsh, J. and O'Flynn J. (1999) *Managing Through Contracts: The Employment Effects of Compulsory Competitive Tendering in Australian Local Government* (University of Melbourne: Department of Management).

Walsh, K. (1995) *Public Services and Market Mechanisms: Competition, Contracting and the New Public Management* (Basingstoke: Macmillan).

Waters, M. (1995) *Globalisation* (London: Routledge).

Watkins, K. (1997) *Globalisation and Liberalisation: Implications for Poverty, Distribution and Inequality*, Occasional Paper 32 (Geneva: United Nations Development Programme).

Waylen, G. (1997) 'Gender, Feminism and Political Economy', *New Political Economy*, Vol. 2, No. 2.

Weiss, L. (1997) 'Globalisation and the Myth of the Powerless State', *New Left Review*, No. 225.

Weiss, L. (1998) *The Myth of the Powerless State* (Cambridge: Polity Press).

Wes, M. (1996)*Globalisation: Winners and Losers* (London: Institute for Public Policy Research).

Whitfield, D. (1983) *Making it Public: Evidence and Action Against Privatisation* (London: Pluto Press).

Whitfield, D. (1985) 'Privatisation and International Restructuring', in *World View 1985* (London: Pluto Press).

Whitfield, D. (1991) 'Strategies to Rebuild the Public Sector: Alternatives to Privatisation, Deregulation and Commercialisation', in *Labour Movement: Strategies for the 21st Century* (Sydney: Evatt Foundation).

Whitfield, D. (1992)*The Welfare State: Privatisation, Deregulation, Commercialisation of Public Services* (London: Pluto Press).

Whitfield, D. (1999) 'Private Finance Initiative: The Commodification and Marketisation of Education', *Education & Social Justice*, No. 2, Spring.

Wilkinson, F. (1997) 'Changes in the Notion of Unemployment and what that means for the Poor', in Arestis, P., Palma, G. and Sawyer, M. (eds) *Markets, Unemployment and Economic Policy, Essays in honour of Geoff Harcourt*, Vol. 2 (London: Routledge).

Wilkinson, A., Godfrey, G. and Marchington, M. (1995) *Bouquets, Brickbats and Blinkers: TQM and EI in Practice* (Manchester: UMIST School of Management).

Wilks, A. (1997) *The World Bank's Promotion of Privatisation and Private Sector Development: Issues and Concerns* (London: Bretton Woods Project).

Williamson, J. (1996) 'Globalisation and Inequality Then and Now: The Late 19th and Late 20th Centuries Compared', Working Paper 5491 (Cambridge, MA: National Bureau of Economic Research).

Williamson, O.E. (1975) *Markets and Hierarchies: Analysis and Anti-Trust Implications* (New York: Free Press).

Williamson, O.E. (1985) *The Economic Institutions of Capitalism* (New York: Free Press).

Wilson, W. (1999) 'The Right to Buy', Research Paper 99/36 (London: House of Commons).

Wilson, W. J. (1996) *When Work Disappears: The World of the New Urban Poor* (New York: Knopf).

Wolf, A. (1999) 'Education and Economic Growth', *New Economy*, Vol. 6.

Wood, A. (1994) *North–South Trade, Employment and Inequality: Changing Fortunes in a Skill-Driven World* (Oxford: Clarendon Press).

World Bank (1994a) *Infrastructure for Development, World Development Report 1994* (Washington, DC).

World Bank (1994b) *Averting the Old Age Crisis* (Washington, DC).

World Bank (1995a) 'Civil Service Reform and the World Bank', Discussion Paper No. 161 (Washington, DC).

World Bank (1995b) *World Development Report 1995* (Washington, DC).

World Bank (1995c) *Privatisation: Principles and Practice* (Washington, DC).

World Bank (1995d) *Meeting the Infrastructure Challenge in Latin America and the Caribbean* (Washington, DC).

World Bank (1996) *Public Policy for the Private Sector*, Note No. 95 (Washington, DC).

World Bank (1997) *The State in a Changing World, World Development Report 1997* (Washington, DC).

World Bank, (1998a) *East Asia: The Road to Recovery*, (Washington, DC).

World Bank (1998b) *Partnership for Development: Proposed Actions for the World Bank* (Washington, DC).

World Bank (1999a) *Poverty Update: Trends in Poverty* (Washington, DC).

World Bank (1999b) *Macroeconomic Crises and Poverty: Transmission Mechanisms and Policy Responses*, Working Paper (Washington, DC).

World Bank (1999c) *Global Development Finance* (Washington, DC).

World Bank (2000) 'World Development Report 2000', Draft (Washington, DC).

World Trade Organisation, Council for Trade in Services (1998a) 'Education Services', Background Note by the Secretariat, S/C/W/49 (Washington, DC).

World Trade Organisation, Council for Trade in Services (1998b) 'Health and Social Services', Background Note by the Secretariat, S/C/W/50 (Washington, DC).

Wyplosz, Charles (1998) *International Financial Instability* in Global Public Goods (UNDP).

Yergin, D. and Stanislaw, J. (1999) *The Commanding Heights: The Battle between Government and the Marketplace that is Remaking the Modern World* (New York: Touchstone).

Zahariadis, N. (1999) 'The Rise and Fall of British State Ownership', *Comparative Politics*, July.

Zysman, J. (1996) 'The Myth of a "Global" Economy: Enduring National Foundations and Emerging Regional Realities', *New Political Economy*, Vol. 1, No. 2.

Index